A GUIDE TO THE
SPIDERS
of Australia

First published in 2014 by Reed New Holland Publishers
Sydney • Auckland

Level 1, 178 Fox Valley Road, Wahroonga, NSW 2076, Australia
5/39 Woodside Avenue, Northcote, Auckland 0627, New Zealand

newhollandpublishers.com

Copyright © 2014 New Holland Publishers
Copyright © 2014 in text: Volker W. Framenau, Barbara C. Baehr and Paul Zborowski
Copyright © 2014 in images: as credited

Front cover image: Males in the Jumping Spider genus *Maratus*, the Peacock Spiders, belong to the most spectacularly coloured spiders in Australia. *Maratus speciosus* is known from sand dune habitats in south-west Western Australia. Males extend abdominal flaps when courting a female and only during this display the bright orange fringing setae of this species can be seen. [J. Otto]
Back cover images: (left) White Crab Spider, *Thomisus spectabilis*; (right) unidentified Spiny Orb-weaver from the genus *Gasteracantha* [both images: P. Zborowski]

All rights reserved. No part of this publication may be reproduced, stored in a retrieval system or transmitted, in any form or by any means, electronic, mechanical, photocopying, recording or otherwise, without the prior written permission of the publishers and copyright holders.

A record of this book is held at the National Library of Australia.

ISBN 9781921517242

Group Managing Director: Fiona Schultz
Publisher and Project Editor: Simon Papps
Designers: Kim Pearce and Lorena Susak
Production Director: Arlene Gippert
Printed in China

10 9 8 7 6 5 4

Keep up with Reed New Holland and New Holland Publishers

ReedNewHolland
@NewHollandPublishers and @ReedNewHolland

A GUIDE TO THE
SPIDERS
of Australia

Volker W. Framenau, Barbara C. Baehr and Paul Zborowski

CONTENTS

Foreword ... 7

INTRODUCTION ... 8

Spiders are arachnids ... 9
Spider body ... 14
Spider silk ... 19
Spider reproduction and growth ... 31
Spider venom ... 41
Evolution and systematics of spiders ... 43
Naming of spiders ... 45
Spiders of Australia – peculiarities ... 49
How to identify spiders, how to use this book ... 50

MYGALOMORPHAE – TRAPDOOR SPIDERS ... 51

Hexathelidae – Funnel-web Spiders ... 54
Dipluridae – Curtain-web Spiders ... 59
Actinopodidae – Mouse Spiders ... 63
Ctenizidae – Cork-lid Trapdoor Spiders ... 68
Migidae – Tree Trapdoor Spiders ... 72
Idiopidae – True Trapdoor Spiders ... 75
Nemesiidae – Wishbone Trapdoor Spiders ... 82
Barychelidae – Brush-footed Trapdoor Spiders ... 87
Theraphosidae – Australian Tarantulas, Bird-eating Spiders, Whistling or Barking Spiders ... 91

ARANEOMORPHAE – MODERN SPIDERS ... 95

Austrochiloidea ... 98

Austrochilidae – Junction-web Weavers ... 99
Gradungulidae – Long-clawed Spiders ... 102

Haplogynae ... 105

Filistatidae – Crevice Weavers ... 107
Sicariidae – Recluse Spiders, Fiddle-back Spiders ... 110

Scytodidae – Spitting Spiders	112
Periegopidae – Relictual Spiders	115
Ochyroceratidae	117
Pholcidae – Daddy Long-legs Spiders	119
Tetrablemmidae – Armoured Spiders	123
Segestriidae – Tube-web Spiders	125
Dysderidae – Woodlouse Hunters	127
Oonopidae – Goblin Spiders	129
Orsolobidae – Six-eyed Ground Spiders	134

Entelegynae – Advanced Modern Spiders   137

Archaeidae – Assassin or Pelican Spiders	139
Stenochilidae	142
Araneidae – Orb-weaving Spiders	144
Nephilidae – Golden Orb-weavers, Hermit Spiders, Coin Spiders	180
Linyphiidae – Sheet-web Spiders, Money Spiders	186
Cyatholipidae	190
Tetragnathidae – Long-jawed Spiders	192
Mimetidae – Pirate Spiders	200
Holarchaeidae – Minute Long-jawed Spiders	202
Pararchaeidae – Tiny Thick-necked Spiders	204
Synotaxidae – Chickenwire-web Spiders	208
Malkaridae – Shield Spiders	210
Theridiosomatidae – Ray Orb-weaving Spiders	212
Mysmenidae – Minute Clasping-weavers	214
Anapidae – Ground Orb-weaving Spiders, Micro Gondwanan Spiders	217
Symphytognathidae – Dwarf Orb-weaving Spiders	223
Nesticidae – Scaffold-web Spiders	227
Theridiidae – Comb-footed spiders, Cob-web Spiders	229
Nicodamidae – Red-and-black Spiders	243
Deinopidae – Net-casting Spiders, Ogre-faced Spiders, Retarius Spider, Hump-backed Spiders	246
Uloboridae – Venomless Spiders, Feather-legged Spiders	250
Hersiliidae – Long-spinneret Bark Spiders, Two-tailed Spiders	253
Oecobiidae – Wall Spiders	258
Hahniidae – Comb-tailed Spiders, Dwarf Sheet Spiders	262
Dictynidae – Mesh-web Spiders	264
Sparassidae – Huntsman Spiders, Giant Crab Spiders	266
Desidae – Intertidal Spiders, House Spiders	276
Stiphidiidae – Platform Spiders, Cone-web Spiders, Sombrero Spiders, Labyrinth Spiders	284
Amphinectidae – Forest Hunters	289

Agelenidae – Funnel-web Weavers	291
Amaurobiidae – Hackled-mesh Weavers	292
Cycloctenidae – Scuttling Spiders	295
Zodariidae – Ant-eating Spiders	297
Lycosidae – Wolf Spiders	304
Pisauridae – Fishing Spiders, Nursery-web Spiders	319
Ctenidae – Tropical Wolf Spiders	325
Oxyopidae – Lynx Spiders	327
Miturgidae – False Wolf Spiders, Prowling Spiders	331
Zoridae – Spiny-leg Spiders, Wandering Ghosts	335
Thomisidae – Crab Spiders, Flower Spiders	339
Psechridae – Pseudo-Orbweaving Spiders, Lace-sheet Weaving Spider	353
Zoropsidae – False Wolf Spiders, False Huntsman Spiders	356
Tengellidae – False Water Spiders, Host Spiders	358
Anyphaenidae – Ghost Spiders, Phantom Spiders, Sea-shore Spiders	360
Clubionidae – Sac Spiders	362
Corinnidae – Swift Spiders, Ant-mimics	366
Liocranidae – Spiny-legged Sac Spiders	371
Selenopidae – Wall Crab Spiders	372
Salticidae – Jumping Spiders	376
Philodromidae – Running Crab Spiders	390
Gnaphosidae – Ground Spiders	393
Prodidomidae – Long-spinneret Ground Spiders	398
Lamponidae – White-tailed Spiders	400
Ammoxenidae – Termite Hunters	406
Gallieniellidae – Long-jawed Ground Spiders	408
Trochanteriidae – Scorpion Spiders	411
Cithaeronidae – Swift Ground Spiders	414
FURTHER READING	416
Glossary	443
Acknowledgements	446
About the Authors	447
Index of Family Names	448

Foreword

For the naturalist or aspiring araneologist, the diversity of Australian spiders can be daunting. Some 3,500 species in about 650 genera and 79 families of spiders are currently described from Australia and the numbers are ever increasing. Our estimates suggest that about 8,500 species in about 850 genera occur in Australia.

We hope that this book will serve as a great launching pad for the reader's journey into the fascinating world of Australian Spiders. However, we believe it will also provide valuable information for those who have already been ensnared by the fascinating biology of these animals. We have not tried to represent as many species as we could, but to illustrate the diversity at all levels including genera and families. Indeed, to our knowledge this is the first book on Australian spiders that covers all families recognised at the time of the compilation of this book and has images for all of them bar one, the Liocranidae.

We not only provide an overview of the taxonomic diversity of spiders, but also elaborate on the most intriguing behavioural and ecological aspects of the members in each family. We provide a comprehensive section at the back of this volume that lists the core studies that were consulted to compile this book. With the help of the Internet, where many of these studies are available for Open Access download, the reader can further delve into the fascinating world of Australian spiders.

This book is as much a compilation of what we know about Australian spiders, as it provides an overview of what we do not know. We have consulted many experts on Australian spiders but as with any publication such as this, any mistakes and errors are of the making of the authors and we are taking full responsibility for these. We encourage the reader to inform us of any inaccuracy within the pages of this book to make sure these are iron out in future work.

Research on Australian spiders is in constant progress. It will therefore not surprise that this book represents only a snapshot of the taxonomy at the time it was compiled. It is obvious that work has already started on the second edition of this volume.

PART 1
INTRODUCTION

Spiders are arachnids

The extraordinary spinning behaviour of spiders is the source of the scientific name of the class Arachnida to which spiders belong. Arachne was a Greco-Roman mythological character, a most beautiful girl and highly-skilled weaver. So proud was she of her talent, that she challenged Athena, goddess of wisdom, weaving and strategy, to a contest. Arachne's tapestry made fun of the love affairs and misbehaviours of the gods and its magnificent beauty apparently offended Athena, who retaliated by transforming Arachne into a spider.

The arachnids, which amongst others also include scorpions and harvestmen, are a class within the arthropods. Arthropoda are the largest animal phylum and include crustaceans (for example crabs and prawns), myriapods (including millipedes and centipedes), insects and arachnids. They have a hardened chitinous shell, the exoskeleton, and few to very many jointed legs (from Greek: *árthron* = joint, and *podos* = foot, leg).

Arachnids generally have four pairs of legs (in contrast to insects which have three pairs) in addition to two frontal appendages, the chelicerae and pedipalps which both assist in prey capture, feeding, defence, sensory perception and reproduction. Chelicerae may be scissor-shaped, like in scorpions, pseudoscorpions and harvestman, or may carry needle-shaped fangs as in some mites and spiders. Pedipalps are similarly diverse in form and function and include the pincers of scorpions and pseudoscorpions and the secondary reproductive organs of male spiders. With few exceptions arachnids are predators. Some mites are detritus feeders (e.g. dust mites) or parasites (e.g. ticks), and a few spiders may re-ingest their own silk with airborne high-energy plant material such as pollen attached to it, but this does not contribute majorly to their diet.

Of the eleven groups of arachnids, eight occur in Australia, although some like the micro whipscorpions (Palpigradi) and short-tailed whipscorpions (Schizomida) are rarely encountered by the public due to their cryptic lifestyle and small size.

With some 44,000 described species worldwide, the spiders (Araneae) are

Opposite: *Cyrtophora moluccensis* is a highly variable Orb-weaving Spider (family Araneidae) that occurs from India into Asia, and from northern tropical Australia along the Queensland coast. A number of subspecies are described from South-East Asia and the Pacific region pointing to an unsatisfactory taxonomic status of spiders in this group. [P. Zborowski]

currently the largest order of arachnids, if it is considered that mites are composed of a number of orders and may not form a single evolutionary unit. A number of unique characters identify spiders in contrast to all other arachnids, most remarkably the presence of spinnerets at the back of the abdomen, venomous chelicerae and the use of the male pedipalp as secondary genitalia for sperm transfer. These three peculiarities are treated in detail below after a short introduction to the body plan of spiders.

In Australia, some 3,500 species of spiders are currently described but realistic estimates suggest that about 8,500 species inhabit this continent (and some published calculations report that up to 20,000 species may exist). This means that more than half of the fauna, whilst often present in vast museum collections, still needs scientific scrutiny; a lot to do for the handful of arachnologists working on the spider fauna of this country.

Groups of Arachnida:

- Acari (mites and ticks)
- Amblypygi (whip spiders and tail-less whipscorpions)
- Araneae (spiders)
- Opiliones (harvestmen)
- Palpigradi (micro whipscorpions)
- Pseudoscorpiones (false scorpions, pseudoscorpions)
- Ricinulei (hooded tick spiders) *
- Schizomida (short-tailed whipscorpions)
- Scorpiones (scorpions)
- Solifugae (camel or sun spiders) *
- Thelyphonida (vinegaroons)*

*not in Australia.

Mites (Acariformes) are extremely diverse and include velvet mites (family Trombidiidae) (illustrated here), chiggers (family Trombiculidae) and water mites (Hydracarina or Hydrachnidia) amongst many others. [P. Zborowski]

Ticks belong to the superorder Parasitiformes (ticks and some mites) which together with most mites (Acariformes) form the traditional subclass Acari within the Arachnida. There is strong evidence that Acari do not have a common ancestry, but exact evolutionary relationships within this group and to the other arachnid orders remain unclear. Illustrated here is a paralysis tick. [P. Zborowski]

Spiders (order Araneae), here a *Cyclosa* male from Brisbane, differ from all other arachnids by the ability to spin silk from abdominal glands, the presence of venomous chelicerae and the use of the male pedipalp as secondary sexual organ. They are the largest arachnid order with some 44,000 described species worldwide of which about 3,500 have so far been named in Australia. [V.W. Framenau, Phoenix Environmental Sciences]

Tail-less whipscorpions or whip spiders (order Amblypygi) are a small order of comparatively large tropical arachnids characterised by their flattened body, long whip-like first pair of legs and raptorial pedipalps. Four species in two genera, *Charinus* and *Charon*, are currently described from the Australian tropics including Christmas Island. [P. Zborowski]

Harvestmen (order Opiliones), here an undescribed species of *Dampetrus* from the Pilbara region of Western Australia, differ from spiders, amongst many other characters, by the lack of a constriction between the two main body parts, carapace and abdomen. Long-legged harvestmen are often referred to as daddy long-legs, but they should not be confused with the spider family Pholcidae which carries the same colloquial name. [F. Bokhari]

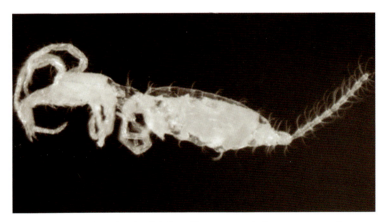

Micro Whipscorpions (order Palpigradi) are a poorly known group of very small arachnids. They live in soil, leaf litter, caves and semi-aquatic interstitial environments. *Eukoenenia mirabilis*, illustrated here, is one of two species introduced to Australia (possibly in the soil of pot plants) and has been found near Adelaide and Perth. The first indigenous Australian palpigrade was only described very recently from subterranean environments in central Western Australia. [V.W. Framenau, Western Australian Museum]

False or book scorpions (order Pseudocorpiones) are small arachnids that resemble tiny scorpions, but lack a venomous tail. They are common throughout Australia where they can be found under rocks, in leaf litter, in soil, under bark of tree or in caves, often in family groups. [P. Zborowski]

Short-tailed whipscorpions (order Schizomida), here a subterranean female *Draculoides* from the Pilbara region of Western Australia, are a group of small arachnids measuring less than about 10 mm in body length. They occur throughout the world tropics in leaf litter, under rocks or in caves. A diverse subterranean fauna has been discovered with many undescribed species of very restricted distributions in northern Western Australia. [V.W. Framenau, Phoenix Environmental Sciences]

Scorpions, here *Urodacus novaehollandiae* from southern Western Australia, are characterised by the presence of chelate pedipalps and an elongate metasoma furnished with a venomous sting. Scorpions are important components of arid ecosystems because their levels of diversity and abundance contribute significantly to the biomass of animal assemblages and they are important predators and prey for other species. [V.W. Framenau, Phoenix Environmental Sciences]

Spider body

An arachnid body consists of two body parts, although these may be fused into one in many groups such as mites (Acari) or harvestmen (Opiliones). The frontal part of the spider is called the cephalothorax (or prosoma) and the rear is the abdomen (or opisthosoma). Both parts are connected by a slim tube called a pedicel.

Carapace

The upper chitinous plate of the prosoma is the carapace, whereas the plate on the underside is called sternum. A central depression on the carapace is called the fovea. It is of varying, sometimes diagnostic shape, and marks internal attachment points for muscles contracting the stomach.

One of the most important characters to identify spider families is the number and arrangement of the eyes. The systematic rank of family is the most recognisable level for spider identification in the field, somewhat equivalent to insect orders. For example, Jumping Spiders (Salticidae), Orb-weaving Spiders (Araneidae) and Huntsman Spiders (Sparassidae) are well-known spider families in Australia.

Most spiders have eight similarly-sized eyes arranged in two rows at the front of their carapace, although in some families these are reduced to six (and some subterranean spiders have lost their eyes altogether). Some families have the back eye row (= posterior eyes) extremely curved so that the eyes at the side (= lateral eyes) are either situated well in front of or behind the central (= median) eyes and these appear to represent two rows in addition to the frontal (= anterior) eyes. For example, in Wolf Spiders (Lycosidae) the posterior lateral eyes are situated well behind the posterior median eyes, to the extent that the posterior eyes in Wolf Spiders have been described as forming a square. [F. Bokhari]

In some spider families, some of the eyes are extremely enlarged and spiders can see very well, although spiders largely rely on other sensory cues such as substrate or web vibration or movements of the air. In Jumping Spiders (Salticidae), the anterior median eyes are enlarged, whereas in Net-casting Spiders (Deinopidae) it is the posterior median eyes that are much bigger than the others.

Finally, there are families with a somewhat different eye pattern, such as the Lynx Spiders (Oxyopidae) with four rows of eyes arranged in a hexagonal pattern. Six-eyed Daddy Long-legs (Pholcidae) have a median pair of tiny eyes and two lateral eye groups of three. Other six-eyed spider families include the Spitting Spiders (Scytodidae), Louse Hunters (Dysderidae) and Goblin Spiders (Oonopidae) and many of these have their eyes in three groups of two.

The prosoma bears six pairs of appendages. The first pair, the chelicerae, consists of a large basal part, the paturon, and the terminal fang. The orientation of the chelicerae is important in separating the more primitive Trapdoor Spiders (Mygalomorphae) from the Modern Spiders (Araneomorphae). The Mygalomorphae have the chelicerae directed frontally and the fangs directed backward in a parallel position. In contrast, in the Araneomorphae, with few exceptions, the fangs are oriented transverse or against each other. This has biomechanical advantages for the strike of a spider. Whereas mygalomorphs strike downwards and need the substrate to pin their prey, araneomorphs can hunt away from the ground, as they can catch their prey between their fangs. Not surprisingly, few mygalomorph spiders are arboreal. The paturon may be very large and in some spiders, such as the mygalomorphs, contain the venom gland. The fangs have a syringe-like opening near the tip to inject the venom into the prey.

The second pair of appendages is called pedipalps. In male spiders, these serve as a secondary sexual organ to transfer sperm from the abdominal sperm gland via a sperm transfer web to the female. The basal segment of the pedipalps, the endites, cover the mouth opening from the side, assisted by the labium which covers the mouth from behind. This cover is important as spiders use excretory enzymes to digest their prey externally, assisted often by mechanical chewing with the chelicerae. They then literally suck up the pre-digested liquid with their stomach, which has circular and dilating muscles to compress and expand the stomach to create the sucking effect.

There are four pairs of walking legs and each leg consists of seven segments. At the base is the coxa followed by trochanter, femur, patella, tibia, metatarsus and tarsus. Each leg tarsus bears two or three terminal claws. The front legs can be armed with specific hairs, spines or other structures, in particular in males, and these are invariably used in courtship or mating.

Abdomen

The abdomen accommodates, amongst other functions, the respiratory and primary reproductive organs, which are visible from the underside, and terminal appendages, the spinnerets.

The respiratory organ consists of booklungs and tracheal tubes. The primitive trapdoor spiders (Mygalomorphae) generally have two pairs of booklungs and no tracheal tubes. In contrast, the modern spiders (Araneomorphae) normally

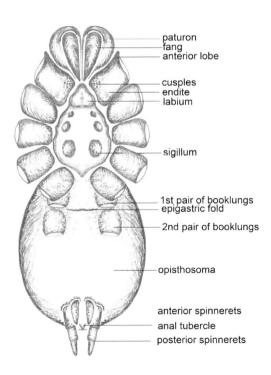

Primitive Trapdoor Spiders (Mygalomorphae) (above) and the Modern Spiders (Araneomorphae) (opposite) differ by the orientation of the fangs (parallel or paraxial vs. transverse or diaxial) and the number of booklungs (four vs. two). [B.C. Baehr]

have one pair of booklungs and a pair of tracheal tubes, which end in a slit-like tracheal spiracle just in front of the spinnerets.

The most primitive spiders, the pseudo-segmented Mesothelae (today only found in South-East Asia, China and Japan) retain four pairs of spinnerets placed under the centre of the abdomen. In all other spiders, these have moved to the end of the abdomen. The anterior median spinnerets are reduced either to a porous spinning plate (cribellum), a tiny unpaired lobe (colulus), or may be completely lost. Mygalomorph spiders may have four or six spinnerets.

The epigastric fold on the ventral side of the abdomen includes the genital opening of the reproductive tract. In males the epigastric fold is just a slit. Male spiders cannot transfer their sperm directly into the female genitalia from this slit. They use their highly modified pedipalps as sperm transfer organ (see below).

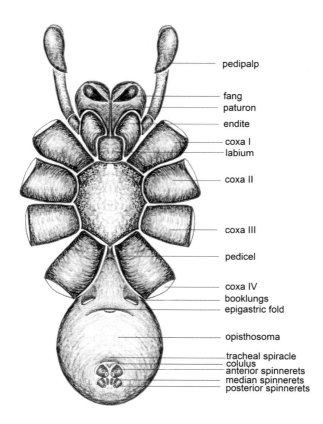

The female epigastric fold shows no specific external structures in the Mygalomorphae or the more primitive spiders within the Araneomorphae, the Haplogynae. In contrast, in the more derived Entelegynae within the Araneomorphae, the female genitalia are characterised by an ornate plate of hard ridges and grooves of often species-specific shape. This plate (epigyne) matches the male's features on the pedipalp to only allow mating between females and males of the same species. Therefore this combination is often considered a matching 'lock-and-key' system.

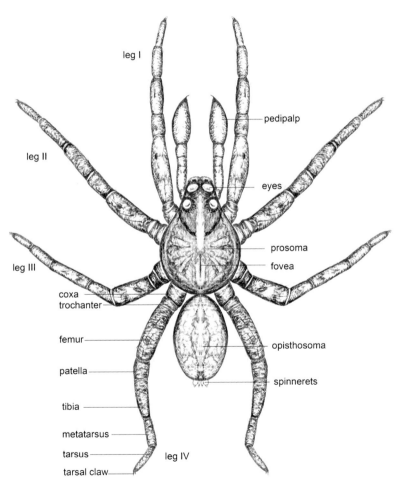

External morphology of a spider, here illustrated for a Wolf Spider (Lycosidae). [B.C. Baehr]

 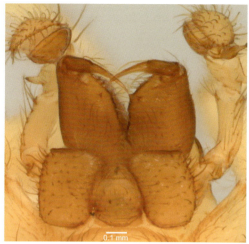

The more ancient Trapdoor Spiders (Mygalomorphae) (left) have the fangs directed backwards in a parallel (paraxial) position, whereas the fangs of Modern Spiders (Araneomorphae) (right) work against each other (diaxial). Small teeth on the base segment of the chelicerae (paturon) pointing towards the fangs are believed to assist in holding and chewing prey in many spiders. [B.C. Baehr]

Spider silk

The ability to produce silk from abdominal spinnerets is one of the three main features that make a spider. No other group of animals has developed this extraordinary skill to such perfection. And it is not just one type of silk from one type of silk gland that spiders produce. They are able to simultaneously produce multiple, chemically and functionally distinct types of silk for a variety of purposes during their life span. In contrast, some insects, mites and pseudoscorpions may be able to produce silk, but generally only of a single type and at a particular time of their life (i.e. silkworm pupal case).

Different types of spider silk have very different mechanical properties and are used for a large array of functions, such as prey capture, safety lines, the lining of burrows, protection of eggs, and aerial dispersal via ballooning. The astonishing diversity in the use of silk is thought to be the evolutionary key to the spiders' ecological success. They colonize all terrestrial habitats from sea shores and reefs, to the nival zones of the highest mountain chains.

Silk glands and spinnerets

Spider silk is a protein-based secretion. The silk is stored in an aqueous solution in the lumen of the abdominal glands that produce the proteins. The glands open to narrowing ducts that lead to the spigots. Whilst passing through the duct, the proteins are subject to strong mechanical forces, elimination of water and ion exchange resulting in a parallel alignment of the proteins. These liquid proteins form the silk fibres at the time when they are pulled out of the spigots. Artificially mimicking the production of spider silk has not yet been accomplished despite extensive research into this topic, partly out of military interest. Some spider silk has extraordinary mechanical properties surpassing most other materials including Kevlar and steel in toughness.

The silk of orb-web building spiders, for example in the families Nephilidae (Golden Orb-weavers) and Araneidae (Orb-weavers), has attracted the most detailed research attention and the spinning abilities of these spiders are best understood amongst all spiders. Spiders originally have eight spinnerets; however, spinneret number is reduced to six in most modern spiders including orb-weavers. Each spinneret has a number of different types of spigots, which are connected to internal silk glands. Up to seven different types of silk are produced by female orb-weavers: dragline silk and structural silk for the web ('major ampullate gland' and associated spigots), temporary capture spiral of the orb-web ('minor ampullate gland), the core fibre of the capture spiral of the web ('flagelliform gland'), sticky droplets of the web ('aggregate gland'), egg-case fibres ('cylindrical gland'), prey-wrapping silk ('aciniform gland'), and cementing silk for fixing fibres ('pyriform glands'). Male spiders, in addition, have so-called epiandrous spigots near the epigastral fold and their silk contributes to the construction of the sperm transfer web.

Each spinneret of a spider is armed with a variety of different spigots that produce different types of silk. The general pattern of Orb-weaving Spiders (family Araneidae) and allies, such as *Eriophora biapicata* shown here, has two different spigot types on the frontal (anterior) spinnerets (major ampullate and pyriform), three on the central back (posterior median) spinnerets (minor ampullate, cylindriform and aciniform) and three on the central side (posterior lateral) spinnerets (aggregate, cylindriform and aciniform). All types produce different types of silk with specific function and material properties. [F. Bokhari]

Cribellum and calamistrum

Most spiders have six functional spinnerets with the original anterior median pair absent or forming a non-functional colulus. However, some Modern Spiders retained this pair of spinnerets in the form of a spinning field, the cribellum. As ancestral trait, the cribellum can be found throughout many Araneomorphae, and spiders with this field are called cribellate spiders. The cribellum may be single or divided and is covered with thousands of tiny spigots, which produce extremely fine cribellate silk. These strands are pulled out by the spiders' calamistrum, a comb of setae on the metatarsus of the fourth leg. The silk has a woolly and messy texture so that prey can easily become entangled. Cribellate capture threads represent a non-drying alternative to the sticky droplets produced by the aggregate gland spigots of non-cribellate spiders.

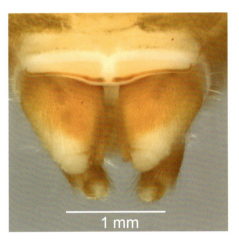

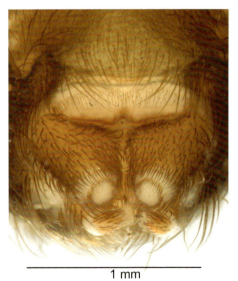

The cribellum is a spinning field in front of the anterior pair of spinnerets. It evolved from the anterior median spinnerets. The cribellum is either divided in two spinning fields (left) or undivided, sometimes with a central indentation (right). [B.C. Baehr]

The calamistrum, here seen along the top edge of the metatarsus, generally consists of a single row of curved bristles, which the cribellate spiders use to pull the woolly strands out of the cribellum. Mature males, who abandon prey capture webs in search for a mate, have no cribellum, or only a reduced version [B.C. Baehr]

The messy web of the Black House Spider, *Badumna insignis*, is living proof of the efficiency of cribellate silk. The capture webs of these spiders often extensively adorn edges, corners and crevices around dwellings throughout Australia, and removing them is a very sticky undertaking. [P. Zborowski]

Hunting with a web

The variety of silk types that spiders can produce is reflected in the multitude of uses spiders employ it for, in particular in the pursuit of prey. Most admiration is evoked by the intricate orb-web, a truly amazing design, and the archetypical symbol for spiders in general. The evolution of the morphological and behavioural components which result in such an architectural masterpiece is difficult to comprehend. But spiders did not stop there; indeed, in Australia some groups such as the Bolas Spiders (genus *Ordgarius* within the family Araneidae) and Net-casting Spiders (family Deinopidae) reduced the orb, took what was left of it into their own 'hands' (for lack of a better word) and now actively chase their prey with it. Others, like Money Spiders (family Linyphiidae) and Comb-footed Spiders (Theridiidae) laid the orb-web flat down and now construct a tangle web of irregular threads above and sometimes below to entangle their prey.

The construction of the web in the family Araneidae commences with a strong, more or less horizontal bridge thread. From the centre of that thread, a third line is dropped as anchor point to the bottom. Further framing threads around the future web are added before more and more radial lines are constructed. After setting some tight centre spirals, the spider now constructs a widely spaced temporary (auxiliary) spiral from the inside to the outside. This is finally followed by setting much tighter sticky spirals from the outside back in, and at the same time eating up the temporary spiral. Most orb-webs have a flagelliform silk spiral with glue drops from the aggregate gland spigots; cribellate orb-weavers such as the Venomless Spiders (family Uloboridae) incorporate cribellate silk onto a pseudoflagelliform silk spiral to entangle prey.

The orb-web is possibly the most efficient way for a spider to use silk in its hunt for prey. Spiders need to invest silk only in a single vertical plane, which will perfectly intercept horizontally flying insects. The mechanical properties of the silk disseminate the energy of the impact without the web being destroyed, and the glue will keep the prey in the web until subdued by the spider.
[P. Zborowski]

There are a multitude of variations to the conventional orb-web. Leaf-curling Spiders in the genus *Phonognatha* (family Araneidae) incorporate a rolled leaf into the centre of the web where the spider hides from predation. [P. Zborowski]

Some orb-weaving spiders, such as *Plebs cyphoxis* from Western Australia, place a silk decoration (stabilimentum) into their web, at times in combination with prey remains. These decorations are mainly found in those spiders that remain in the web during the day. A number of functions for the stabilimenta have been proposed, including prey attraction (by reflecting light frequencies to which prey are attracted), predator avoidance (by blending the shape of the spider into the decoration), web protection (web is more easily seen by large birds), excess removal of silk, or thermoregulation. [V. W. Framenau, Phoenix Environmental Sciences]

The horizontal, tightly meshed tent webs of the orb-weaving spider genus *Cyrtophora* (family Araneidae), here that of *C. unicolor* from Christmas Island, are thought to have evolved from a vertical orb-web, laid down flat and equipped with tangle threads to ensnare prey above the orb. A number of other spider families have followed a similar evolutionary path, such as the Money Spiders (family Linypiidae) or the Comb-footed Spiders (Theridiidae). [V.W. Framenau, Phoenix Environmental Sciences]

The construction of prey capture webs is of course not limited to Orb-weaving Spiders and their relatives. A large variety in snare designs is found throughout almost all groups of spiders. The evolution of the prey capture web is believed to have evolved from the burrowing primitive spiders, that often cover the entire burrow interior with silk, by expanding the prey capture area from the immediate entrance of the burrow to the outside using silk as prey detector.

In the simplest case, some signalling threads are spun from a subterranean burrow alerting the spider in the burrow if prey touches them. These are used in many mygalomorph spiders such as the Funnel-web Spiders (family Hexathelidae)

Burrowing spiders often cover the interior wall of their tube with more or less thick layers of silk. This *Misgolas* female, an east Australian member of the mygalomorph family Idiopidae, has a particularly thick internal silk cover in her burrow. This large investment in burrow construction reflects the fact that mygalomorph spiders rarely, if ever, abandon their burrow due to the higher risk of desiccation in comparison to Modern Spiders (Araneomorphae). [P. Zborowski]

or in araneomorph spiders such as the Tube-web Spiders (family Segestriidae).

These single tangle threads may be interconnected and a very loose sheet-like structure is being constructed, either on the ground or in vegetation. Typical representative of this type of web can be found in the Crevice Weavers (family Filistatidae) or in some House Spiders (family Desidae).

As the next level of complexity, spiders in burrows or arboreal funnels may not just use single threads and few interconnecting lines, but extend a dense sheet-web from their hide-out. These are, for example, constructed in the Platform Spiders of the family Stiphidiidae or House Spiders in the genus *Badumna* (family Desidae).

The Net-casting Spiders (family Deinopidae) construct an extremely derived orb-web that they subsequently hold between their legs to catch their prey. [F. Bokhari]

The web and funnel-shape retreat may then go completely airborne within the vegetation such as in some Fishing Spiders (family Pisauridae).

Sheet-webs may become three-dimensional and in some instances may harbour more than a single spider. Some primitive forms of sociality have been described in spiders such as the Huntsmen Spiders (family Sparassidae), Crab Spiders (family Thomisidae) and House Spiders (family Desidae). This social behaviour is generally associated with prolonged maternal care. Large aggregations of spiders can be found in three dimensional webs in *Phryganoporus* (Desidae) whereas aggregations of *Diaea* (Thomisidae) in Western Australia are much smaller.

Sheet-webs are a common prey capture web in spiders and occur in a large number of families. Sheet-webs often originate from a funnel-like retreat in which the spider hides until it senses the movement of prey on the snare. [P. Zborowski]

Venonia micariodes (Lycosidae) is an unusual sheet-web builder in a family that generally includes vagrant hunters or spiders living in a permanent burrow. The sheet-web may be the ancestral way of hunting in Wolf Spiders as these spiders retain a third tarsal claw that is usually used to walk on silk. [P. Zborowski]

Phryganoporus candidus occurs throughout Australia and lives in aggregations of dozens of spiders. They build a messy colonial web with cribellate silk on trees or bushes. [V.W. Framenau, Phoenix Environmental Sciences]

Other uses of silk

Not all spiders build a capture web, in fact a large number of spiders are vagrant hunters or ambushers. These include the very diverse families of Wolf Spiders (Lycosidae), the Jumping Spiders (Salticidae), the Ground Spiders (Gnaphosidae), most Crab Spiders (Thomisidae), or the lesser known Assassin Spiders (Archaeidae), Pirate Spiders (Mimetidae) (both specialist hunters of other spiders) and the highly specialised Spitting Spiders (Scytodidae). However, all these spiders use silk for a variety of applications other than prey capture.

Wandering spiders such as Wolf Spiders or Jumping Spiders may continuously release a silk thread on the move, the dragline. This serves as security blanket, for example in case of an accidental fall or if a fast retreat is required during a botched prey attack, and also helps male spiders to find a female. Her dragline appears to be covered by chemicals that serve as pheromones to alert him of her presence.

Spider silk plays a very important part in reproduction as the eggs are invariably enclosed in a more or less complex eggsac. This eggsac is often of family-, genus- or species-specific architecture. In some cases, it may be easier to initially locate the eggs than the often cryptic spiders, for example in the Orchard Spiders (genus *Celaenia*) and Bola Spiders (genus *Ordgarius*). Both belong to the Orb-weaving Spiders (family Araneidae) but have largely abandoned building an orb-web. More on the diversity of eggsacs can be found in the chapter on reproduction below.

Spiders cannot fly but some groups have managed to use the movement of the air such as updrifts and wind for dispersal, in particular in the early immature stages. When dispersing spiders sense wind movements or warm air rising, they climb up grasses or trees as launching points. They point their spinnerets into the air and pull long strands of silk from their spinnerets. If the strand is long enough and has enough lift, they let go of the substrate and rise into the air, sometimes to several thousands of metres in altitude until they descent to their new destinations. This phenomenon is called ballooning and the specialised thread is called gossamer. News reports sometimes show thousands of young spiders forced out of their homes due to river flooding. Spiders apparently ballooned to the nearest high ground and the gossamer threads, together with thousands of draglines, place a carpet of silk over the low vegetation.

Many spider families practice ballooning. In the Trapdoor Spiders (Mygalomorphae), immatures in the genera *Missulena* (Actinopodidae) and

Conothele (Ctenizidae) have been observed to release gossamer. Within Modern Spiders (Araneomorphae) an analysis of the composition of the 'aerial spider fauna' in eastern Australia has shown that it is composed mainly of Sheet-web Spiders (Linypiidae), Orb-web Spiders (Araneidae) and Wolf Spiders (Lycosidae), but also Crab Spiders (Thomisidae) and Sac Spiders (Clubionidae) dependent upon the habitat investigated.

Spider reproduction and growth

The way in which spiders reproduce, in particular through the use of the male pedipalp as a secondary sexual organ, is unique at least in the Arachnida. Males use the pedipalps to transfer their sperm from a temporary sperm transfer web to the female genitalia. The reproductive behaviour of many spiders can be complex and this, in combination with a number of remarkable evolutionary phenomena such as pronounced sexual size dimorphism and sexual cannibalism, has resulted in spiders being frequently used as model organisms by evolutionary scientists.

The structures in the male pedipalp that transfer sperm are located in the bulb, although other hook-like sclerotisations, for example on the pedipalp tibia, may assist in locking the pedipalp onto the female epigyne. The bulb has a more or less S-shaped tubular duct (sperm duct) that ends in a sharp hollow needle of varying length and shape, the embolus. The pedipalp attains its final, often extremely complicated shape only during the last moult. Before copulation, the male weaves a small triangular sperm transfer web, deposits his sperm onto the web and then takes the sperm into the embolus. As part of a sometimes complex mating ritual, the male ejects the sperm with the embolus into the female genitalia.

In the more ancient Trapdoor Spiders (Mygalomorphae) and the primitive Modern Spiders (Araneomorphae), the Haplogynae, the male bulb looks like a simple sac with a pointed end forming the embolus. In these spiders, females do not have structured external genitalia and sperm transfer is straightforward. In contrast, the bulb can be extremely complex in the advanced Modern Spiders, the Entelegynae. Complicated interlocking structures on the bulb connect to female sclerotised external structures, the epigyne. During copulation, the bulb, which consists of a number of different rigid parts connected by extensible lamellas, expands and changes its shape greatly to provide a good connection to the epigyne. As the pedipalp bulb and epigyne are of species-specific shape, the embolus can generally only be inserted in a female epigyne of the same species. Hence, these extraordinary features, together with the internal structure of the epigyne, are the most important characters for identifying spiders at the species level.

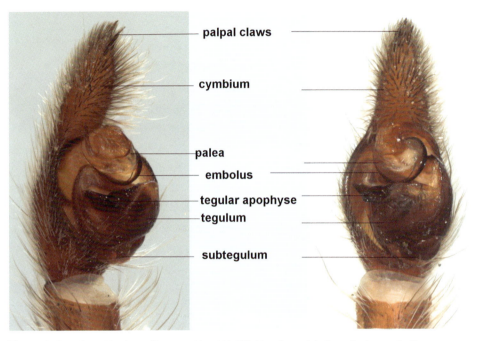

The embolus of a spider, here illustrated in a Wolf Spider (Lycosidae) pedipalp, works like a syringe with which the male transfers the sperm into the female epigyne. Male pedipalps and the female epigyne have been described as a key-and-lock system. Males can only mate with conspecific females, although species-specific behavioural sequences will generally not allow a male and female from different species to copulate. [B.C. Baehr]

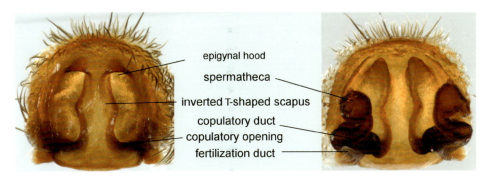

The female epigyne, here illustrated for a Wolf Spider (Lycosidae), varies from species to species, and is often an excellent feature to identify a spider species, although this requires the use of a stereomicroscope. The external view (left) shows a chitinous median plate (scapus). The internal view cleared from muscular and connective tissue (right) shows copulatory ducts and spermatheca. [B.C. Baehr]

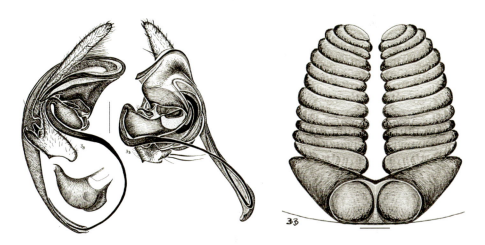

Some entelegyne spiders, here *Masasteron complector* from Western Australia, have extremely complicated pedipalp structures (left) and corresponding strongly coiled internal genitalia (right). [B.C. Baehr]

Mating is inherently dangerous for male spiders as females may mistake them for prey. Copulation is therefore often preceded by complicated behavioural sequences initiated by the male. These differ greatly between species. Spiders use a great number of sensory channels to communicate, such as visual cues, chemical cues, and vibratory cues including web-borne signals or drumming on the surface with pedipalps or abdomen in vagrant spiders. Often these signals are used by single males in combination and these multimodal male mating displays may reflect the reproductive fitness of a male.

Maternal care

All female spiders protect their eggs by encasing them into a more or less complicated case of silk, the eggsac. In their simplest form, these sacs may just be a few strands of silk that hold the eggs together and the eggs are clearly visible, such as in the Daddy Long-legs (Pholcidae) or Spitting Spiders (Scytodidae). However, most spiders construct a fairly dense case of varying shape to maintain optimal climatic conditions for the eggs and to protect them from fungal growth and parasites.

Most spiders fix their eggsacs to the substrate or suspend it in or near the web. They may abandon it immediately, but in many spiders, the mother provides maternal care and will defend the clutch against potential predators. In some vagrant spiders, females will construct their eggsac in a silken retreat in which they stay until the spiderlings hatch. The mother may have to help the young to escape the eggsac.

This female Twin-peaked Thwaitesia, *Thwaitesia argiopunctata* (family Theridiidae), from Queensland has placed her eggs in a fluffy eggsac attached to the underside of a leaf [P. Zborowski]

The architecture of spider eggsacs may vary greatly, even within families. Both Jumping Spider (Salticidae) females shown on this page have attached their eggsac to the underside of a leaf and remain with it and defend it. However, the eggsacs differ greatly in shape either forming a compact disc with short strands to secure it to the leaf (left) or a fluffy, loose eggsac through which the eggs can be seen (below). [P. Zborowski]

This female Cat-eye Spider, *Chrysso nigra* (family Theridiidae), produces a pear-shaped eggsac which is attached to the underside of a leaf [P. Zborowski]

Female Daddy Long-legs Spiders (family Pholcidae), here possibly *Belisana australis* photographed in Queensland, carry their eggsac between their chelicerae. However, the eggsacs are very flimsy without much of a protective silk layer. [P. Zborowski]

Below: Crab Spiders (family Thomisidae), such as this *Diaea* female, fix their eggsac under a protective cover of silk on the upperside of a leaf. [P. Zborowski]

Mobile maternal care is comparatively rare in spiders and occurs in families such as the Spitting Spiders (Scytodidae), Daddy Long-legs (Pholcidae) and the Fishing Spiders (Pisauridae) in which females carry their eggsac between their chelicerae. In contrast, Wolf Spider (Lycosidae) mothers attach the eggsac to their spinnerets. Mobile brood care is of great advantage as the female is able to seek optimal physical condition for the development of the eggs and she can remove her clutch from danger. For example, Fishing Spiders and Wolf Spiders are very abundant near water in habitats in constant danger of inundation, and their ecological success in these environments may be partly due to the ability to protect their eggsac from rising water levels by simply moving them away from the shore. A limitation of this strategy is that only one eggsac can be built at a time, whereas many other spiders construct multiple eggsacs simultaneously.

Fishing Spider (family Pisauridae) mothers, here *Hygropoda lineata* from Queensland, carry the eggsac between their chelicerae. The advantage of providing well for her clutch is traded against the limited ability to catch prey. Before the spiderlings hatch, pisaurids construct a special nursery web in which the initial stages of the young reside under the protection of the mother. [P. Zborowski]

Wolf Spiders (family Lycosidae), here *Venatrix arenaris* from Western Australia, carry their eggsac attached to the spinnerets so that she can seek optimal conditions for the development of the eggs in relation to temperature and humidity. She is also able to remove her clutch from any danger such as predators or inundation. [V.W. Framenau, Phoenix Environmental Sciences]

Some spiders continue caring for the brood after the spiderlings hatch. For example, in many mygalomorph spiders, the young spiderlings will stay in the maternal burrow until favourable conditions occur, often the first seasonal rainfalls that allow the spiders to establish their own burrow in softer soil and with less danger of desiccation. Wolf Spiders (Lycosidae) have taken maternal brood care to the next level. After the spiderlings hatch, they climb onto the females back and remain there for about two to four weeks, depending on species, until they disperse. Wolf Spider mothers can often be seen completely covered by multiple layers of spiderlings.

The female Black House Spider, *Badumna insignis* (family Desidae), builds a few eggsacs within a cribellate sheet-web. She stays with them until the young hatch and disperse. [P. Zborowski]

Juveniles in the genus *Phryganoporus* (family Desidae), here *P. nigrinus* from Western Australia, remain in the maternal nest for extended periods of time. In some species of the genus this leads to colonies of related mature animals, representing a primitive form of sociality in spiders. [V.W. Framenau, Phoenix Environmental Sciences]

Wolf Spider females, here an unidentified *Artoria*, carry their young on their back after they hatch from the eggsac. Spiderlings have a free ride until they moult for the first time and disperse, often by ballooning on gossamer. [P. Zborowski]

Moult

A rigid exoskeleton does not allow unlimited growth. Spiders, as other arthropods, solve this issue by regularly shedding their skin during their development (moult or ecdysis). In araneomorph and male mygalomorph spiders, growth stops when they reach maturity; once genitalia are fully developed, spiders mate (maybe with more than one female) and die. In contrast, female Mygalomorphae grow their entire life. These females lay eggs after copulation, care for their brood and become virgin again after their next moult.

Life span greatly varies between spiders. Typically, araneomorph spiders may reach maturity and reproduce within one or two years and their life cycle, in particular in temperate zones, is often tightly synchronised with the seasons. For example, the Christmas or Jewel Spider (*Austracantha minax*) is generally found as adult spider in early summer before Christmas, which is reflected in one of the common names for this spider. After reproduction, adults die and the smaller juveniles live lower in the vegetation unnoticed by most nature lovers. They rise up with larger and higher webs after winter to be noticed again just before Christmas. In contrast, the little Yellow-handed Artoria (*Artoria flavimana*), a Wolf Spider, is winter mature. Despite its wide distribution along the southern coast of Australia including Tasmania, specimens are rare in collections because most ecological work is limited to the warmer seasons. Mygalomorph males may live five to seven years before reaching maturity and their female counterparts may live up to 40 years. Overall, little is currently known about the exact life cycle of many Australian spiders.

Arboreal spiders often moult suspended on a strand of silk. This Huntsman Spider (family Sparassidae) hangs upside down while its prosoma splits open between carapace and sternum. Gravity helps the soft spider to gently slip out of the old skin. [both images: P. Zborowski]

Female mygalomorph spiders, here an unidentified *Selenotholus* (family Theraphosidae) from north-western Australia, are very long-lived and grow their entire life even after reaching maturity. Before the moult, she spins a fine sheet-web on which she places herself upside down. The prosoma splits open along the side where the legs attach. Slowly, the female wiggles out of her old skin, shedding booklungs and genitalia to become a virgin once more. [V.W. Framenau, Phoenix Environmental Sciences]

Spider venom

In addition to the production of silk from abdominal gland spigots and reproduction assisted by male pedipalps functioning as secondary genitalia, cheliceral venom glands are the third major feature that makes a spider.

All spiders, with a few exceptions such as the Venomless Spiders (family Uloboridae) and the Minute Long-jawed Spiders (Holarchaeidae), have venom glands in their paturon or cephalothorax. The venom has primarily evolved to succumb prey but it is also very useful for defence. The venom of most spiders has a neurotoxic component, but the way in which this affects the nervous system of their prey varies greatly. The alpha-latrotoxins of the Redback Spiders (genus *Latrodectus*) cause the release of neurotransmitters such as acetylcholine or norepinephrine which stimulate muscle contractions. The atratoxins of the Funnel-web Spiders (family Hexathelidae) open sodium channels which in turn causes excessive neural activity. Mouse Spiders (family

Actinopodidae) have a venom similar to atratoxin.

Recluse Spiders (family Sicariidae) have a necrotic enzyme in their venom, sphingomyelinase D, which can result in excessive skin lesions or ulcers that can take a long time to heal. In rare cases, systemic effects can occur. The White-tailed Spiders (family Lamponidae) and Wolf Spiders (family Lycosidae) have been associated with necrotic ulcers after bites but these effects have not been confirmed in medical studies in which spiders where collected and identified by an expert arachnologist. It is more likely that secondary bacterial infections are responsible for necrotic ulcers following the bites of these spiders, as sphingomyelinase D is also reported from some pathogenic soil-borne bacteria.

Members of only two Australian spider groups are known to cause fatal envenomations in humans, these being the Funnel-web Spiders (genera *Atrax* and *Hadronyche*, family Hexathelidae) and the Redback Spiders (*Latrodectus hasseltii*, Theridiidae). However, antivenom is available for both groups, but may only be given in severe envenomations. More detailed information on the toxicity of spider venom can be found in the family chapters of this book.

Most spiders produce a neurotoxic venom that allows them to overcome prey much bigger than themselves. This tiny *Euryopis* female, a Comb-footed Spider (family Theridiidae), is feeding on an ant, *Camponotus chalceus*, which is about five times its own size. [F. Bokhari]

Evolution and systematics of spiders

Currently 112 families of spiders are recognised worldwide, of which 79 have been reported from Australia. This book deals with spider families as a core unit and there is a necessity to provide some order to this diversity. The most logical way to structure a guide book is to place similar groups together for easy comparison, and we have followed this pattern here. Similar families are often closely related and therefore the order of families in this book follows our current understanding of the evolutionary history of the spider families. The most ancient group known from Australia, the Mygalomorphae, are treated first and the most advanced spiders, the Entelegynae, within the Araneomorphae, are dealt with in the later parts of the book. A short discourse into the evolution and systematics of spiders will help to understand the layout of this book.

Spiders are one of the better-understood mega-diverse arthropod orders. The inter-relationships of almost all spider families have been treated in systematic studies and placed in an evolutionary context. However, new methods, in particular the ever-increasing number of studies of DNA, now challenge some of the concepts that have been developed by studying morphological traits in the past.

Spider-like arthropods found in the Devonian period from about 380 million years ago could produce silk but did not have spinnerets and are therefore not considered to be spiders. They belong into a separate extinct order, the Uraraneida. Fossils of the first true spiders, similar to the basal segmented Mesothelae, date back to the Carboniferous period some 300 million years ago. The first spiders with spinnerets at the end of the abdomen appeared some 250 million years ago with representatives of the mygalomorph spider family Hexathelidae in the Triassic period. The first Orb-web Spiders have been dated to the Cretaceous period some 136 million years ago, although a giant spider, initially thought to be a *Nephila* and named *Nephila jurassica*, dates back earlier, to the Jurassic period about 165 million years ago. It is now believed that Nephilidae did not evolve before about 50 million years ago and therefore *N. jurassica* belongs to a much earlier, possibly orb-weaving, lineage.

The ancient Mesothelae, today only known from some 90 species in South-East Asia, China and Japan, feature a segmented abdomen reminiscent of segmented spider-ancestors. All other spiders, the Opisthothelae, lost any obvious segmentation and can be divided into the more primitive Mygalomorphae (Trapdoor Spiders) and the more advanced Araneomorphae (Modern Spiders). The Mygalomorphae retained the forward-directed chelicerae with parallel fangs similar to those of the Mesothelae. The Araneomorphae changed to ventrally directed chelicerae with fangs working against each other, and the evolutionary advantage of this is discussed in the introductory chapters for these groups.

Whilst there is good scientific consensus on the above higher level systematic groupings of spiders, the evolutionary relationships between some spider families, and in some cases even the validity of these, remains unresolved. Recent systematic analyses employing modern molecular methods have cast doubt on some traditional concepts within both the Mygalomorphae and Araneomorphae. It is therefore impossible to provide a family number and order for this book to which all arachnologists would agree. However, we have endeavoured to list competing hypotheses within each family chapter

Traditionally, the Araneomorphae have been divided into the basal Hypochiloidea (only known from North America and China), the Austrochiloidea (Australasia and South America) and a third clade that consists of the Haplogynae and Entelegyne. Hypochiloidea and Austrochiloidea both retain two pairs of book lungs (as Mesothelae and Mygalomorphae) suggesting these to be the more ancient representatives within the Araneomorphae. Most other araneomorph spiders have only retained the frontal one pair of booklungs, whereas the rear pair has evolved into a tracheal system. Within these, the Haplogynae have simple genitalia, in particular they lack an external, well-developed female epigyne. In terms of evolution they are considered the less developed spiders, in comparison to the Entelegynae in which females have well developed, sclerotised external genitalia.

Following the above phylogenetic order, this book deals with the families within the Mygalomorphae first (9 families) and then the Araneomorphae (70 families). Here Austrochiloidea (2 families) are treated before the Haplogynae (11 families) and then the Entelegynae (57 families).

About one quarter of the Australian spider families have been taxonomically revised recently, where comprehensive studies that allow genus- and species-level identification have been published using modern taxonomic methods and concepts. However, that does not mean that all species of these families occurring in Australia have a scientific name. Comprehensive revisions are based on spider material present in museum collections at the time, and species never collected or preserved would not have been treated. Well-known faunas include the Golden Orb-weaving Spiders and allies (Nephilidae), the Red-and-black Spiders (Nicodamidae), White-tailed Spiders (Lamponidae) and lesser known families such as the Long-spinneret Ground Spiders (Prodidomidae). About 30 families had a partial taxonomic reassessment in recent times. In these groups, selected genera may have been revised, but genus-level identifications may not be possible, or species-level identifications in many genera remain obscure. This is the case, for example, for True Trapdoor Spiders (Idiopidae), Jumping Spiders (Salticidae), Wolf Spiders (Lycosidae) and Daddy Long-legs Spiders (Pholcidae). About 24 spider families are so poorly known that identifying species, if at all possible, requires detective work and familiarisation with historical arachnological literature. The nomenclature for the described species is often out of date (for example, species are historically listed in genera which we now know do not occur in Australia), but most species will simply not be named at all. Some of the more conspicuous of these are the Crab or Flower Spiders (Thomisidae), Comb-footed Spiders (Theridiidae) and Sheet-web Spiders (Linyphiidae).

Five families occur in Australia based on introduced species only, and as these are generally widespread and synanthropic species, identification is often possible. They include the Recluse Spiders (Sicariidae), Woodlouse Hunters (Dysderidae) and Flat-mesh Weavers (Oecobiidae). The level of taxonomic resolution is identified for each family in this book and although it is somewhat arbitrary, here referred to as "taxonomy revised", "partially revised", "taxonomy poorly resolved" or "introduced species only".

Naming of spiders

Below family level, only a few spiders have common or colloquial names. These are generally the spiders that are of some relevance to the public, for example because they are venomous (Australian Redback Spider, Sydney Funnel-web Spider) or because they are ubiquitous and often seen around houses (Black House Spider, Daddy Long-legs). Unlike for scientific nomenclature, which is strongly governed by the International Committee for Zoological Nomenclature (ICZN), there is no organisation that rules on the validity of common names, and there might be a wide variety of names for the same thing. Despite that, the use of colloquial names facilitates communication about spiders with the public and makes Araneology more accessible. Therefore, we use colloquial names as much as possible and in some cases we may even have coined new ones whilst writing this book. We do not claim final wisdom on common names in spiders, but we have used those which we believe are in common usage and have attempted to provide names that are logical. In some cases, for example in the Golden Orb-weavers (family Nephilidae) or Assassin Spiders (family Archaeidae), the recent scientific literature has proposed colloquial names. There is no rule if colloquial names are capitalised or not. We have followed the common application for vertebrates, such as birds and mammals, and capitalise all colloquial species names used in this book.

As we have to deal with a large number of scientific names, it will be helpful to some readers to introduce the most important principles of zoological nomenclature. Here is an example of the most important taxonomic levels in spiders:

Taxonomic level	Scientific name	Colloquial name
Order	Araneae	Spiders
Suborder	Opisthothelae	Unsegmented Spiders
Infraorder	Araneomorphae	Modern Spiders
Family	Theridiidae	Comb-footed Spiders
Subfamily	Latrodectinae	
Genus	*Latrodectus*	
Species	*hasseltii*	Australian Redback Spider

The scientific naming of some of these levels is governed by the ICZN. For example, the ending of a scientific family name is always –**idae**, such as Theridiidae above. Other family names are for the Brush-footed Trapdoor Spiders: Barychel**idae**, Goblin Spiders: Oonop**idae**, and Jumping Spiders: Saltic**idae**.

For most Australian spiders, their association with a particular spider family is settled, but there are exceptions, and in some cases scientists argue about it depending on what evidence they follow. Recent molecular studies based on the analyses of DNA challenge a number of systematic concepts derived from studies of the morphology of spiders and these may not yet be widely accepted. A typical example is the current placement of the Australian genus *Kiama* in the Nemesiidae (based on mainly molecular evidence of selected genes), in contrast to its placement in the Cyrtaucheniidae based on morphological evidence. Another example concerns the Leaf-curling Spiders (genera *Phonognatha* and *Deliochus*) which have at times been argued to belong to the Long-jawed Spiders (Tetragnathidae), the Orb-weaving Spiders (Araneidae) and at the time of the writing of this book, suggested to belong in the Zygiellidae, a family currently not listed in the *World Spider Catalog* by Norman Platnick of the American Museum of Natural History (http://research.amnh.org/iz/spiders/catalog/INTRO3.html), which is the authoritative taxonomic reference for spiders worldwide. It is beyond the scope of this book to assess the merit of controversial taxonomic or systematic issues. If appropriate we alert to problems within certain family placements of genera.

Some spider families are very large and it helps to break these down into recognisable smaller units, the subfamilies, before tackling an overview at genus level. Subfamily names have the ending **–inae**. A typical example where this is helpful is the Orb-weaving Spiders (family Araneidae). A number of subfamilies are recognised, such as the Gasteracanth**inae** (which includes the spiny Jewel or Christmas Spiders), Argiop**inae** (which includes the St Andrew's Cross Spiders), Mastophor**inae** (which includes the Magnificent or Bola-Spiders) and Arane**inae** (representing the typical nocturnal orb-weavers). In general, the systematic resolution at subfamily level is even less resolved than at the family level, and a subfamily classification may not exist at all. Hence, subfamilies are here mentioned only within each family if they assist in providing an overview of the composition of the family.

A genus unites species into a group which share a common ancestry, and are overall more similar within this group than outside. In some cases, species are so different from any other that they are placed in a genus by themselves. A typical example is the Tasmanian Cave Spider, *Hickmania troglodytes*. No other species is placed in the genus *Hickmania*. The level of difference from one genus to another is somewhat arbitrary and is best made within the context of the same family, i.e.

how do species in a family group the best, and what defines a genus within this family. About 650 spider genera are currently described for Australia, and taking into account that many families have not been revised taxonomically, this number is a testament for the incredible diversity of spiders in this country. The most genus-rich family is the Jumping Spiders (Salticidae) with 80 genera, followed by the Orb-weaving Spiders (Araneidae) with 40 genera, Wolf Spiders (Lycosidae) and Ant-eating Spiders (Zodaridae) with 30 genera each, and Crab or Flower Spiders (Thomisidae) with 23 genera. However, none of these are completely revised and the number of genera will clearly increase. The number of estimated genera are given in each family chapter. The naming of a genus rests with the scientist describing it and although there are some guiding rules through the ICZN, generic names might be somewhat peculiar. For example, *Abracadabrella* is a genus of Jumping Spiders (Salticidae), *Kangarosa* a genus of Wolf Spiders (Lycosidae) and *Pinkfloydia* a genus in the Long-jawed Spiders (Tetragnthidae). The late Tasmanian arachnologist V.V. Hickman had at least three genera named after him, *Hickmanapis* (Ground Orb-web Spiders, Anapidae), *Hickmania* (Junction-web Weavers, Austrochilidae) and *Hickmanolobus* (Six-eyed Ground Spiders, Orsolobidae).

There a currently some 3,500 species of spiders described from Australia, although this only represents half to a third of the estimated diversity. Based on the number of described species, the largest families are the Jumping Spiders (Salticidae) (385 species), Orb-weaving Spiders (Araneidae) (268 species) and Ant-eating Spiders (Zodariidae) (252 species). However, there is still a considerable undocumented fauna in each of these families.

The most prolific taxonomists dealing with the Australian fauna are so far Barbara Baehr (Queensland Museum), one of the authors of this book, who described 523 currently recognised species, followed by Norman Platnick (American Museum of Natural History) with 506 species, although both have published a number of species as co-authors. Still the third in line is the German arachnologist and entomologist Ludwig C. C. Koch (1825–1908) who described 370 currently valid species, mostly between 1871 and 1881 as author of the monumental "*Die Arachniden Australiens*", which was continued by Eugen von Keyserling (1833–1889) between 1885 and 1889; von Keyserling himself is the author of 130 valid species.

Spiders of Australia - peculiarities

The Australian spider fauna can generally be divided into three major elements. The oldest element is the indigenous Australian fauna that often has biogeographic affinities to Gondwana, the old southerly supercontinent. Gondwana, composed nowadays of South America, Africa, Madagascar, India, Australia, New Zealand and Antarctica, began to break up in the early Jurassic period (184 million years ago). Australia together with New Guinea, the Sahul Shelf, is believed to have separated from Antarctica between 80–55 million years ago, and was then isolated for about 40 million years. Spider families that show a typical Gondwana distribution are the Junction Orb-weavers (Austrochilidae) with representatives currently only known from Tasmania, Chile and Argentina. Similarly, the Mouse Spiders (Actinopodidae) are only known from Australia and South America. Many other examples of spider families with Gondwanan affinities exist.

From about 15 million. years ago, the Sahul Shelf moved into South-East Asia's Sunda Shelf. The close proximity to Asia allowed species to invade Australia from the north, and these invaders represent the second major faunal element in Australia. For example, the Wolf Spider (Lycosidae) subfamily Lycosinae, which represents the larger, burrowing species, can be divided in a large clade with relatives found in South America and a smaller group that has affinities with spiders from the Northern Hemisphere. Many of these spiders have moved south along the east coast of Australia and can now be found into Tasmania.

The third, much smaller faunal element includes those species that have been carried into Australia mainly by human activity. As these are generally synanthropic and thrive around human dwellings, they often represent a very conspicuous fauna. Typical examples include some Daddy Long-legs (Pholcidae), the Woodlouse Hunter (Dysderidae) and the Recluse Spiders (Sicariidae).

Australia is a very old continent and a vast part of its arid landscape has never been inundated or been covered by glaciation. Hence, Australia has a very diverse ancient fauna, in particular within the Mygalomorphae. The Wishbone Spiders (Nemesiidae) are extremely diverse in the north-western parts of the country, and the number of undescribed species runs into the hundreds. Conversely, some spider families that are dominant in other parts of the world, in particular the northern hemisphere, have a poor representation in Australia. The Sheet-web

Weavers (Linyphiidae) represent almost half of the species diversity in Central Europe, and at a world-scale are the second largest spider family based on the number of described species. Yet, they represent only a very small fraction of the Australian fauna with an estimated 200 species.

Some originally Australian spiders have been exported by humans. For example, the Australian Redback Spider, *Latrodectus hasseltii* (family Theridiidae), now has well-established populations in Japan and the Brown House Spider, *Badumna longiqua* (family Desidae) has been found in California and Europe. Many Australian species of spiders can be found in New Zealand and some, such as White-tailed Spider, *Lampona cylindrata* (family Lamponidae), were possibly spread by humans.

How to identify spiders, how to use this book

The main aim of this book is to provide an overview of the enormous and fascinating diversity of Australian Spiders. To do all Australian spiders justice, we have included all families known from this continent, even if spiders in some families are so cryptic, rare or small that they are almost never encountered by the passionate naturalist. As such, this is not a simple field guide, it goes much beyond.

Many, indeed most Australian spiders, cannot be identified to species level by comparison with a photograph and the naked eye, although family and sometimes genus level identification is possible in the field. However, we hope this book will help to put any given spider at hand at least into the vicinity of its true identity, and for many common and distinctive species this can be the species it belongs to.

At the end of the book we have provided some suggestions for further reading relating to each chapter. In many cases, these are the scientific papers which have been used to compile this book. These references often provide much more detail on the distribution of species or how to identify them. Many of these references are available as Adobe® PDF-files, free of charge on the Internet. We have not included the respective web address (URL) as this might change. But simply putting the title of a publication into your preferred Internet search engine will quickly provide a link to the publication. From this book, this is the next step to delve further into the fascinating world of Australian spiders.

PART 2
MYGALOMORPHAE - TRAPDOOR SPIDERS

One of the characteristics of spiders in the Infraorder Mygalomorphae, the Trapdoor Spiders, is the orientation of the fangs which are situated more or less parallel to each other designed for a downward stroke. [V.W. Framenau, Phoenix Environmental Sciences]

MYGALOMORPHAE
Trapdoor Spiders

The common name for the ancient infraorder Mygalomorphae applied in this book is Trapdoor Spider, although it is recognised that not all of these spiders close their burrow with a trapdoor; indeed, not all even construct a true burrow. The combination of two characters identifies the Mygalomorphae, two pairs of booklungs and paraxial (downward-striking) fangs. These characters also occur in the Araneomorphae; for example, the ancient Austrochilidae and Gradungulidae have two pairs of booklungs and the Gallieniellidae have paraxial fangs, but the two characters are never seen together in Modern Spiders.

There are 17 families of mygalomorph spiders worldwide, of which nine occur in Australia, if we accept that the genus *Kiama* belongs to the Nemesiidae. This placement is controversial and if the genus is considered a member of the Cyrtaucheniidae, the number of mygalomorph spider families in Australia rises to

The paraxial orientation of the fangs in mygalomorph spiders, here an undescribed *Aname* male (family Nemesiidae) from Western Australia, necessitates a downward stroke to attack prey or for defence. This attack is most effective against a solid substrate and will not work well in an elastic prey capture web. This foraging limitation in combination with the higher risk of desiccation due to two pairs instead of one pair of booklungs most likely kept mygalomorph spiders in burrows and on the ground [V.W. Framenau, Phoenix Environmental Sciences]

ten. Eastern Australia is home to all nine Trapdoor Spider families, a notable and welcome absence from Western Australia is the family Hexathelidae (Funnel-web Spiders) which includes the most venomous spiders in the world.

The two characters mentioned above limit Trapdoor Spiders to a largely ground-dwelling lifestyle in permanent burrows or retreats. The four booklungs expose a large surface area to the air, which leaves these spiders extremely susceptible to desiccation. A closed burrow helps maintain temperature and humidity at levels that reduce water loss. Spiders are most active in favourable conditions, mainly at night. An effective strike with paraxial fangs is only possible when the prey item is pushed against solid ground, and therefore Mygalomorphae generally don't build a prey capture web. Web elasticity would simply not provide sufficient resistance to penetrate the prey. In contrast, the fangs of Araneomorphae work against each other allowing to efficiently bite prey anywhere without ground support.

Females and developing juveniles of most species stay in the same permanent burrow as long as they are not disturbed and sufficient food remains available. This means that mature males need to leave the burrow to find a mate. Male ground-dwelling spiders often have comparatively longer legs than females, as higher mobility appears to be advantageous in their evolutionary arms race. Interestingly, experimental evidence that longer-legged males mate successfully with more females and produce relatively more offspring, prerequisite for higher evolutionary fitness, has never been brought forward. Due to the physiological restrictions mentioned above, males may spend a considerable time waiting in the burrow after their final moult, until favourable conditions arrive. In particular in arid environments, males are usually found wandering after the first seasonal rainfalls, and then generally leave the burrow at night. Whilst many spiders, including Trapdoor Spiders, show seasonal patterns in their lifecycle, detailed studies on this are very rare.

Unlike most Araneomorphae, the Trapdoor Spiders are very long-lived. Field surveys suggest lifespans of up to 40 years, with an average time to maturation of maybe five to seven years. They generally moult only once per year, and females continue renewing their skin even after reaching maturity. In contrast, the male's life is over after mating, possibly more than once with multiple females. In some cases they may fall prey to the female they mated with. Sexual cannibalism is not uncommon in spiders generally.

HEXATHELIDAE
Funnel-web Spiders

- Eight eyes in a compact rectangular group
- Carapace shiny and sparsely haired
- Labium with short and stout spines
- Two or three pairs of spinnerets, posterior lateral pair elongated
- Nocturnal hunters in a silken funnel with trip-lines at the burrow entrance
- Body length: 14–50 mm

Australia:
Taxonomy revised
Current: 50 species in 7 genera
Estimated: 53 species in 7 genera
World: 112 species in 12 genera

The Funnel-web Spiders, family Hexathelidae, are probably Australia's most notorious spiders, with their name striking fear into the hearts of many. However, their venom is harmless to many animals, like dogs, cats, guinea pigs and sheep, which neutralise the venom within 20–30 minutes. Coincidentally, it may be fatal to primates, including humans, who presumably lost the neutralising enzyme. The high toxicity of Funnel-web Spider venom to humans is therefore an evolutionary oddity. Funnel-web Spiders have been responsible for at least 13 deaths in Australia, although no fatalities have occurred since the introduction of an antivenom in the early 1980s.

The Hexathelidae fall into three distinct subfamilies. The Atracinae have two pairs of spinnerets and possibly include the world's three most dangerous spider genera: *Atrax*, *Hadronyche* and *Illawarra*. The Hexathelinae (including *Bymainiella*, *Paraembolides* and *Teranodes*) and the Plesiothelinae (with the single genus *Plesiothele*) have three pairs of spinnerets. The latter two subfamilies include spiders with much more ornate body patterns than the generally black to brown atracine Funnel-web Spiders.

Hexathelidae are only found in the eastern mainland states of Australia and Tasmania. Their distribution is very much governed by temperature and humidity. The Sydney region is lucky enough to accommodate all the highly venomous genera of the **Atracinae**. The Sydney Funnel-web Spider, *Atrax robustus*, occurs only within approximately a 120 km radius of Sydney and the

The Sydney Funnel-web Spider, *Atrax robustus*, is only found within a 120 km radius around Sydney. The male of this species illustrated here is one of the most venomous spiders in the world. People are mainly bitten between October and December when males roam in search of a mate. Males are about 20 mm long. [M.R. Gray, Australian Museum]

other two species of *Atrax* are found only in southern New South Wales, Victoria and the Australian Capital Territory. *Illawarra* includes a single species from near Wollongong. The most diverse and widespread genus is *Hadronyche*, which includes 31 described species localised in various regions across the entire range of the family. In Queensland, they tend to be found in the cooler rainforests or mountains, and one species, *Hadronyche anzses*, occurs in the remote high mountains west of Mossman. On Fraser Island, *Hadronyche infensa* lives both in moist rainforest and the heath covered hills. Further south, they occur in lowland coastal areas in New South Wales, the ACT, Victoria and Tasmania. Two species occur in very localised areas of South Australia, the Flinders Range (*H. flindersi*) and Eyre Peninsula (*H. eyrei*). At present, *Hadronyche pulvinator*, from the Cascades area of Hobart, despite frequent searches, has not been found since 1927.

The 19 species of the less venomous **Hexathelinae** and **Plesiothelinae** occur across a similar range. Among these, *Plesiothele* and *Teranodes* survived the Pleistocene glaciations in Tasmania. The single species of *Plesiothele*, known only from the Central Highlands of Tasmania, is probably the most ancient mygalomorph spider alive.

The Hexathelidae have been well studied, so we are confident they are not present in Western Australia or the Northern Territory.

Funnel-web Spiders can be transported accidentally in hollow soil-filled logs and staghorn ferns, where they natively live. Hence, if you transport large plants, logs or large amounts of soil from the wild, you may have a surprise hitchhiker. In one case, a male Funnel-web Spider hopped on clothing in New South Wales and travelled by caravan to Hobart where it was found still alive and well.

Funnel-web spider burrows can predominantly be found in moist, cool and sheltered habitats where they burrow under and in logs, rocks, and the crevices

Female Sydney Funnel-web Spiders, *Atrax robustus*, are considerably larger than their male counterparts and their body length may exceed 30 mm. They rarely leave the vicinity of their burrow, usually when disturbed naturally (for example, due to flooding) or by human interference. The female lacks the fatal neurotoxin of the male and therefore her bites are less severe. [M.R. Gray, Australian Museum]

of trees. Most species are ground-dwellers, but some, like the Southern Tree Funnel-web Spider, *Hadronyche cerberea*, and the Northern Tree Funnel-web Spider, *Hadronyche formidabilis*, may be entirely arboreal, excavating burrows within decomposing wood of logs or trees. *Hadronyche formidabilis* is the largest of all Funnel-web Spiders in Australia, reaching up to 50 mm body length.

Funnel-web spiders are vibration-sensitive animals, which feed on insects, such as beetles or cockroaches, and other arthropods such as millipedes. Vertebrates such as small skinks are also taken.

A number of predators have been reported taking Funnel-web Spiders. For example, males are fed upon by Land Mullets (*Egernia major*), large black bluetongue-like lizards of rainforests and cooler zones. Females fall prey to large centipedes that seem to find them as they hunt through the soil. The delicate, beautiful and deceptively harmless Velvet Worms (Onychophora) and Flat Worms (Platyhelminthes, Geoplanidae species) enter the burrow so slowly the spider does not respond. They then quietly attack the spider at the soft leg joints, and kill and eat their insides. As with many other big spiders, Funnel-web Spiders also fall prey to White-tailed Spiders (*Lampona* species, family Lamponidae).

The most dangerous species is the Sydney Funnel-web Spider, *Atrax robustus*, but any bite from a Funnel-web Spider should be treated seriously. Unlike snakes, Funnel-web Spiders do not inject venom. The drops are produced on the fang tips. Hence, most of the venom can be easily lost in clothing or bumped off. Equally, as venom milkers know well, only a limited amount of venom is produced at any time, and once used, it is a month before the spider can be milked again. Until then only 'dry' (venom-free) bites occur.

Severe Funnel-web Spider envenomation is limited to New South Wales and southern Queensland and mainly involves the Sydney Funnel-web Spider and the two tree-dwelling *Hadronyche* species mentioned above, in addition to a few other *Hadronyche*. Severe envenomation in humans has only been reported for bites from male Funnel-web Spiders. These are more likely to get into contact with humans while searching for females, which generally remain sedentary in and around their burrows. In addition, at least valid for the Sydney Funnel-web Spider, the female venom does not include the component that is responsible for the fatal neurological effects of the male spider's atratoxin.

Funnel-web Spiders, like this *Hadronyche* male from southern Queensland, are generally black and have strong legs that are usually quick to rise to the attack pose; however, they cannot jump, even short distances. They are poorly sighted. When they attack they are virtually blind as the head is angled back so the eyes detect only shadows. [J. Haider]

The colloquial name Funnel-web Spiders refers to the silken, funnel-like burrows that are not armed with a door. This *Hadronyche* web was found on the cooler eastern slopes of Fraser Island, Queensland. [R.J. Raven]

Hadronyche male showing the heart-shaped sternum with three dark pairs of sigillae. The abdomen bears two pairs of orange booklungs. [J. Haider]

The female of *Teranodes montanus*, a member of the subfamily Hexathelinae, is a rather slender Funnel-web Spider with brown rings on the legs and pale chevrons on top of the abdomen. This species is currently known only from Tasmania and southern Victoria. The second and similar species in the genus, *T. otwayensis*, also occurs in wet sclerophyll forests of southern Victoria. [R.J. Raven]

DIPLURIDAE
Curtain-web Spiders

- Six or eight eyes in two rows (*Troglodiplura* is blind)
- Carapace very low and hairy
- Legs slender
- Very long, three-segmented posterior lateral spinnerets
- Nocturnal hunters with curtain web
- Body length: 3–30 mm

Australia:
Partially revised
Current: 30 species in 7 genera
Estimated: 50 species in 9 genera
World: 179 species in 24 genera

Unlike most other mygalomorph spiders that lead a largely cryptic lifestyle, Curtain-web Spiders (family Dipluridae) use an extensive sheet- or curtain-web outside their burrow for prey capture. The silken tube of the burrow opens in one or several funnel-like mouths. It may also lead to a massive, curtain-like web against tree stumps, shrubs, embankments and rocks. Corridors or tubes may be incorporated into the webs to facilitate movement.

Seven genera of Curtain-web Spiders are currently known from Australia, but four of these (*Caledothele*, *Carrai*, *Masteria*, and *Troglodiplura*) include only a single species each. With 12 described species, *Cethegus* is the largest and most widespread genus. *Australothele* and *Namirea*, both only found in Queensland and New South Wales, currently include seven species each. Genus and species identification can be difficult and may require the use of a stereomicroscope.

Diplurids live in tropical and subtropical regions worldwide, and occur throughout mainland Australia in most habitats from rainforest to arid grassland. They have not been recorded from Tasmania. The highest diversity is in eastern Queensland where five of the seven genera occur. *Carrai afoveolata* is known only from near Kempsey, New South Wales, where it is usually found under logs in black, friable soils. *Masteria toddae* is a tiny, litter-dwelling spider from northern Queensland. *Caledothele australiensis* is known from eastern Victorian sclerophyll fern forest. This genus is most diverse in New Caledonia. *Cethegus* is the only genus of Curtain-web Spiders found in Western Australia, although the northern tropical fauna of the state remains poorly investigated and may harbour additional genera.

The Nullarbor Cave Trapdoor Spider, *Troglodiplura lowryi*, only known from caves on the Nullarbor Plain in Western Australia, is the only known true troglobitic (cave-adapted) mygalomorph spider in Australia. It is completely blind. The species is currently considered to belong to the Dipluridae, although it has previously been regarded as member of the family Nemesiidae based on the presence of two rows of teeth on the tarsal claws.

Males of many Curtain-web Spiders have a mating spine on the first and sometimes also the second legs. These spines are used during mating, when the males attain a precarious geometry to prevent the extended female fangs from descending unceremoniously through their head. One pair of spines safely holds the female's fangs, and the other pair arrests a pair of her legs.

Nothing is known of the bite of Curtain-web Spiders, as they seem to be timid and rarely, if ever, attack when disturbed.

Curtain Web Spiders, here *Namirea planipes* from south-eastern Queensland, spin delicate silk with their two long finger-like spinnerets. The webs fill spaces from the size of a matchbox to the size of an oven. *Namirea* species tend to be more common along open forest edges. [J. Haider]

The genus *Australothele*, here an *Australothele jamiesoni* female from south-eastern Queensland, occurs in highest numbers in moist forest corridors or rainforests in Queensland. [J. Haider]

Jamieson's Curtain-web Spider, *Australothele jamiesoni*, builds a filmy white curtain web around the bases of trees, clumps of rocks and on embankments. Several tunnels are usually seen from the outside. Judged by piles of small charopid and pupinid snail shells in the deepest part of the web, snails form part of their diet. Experiments with the introduced garden snail, *Helix aspersa*, placed in their web showed that the spiders bite the soft extended foot of the snail and then rotate their body around the head, spinning silk from their long spinnerets as they go. That swathes the prey in silk, the hard way (Modern Spiders generally rotate the prey). [R.J. Raven]

This undescribed male *Cethegus* from Barrow Island, Western Australia, displays the typical flat and hairy carapace of the Dipluridae. In contrast to the dark species typical for forest habitats, the dry forest and desert forms are generally pale brown to almost orange. [V.W. Framenau, Phoenix Environmental Sciences]

Extremely elongated spinnerets are characteristic for species in the family Dipluridae, here seen in a male *Cethegus* from north-west Western Australia [V.W. Framenau, Phoenix Environmental Sciences]

A common modification of the *Cethegus* curtain-webs in Western Australia incorporates large amounts of soil in vertical strands. These types of webs are reported for *C. fugax*. [P.R. Langlands, Phoenix Environmental Sciences]

ACTINOPODIDAE
Mouse Spiders

- Eight eyes in two rows in wide rectangular arrangement
- Carapace highly elevated in front
- Chelicerae massive
- Night and day active hunters without prey capture web
- Burrow with single trapdoor or double-door
- Spinnerets short
- Body length: 10–30 mm

Australia:
Partially revised
Current: 16 species in 1 genus
Estimated: 40 species in 1 genus
World: 46 species in 3 genera

It is unclear how Mouse Spiders (family Actinopodidae) received their common name, but the legends go that somebody either found one of these spiders in a burrow presumed to be that of a mouse, or that they eat mice, or that the stocky females look like mice. In any case, the males of the red-headed species of *Missulena*, the only genus of the family in Australia, belong to one of the most recognisable spiders in this country, and are some of the most colourful mygalomorph spiders. Actinopodidae have Gondwanan affinities, only occurring in Australia and South and Central America.

Mouse Spiders cannot really be mistaken for any other family in Australia, as they are the only mygalomorph family in Australia with their eight eyes spread out across almost the whole width of the highly elevated head region. They are stout spiders with huge chelicerae. Whilst most species are black or dark brown, males of some species, such as the common Red-headed Mouse Spider, *Missulena occatoria*, have spectacular, bright red frontal parts of the body; either just the chelicerae, chelicerae and head region, or the complete carapace. Females of all species are usually uniformly dark brown to black, but in species with red-headed males the brown chelicerae might also have a reddish-orange tinge. The carapace is often shiny and with few or no hairs, but in some species it has a dimpled or rugose, matt appearance.

A total of 16 species in the genus *Missulena* are currently described throughout mainland Australia. Western Australia is the centre of this diversity, as all but two of the named species occur there, and a fair number of undescribed species are known from the state. *Missulena* has not been reported from Tasmania, but occurs on offshore islands such as Kangaroo Island (South Australia) and Groote Eylandt (Northern Territory). Many species of Mouse Spiders are widespread, probably facilitated by young spiderlings ballooning by gossamer, at least for small distances.

Species identification may be difficult, in particular in Western Australia where many similar species occur. Detailed examination of genitalia may be required to accurately establish the identity of males. Female taxonomy is even more problematic.

Mouse spiders are quite common in the suburbs of all Australian towns, but their burrows are not often obvious. Some species make a soil-encrusted, well-camouflaged web tube which flops onto the ground in lawns or open ground. Sometimes one may find a small pyramid of soil beside the well-concealed tube. In Western Australia, many species construct hinged double-doors to close their single burrow. The spiders are often found while gardens are being dug or soil turned over. Males of most species wander from late summer into winter. Unlike other mygalomorph spiders they can often be seen roaming around during the day, indicating a comparably low tendency for desiccation. It appears that they find the females based on airborne pheromones. They wander with raised pedipalps that presumably contain chemosensory organs, and often fall into suburban swimming pools whilst searching for females.

Mouse Spiders normally eat insects. Their main predators are bandicoots, scorpions, centipedes, flatworms, velvet worms and wasps.

Cases of Mouse Spiders biting humans are rare but can result in serious symptoms similar to those of Funnel-web Spiders (family Hexathelidae). The venom of *Missulena bradleyi* was found to be of similar composition to the venom of the Sydney Funnel-web Spider *Atrax robustus*. One serious bite from a Mouse Spider in Queensland was successfully treated with Funnel-web Spider antivenom. However, although Mouse Spiders are quite aggressive and bites are not uncommon, severe envenomation is rare, most likely as spiders commonly give 'dry' (venom-free) bites like some Funnel-web Spiders.

The male of the Red-headed Mouse Spider, *Missulena occatoria*, here photographed in Minnivale, Western Australia, shares with a number of other *Missulena* species a bright red coloration of frontal parts of the body and a dark royal blue abdomen. *Missulena occatoria* occurs in all Australian mainland states. The red coloration may convey a warning to potential predators as these spiders have a potent venom. Unusually for mygalomorph spiders, the males may wander during the day in search of a female, making the warning coloration more important. [V.W. Framenau, Phoenix Environmental Sciences]

Missulena females do not display the intense bright coloration of some males. However, in species with red-headed males, females like this, of an undescribed species from the Pilbara region in Western Australia, may display a reddish-brown tinge on the chelicerae. Females are generally larger and stouter than males and less colourful. [V.W. Framenau, Phoenix Environmental Sciences]

An unidentified *Missulena* female from southern Western Australia. When provoked, *Missulena* rises quickly into the striking position. From underneath, the fangs of *Missulena* tend to cross at the tips whereas the fangs of other Mygalomorphae are parallel when closed. [V.W. Framenau, Phoenix Environmental Sciences]

Unusual amongst *Missulena*, this male Northern Mouse Spider, *Missulena pruinosa*, has a completely white upper abdomen. The species is found in tropical Western Australia, the Northern Territory and Queensland. [K. Lowe, Australian Museum]

The male of *Missulena bradleyi* has a pale patch in the frontal half of the abdomen. The female is uniformly black. This species is found in Queensland, New South Wales and Victoria. [M.R. Gray, Australian Museum]

Many species of *Missulena*, in particular in Western Australia, construct a burrow with a characteristic double-door. The upper part of the burrow is oval in cross-section, but becomes circular towards the bottom, below a horizontal side shaft that can be closed from the main shaft with a hinged door. Juvenile spiders inside the burrow are generally found in the side shaft. Trip lines may radiate from the burrow to facilitate the detection of passing prey. [P.R. Langlands, Phoenix Environmental Sciences]

This more unusual *Missulena* burrow entrance, seen in Western Australia, combines a larger double door with two additional smaller doors. [P.R. Langlands, Phoenix Environmental Sciences]

CTENIZIDAE
Cork-lid Trapdoor Spiders

- Eye group small, in widely rectangular arrangement
- Chelicerae with distinct rastellum
- Carapace ovoid with raised head region and U-shaped fovea
- Saddle-shaped depression in the tibia of the third leg
- Spinnerets short
- Night active without prey-capture web
- Burrow with cork- or bathplug-like hinged door
- Body length: 15–35 mm

Australia:
Taxonomy poorly resolved
Current: 2 species in 1 genus
Estimated: 30 species in 1 genus
World: 128 species in 9 genera

The common name of the Cork-lid Trapdoor Spiders (family Ctenizidae) refers to the characteristic, cork- or bathplug-like, slightly convex trapdoor that these spiders use to tightly close their burrow. The burrow itself is a simple vertical tube in the ground. It has a tough silk lining, although at least one species found in Australia, *Conothele arboricola*, constructs its cigar-shaped burrow into the bark of trees.

A single genus, *Conothele*, is currently known from Australia. The genus is found from India, throughout South-East Asia and into the Pacific. However, it is doubtful if *Conothele* species differ sufficiently from those of the Nearctic and Palaearctic genus *Ummidia* to consider both different genera. Future taxonomic work may show them all to belong to a then almost cosmopolitan genus *Ummidia* (which is the older available name).

Conothele is easily distinguished from other Australian mygalomorph spiders by a saddle-like, sometimes darker depression on the tibia of the third leg. This depression apparently aids the spider in bracing itself against the nest wall when holding the trapdoor down with their chelicerae and first legs, for example in defence from predators. The carapace often has a roundish appearance and the central part of the head region is convex. It is shiny and armed with few hairs. Males are sometimes strikingly coloured with orange leg segments and abdomen contrasting with a black carapace. The species found

Female *Conothele*, here a heavily mite infested spider from the Pilbara in Western Australia, rarely move far from their burrow. Parental care has been reported in the Ctenizidae as females apparently feed spiderlings with regurgitated prey liquid. However, this behaviour has not been confirmed for Australian *Conothele*. [V.W. Framenau, Phoenix Environmental Sciences]

in arid environments are generally of fairly uniform light brown coloration.

Two species are described from Australia, *Conothele doleschalli* from Cape York and *Conothele arboricola* from Thursday Island (the species also occurs in Papua New Guinea). *Conothele malayana* may also occur in northern Australia (known from the Moluccas, Solomon Islands and Papua New Guinea). Whilst all described species are from the tropical north, the genus has a much wider distribution into the arid inland of Australia, where many undescribed species are known to live. *Conothele* is not known from the coastal areas in the south-east or the south-west of the country. Within their range, the spiders are found from the seashore through to central deserts, including mangroves and trees in rainforests. Like *Missulena* spiderlings (family Actinopodidae), those of *Conothele* are reported to balloon on gossamer for short distances. This is an unusual behaviour for mygalomorph spiders and facilitates species dispersal.

During the day, Cork-lid Trapdoor Spiders normally hold the lid shut with their fangs. At night, they wait at the top of the burrow for potential prey like insects or other small invertebrates. *Conothele* dispatches food remains outside the burrow instead of incorporating them into the wall or leaving them at the base. The thick door of the burrow fits so well to the burrow entrance that the spiders are able to survive flash flooding as long as it is not prolonged. With the onset of the dry season, the spider seals the burrow door with silk. Later dust quickly perfects the camouflage.

Conothele are not aggressive, and as they are rarely encountered by humans, bites are uncommon and severe envenomation has not been reported.

The cryptic Cork-lid Trapdoor Spiders, here an undescribed *Conothele* female from Barrow Island in Western Australia, are easily recognised by the saddle-like depression on the tibia of the third leg. Other features include the convex head region and the U-shaped fovea which marks the attachment point of the sucking stomach that forms a donut around the brain. [V.W. Framenau, Phoenix Environmental Sciences]

The cork-like, hinged door of a *Conothele* species' burrow is made of soil bound together with silk. During the day, the spider normally holds the lid shut with its fangs. [R.J. Raven]

Arid zone *Conothele* construct simple vertical burrows of up the 20 cm depth, which are closed with a strong, slightly convex door that perfectly fits into the entrance of the burrow [P.R. Langlands, Phoenix Environmental Sciences]

MIGIDAE
Tree-trapdoor Spiders

- Eight eyes in two rows, in a group about three times wider than long
- Carapace frontally squared, shiny with few hairs
- Abdomen with cinnamon and pale chevrons
- Fangs with two ridges along the outer edges
- Legs fairly strong with strong spines on the front legs
- Tubular retreat with trapdoor
- Body length: 5–10 mm

Australia:
Partially revised
Current: 7 species in 3 genera
Estimated: 20 species in 4 genera
World: 91 species in 10 genera

Tree-trapdoor Spiders (family Migidae) build their vertical burrows directly on the surface of tree trunks and sometimes into a gap in the bark. Some species also burrow into the ground, and with their well-camouflaged trapdoor, these spiders are very difficult to find. In Australia, Tree-trapdoor Spiders are represented by species with few hairs, but a more subtle character, two ridges on the outer edge of the fangs, unmistakably identifies the family.

Migids have a southern continental distribution that includes Australia, Tasmania, New Caledonia, New Zealand, South America, South Africa and Madagascar. This points to an evolutionary origin on the prehistoric southern supercontinent Gondwana.

The Australian fauna is small and includes only three genera. *Migas* is predominantly found in New Zealand and only three species from Queensland and Tasmania are currently named for Australia. *Heteromigas* is only known from two Australian species: *Heteromigas dovei* from Tasmania and *Heteromigas terrareginae* from Queensland. *Migas* is distinguished from *Heteromigas* by an inclined thoracic portion of the carapace, and the ridge between the fovea and the eyes is almost horizontal. In contrast, this ridge is arched in *Heteromigas*. Both genera occur in cooler, usually montane, forest along the east coast of Australia. *Moggridgea*, a genus also found in South Africa, occurs in coastal South Australia with *Moggridgea australis*, and in south-western Western Australia with *Moggridgea tingle*. Unlike the other genera, *Moggridgea* has a slight saddle-shaped depression on the third tibia.

Little is known about prey and predators of Tree-trapdoor Spiders, and no bites on humans have been reported for these elusive little spiders.

Some Tree-trapdoor Spiders, like this undescribed *Heteromigas* species from Queensland, create their burrows on the ground. In contrast to *Migas*, species of *Heteromigas* have an arched head region. [R.J. Raven]

Vertical burrows of Tree-trapdoor Spiders, here an unknown species from Lamington National Park in Queensland, are secured with a small hinged lid and camouflaged with tiny bark pieces. The spiders spend their daytime in their burrow with the door closed. At night they peek out of their burrow waiting for insects. [R.J. Raven]

The slightly lighter, small trapdoors of *Moggridgea tingle*, in a compacted creek embankment of the Stirling Range National Park in Western Australia, are perfectly camouflaged and almost invisible. Recent molecular studies on *Moggridgea tingle* showed considerable genetic differences between neighbouring populations, with evidence for long-term (>3 million years) isolation of at least nine geographically very close populations. [V.W. Framenau, Phoenix Environmental Sciences]

IDIOPIDAE
True Trapdoor Spiders

- Eight eyes in small rectangular, square or trapezoidal arrangement
- Mostly uniformly light brown to black spiders
- Spinnerets short
- Burrows generally with trap door
- Body length: 10–40+ mm

Australia:
Partially revised
Current: 113 species in 9 genera
Estimated: 200+ species in 15 genera
World: 318 species in 22 genera

The True Trapdoor Spiders (family Idiopidae) include the typical trapdoor spiders that usually close the burrow with a hinged door, although some may have an open burrow. Family-level identification relies on a combination of characters rather than a particular feature and these include short posterior lateral spinnerets, the presence of a rastellum on the chelicerae, the absence of tarsal claw tufts and a single row of teeth on the tarsal claws.

The Idiopidae have a largely Gondwanan distribution and have so far been recorded from South America, Africa, Madagascar, the Middle East, India and Sri Lanka, South-East Asia and New Zealand. However, all Australian idiopid genera are endemic to this country. The Australian fauna is most diverse in south-eastern Queensland, eastern New South Wales and south-western Australia, and the family is largely absent from the tropical north.

All Australian representatives belong to the subfamily **Arbanitinae** and this is divided into two tribes based on the length of the labium and the eye pattern. The Aganippini (*Aganippe*, *Anidiops*, *Eucyrtops*, *Idiosoma*) have a broad, indented labium and often their posterior eye row is wider than the eyes at the front. With the exception of *Aganippe*, this tribe is largely confined to the western parts of the country. In contrast, the Arbaniti (*Arbanitis*, *Blakistonia*, *Euoplos*, *Misgolas*, *Cataxia*) have an elongated labium and the anterior and posterior eye rows are of similar width. Their centre of diversity is in eastern Australia.

However, systematic relationships within the Australian Idiopidae and their genus-level taxonomy are not settled. Arguably, some genera currently placed in synonymy with the ones listed above should be re-validated (such as *Albaniana*,

Gaius, *Homogona*, and *Neohomogona*), and a number of undescribed genera, including some illustrated here, need to be named.

Anidiops is restricted to Western Australia and into South Australia and includes the largest idiopids. Females reach more than 40 mm in body length and long-term observation of *Anidiops villosus* populations suggests that females live up to 40 years. The currently most species-rich genus in the family is *Misgolas*, which occurs in eastern Australia from Queensland into Tasmania. Some 60 species are currently described, with more waiting to be named. Up to six species have been found to co-occur. Some species are relatively widely distributed but most are highly localised and sometimes occur only in the confinement of a small valley.

Whilst some genera, such as *Misgolas*, rarely have a trapdoor, there are a variety of burrow modifications, which may allow at least genus level identification in the field. Burrow morphology of idiopids is probably best studied in Western Australia, one of the centres of diversity for the family. For example, *Anidiops villosus* and *Anidiops manstridgei* have a trapdoor armed with radiating leaves. Halfway down the burrow is a collapsible silk sock that can be used to close the burrow in defence from predators. Old prey items conceal this false bottom under which the spider sits in relative safety. The Treestem Trapdoor Spider, *Aganippe castellum*, restricted largely to the Western Australian Avon Wheatbelt, builds a tube up a tree or shrub, which is also closed with a twig-lined trapdoor. *Idiosoma nigrum* has a constriction in the upper parts of the burrow in which the truncated posterior end of the highly sclerotised abdomen perfectly fits to seal the burrow against intruders. The trapdoor also has a moustache-like decoration of leaves or twigs.

The burrows of these spiders are constructed using the cheliceral claws, not the rake-like spines on the chelicerae, the rastellum, as once suggested. The rastellum is used to compact the walls of the burrow, which is lined with a dense layer of silk.

Main predators of idiopids include *Isometroides* scorpions and *Cormocephalus* centipedes, but they also fall prey to spider wasps (Pompilidae) and birds, such as the Australian Magpie. True Trapdoor Spiders prey in particular on beetles and ants, but also on various other insects and arthropods.

Due to their often large size, bites by idiopid spiders can be painful, but they appear to only cause minor local effects.

The carapace of this female *Arbanitis robertcollinsi* is clothed with golden hairs. This species is only known from Lamington National Park in south-eastern Queensland. [J. Haider]

An unidentified *Misgolas* female from north Queensland, waiting for prey at the entrance to the burrow. Idiopids make a diversity of burrows and many species build doors with a variety of modifications. In contrast, most *Misgolas* have an open burrow which may extend up to 20 cm above the ground. [P. Zborowski]

Cataxia pulleinei is found in Queensland and New South Wales. This species constructs thin doors that are like the extension of an upper silken flap. The species was originally described in the genus *Homogona* and the synonymy of this genus with *Cataxia* is doubtful. [J. Haider]

The rectangular eye-pattern identifies this male *Euoplos* from Barrow Island in Western Australia as a member of the tribe Arbanitini. Members of this tribe are not very common in Western Australia and much more diverse in the eastern states. [V.W. Framenau, Phoenix Environmental Sciences]

Males of some Western Australian Idiopidae have a spectacular white carapace, which gained them the colloquial name Albino Spiders. They are currently placed in the genus *Euoplos* but it is perceivable that future systematic studies will reclassify them into their own genus. This image shows an undescribed species from Northam, but two Albino Spiders are named from south-western Western Australia: *Euoplos ballidu* (from Ballidu) and *Euoplos mcmillani* (from Eneabba). [V.W. Framenau, Phoenix Environmental Sciences]

The Idiopidae have a diverse array of burrow modifications. The Tree-stem Trapdoor Spider, *Aganippe castellum*, from south-western Western Australia, constructs a tube up trees, or parts of vegetation, which is armed with a trapdoor. [V.W. Framenau, Phoenix Environmental Sciences]

Species in the genus *Aganippe*, here an unidentified female from Western Australia, can be recognised by their trapezoidal eye pattern, i.e. the eye group is wider at the back than at the front, and by two or three distinct pairs of sigillae on the abdomen. These are hairless, sclerotised spots of variable size. The genus is widespread in southern Australia south of the Tropic of Capricorn. [V.W Framenau, Phoenix Environmental Sciences]

Females of the Shield-backed Trapdoor Spider, *Idiosoma nigrum*, have a heavily sclerotised abdomen that is deeply ridged and truncated at the back of the spider. This morphological feature is thought to preserve moisture in arid environments. In addition, the abdomen is used to plug a constriction in the spider's burrow in protection against intruders. The genus is endemic to Western Australia, from where two other species are named: *I. sigillatum* and *I. hirsutum* from the Perth Coastal Plain. [V.W. Framenau, Phoenix Environmental Sciences]

Anidiops villosus occurs in the semi-arid regions of south-western Western Australia. It is one of the largest species of True Trapdoor Spiders and females reach more than 40 mm body length. This species was originally placed in the genus *Gaius* and distinct differences in the male pedipalp morphology suggest both *Anidiops* and *Gaius* to be valid genera; however, females are almost indistinguishable. Both genera may include up to ten species, but only one in each is currently named. [V.W. Framenau, Phoenix Environmental Sciences]

The burrow of *Anidiops villosus* is closed by a trapdoor and is armed with radiating leaves, which increase the area to detect prey. Halfway down the burrow is a silk sock that the spider can close as a false bottom to fool intruding predators. [V.W. Framenau, Phoenix Environmental Sciences]

The relatively poor taxonomic knowledge of the Idiopidae is exemplified by this spectacularly shaped female of an undescribed genus and species, which is currently only known from central Western Australia. These small idiopid spiders superficially resemble members of the African genus *Galeosoma* from the subfamily Idiopinae, which is believed not to occur in Australia. Similar to the sclerotised abdomen in *Idiosoma*, these spiders possibly plug their burrow with their rear end to avoid predation and desiccation. The males of this species are currently unknown. [V.W. Framenau, Phoenix Environmental Sciences]

Females in the genus *Eucyrtops*, here an unidentified species from Fitzgerald River National Park in south-western Western Australia, differ from other genera in the tribe Aganippini, such as. *Anidiops*, *Aganippe* and *Idiosoma*, by a highly arched head region and more globular abdomen. There are many undescribed species in this genus in Western Australia. [V.W. Framenau, Phoenix Environmental Sciences]

NEMESIIDAE
Wishbone Trapdoor Spiders

- Eight eyes in two rows in rectangular arrangement about twice as wide as long
- Carapace low, cephalic region slightly arched, fovea short and more or less straight or slightly procurved
- Four spinnerets, posterior lateral pair with long apical segment
- Legs long with scopulae on tarsi
- Superior tarsal claws with two rows of teeth
- Chelicerae without rastellum
- Night active hunters without prey capture web
- Body length: 5–30 mm

Australia:
Partially revised
current: 98 species in 14 genera
estimated: 250 species in 20 genera
World: 364 species in 43 genera

The common name Wishbone Trapdoor Spiders for the spider family Nemesiidae refers to the Y-shaped silk-lined burrow, that some of the species within this family inhabit. However, burrow morphology is very diverse within the Nemesiidae and also includes simple vertical tubes, with and without doors. The main morphological feature that unites this family is the presence of two rows of teeth on the two main tarsal claws. However, this character has also been found in other mygalomorph spider families and it has been argued that the members of the Nemesiidae do not form a natural group.

Most nemesiids are relatively large with uniform pale, brown or black coloration. Females have robust legs although these are relatively longer and slimmer in males. Some representatives of the family, for example in the genera *Teyl* or *Swolnpes*, may be fairly small; males may not exceed more than 5 mm in body length.

The large and black representatives of the Wishbone Trapdoor Spiders in the genus *Aname* are often confused with the notorious Funnel-web Spiders (family Hexathelidae), but unlike the shiny hexathelids, *Aname* often have golden or silvery hairs on the carapace. Males have a prominent spine on the middle joint (tibia) of the first leg; the only bump on the legs of Funnel-web Spiders is on the second leg.

Black Wishbone Spiders, *Aname mainae*, represent the 'typical' Wishbone Trapdoor Spiders, as they build a Y-shaped burrow. A side shaft from the slanting main tube reaches just below the surface and is covered lightly with soil and litter to allow an escape if threatened from the main entrance. *Aname mainae* occurs from Western Australia to the Eyre Peninsula in South Australia, although many very similar species are known from Western Australia and the group requires taxonomic revision. [V.W. Framenau, Phoenix Environmental Sciences]

Fourteen genera in the Nemesiidae are currently described from Australia. All of these are endemic to the country with the exception of *Stanwellia*, which also occurs in New Zealand. Characters that differentiate the genera are often difficult to establish in the field, and relate to the patterns of cuspules on the maxillae or details of male pedipalp morphology.

The distribution of some of the genera shows some geographic patterns also observed in other mygalomorph spider, i.e. there are genera limited to eastern Australia (*Namea, Ixamatus, Xamiatus, Kiama*) and others currently known only from the west, possibly reaching into South Australia (*Kwonkan, Merredinia, Pseudoteyl, Swolnpes, Yilgarnia*). However, some of these distribution patterns may be an artefact of the poor knowledge of the family.

Aname is the most widely distributed and species-rich genus with 36 currently described species. These spiders prefer dry open country and occur throughout much of Australia, in particular the dry interior. Many further species await formal description. *Chenistonia* is also known from the east to the west coast and species of *Teyl* have been described from Western Australia and Victoria. *Stanwellia* has a typical south-coastal distribution although it is not well represented in Western Australia.

Kiama lachrymoides has so far only been found at Kiama in New South Wales and is the only species in the genus. The family placement of *Kiama* is controversial and it has also been considered a member of the Cyrtaucheniidae (Wafer Trapdoor Spiders), which is otherwise absent from Australia.

Nemesiids are nocturnal hunters but will generally not venture far from the burrow. Like many burrowing mygalomorphs, the spiders often rest at some distance down from the entrance. However, little is known about the natural history of many species and genera.

Whilst Wishbone Trapdoor Spiders can be very aggressive when disturbed, their venom does not appear to cause any severe effects in humans.

When disturbed, *Aname* are fairly aggressive, raising their first pair of legs and prosoma ready for a downward strike with their chelicerae. However, Wishbone Trapdoor Spiders are not known to cause severe envenomations in humans. *Aname mellosa*, here a female in striking position, occurs in the central and northern semi-arid landscapes of Western Australia. [V.W. Framenau, Phoenix Environmental Sciences]

Nemesiidae, here an unidentified *Aname* female from Western Australia, usually remain in their burrows or hunt within a body length of the burrow entrance. The burrow generally does not have a trapdoor, as can be seen here in the bottom right corner of the photograph. [F. Bokhari]

Ixamatus webbae is known from the McPherson Ranges in southern Queensland. This species usually makes a simple sinuous tube of web under logs. There is no true burrow but merely a silk-lined impression about the same depth as the spider's body length. Ten species of *Ixamatus* are currently described from New South Wales and Queensland. [J. Haider]

The genus *Kwonkan*, here a male from South Australia, is currently defined by the presence of spines on the leg tarsi. This unites a number of morphologically otherwise very different species and it must be questioned if the genus as currently defined is valid. The species illustrated here is dark brown with a hairy prosoma. Six species of *Kwonkan* are currently described, five from Western Australia and one from South Australia. [B.C. Baehr]

This *Kwonkan* female of an undescribed species from Barrow Island, Western Australia, is very different in its light brown coloration compared to the species from South Australia illustrated above. It may represent a different genus altogether. Many light reddish-brown nemesiids from arid environments, such as those in the genera *Aname*, *Yilgarnia* and *Kwonkan*, look superficially very similar and require closer morphological examination for genus-level identification. [V.W. Framenau, Phoenix Environmental Sciences]

The genus *Yilgarnia*, here an undescribed species from Western Australia, is identified by fields of cuspules on the coxa of the third and fourth leg. They often have a uniform dark purplish abdomen. Two species are currently described from Western Australia, *Y. currycomboides* and *Y. linnaei*. [V.W. Framenau, Phoenix Environmental Sciences]

The carapace of this male *Aname tepperi* is covered with dense golden hairs. This species ranges from southern Western Australia across the Nullarbor Plain to the Adelaide Hills, although molecular data suggest that more than a single species is involved. [V.W. Framenau, Phoenix Environmental Sciences]

Aname tepperi makes a sinuous burrow with an almost horizontal sitting chamber just below the entrance [S. Blane]

BARYCHELIDAE
Brush-footed Trapdoor Spiders

- Eight eyes in two or three rows in rectangular, subquadrate or trapezoidal arrangement
- Two or four short spinnerets
- Claw tufts
- Dense scopulae on tarsus and metatarsus of the first and second leg
- Cheliceral rastellum on low process or absent
- Burrow cryptic and camouflaged, often under rocks and logs
- Body length: 10–35 mm

Australia:
Partially revised
Current: 112 species in 12 genera
Estimated: 150 species in 13 genera
World: 307 species in 44 genera

Brush-footed Trapdoor Spiders (family Barychelidae) gained their name due to the presence of dense scopulae or 'brushes' on the first two pairs of legs. Barychelids look like small Australian Tarantulas (family Theraphosidae) but have much shorter posterior lateral spinnerets.

Australia has the most diverse barychelid fauna by world standards, although the family is also known from South and Central America, central Africa, Madagascar, India, Papua New Guinea and Pacific islands. In Australia, the highest diversity is found in the tropical rainforests of the far north, but barychelids are equally at home in the arid centre. Considerably more new species are yet to be named, in particular in the genus *Idiommata* which includes some of the largest barychelids. Spiders in this genus have a dense layer of silver (or sometimes golden) hairs in males, which won them the common name Silverback.

All Australian barychelids belong to the subfamily Barychelinae, with the exception of a single species of *Sason*, *S. colemani* from Queensland, which is a member of the Sasoninae. In the **Sasoninae**, unlike in the Barychelinae, the eyes do not sit on a tubercle and males have only one row of teeth on the tarsal claws (compared with two in the Barychelinae).

Like many mygalomorph spiders, the genera in the **Barychelinae** show distinct geographical patterns in their distributions. *Ozicrypta*, *Moruga* and *Mandjelia* occur predominantly in the tropical and arid parts of Queensland and the

Northern Territory although *Mandjelia* crosses the country into south-eastern Western Australia. *Aurecocrypta* is only known from Western Australia and, likewise, *Synothele* is predominantly found in this state although its range also extends into South Australia and the Northern Territory. *Tungari* and *Zophorame* are only known from Queensland's tropical north. *Sequocrypta* and *Trittame* are east coast genera. The most widespread genus is *Idiommata*, which is known from throughout the country, although its taxonomy is the least resolved. Overall, many barychelid species have very small distributions, suggesting poor dispersal capabilities and possibly narrow environmental tolerances.

Idioctis represents an intriguing Brush-footed Trapdoor Spider genus as these species are generally found along the seashore below the high-water mark. *Idioctis xmas* is found on Christmas Island in the Indian Ocean and *I. yerlata* along the northern Queensland coast. Additional intertidal *Idioctis* species are known from Madagascar east to Hawaii. These spiders depend on a neatly fitting lid to keep the burrow dry when the water level rises.

Despite their considerable diversity, very little is known about the biology of the Brush-footed Trapdoor Spiders. Like most mygalomorph spiders, they tend to be more active in the cooler off-summer periods. Barychelids are most easily found by brushing the surface of the ground with a wide brush, which may expose their burrow.

Brush-footed Trapdoor Spiders belong to the least aggressive mygalomorph spiders and therefore bites are rare.

The genus *Idiommata*, here an unidentified male, is the most widespread of all Australian Brush-footed Trapdoor Spider genera, and occurs throughout much of the country. These include the largest barychelids with a body length of up to about 35 mm in females. Males are often covered by a layer of silver hair, hence their common name Silverback. [V.W. Framenau, Phoenix Environmental Sciences]

The burrow of the *Idiommata* species is open, but has a substantial door a few cm into the tube. Barychelids are among the more cryptic trapdoor spiders, because their door is often quite floppy and melds invisibly into the environment into which it opens. [R.J. Raven]

Spiders in the genus *Synothele*, here a female of an undescribed species from Fitzgerald River National Park in Western Australia, make thin doors that are difficult to spot. Females hunt with the front legs extended just beyond the burrow door and therefore predominantly rely on vibration. *Synothele* are found in arid and semi-arid landscapes from Northern Territory into South Australia, but are most diverse in Western Australia. [V.W. Framenau, Phoenix Environmental Sciences]

In the subfamily Barychelinae, such as this unidentified female *Synothele* from Western Australia, the eyes are somewhat raised on a tubercle, which differentiates them from the Sasoninae. [V.W. Framenau, Phoenix Environmental Sciences]

Synothele often have a mottled pattern on the abdomen, and it can be more distinct in juvenile spiders. [F. Bokhari]

This *Synothele mullaloo* male represents a comparatively dark species of *Synothele*. These spiders are found on the Swan Coastal Plain north of Perth into the Darling Escarpment. [V.W. Framenau, Phoenix Environmental Sciences]

This dark Brush-footed Trapdoor Spider male from Queensland belongs to the genus *Idiommata*. Spiders in this genus have maxillary lyra, which are a set of specialised spines on the anterior face of the maxillae. These interact with a line of fine pins along the cheliceral furrow to produce sound. Similar structures are also found, for example, in the Tarantulas (family Theraphosidae). [P. Zborowski]

Spiders in the genus *Trittame*, here possibly a *T. loki* female, are among the largest of the Barychelidae. They build open burrows with raised leafy collars. They hunt from their burrow at night, with the pedipalps and the first two pairs of legs sitting just outside the edge of the burrow. They launch out of the burrow often with the long fourth legs still in the burrow entrance. A series of small spines across the chelicerae tip, the rastellum, serves to compact the soil and better bind it to the silk that lines the burrow. *Trittame* is only known from eastern Australia. [P. Zborowoski]

THERAPHOSIDAE
Australian Tarantulas, Bird-eating Spiders, Whistling or Barking Spiders

- Eight eyes in two rows in rectangular arrangement
- Legs with two claws on the front legs, often three claws on back legs, all claws well hidden by dense claw tufts
- Very hairy with strong legs, various shades of brown and black, sometimes with darker base parts of the legs
- Sound-making lyra on the front of endites
- Four spinnerets, apical segment of posterior lateral spinnerets long
- Nocturnal hunters without prey capture web
- Silk-lined open burrow
- Body length: 20–60+ mm

Australia:
Taxonomy poorly resolved
Current: 7 species in 4 genera
Estimated: 30 species in 6 genera
World: 950 species in 124 genera

The Australian Tarantulas (family Theraphosidae) include the largest Australian spiders and are native to northern tropical and inland arid parts of the country. They are also known as Barking and Whistling spiders. Barking may simply refer to dogs agitated by the spider, whose venom is dangerous to them as well as to cats. The whistling refers to a sound-making organ (lyra) on the front of the endites, the basal segment of the pedipalps. It can produce different sounds such as a high-pitched hiss, a sound like a ticker on a slow turning bicycle wheel or fast castanettes. A common sound resembles the sound made by quickly ripping a fingertip across a plastic hair comb.

Together with the Barychelidae, Australian Tarantulas are the only mygalomorph family in which spiders have claw tufts on their tarsi. In contrast to the Barychelidae, Australian Tarantulas have much longer posterior lateral spinnerets and can therefore reliably be identified in the field.

All Australian Tarantulas belong to the subfamily **Selenocosmiinae** and this includes the genera *Phlogius*, *Selenotypus*, *Selenotholus*, *Coremiocnemis* and *Phlogiellus*. Characters to identify genera are subtle and are difficult to establish in the field. They include the shape of the fovea, length and thickness of legs, shape of setae on the chelicerae and the presence of a 'tarsal crack' on the fourth leg.

Australian Tarantulas excavate long burrows, up to one metre deep, from which they emerge at night to ambush prey, which includes spiders, insects, frogs, lizards and birds. The burrows are generally open but may be plugged during the colder and very hot months.

Theraphosids are highly threatened by the pet trade, which is responsible for around 2,000 spiders being sold in each state every year. This has serious conservation implications, as many of the Australian Tarantulas are only known from small ranges. Their role as pets also increases the likelihood of bites by these large spiders.

Symptoms of a bite include queasiness, vomiting, sweating and general malaise. Dogs and cats have been bitten fatally. There is no antivenom required or available.

Australian Tarantulas, like this *Phlogius crassipes* male from northern Queensland, can cling to smooth surfaces and even glass with their dense claw tufts on the tips of their legs. [P. Zborowski]

This unidentified *Selenotholus* female from Queensland has created a large silky retreat under stones where it is hiding during the daytime. It may belong to the genus *Phlogius*, but even genus level identification based on images is difficult. [P. Zborowski]

This tarantula from South Australian is probably the Australian Common Whistling Spider, currently referred to *Selenocosmia stirlingi*, a widespread species throughout the semi-arid and arid zone. However, *Selenocosmia* is believed not to occur in Australia and this species probably belongs to the genus *Selenotholus*. [P. Zborowski]

Species in *Selenotholus*, here an unidentified male from Western Australia, have a recurved fovea. The genus has currently only a single species described, *S. foelschei*, which mainly occurs in the western half of the country. However, the genus is clearly more diverse. [V.W. Framenau, Phoenix Environmental Sciences]

The burrow of *Selenotholus foelschei* is open with a raised, silk-cemented rim. [P.R. Langlands, Phoenix Environmental Sciences]

This image of a male *Selenotholus foelschei* from Western Australia shows the long posterior lateral spinnerets that distinguish Australian Tarantulas from spiders in the family Barychelidae. This species has been reported from Western Australia and the Northern Territory [V.W. Framenau, Phoenix Environmental Sciences]

PART 3
ARANEOMORPHAE - MODERN SPIDERS

This face of the Shield Huntsman, *Neosparassus*, shows the long chelicerae tipped with fangs that point toward each other, the diaxial condition. [P. Zborowski]

ARANEOMORPHAE
Modern Spiders

The Modern Spiders (Araneomorphae) differ from the Trapdoor Spiders (Mygalomorphae) by a transverse (diaxial) orientation of the fangs. Other characters often used to characterise Modern Spiders, such as the reduction of the posterior pairs of booklungs and complex genitalia, are not present in all Modern Spiders. It is worthwhile to note that a reversal to the paraxial fangs has occurred at least once in Modern Spiders in Australia, in the Long-jawed Ground Spiders (family Gallieniellidae). Hence more than one of the above mentioned characters has to be used when differentiating between Trapdoor and Modern Spiders.

The cribellum, the spinning field evolved from the anterior median spinnerets, is a character that has probably evolved at the base of the Araneomorphae. It is a complex morphological feature and unlikely to have evolved twice. However, in most Modern Spiders it is reduced to a vestigial hump (colulus) or is absent altogether and therefore not helpful in identifying this group. A number of spider families have both cribellate and ecribellate members. Australia has a comparatively diverse cribellate spider fauna, in particular within the Amaurobioidea. This group includes the Hackled-mesh Weavers (family Amaurobiidae), but family-level relationships within Australian genera are poorly resolved.

The transverse orientation of the fangs has allowed Modern Spiders to move away from the ground, which is a requirement for Trapdoor Spiders to provide resistance to pin down prey in the downward strike of the fangs. Attacking prey in a more or less elastic prey capture web would not be possible with paraxial fangs. Taking into the vegetation was assisted by the reduction of the posterior booklungs which reduces water loss for spiders after leaving the burrow in which the micro-climate can be actively manipulated by opening and closing the entrance.

The Araneomorphae are divided into four groups. Two of these retain four booklungs and are therefore considered the most primitive within the Modern Spiders. The Hypochiloidea, only represented by a single family, Hypochilidae, can only be found in the Nearctic and China. The Austrochiloidea are the southern hemisphere equivalent and occur in South America, Australia and New Zealand. Both superfamilies do not appear to share a common ancestry and are therefore considered to represent separate ancient lineages within the Araneomorphae. The other two araneomorph groups, the Haplogynae and the Entelegynae, share

The reduction of the second pair of booklungs to tracheae decreased water loss during respiration and allowed members of the Araneomorphae to leave the protective, climate controlled underground burrows which are home to most Mygalomorphae. The construction of aerial webs, here the orb-web of an unidentified *Cyclosa* (family Araneidae), allows aerial hunting and therefore access to a never-ending supply of flying insects. [V.W. Framenau, Phoenix Environmental Sciences]

a single pair of booklungs, but differ in the complexity of their genitalia. The more primitive Haplogynae do not have sclerotised external genitalia, an epigyne, whereas this is well-developed in most Entelegynae.

The Haplogynae are a comparatively small group of often cryptic spiders in Australia and include six-eyed spider families such as the Goblin Spiders (Oonopidae), Six-eyed Ground Spiders (Orsolobidae), Tube-web Spiders (Segestriidae) and the introduced Woodlouse Hunters (Dysderidae), and the mostly eight-eyed Daddy Long-legs Spiders (Pholcidae). The highly diverse Jumping Spiders (Salticidae), Orb-weaving Spiders (Araneidae), Huntsman Spiders (Sparassidae) and Wolf Spiders (Lycosidae) belong to the Entelegynae. Whereas the relationships within and between the more primitive spiders – the Hypochiloidea, Austrochiloidea and the Haplogynae – is not settled, it is widely accepted that the Entelegynae share a common ancestry.

Austrochiloidea

The Austrochiloidea are the ancient cousins of all other Modern Spiders within the Araneomorphae. They retain four booklungs, like the Mygalomorphae, but have diaxial fangs (i.e. they close against each other). The Austrochiloidea are a Gondwanan lineage and only occur in Australia, New Zealand and Chile. They find their Northern Hemisphere four-lunged counterparts in the Hypochiloidea from Northern America and China. Both these ancient araneomorph lineages do not seem to be immediately related, but independently retained their primitive features.

The Austrochiloidea are represented by two families in Australia, the Austrochilidae (Junction-web Weavers) and the Gradungulidae (Long-clawed Spiders). The Austrochilidae, which also occur in Chile, are here only represented by the enigmatic Tasmanian Cave Spider, *Hickmania troglodytes*, whereas the Gradungulidae include cribellate web-builders and ecribellate vagrant hunters along the east coast of Australia, including Tasmania.

The Austrochiloidea include the Long-clawed Spiders (family Gradungulidae), a poorly known family of ancient spiders, some of which, such as *Progradungulia carraiensis*, developed a rather sophisticated prey capture strategy. With their two pairs of frontlegs they throw passing prey items into a cribbelate web that is positioned between their two pairs of hindlegs. [M.R. Gray, Australian Museum]

AUSTROCHILIDAE
Junction-web Weavers

- Eight similar-sized eyes in two rows
- Legs long, metatarsus of second leg flexible in males
- Active day or night in cave entrances and twilight zones
- Extensive cribellate sheet-webs
- Two pairs of book lungs
- Body length: 13–25 mm (leg-span up to 180 mm)

Australia:
Taxonomy revised
Current: 1 species in 1 genus
Estimated: 1 species in 1 genus
World: 9 species in 3 genera

The enigmatic Tasmanian Cave Spider, *Hickmania troglodytes*, is the only representative of the Junction-web Weavers (family Austrochilidae) in Australia. It is a relict of an old Gondwanan fauna, and the two other austrochilid genera, *Austrochilus* and *Thaida*, are only found in Chile and Argentina.

These Tasmanian endemics cannot be mistaken for any other spider. With a body length up to 30 mm and a leg-span up to 180 mm, Tasmanian Cave Spiders faintly resemble giant Daddy Long-legs (family Pholcidae) hanging upside down in dark shady places in their massive sheet-webs. The carapace is reddish-brown and the abdomen dark greyish-brown. Males are smaller than females but with relatively longer legs. As member of the Austrochiloidea, *Hickmania troglodytes* has retained two pairs of booklungs similar to the Mygalomorphae. They are cribellate spiders with an undivided cribellum.

Hickmania troglodytes, an iconic species for faunal preservation, is widely distributed in Tasmania and common in shady places such as cave entrances, inside large hollow logs, or dark spaces in rainforests. Most spiders are found under old and decaying tree trunks and logs, in between old and decayed man-ferns and in small natural ground hollows. In Hobart they are also found under houses.

The cribellate sheet-web of *Hickmania troglodytes* can be more than a metre across and catches prey items such as crickets, beetles, flies, millipedes and other spiders. They are able to repair their damaged webs in just a few hours, laying out single strands first seemingly in any fashion, then adding the fuzzy cribellate threads. This large spider was first collected in 1883 in a cave near Launceston.

The eggsac of the Tasmanian Cave Spider is pear-shaped and suspended by a narrow stalk. In caves it is pure white but often disguised with woody and leaf debris at places where that is present. The eggsac is structured in two main layers, the inner thimble-like structure does not touch the outer shell. Juveniles hatch out of the eggsacs after about nine months, an astonishingly long development time in comparison to other spiders. The spiders themselves are said to be very long-lived, although the sometimes claimed 'several decades' appears to be an exaggeration.

A female *Hickmania troglodytes* from Mystery Creek Cave walks over moonmilk, a white, creamy substance found inside caves. [A. Clarke]

Hickmania troglodytes males, here photographed at Bubs Hill, have a smaller body and comparatively longer legs, but the same coloration as the female. The male has a bent, flexible metatarsus on the second leg that is used for locking the female's head and pinning her fangs for safety during copulation. [A. Clarke]

Hickmania troglodytes female in a sandstone cave, under a rotting log in rainforest at Francistown, in southern Tasmania. Females produce pear-shaped eggsacs, which can be camouflaged with leaves or debris. The female stays with the eggsac until the young hatch and disperse. [A. Clarke]

GRADUNGULIDAE
Long-clawed Spiders

- Eight similar-sized eyes in two rows
- Legs long
- Superior tarsal claws on first and second leg elongated, with the frontal one largest
- Specialised prey capture web or vagrant hunters
- Two pairs of booklungs
- Cribellum present (in web-builders) or absent (in hunters)
- Body length: 7–25 mm

Australia:
Partially revised
Current: 13 species in 4 genera
Estimated 31 species in 5 genera
World: 16 species in 7 genera

The common name of the Long-clawed Spiders (family Gradungulidae) is derived from their elongated main tarsal claws on the first and second pairs of legs. Of these, the one to the front is particularly large. These claws are associated with a somewhat swollen tarsus and strong spines on its underside. These morphological adaptations have possibly evolved in concurrence with a specialized form of web-based prey capture described below. The presence of two pairs of book lungs reveals the Long-clawed Spiders to belong to an ancient araneomorph spider lineage and sister group to the Austrochilidae (with the Tasmanian Cave Spider).

Gradungulidae is a small spider family found only in Australia and New Zealand. The Australian fauna consist of 13 species in four endemic genera with two distinctly different hunting strategies. The web-builders *Progradungula* and *Macrogradungula* retained a cribellum and they incorporate the fine cribellate silk into the capture structures of their web. In contrast the litter-dwelling vagrant hunters, *Kaiya* and *Tarlina,* lost the cribellum. The New Zealand fauna consists of three endemic species in three genera, *Gradungula*, *Pianoa* and *Spedungula*.

Progradungula includes two species, *P. carraiensis* from northern New South Wales and *P. otwayensis* from Southern Beech (*Nothofagus*) forests in the Otway Ranges in Victoria. Growing up to 25 mm in body length, *Macrogradungula moonya* is the largest gradungulid in Australia. It occurs in northern Queensland, inhabiting rock overhangs in the dense rainforests of the Atherton Tableland and

The prey capture strategy of *Progradungula carraiensis* is somewhat reminiscent of that of the Net-casting Spiders (family Deinopidae). In contrast to the deinopids, however, which carry their cribellate web completely between their legs, the capture threads of *Progradungula* are suspended between two fixed threads. When prey approaches within range it is thrown into the snare facilitated by the large raptorial claws. The prey capture strategy is similar in *Macrogradungula*. [M.R. Gray, Australian Museum]

Black Mountain National Park, near Cooktown, these areas being characterised by mountains of giant granite boulders. In Queensland, gradungulids are usually found on mountains at least 700 metres above sea level. In the cooler southern states, they can be found at lower elevations.

Progradungula carraiensis construct their webs among rocks or under wall overhangs of caves, although this species is possibly not an obligate cave-dweller. The web consists of an upper retreat network from which two semi-vertical lateral support threads run to the substrate 20–130 cm below. The lower parts of these support threads are held almost parallel to each other by short bridging threads and between them is a narrow ladder-like platform consisting of an irregular zigzag of cribellate silk, forming the comparatively small prey capture area of the web. The spider hunts head-down on the lower side of this semi-vertical springy catching ladder, with the front legs just above the substrate and the third legs stretching the capture area of the web. A prey item daring to approach the spider too closely is grasped with the two forelegs facilitated by the long claws, and thrown into the silk ladder. Cave-dwelling *P. carraiensis* appears to prey largely on moths in the family Tineidae, which are common members of the guanophilic cave-floor fauna.

The webs of *P. otwayensis* and *M. moonya* are similar. *Macrogradungula* webs have been found covering rock faces and tree trunks in tropical forests. The actual capture structure is also small and there are fewer cribellate threads than in *Progradungula*. The threads leading from the catching platform of an adult female extend approximately two metres up the side of a tree trunk to the retreat. In *P. otwayenis*, webs are generally supported by *Nothofagus* trees and the catching ladder in the supporting web may be constructed several metres from the retreat to which it is attached by a single, sturdy guideline.

The described species of the two genera of ecribellate ground hunters, *Tarlina* and *Kaiya*, have a disjunct distribution. The six species of *Tarlina* occur in many rainforests from northern Queensland to mid-northern New South Wales. The four species of *Kaiya* occur from the mid-eastern highland region in New South Wales into Victoria, where they have been reported from the Grampians National Park.

Tarlina woodwardi, here a female from Lamington National Park in Queensland, is a litter-dweller in south-eastern Queensland. The photo illustrates well the extremely long claw on the second right leg, which is typical for the Long-clawed Spiders. The frontal of the two superior claws of the first and second leg are extremely elongated in spiders of this family. [J. Haider]

Haplogynae

The Haplogynae traditionally included those spider families within the Modern Spiders (Araneomorphae) without sclerotised external female genitalia, in contrast to the Entelegynae which have a sclerotised epigyne and separate copulatory and fertilisation ducts. The haplogyne condition is primitive, it also occurs for example in the Mygalomorphae, and is therefore not a good character to trace the evolutionary history of a group. For example, the haplogyne epigyne is also evident in some entelegyne spiders, for example in some Triangle-web Spiders (family Uloboridae), Long-jawed Spiders (Tetragnathidae) and Ground Orb-web Spiders (Anapidae) and it is unclear if these spiders ever had a sclerotised epigyne or if has been secondarily lost. Characters that have evolved in haplogynes and may point to a common ancestry are, for example, the fusion of the chelicerae at their base and, possibly, a lamina on the chelicerae; both characters, however, have subsequently been lost in some haplogyne groups. Monophyly of the Haplogynae has been recently questioned and new hypotheses on their phylogenetic relationships, in particular with the respect to the Austrochiloidea, require further investigation. Interestingly, many haplogyne spiders have only six eyes. In Australia this is the case in all families except the Crevice Weavers (Filistatidae) and Daddy Long-legs (Pholcidae), which may retain the primitive pattern of eight eyes. These two families are also the only groups that build prey capture webs within the Australian haplogynes.

Eleven of the 18 currently recognised families of haplogyne spiders are found in Australia. Three of these are represented only by a single introduced species; the Dysderidae with the cosmopolitan Woodlouse Hunter *Dysdera crocata*, the Sicariidae with the Mediterranean Recluse Spider *Loxosceles rufescens,* and the Ochyroceratidae with the pantropical *Theotima minutissima*.

The Crevice Weavers (family Filistatidae) are the only spider family within the Haplogynae that retained a cribellum. They are generally accepted as the sister group to all other haplogyne families combined.

Four Australian haplogyne families represent the superfamily Dysderoidea. Their common characters relate mainly to internal morphology, i.e. their posterior tracheal spiracles are very close to the booklung spiracle and they have a peculiar specialization of the internal female genitalia. In addition to the above-mentioned introduced Woodlouse Hunter, the Australian Dysderoidea also includes the Tube-web Spiders (Segestriidae), the tiny, closely related Goblin Spiders

(Oonopidae) and the Six-eyed Ground Spiders (Orsolobidae).

The superfamily Sicarioidea includes three families in Australia. They have slender maxillary lobes that reach across the labium and a limited development of posterior tracheal respiratory system. They include the Spitting Spiders (Scytodidae), and the enigmatic Relictual Spiders (Periegopidae), in addition to the above-mentioned introduced Mediterranean Recluse Spider (Sicariidae) that has established populations in South Australia.

Some analyses place the Armoured Spiders (family Tetrablemmidae) together with the Afrotropical and Nearctic family Caponiidae as sister group to the Dysderoidea based on the loss of the anterior median eyes and the loss of a fusion of the chelicerae. However, the presence of a cheliceral lamella and reduced posterior tracheal system indicates closer relationships to the Sicarioidea. The tiny Armoured Spiders have only a few named species in Australia, including enigmatic subterranean representatives.

The closest relatives of the Daddy Long-legs (Pholcidae) within the Haplogynes do not occur in Australia. The Plectreuridae and the Diguetidae are only found in the Americas and Cuba. All three families have a peculiar structure on the posterior median spinneret, a distal ring that is composed of fused spigot bases. The Pholcidae include a large indigenous fauna in Australia, but the most commonly encountered species are cosmopolitan tramp species.

Daddy Long-legs (family Pholcidae) are probably the most prominent members of the haplogyne spiders in Australia. *Pholcus phalangioides*, here a female with eggs, is a cosmopolitan tramp species that can possibly be found in every house in Australia. Daddy Long-legs have eight or six eyes. Haplogynes have evolved to utilise a variety of predatory styles, including vagrant hunters and web-builders. [V.W. Framenau, Phoenix Environmental Sciences]

FILISTATIDAE
Crevice Weavers

- Eight eyes in compact arrangement
- Carapace broadly oval with snout-like front
- Abdomen oval with cinnamon and pale chevrons
- Legs comparatively long without spines
- Cribellum divided, short biseriate calamistrum on metatarsus of fourth leg
- Nocturnal
- Tubular retreat and capture web with radiate lines layered with cribellate silk
- Body length: 3–9 mm

Australia:
Partially revised
Current: 13 species in 3 genera
Estimated: 40 species in 6 genera
World: 115 species in 17 genera

Crevice Weavers (family Filistatidae) are the only cribellate spiders within the Haplogynae, the modern spiders with simple genitalia. The cribellum is divided and, unique within cribellate spiders, the calamistrum consists of three rows of setae in some Crevice Weavers. Filistatidae appear to represent a basal lineage within the Haplogynae, possibly sister taxon to all other families. They have a worldwide distribution and are most diverse in subtropical and tropical regions.

Two subfamilies are recognised in Australia, the Filistatinae and the Prithinae. The **Filistatinae** are generally larger and a fovea is present. They are represented in Australia only by a single species, *Filistata gibsonhilli* from Christmas Island. However, the generic placement of this species remains questionable and it may represent a new genus with Indo-Pacific distribution. **Prithinae** include *Wandella* and *Yardiella*. *Wandella* is the most diverse genus in Australia and currently includes 11 species. They are widely distributed in habitats ranging from the arid zone into tropical rainforest. *Yardiella humphreysi* is the only representative of *Yardiella* and only found in caves along Cape Range in Western Australia. It appears to be an obligate cave inhabitant.

Crevice Weavers make small, irregular, cribellate sheet-webs under loose bark of trees, in crevices on tree trunks and rocks, and in caves. These webs may have up to four entrances and are sometimes reminiscent of the webs of the Black House Spider, *Badumna insignis* (family Desidae).

Left: Most Crevice Weavers, such as this male *Wandella stuartensis* from South Australia, have their cephalic area narrowed to a snout-shaped tip. This species occurs throughout the arid south of the continent. [B.C. Baehr]

Below: *Wandella* constructs its web with silk-lined tubular retreats in cracks or gaps of bark, rocks or walls. Cribellate signal-lines radiate in all directions, layered with thick cribellate silk. At night, the spider waits close to the entrance until prey entangles its feet in the woollen silk. [R.J. Raven]

A *Wandella barbarella* female from Walyunga National Park, Western Australia, has just shed its skin under the protection of a piece of bark. The flimsy, cribellate silk provides only minimal protection. This species is known from the Swan Coastal Plain north to Geraldton and onto the Darling Escarpment in Western Australia [H. McLennan, Australian Museum]

A male of *Wandella orana* from Mount Colah, New South Wales, shows the large pedipalps in front of the eyes. This species occurs in forest habitats in north-eastern New South Wales. It has very localised populations, presumably introduced, associated with old farm buildings in outer suburban Sydney and central coastal New South Wales [H. McLennan, Australian Museum]

SICARIIDAE
Recluse Spiders, Fiddle-back Spiders

- Six eyes in three groups of two
- Carapace low, about as long as wide
- Legs long and slender, two claws
- Vagrant with flimsy silken retreat
- Body length: 6–10 mm

Australia: Single introduced species
World: 130 species in 2 genera

The Recluse Spiders (family Sicariidae) have gained notorious fame as their bites can occasionally cause severe necrotic lesions. The natural distribution of the Sicariidae, represented by the genera *Sicarius* and *Loxosceles*, includes the Americas, and in the Old World the Mediterranean region into temperate southern Africa, thereby hinting at a western Gondwanan origin.

Two species in the genus *Loxosceles* have been found in Australia. The Mediterranean Recluse Spider, *Loxosceles rufescens*, has established populations in South Australia at least since the 1930s and has been found once in Perth in the 1950s. The Chilean Recluse Spider, *Loxosceles laeta*, originally from South America, has only been reported once in Sydney. Both species have been widely distributed outside their native ranges and are typical synanthropic, almost cosmopolitan tramp species.

Loxosceles rufescens is a long-legged reddish-brown spider with characteristic darker coloration of the head region and a uniformly olive-brown abdomen that has a darker cardiac mark in its frontal half. It lives in buildings and accumulated litter outside houses. They build a flimsy retreat of irregular strands of silk under objects on the ground or in the dark corners of buildings and caves.

Bites of some *Loxosceles* species may cause serious necrotic skin lesions (loxoscelism) caused by sphingomyelinase D, a dermonecrotic component of the venom that in addition to sicariids also occurs in some pathogenic bacteria. Severe cases of loxoscelism, including fatal bites, are known from *L. reclusa* and *L. laeta*. Skin ulcerations due to Mediterranean Recluse Spider bites, the only species resident in Australia, appear to be much milder. In any case, the risk of a *Loxosceles* bite, even in heavily infested buildings, appears low as spiders mainly bite in defence.

The Mediterranean Recluse Spider, *Loxosceles rufescens*, is an introduced species in South Australia and it has been present there since at least the 1930s. This six-eyed, long-legged spider has a characteristic darker cephalic region on a low carapace. In this image a male is cleaning its left front leg with its fangs. [A. Lance]

SCYTODIDAE
Spitting Spiders

- Six eyes arranged in three groups of two
- Prosoma low in eye region but domed towards thoracic region
- Anterior spinnerets short, conical, contiguous
- Legs spineless, long and slender, directed sideways with 3 claws
- Night active without prey capture web
- Spit venom-glue mixture from their venom glands to pin down prey in zig-zag pattern
- Body length: 4–11 mm

Australia:
Taxonomy poorly resolved
Current: 6 species in 2 genera
Estimated: 30 species in 3 genera
World: 228 species in 5 genera

The Spitting Spiders (family Scytodidae) have inspired awe amongst arachnologists due to their unusual and fascinating prey capture strategy. They spit venomous glue in a zig-zag pattern over their prey, thereby pinning it down and at the same time paralysing it. The spitting action is driven by rapid contraction of carapace muscles, which compress the large venom glands that include a compartment to produce the gluey silk. Spitting spiders are the only spiders that produce silk in their prosoma. Spitting is enormously fast and an attack sequence consisting of between 5–57 fang cycles (one upsweep of a chelicera) typically lasts less than 30 milliseconds in *Scytodes thoracica*. It involves fang oscillations at 278–1781 Hertz.

Spitting Spiders have six eyes arranged as three pairs. They have a dome-shaped carapace with a very low eye region and generally a characteristic pattern of dark spots and lines on a lighter body.

Scytodids are pantropical and include a number of cosmopolitan species. Most of the described species are from Brazil, where recent revisions are available. The Australian scytodid fauna has not been revised and only six species in two genera, *Dictis* and *Scytodes*, are known. All of these are known from well outside the country.

Dictis striatipes is the only Australian member of *Dictis* and was initially described from the Pacific. It has since been found to occur from China throughout South-East Asia into Australia. All other currently named Spitting Spiders in Australia belong to the cosmopolitan genus *Scytodes* and all are more or less pantropical in their distribution. Probably the most common species in Australia is the synanthropic *Scytodes thoracica*. *Scytodes tardigrada* has been initially described from northern Queensland but is now known to occur in South-East Asia. Little to nothing is known about the indigenous fauna of spitting spiders.

Most scytodids are cursorial, although some species build webs. Some form of sociality with extended maternal care has been reported in some species. Maternal care in these spiders is pronounced with females carrying their eggsac between their chelicerae.

Scytodes thoracica is a cosmopolitan species that is often found in or near houses (it is synanthropic). Spitting spiders have a domed prosoma and six eyes arranged in three groups of two each. [F. Bokhari]

Spitting Spiders often have a very characteristic pattern of dark spots and lines on an otherwise light brown body. With her extremely long legs this *Scytodes thoracica* female silently creeps up to her prey until she is close enough to pin it down with a zig-zag line of venomous glue. [V.W. Framenau, Phoenix Environmental Sciences]

With her specialised prey capture strategy, *Scytodes thoracica* is able to prey on animals that are larger or equally venomous, such as Daddy Long-legs Spiders (family Pholcidae). [H. Smith, Australian Museum]

PERIEGOPIDAE
Relictual Spiders

- Six eyes arranged in three widely separated groups of two
- Chelicerae not fused and with cheliceral teeth
- Possibly tubular retreats under logs
- Body length: 6–8 mm

Australia:
Taxonomy revised
Current: 1 species in 1 genus
Estimated: 1 species in 1 genus
World: 3 species in 1 genus

The Periegopidae is one of the world's smallest spider families. It currently includes three species in a single genus, *Periegops*: one from Australia (*P. australia*) and two from New Zealand (*P. suterii*, *P. keani*), and it is unlikely that many more, if any, will be discovered. In Australasia, only the Holarchaeidae with two species, one each from Australia and New Zealand, is a smaller family.

Periegops has previously been included in the Recluse Spiders (Sicariidae) or the Tube-web Spiders (Segestriidae), but differs from those and other related haplogyne families due to the lack of a fusion of the chelicerae and cheliceral teeth in addition to some characters of the internal female genitalia. The family is currently considered the sister taxon to the Nearctic/Afrotropical False Violin Spiders (Drymusidae), and together they are most closely related to the Spitting Spiders (Scytodidae).

The three known species of *Periegops* have highly limited distributions. *Periegops australia* has only been found at two small locations in south-eastern Queensland, *P. suterii* is only known from Banks Peninsula and inner-city Christchurch and *P. keani* from Aldermen Island and East Cape in New Zealand.

Very little is known about the ecology of *Periegops*. They appear to be cursorial spiders in deep leaf litter on well-drained soil. They do not construct prey-capture webs but have tubular retreats. The Australian specimens have been found in pitfall traps and a female was extracted from a rotten root cavity.

Periegops suterii from New Zealand is one of only three known species of Relictual Spider (family Periegopidae). This species differs only marginally in genitalic structure from the Australian representative, *P. australia*, from south-eastern Queensland. [B. McQuillan]

OCHYROCERATIDAE
No common name

- Six eyes, four in anterior row and two behind
- Chelicerae free and with several denticles in addition to a lamella
- Genital opening of females extends laterally and is connected to tracheal spiracle
- Irregular space webs in dark and moist places
- Body length: ca. 1 mm

Australia: Single introduced species
World: 161 species in 14 genera

The Ochyroceratidae is a family of small spiders from the tropical and subtropical regions. As members of the superfamily Leptonetoidea, they are most closely related to two spider families otherwise not present in Australia, Leptonetidae and Telemidae.

The only representative of the Ochyroceratidae in Australia is *Theotima minutissima* which was collected along the central Mackay coast in Queensland. It has a pantropical distribution. Males of *T. minutissima* have rarely been found and the species has been shown to reproduce parthenogenetically.

Ochyroceratidae are common in tropical forest litter and caves in South Africa, the Caribbean and Asia and are especially diverse in the Indo-Pacific region. They build small, irregular sheet-webs in dark, damp places around leaves, sticks and logs.

Members of the Ochyroceratidae typically carry their eggs in their chelicerae; however, the biology of these species is otherwise very poorly known.

Theotima minutissima is a pantropical species that has been found in Queensland. It is the only representative of the family Ochyroceratidae in Australia. It is believed to mainly reproduce parthenogenetically as only few males have ever been found. [B.C. Baehr]

PHOLCIDAE
Daddy Long-legs Spiders

- Six or eight eyes in two groups each forming a triangle on a high or low mount; the two anterior median eyes are small or reduced
- Legs very long and slender with flexible tarsi
- Chelicerae small and joined at base
- Tangled space webs
- Body length: 3–10 mm

Australia:
Partially revised
Current: 69 species in 16 genera
Estimated: 150 species in 20 genera
World: 1,340 species in 90 genera

Daddy Long-legs Spiders (family Pholcidae), as their colloquial name suggests, have exceptionally long and slender legs. Their eyes are arranged in two laterally situated groups that form triangles and this eye arrangement distinguishes them from similar spiders in the families Synotaxidae and possibly Linyphiidae (Money Spiders). The chelicerae of pholcids are joined together at the base, which is very unusual in spiders, but also occurs for example in the Crevice Weavers (family Filistatidae) and Dwarf Orb-weaving Spiders (Symphytognathidae).

The relationships between the genera of the Pholcidae is not well understood; however, three different subfamilies currently accommodate the most common genera with indigenous species: *Wugigarra* belongs to the **Modisiminae**, *Trichocyclus* to the **Arteminae** and *Micromerys* to the **Pholcinae**.

Whilst Australia hosts a diverse indigenous fauna, the species of Daddy Long-legs most commonly encountered are those living in and near houses. Daddy Long-legs are among the most common spiders in houses worldwide and most of the synanthropic species have been found in this country. At least nine species have been introduced to Australia, including the very common *Pholcus phalangioides* (from the Palaearctic), *Smeringopus pallidus* (of African origin), the biggest of all pholcids: *Artema atlanta* (from the Middle East), and *Holocnemus pluchei* (from the Mediterranean).

The indigenous fauna is dominated by two genera, *Trichocyclus* and *Wugigarra*. Both are apparently of Gondwanan origin but their distribution patterns are largely separated in Australia. The currently 21 described species of *Wugigarra* have an eastern Australian distribution from Cape York Peninsula in northern Queensland to the Eyre Peninsula in South Australia. In contrast, *Trichocyclus* (23 species) covers the entire west of the continent, with gaps only in the driest deserts and very few records along the east coast.

Micromerys includes seven Australian species and its presence in Australia is probably based on post-Pleistocene immigrations from the north, similar to other smaller genera related to *Pholcus* such as *Panjange*, *Belisana* and *Spermophora*.

The mostly silver-coloured slender pholcids live in tangled space-webs, usually incorporating some form of sheet, in which they hang upside down. Some Australian rainforest species build a high dome in the centre of the tangled snare.

Disturbance of the web unfailingly causes the occupant to vibrate vigorously. This behaviour possibly serves two purposes. It clearly helps in avoiding predation as the wildly shaking spider is very hard to focus on. In addition, a prey item will entangle much more quickly and efficiently if the web is constantly moving.

Daddy Long-legs have shown to be very adaptable when it comes to catching prey. Whilst their tangle-web provides for the most common way to subdue prey, *Pholcus phalangioides* has also been reported to invade other spiders' webs where it consumes the other spiders' prey or the resident spider itself. This species may also capture walking prey in the periphery of the web and has been shown to use specialised gluey gumfoot lines for this purpose in addition the tangle mesh itself.

Prey items are quickly wrapped in silk and only then the spider inflicts the fatal bite. The prey may be eaten immediately or stored for later consumption. With their joined chelicerae and short fangs, Daddy Long-legs can bite their arthropod prey only on the thin tubular legs. Despite this limitation, pholcids are well known to be able to subdue other, even much larger spiders such as Huntsman Spiders (Sparassidae) and Australian Redback Spiders (family Theridiidae).

Daddy Long-legs are subject to the urban myth that their venom is the most potent of all spiders, but that their fangs are too small to penetrate human skin. This is clearly not true and subsequent 'experiments' with these spiders showed the bite of the Daddy Long-legs to only cause very minor irritations.

Pholcus phalangioides is a cosmopolitan species and probably the most common species in or around houses. Adults have been collected throughout the year. Daddy Long-legs show maternal brood care. Females carry their cluster of eggs between their chelicerae. The silk of the eggsac is so thin that the individual eggs shine through. The female carries the eggsac until the young are ready to disperse over the tangled space web. She will care for them until they are ready to disperse out of the web. [V.W. Framenau, Phoenix Environmental Sciences]

The genus *Smeringopus*, here a penultimate male photographed in Perth, Western Australia, was introduced into Australia by humans. Two species in this genus have been reported from Australia, *S. pallidus* and *S. natalensis*, which are both of African origin [V.W. Framenau, Phoenix Environmental Sciences]

The Australian Pholcidae include a large indigenous element, but the most commonly encountered species are introduced and synanthropic. The spider pictured here was not collected and remained unidentified as genus- and species-level identification often requires the use of a stereo microscope. [F. Bokhari]

The unique endemic rainforest pholcid, *Micromerys gracilis*, is one of the most colourful species in the family. Here, an individual is hiding under a leaf in a rainforest at Mossman Gorge, north Queensland. [P. Zborowski]

TETRABLEMMIDAE
Armoured Spiders

- Six eyes, but number often reduced (no eyes in subterranean species)
- Carapace raised, with modifications in males
- Chelicerae often with horns in males
- Abdomen oval with lateral sclerotised ridges between dorsal and ventral scutes
- Small sheet-web or free living hunters
- Body length: 0.7–4 mm

Australia:
Taxonomy poorly resolved
Current: 3 species in 1 genus
Estimated: 60 species in 4 genera
World: 144 species in 30 genera

Armoured Spiders (family Tetrablemmidae) are characterised by their small size – they are amongst the smallest of spiders – and the presence of distinctive lateral sclerotized plates between the dorsal and ventral main plates (scutes) of the abdomen.

They are a largely tropical and subtropical family of litter dwellers with the centre of diversity in South-East Asia; they are poorly studied in Australia. The local fauna only includes three described species, *Tetrablemma okei* from Victoria, *Tetrablemma magister* from Queensland and the subterranean *Tetrablemma alaus* from the Pilbara region in Western Australia.

Eye reduction is not uncommon in Armoured Spiders. Most species have six eyes, but four-eyed and two-eyed species occur throughout many different genera. Their small size may contribute to the reduction in the number of eyes. The total loss of eyes is uncommon in tetrablemmids and is only known from cave-dwelling and subterranean species from Thailand, Mexico and Australia. The blind *Tetrablemma alaus* was discovered during troglofauna surveys in exploration bore holes in the mineral-rich Pilbara region of Western Australia. It belongs to a diverse troglofauna that inhabits the underground fissures and crevices in the extremely old geology of this landscape. Further blind *Tetrablemma* species have since been found in the region.

The genus *Tetrablemma* contains 25 named species and is known from Australia, central and south-eastern Asia, Micronesia, Polynesia, the Caribbean and North Africa.

Little is known about the biology of the Armoured Spiders. Most species appear to be vagrant hunters, but some create tiny sheet-webs in leaf litter or moss, or under bark, mainly in rainforests.

Tetrablemma males, here an undescribed male from leaf litter in the rainforest of Lamington National Park in Queensland, often have a strongly raised carapace with an elevated eye-mount. Their chelicerae are armed with an elongated horn on the front. The scale bar of just 1 mm illustrates the very small size of these spiders. [B.C. Baehr]

The Armoured Spiders can be recognised by the sclerotised ridges between the dorsal and ventral plates of the abdomen. This *Tetrablemma* female from Lamington National Park has only a slightly raised carapace, in contrast to the male illustrated above. [B.C. Baehr]

SEGESTRIIDAE
Tube-web Spiders

- Six eyes in three separate groups of two
- Chelicerae long and directed forward with small fangs
- First three pairs of legs directed forwards
- Nocturnal
- Tubular retreats and radiating trip lines
- Body length: 6–15 mm

Australia:
Taxonomically poorly known
Current: 9 species in 2 genera
Estimated: 70 species in 4 genera
World: 119 species in 3 genera

Tube-web Spiders (family Segestriidae) are six-eyed haplogyne spiders that are characterised by the position of their legs. When resting, three pairs of legs are directed forward alongside the spider's body.

The taxonomy of the Segestriidae is poorly resolved both at the local scale and worldwide. Australia accommodates two of the three described genera, *Ariadna* and *Gippsicola*. The latter is only known from a single described species, *G. raleighi*, from eastern Victoria but apparently also occurs in New Zealand. There, both genera can easily be separated by the coloration of the abdomen, which is uniform dark purplish or brown in *Ariadna* but light grey with dark patches in *Gippsicola*. We do not know if this separation also applies to the Australian species as the fauna in this country is too poorly known. The most recent description of a species of *Ariadna* in Australia dates back to the 1950s, which was *A. decatetracantha* from Western Australia.

The cylindrical body of the Tube-web Spiders is perfectly adapted to a life in a permanent burrow. These spiders construct their retreat in small holes in bark, under wood, beneath rocks, in cracks, or in wall gaps. The burrow is open and often some radiating trip lines fan out alerting the spiders to passing prey. Segestriids are active at night.

An unidentified female Tube-web Spider from Western Australia shows the typical resting position of the legs along the left hand side of its body, with three of the four pairs being directed forward. This species would possibly be attributed to the genus *Ariadna*; however, the Australian segestriid fauna is poorly known even at the genus level. [V.W. Framenau, Phoenix Environmental Sciences]

Tube-web Spiders construct small, simple burrows often in hollow branches, the vacant holes of boring insects, under logs or rocks, and in cracks and crevices of rocks. The burrows generally have about ten trip-lines radiating from the entrance. [R.J. Raven]

This Tube-web Spider female excavated from an embankment in Tasmania, possibly belonging to the genus *Ariadna*, has a very dark carapace and dark chevrons on the abdomen, contrasting with the colour pattern of the Western Australian species illustrated above. [R.J. Raven]

DYSDERIDAE
Woodlouse Hunters

- Six eyes
- Carapace reddish-brown
- Chelicerae projecting forward
- Abdomen cream-coloured to grey
- Free-living nocturnal hunter that hides in loosely woven silk retreat during day
- Body length: 10–14 mm

Australia:
Single introduced species
World: 528 species in 24 genera

Woodlouse Hunter is the colloquial name for *Dysdera crocata* of the family Dysderidae, as they have been suggested to be specialist hunters of these invertebrates. This concept has been challenged as laboratory experiments showed that these spiders readily attack and eat other arthropods, at least in captivity. Woodlice clearly form a significant proportion of the diet of these spiders and their long chelicerae appear to be well suited to pierce these heavily sclerotised terrestrial crustaceans.

Dysdera crocata is the only member of the Dysderidae currently known from Australia. It is a tramp species with a worldwide distribution which has apparently been introduced to Australia from Europe in the early days of settlement. It was described in Australia in the year 1900 under a different name, *D. australiensis*. Related families are the Six-eyed Ground Spiders (family Orsolobidae) and possibly the Goblin Spiders (family Oonopidae) but their representatives are generally less than half the size of the Woodlouse Hunters.

The introduced species of Woodlouse Hunter is currently known from south-eastern Australia only. These spiders prefer moderately moist conditions and hide, for example, under logs. They can be found in urban environments such as gardens and parks.

The bite *of Dysdera crocata* appears to show only local and minor effects, although it might be initially painful due to the large chelicerae.

Dysdera crocata, here a female from Warwick Farm, New South Wales, has a distinct coloration with dark reddish carapace and cream-coloured to grey abdomen. The chelicerae point forward. Unlike the superficially similar Tube-web Spiders (family Segestriidae), *Dysdera* only keeps two pairs of legs, not three, pointing forward when resting. [M.R. Gray, Australian Museum]

OONOPIDAE
Goblin spiders

- Six eyes in two rows, median eyes large contiguous, posterior eye row normally procurved (eyes reduced in subterranean spiders)
- Abdomen oval, often enclosed in a dorsal and ventral shield (scute)
- Coloration orange-brown, although soft-bodied spiders have pale and cinnamon colours
- Legs generally short and robust with two tarsal claws
- Free-living nocturnal ground,- bark- or tree-dwellers
- Body length: 0.8–4 mm

Australia:
Partially revised
Current: 142 species in 13 genera
Estimated: 300 species in 14 genera
World: 1,135 species in 93 genera

The name Goblin Spiders for the family Oonopidae refers to the somewhat peculiar appearance of these small spiders. They are often hard-bodied with strong sclerotised abdominal plates (scutes) and orange-brown in colour. At a global scale, Goblin Spiders are known for some unusual morphological features, such as bizarre spines on the head, horny extensions on the chelicerae, strange-looking mouthparts, sternal pouches, and hand-like extensions on the posterior coxae, to name just a few. Not much would be known about the tiny litter- and canopy-dwelling goblins if they had not been the object of an international research effort, a Planetary Biodiversity Inventory (PBI), funded by the National Science Foundation (NSF) in the USA.

Goblin Spiders are very similar to the Six-eyed Ground Spiders (Orsolobidae) and some Australian genera were initially placed in the oonopids until the family Orsolobidae was established. Differences between the two families are subtle and include a peculiar, raised morphology of a tarsal chemosensory organ in orsolobids.

Goblin Spiders have a worldwide distribution but are most common in the tropics and subtropics. The Australian fauna currently includes named species in 13 genera, some of which have been treated in extensive revisions as part of the PBI (e.g. *Cavisternum*, *Prethopalpus* and *Opopaea*), others represent the legacy of historical taxonomic work and still require revision (e.g. *Gamasomorpha*, *Oonops* and *Orchestina*), and others are introduced pantropical tramp species (*Brignolia* and *Heteroonops*).

Males in the genus *Cavisternum* have a concave sternum that is covered with leaf-like setae; their fangs are extremely long and have broadened tips. The females are indistinguishable from those from other genera. *Cavisternum* is endemic to Australia and found in tropical northern parts of the country. Most described species are known from single localities. Species of *Grymeus* have setae-bearing booklung covers, and males have a pouch formed by the maxillae, labium and sternum. Three species are described from south-eastern Australia. The genus *Ischnothyreus* is represented by dark spiders and males have very small, strongly sclerotized pedipalp bulbs that are well-separated from the cymbium. The genus includes 34 species in tropical Australia where many species are known to be canopy-dwellers.

The main criterion that distinguishes *Opopaea* from most other Goblin Spiders is the unusual shape of the male pedipalp, which has a greatly enlarged patella. In addition to more than 80 litter-dwelling species, the genus also includes two blind subterranean species from northern Western Australia. *Pelicinus saaristoi*, described from Barrow Island in Western Australia, is currently the only named species of the genus in Australia; however, many more species are known from collections. The genus is particularly species rich in this country.

The genus *Prethopalpus* is restricted to the Australasian tropics. Males are characterised by the swollen pedipalp patella which is one to two times the size of the femur. Most species are recorded from single locations, demonstrating high local endemicity. Of 20 Australian species, 14 are troglobitic and only known from subterranean ecosystems in Western Australia.

The pantropical *Brignolia parumpunctata* and *Heteronoops spinimanus* have been introduced to Australia and are currently known to occur in Queensland. The latter is believed to be able to reproduce parthenogenetically as only two populations with males have so far been found.

Goblin Spiders are found in leaf litter, decaying substratum, under bark and stones, and in foliage among lower vegetation and in the canopy of rainforests. Although they are predominantly tropical and subtropical, they occupy a diversity of habitats ranging from rainforests to deserts. They also represent a significant proportion of the subterranean spider fauna.

Little is known about the biology of these tiny spiders. They are believed to be vagrant hunters, actively pursuing their prey, which includes mites and small hexapods such as springtails. Like many other free-living spiders, some species of Goblin Spiders appear to build small silk nests for resting and moulting. Oonopid eggsacs include only very few, sometimes only one or two, but comparatively large eggs.

This *Opopaea carnarvon* male from central Queensland has big jellybean-like pedipalps, a feature which is one of the main characters of this genus. It is the most species-rich genus in Australia. *Opopaea* species live mostly in leaf litter or on tree trunks, where they hunt springtails and other small insects. [B.C. Baehr]

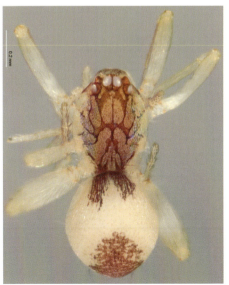

Species in the genus *Orchestina*, here a female from Lamington National Park in south-eastern Queensland, have soft bodies with pale and cinnamon markings. Their massive back legs are believed to enable them to jump, and this feature is the main character of *Orchestina*. Most of the species live in the canopy of rainforests. [B.C. Baehr]

This *Ischnothyreus* male from Lamington National Park in south-eastern Queensland has pairs of strong spines on the front legs possibly assisting in prey capture. They have small, strongly sclerotized male pedipalps. The genus occurs predominantly in leaf litter or tree canopies in rainforests. The genus currently includes 34 described species in Australia. [B.C. Baehr]

The members of the genus *Pelicinus*, here a male from Lamington National Park in south-eastern Queensland, are more soft-bodied than those in *Xestaspis* and the abdomen rises further over their carapace. Their preferred habitat seems to be forest litter, but they also occur in drier areas. *Pelicinus* includes about 70 species, most of which are currently unnamed. [B.C. Baehr]

The genus *Xestaspis* includes the largest Goblin Spiders in Australia. They are orange-brown with heavy abdominal scutes. *Xestaspis* includes at least 60 species known from the collections of Australian museums, almost all of which are currently unnamed. [B.C. Baehr]

Cavisternum ewani is found along the coastal region of Queensland where it lives between cracks in rocks or in leaf litter. All *Cavisternum* species have soft, pale orange scutes, the sternum of the male (image below) is concave and covered with leaf-like setae, and the fangs are extremely long and curved. [B.C. Baehr]

ORSOLOBIDAE
Six-eyed Ground Spiders

- Six eyes in a H-shaped pattern
- Chelicerae with teeth
- Abdomen oval, pale, or with cinnamon and pale chevrons
- Legs slender, tarsi with two biserially dentate claws
- Tarsal organ elevated
- Free-living night active hunters
- Body length: 2–7 mm

Australia:
Taxonomy recently revised
Current: 37 species in 4 genera
Estimated: 50 species in 5 genera
World: 187 species in 30 genera

The Six-eyed Ground Spiders (family Orsolobidae) are superficially similar to the Goblin Spiders (family Oonopidae) and the Woodlouse Hunters (family Dysderidae) and some of the species now in Orsolobidae have been previously placed in these families. However, the presence of an obscure raised sensory organ on the tarsi, a feature which is unique amongst spiders, unites the orsolobids as a separate family.

Orsolobids have a typical Gondwanan distribution and occur in South America (where the family is most diverse in Chile), Africa, Madagascar, New Zealand and Australia. New Zealand is the world centre of diversity of this family, where more than 100 described species still only represent part of the fauna.

The most species-rich genus in Australia is *Tasmanoonops* with 30 described species. These spiders occur mainly in the wet forests of eastern Australia, including, as the name suggests, Tasmania. However, two species in the genus are also recorded from Western Australia. *Hickmanolobus* includes four species from Queensland, New South Wales and Tasmania. Two Australian genera include only a single species, *Australobus torbay* from south-western Western Australia and *Cornifalx insignis* from Tasmania. Differences between the genera relate mainly to abdomen coloration, the shape of the tarsal organ, the presence of leg spines and the morphology of male genitalia.

Orsolobids are an important component of the forest litter fauna in the southern hemisphere, where they pursue a vagrant lifestyle. Some species, for example in the genus *Tasmanoonops*, build a silken purse retreat with a single entrance in which the female constructs the eggsac that she guards until the young hatch. Six-eyed Ground Spiders have been reported to prey on springtails, amphipods and insect larvae, but little of their life history is known.

Hickmanolobus linnaei is only known from Coolah Tops National Park, New South Wales. This species has particularly distinct light chevron marks on the abdomen. [B.C. Baehr]

Below: *Hickmanolobus ibisca* is a relatively small species, being a mere 1.5–2 mm in body length, whereas *Tasmanoonops* species are at least three times as large. Both genera have the H-shaped eye pattern, which is typical for the Orsolobidae. [B.C. Baehr]

Hickmanolobus linnaei has a comparatively low tarsal organ, as is typical for the species in this genus. It is visible here as small circle below the setae towards the top left corner of the image. The presence of a raised tarsal organ and the biserially dentate claws (i.e. claws with two rows of teeth) here almost entirely covered by tarsal setae in the centre of the image, identify the Orsolobidae. [B.C. Baehr]

Entelegyne
Advanced Modern Spiders

The Entelegynae are the most advanced spiders. They have traditionally been defined by the presence of a sclerotised genital plate in females, the epigyne. The development of the epigyne occurred hand in hand with the evolution of a second genital duct, the fertilisation duct, which is absent in the haplogyne spiders. The fertilisation duct is a separate duct into which the male spider inserts its embolus. The female lays the eggs through a different genital opening. In contrast, in haplogyne spiders, the embolus is inserted into the same opening through which the female lays the eggs. There are additional characters which are only present in the Entelegynae, such as cylindrical gland spigots on the posterior spinnerets, the separation of labium and sternum, and features of the respiratory system. Additional evidence for a common ancestry of the Entelegynae is a peculiar cribellate silk-combing behaviour in some families, in which both fourth legs are braced against each other and moved simultaneously.

The Entelegynae is the largest group within the Araneomorphae and it includes the majority of Australian spiders. Fifty-seven of the 79 spider families that occur in Australia are entelegyne. Major groups within the Entelegynae include the Araneoidea, i.e. Orb-weaving Spiders (family Araneidae) and allies, which include 18 families in Australia that share the construction of an orb-web with sticky glue, although often this orb-web is highly modified or reduced. Together with two families of cribellate orb-weavers, the Net-casting Spiders (Deinopidae) and the Venomless Spiders (Uloboridae), the Araneoidea form the Orbiculariae, i.e. all spiders with orb-weaving behaviour believed to have evolved only once within spiders.

A second large group is termed the 'RTA-clade' and this unites those spiders in which the male pedipalp tibia has a distinct outgrowth, the retrolateral tibial apophysis (RTA). This clade includes almost all other entelegyne spiders outside the Araneoidea. Within the RTA-clade there are a number of distinct groups. The Lycosoidea, with 10 Australian families, includes many ground-living spiders related to Wolf Spiders (family Lycosidae), which are classically identified by internal eye morphology. Lycosoidea also include, for example, the Fishing Spiders (Pisauridae), Lynx Spiders (Oxyopidae) and Crab Spiders (Thomisidae). The Gnaphosoidea, with seven Australian families, is represented by spiders closely related to Ground Spiders (Gnaphosidae), and characterised by eye pattern and spinneret morphology. These include, for example, the White-tailed Spiders (Lamponidae) and Long-spinneret Ground Spiders (Prodidomidae).

Superior hunting strategies allow Modern Spiders (Araneomorphae) to overcome prey much larger and potentially more dangerous than themselves. The Entelegynae is the most advanced and most diverse major group of Modern Spiders and includes 57 of the 79 Australian spider families. The Crab Spider *Tharpyna campestrata* (family Thomisidae), which is widespread throughout Australia, is here making a meal of a Bull Ant, *Myrmecia desertorum*. Spiders have been suggested as an important element of an integrated pest management strategy in agriculture. [F. Bokhari]

ARCHAEIDAE
Assassin or Pelican Spiders

- Eight eyes in two rows
- Extremely elevated head-region and elongated fangs
- Long legs with a particularly long patella on first leg
- Vagrant hunters without prey capture web
- Prey specialist, hunts other spiders
- Body length: 2–5 mm

Australia:
Taxonomy recently revised
Current: 38 species in 2 genera
Estimated: 50 species in 2 genera
World: 70 species in 4 genera

The common name Assassin Spiders for the family Archaeidae refers to the predatory behaviour of these spiders as they are specialist spider hunters. They are also called Pelican Spiders due to their extremely elongated chelicerae, which are accommodated by a neck-like extension of the carapace.

Assassin Spiders were originally distributed worldwide and are known from Mesozoic and Tertiary fossil deposits from about 40 million years ago. The family was first described from Europe in the 1840s from fossil specimens enclosed in Baltic amber. In 1881 the first living Assassin Spider was found in Madagascar. Today three diverse, highly endemic faunas are known from southern Africa, Madagascar and Australia.

The Australian Assassin Spider fauna is diverse at a very local scale and many species are restricted to individual mountains or montane systems. This country is home to two endemic genera; *Austrarchaea* with 27 named species and *Zephyrarchaea* with 11 species. *Austrarchaea* species have a comparatively longer carapace in addition to some more subtle morphological differences. Most of the *Austrarchaea* species live in eastern Australia's rainforests and montane wet sclerophyll forests east of the Great Dividing Range, hidden in moss or low vegetation. Species of *Zephyrarchaea* occur west of the Great Dividing Range, in southern Western Australia, South Australia and Victoria. They are usually found in coastal, sub-coastal or montane temperate heathlands, but also in wet eucalypt forests and temperate rainforests.

Assassin Spiders hunt without a web by stabbing their prey with venom-filled fangs that are attached to the end of their extremely elongated jaws. This arrangement allows them to strike spiders without having to approach them too closely. Young Assassin Spiders are generally found in leaf litter, whereas adults seem to be more common on tree trunks in long moss. They have also been found over a metre high on single threads spanning the trees.

Females construct their eggsacs with only a few eggs – usually about a dozen – enclosed in loosely woven silk, and carry them between their third legs. They build a retreat with only a few threads, and attach the eggsac when the young are about to hatch. After hatching they re-attach the eggsac with the young riding on it.

Zephyrarchaea janinae, here a female from south-western Western Australia is, together with *Z. mainae*, the only species in its genus with three distinct pairs of humps on the upper side of the abdomen. The head of *Z. janinae* is a somewhat higher than that of *Z. mainae*. *Z. janinae* is only found in the high-rainfall province of south-west Western Australia, from the Leeuwin-Naturaliste and Wellington National Parks (near Bunbury) east to Pemberton, whereas *Z. mainae* can be found in the wider Albany area. [V.W. Framenau, Phoenix Environmental Sciences]

Opposite page: Species in the genus *Austrarchaea*, here *A. raveni* from rainforest at Mt. Glorious in southern Queensland, differ from *Zephyrarchaea* due to a comparatively higher carapace. These tiny spiders are also known as Pelican Spiders because their carapace, with bizarrely elongated fangs and a long neck, is reminiscent of the bill, head and neck of these distinctive birds. [B.C. Baehr]

STENOCHILIDAE
No common name

- Eight eyes in two rows in oval arrangement
- Carapace diamond-shaped with two thoracic grooves
- Labium fused to sternum
- Scute on the abdominal venter
- Vagrant hunters without prey capture web
- Body length: 3–10 mm

> **Australia:**
> Taxonomy poorly resolved
> Current: no species described
> Estimated: 3 species in 2 genera
> **World:** 13 species in 2 genera

The Stenochilidae is a very small family of spiders with a tropical distribution that covers the Indian subcontinent, including Sri Lanka, and across South-East Asia and into the Pacific region. No species is currently described from Australia, but specimens from northern Queensland are known in collections.

The stenochilids are the only Australian representatives of the superfamily Palpimanoidea. They are characterised by a diamond-shaped carapace with two thoracic grooves. The family includes only two genera. The carapace outline has undulations in the genus *Stenochilus* and is smooth in *Colopea*, although this character appears to be a less reliable way to differentiate the only two known genera of the family than differences in genitalia and tarsus morphology.

Stenochilidae are ground-living spiders that do not build a prey capture web. They most frequently inhabit rainforest litter, although some are known from more open arid habitats. As with many other ground-living spiders, stenochilds have been observed in silken, tube-like retreats.

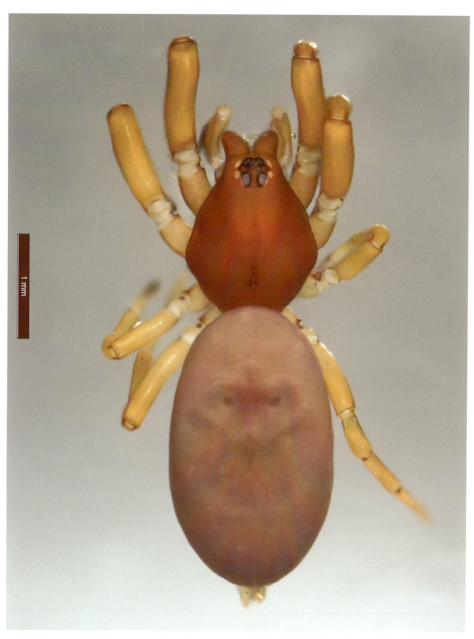

This undescribed species of *Stenochilus* from Cape York illustrates one of the typical characters of the family Stenochilidae, the diamond-shaped carapace. The family is known to occur in tropical Queensland, but no species is currently described from Australia. [B.C. Baehr]

ARANEIDAE
Orb-weaving Spiders

- Eight eyes in two rows, lateral eyes close together (except in *Poltys* and *Micropoltys*)
- Carapace with ocular region elevated, strongly in males, less in females
- Legs strong and spiny, tarsi with 3 claws
- Vertical orb-web with sticky spiral, sometimes with modifications (for example, stabilimentum, curled leaf), reduced (Bola Spiders) or absent (some Cyrtarachninae)
- Body length: 3–35 mm

Australia:
Partially revised
Current: 268 species in 39 genera
Estimated: 500 species in 60 genera
World: 3,030 species in 169 genera

Few spider families rival the Orb-weaving Spiders (family Araneidae) in number of species and diversity of shapes and behaviour. This family includes the typical orb-weavers and for some people these represent the archetypical spiders. The family itself has been diagnosed by a number of characters, including a twisted pedipalp with the cymbium turned to the centreline of the spider, a wide separation of the lateral eyes from the median eyes, and some details in the male pedipalp. Curiously, the limitations of the Araneidae are by no means settled. This is reflected here, for example, by including in this family the leaf-curling genera *Deliochus* and *Phonognatha,* or the enigmatic genus *Paraplectanoides*, all of which, based on recent molecular data, are unlikely to belong to the Araneidae. However, valid alternative family placements were not published at the time this book was compiled. In contrast, we have included the Triangular Spiders, genera *Arkys* and *Demadiana*, not in the Araneidae but in the Long-jawed Spiders (Tetragnathidae), as support for this placement now appears unequivocal.

Opposite page: The Garden Orb-weavers, here *Eriophora biapicata* from Western Australia, represent an undescribed genus of very similar spiders that are impossible to identify in the field unless the fauna of an area is known. The abdomen colour is very variable and does not assist in species identification. It may incorporate white patches or lines of guanine deposits, the principal nitrogenous excretory product of spiders. [V.W. Framenau, Phoenix Environmental Sciences]

Garden Orb-weavers often have reddish-brown, conspicuous leg femora. The most common species, *Eriophora biapicata* and *E. transmarina*, are very often confused as they overlap in their distribution. *Araneus lodicula* and *A. urbana* are other common eastern Australian Garden Orb-weavers in addition to a number of undescribed species, such as this unnamed representative from Victoria. [V.W. Framenau, Phoenix Environmental Sciences]

Male Orb-weaving Spiders, such as this undescribed Garden Orb-weaver from Melbourne, are often seen hanging between vegetation at night, possibly waiting to capture the scent of a female. Mature orb-weavers, similar to most spiders, abandon foraging and invest most of their energy into searching for a mate and courtship. [V.W. Framenau, Phoenix Environmental Sciences]

Not all Orb-weaving Spiders construct an orb-web. For example it is heavily reduced or even absent in the Bola and Orchard Spiders (subfamily Mastophorinae) or in the subfamily Cyrtarachninae, which includes the Two-Spined Spiders (*Poecilopachys*). In contrast, members of other spider families build orb-webs, for example in the Golden Orb-weavers (Nephilidae), Long-jawed Spiders (Tetragnatidae) and Venomless Spiders (Uloboridae). The orb-web has evolved in the evolution of spiders at the base of all these and other spider families, which together represent the Orbiculariae.

The taxonomy of the Araneidae in Australia is still in its infancy. Many species have been described in the early days of Australian arachnological research, in the late 1800s and early 1900s. Orb-weaving Spiders are easily collected and many specimens were submitted to the pioneering scientists who were mainly based in Europe. However, as in many other Australian spider families, species were placed in genera known from the Northern Hemisphere and we know today that this was an inadequate taxonomic treatment, in particular for those groups with Gondwanan origin. For example, some 100 species of Orb-weaving Spiders are currently placed in the genus *Araneus,* and we can confidently say that true representatives of this genus do not occur in Australia. The same is true for *Eriophora*, *Verrucosa* and *Parawixia*, which are genera arguably restricted to the New World.

Orb-weaving Spiders are at home in almost any habitat with vegetation strong enough to fix their snare. Even those groups that have abandoned web-building are generally found in vegetation. Here, Orb-weaving Spiders are absolute masters of disguise. In particular in the Araneinae, a subfamily with largely nocturnal orb-weavers, spiders have evolved the most obscure shapes and behaviours in order to avoid predation when hiding during the day. They pretend to be twigs or gumnuts, they wrap flat around branches, they become elongate and green in grasslands or actively incorporate a leaf as a retreat in their web so that they can hide. Those that do remain in the web during the day also disguise their presence either by including a silk decoration (stabilimentum) and/or prey remains into the web. The Spiny Orb-weavers (family Gasteracanthinae) evolved a spiny abdomen and bright colours to convince birds that they are not good eating.

Literature on the ecology, evolution and behaviour of Orb-weaving Spiders is rife and we have here listed only a fraction of it. They are frequently used as model organisms for a variety of evolutionary marvels, for example sexual size dimorphism (females are often much larger than males) and foraging behaviour (the orb-web provides a measurable currency of foraging investment and its multitude of modifications are often puzzling for evolutionary biologists). The silk of Orb-weaving Spiders, in addition to that of the Golden Orb-weavers (family Nephilidae), is the most studied of all spiders in the quest to replicate its astonishing material properties for human use.

Orb-weaving Spiders do bite humans, but the effects of the bites are generally benign. Most common are bites by the large Garden Orb-weavers (*Eriophora*) and Desert Orb-weavers (*Backobourkia*). Representatives of both love to build their web attached to clothes lines at night and hide in the washing during the day. Bites generally occur when the washing is taken down or the innocent victim puts on their clothes.

This chapter cannot do justice to the diversity of Australian Orb-weaving Spiders and one could fill a whole book with intriguing peculiarities of their biology. Tackling this diversity requires dealing with the subfamilies separately, all of which represent unique lineages of the basic groundplan of the Araneidae. A total of seven subfamilies occur in Australia, although phylogenetic relationships are by no means settled; these are the Araneinae, Argiopinae, Cyrtarachninae, Cyrtophorinae, Gasteracantinae, Mastophorinae, and Phonognathinae.

The **Araneinae** is the largest subfamily of Orb-weaving Spiders in Australia and worldwide. These are the weavers of the typical, vertical orb-web. They are largely nocturnal and generally rebuild their web every night, apparently because the glue of the sticky spiral produced by the aggregate gland spigots loses its stickiness during the day. These spiders are recycling masters as they ingest the old web before constructing the new snare. Radioactive marking of old webs has shown that 80–90 per cent of the radioactivity appears in the new web within 30 minutes. Araneines usually rest in a camouflaged retreat away from the hub. Many genera construct a signal line that connects the retreat to the hub, although they are not the only orb-weavers to do so. Male and female genitalia are the most complicated within the family, rivalling anything else known in spiders.

Molecular analyses suggest that the subfamily Araneinae as defined today does not form a single evolutionary unit, but consists of separate, more or less distantly related lineages, some of which possibly deserve subfamily status in their

The Desert Orb-weavers, genus *Backobourkia*, can be recognised by the white, triangular guanine patches on the front of their abdomen and strong abdominal spines. Like many araneine orb-weavers, these spiders are very variable in coloration. The distribution of the widespread *Backobourkia heroine*, illustrated here, and *B. browni* largely overlap in range and these spiders are indistinguishable in the field. [V.W. Framenau, Phoenix Environmental Sciences]

Modified tibiae of the second leg are typical for males in the subfamily Araneinae. These are often somewhat curved, stronger than all the other legs and at the same time armed with heavy spines or spurs as seen here in *Backobourkia heroine*. This armature is used to fend off females during courtship and mating. [V.W. Framenau, Phoenix Environmental Sciences]

The Grass or Bush Orb-weavers (genus *Plebs*) are very common members of the Australian Araneinae. *Plebs cyphoxis*, illustrated here, is a species from Western and South Australia. Its eastern counterpart, *P. eburnus*, is almost indistinguishable from *P. cyphoxis* and is one of the most commonly collected Orb-weaving Spiders in Australia. A total of seven species of *Plebs* occur in Australia and the genus is also found into Asia as far west as India. Uncommon in the Araneinae but consistent with their diurnal activity pattern, *Plebs* include a stabilimentum in their web. [F. Bokhari]

Below: Whilst the dorsal coloration of Orb-weaving Spiders is generally extremely variable within and between species, the pattern on the underside is often genus-specific. For example, species in the genus *Plebs*, here *P. cyphoxis* from Western Australia, all have a Ü-shaped white mark, with two (or sometimes four) spots beside the spinnerets. Variability of dorsal patterns provides camouflage for the resting spider during the day, whereas ventral coloration does not appear adaptive. [V.W. Framenau, Phoenix Environmental Sciences]

own right. As in many other families, the Australian fauna consists of a large indigenous fauna of Gondwanan origin (e.g. *Eriophora*, *Lariniophora*, *Backobourkia*, *Carepalxis*, *Plebs*) and later immigrants from the Northern Hemisphere (e.g. *Neoscona*, *Larinia*). Some current hypotheses are intriguing, for example the indigenous Wrap-Around Spiders (*Dolophones*) appear to be most closely related to the morphologically very different circumtropical *Cyclosa* and an undescribed Australian genus of leaf-curling spiders to which *Araneus dimidiatus* belongs.

One of the most commonly encountered groups in the subfamily Araneinae include the Garden Orb-weavers, currently referred to *Eriophora* in Australia. Two species are particularly common, the very similar *E. biapicata* and *E. transmarina*. Care must be taken when identifying these species as there are indistinguishable in the field and generally require the examination of genitalia. *Eriophora biapicata* is the more widespread of both species, whilst *E. transmarina* rarely occurs south of Sydney, does not occur in the arid centre and in Western Australia is restricted to the tropical north. Overall, *E. transmarina* is a more northern and coastal species whereas *E. biapicata* is less common towards the tropics and also occurs in the arid zone. However, both species do frequently occur together. There are also a number of other species, both described and undescribed, within the Garden Orb-weavers adding to the identification hurdles for these spiders in the field. As with *Araneus*, true *Eriophora* do not occur in Australia; they are limited to the New World where the genus was described for the first time.

Spiders in the genus *Backobourkia*, the Desert Orb-weavers, are very similar in appearance and behaviour to the Garden Orb-weavers and both groups frequently occur together. Spiders of the genus are mainly characterised by a structure of the main pedipalp; however, *Backobourkia* has a white triangular mark at the front of the abdomen and relatively strong spines on the back. Three species are named, of which the smallest, *B. collina*, is the only one to show extreme sexual size dimorphism. Size reduction of males in this genus has apparently continued along an initial trajectory of size reduction in the species when compared to the two other species of *Backobourkia*. This suggests male dwarfism to be responsible for a small male size in this species rather than female gigantism as, for example, is likely in the Golden Orb-weavers (family Nephilidae).

The Grass or Bush Orb-weavers, genus *Plebs*, are frequently encountered throughout the country. These are comparatively small orb-weavers and, unlike

Cyclosa trilobata, here a specimen from Perth, Western Australia, is the most common representative of the genus in Australia and also occurs in Tasmania and New Zealand. Females in the genus have a conspicuous groove in the carapace behind the eyes, whereas males are considerably smaller and have a very flat carapace. *Cyclosa trilobata* belongs to a group of *Cyclosa* with medium-sized abdomens, and species identification in the field can be difficult. [V.W. Framenau, Phoenix Environmental Sciences]

This unknown *Cyclosa* female from Brisbane, Queensland, belongs to a group of species with very long abdomens. This group includes, amongst others, *C. bacilliformis* and *C. bifida*. *Cyclosa* incorporate prey remains in their web, camouflaging the outline of the spiders. [V.W. Framenau, Phoenix Environmental Sciences]

other members of the Araneinae, are active in their web during the day and include a vertical web-decoration (stabilimentum) into their snare. These spiders, in addition to overall similarity of colour and shape, all share the same pattern on the underside of the abdomen, an Ü-shaped white mark with the two spots beside the spinnerets. Ventral patterns are often much more reliable for genus-level identification in the Araneinae than colour variations on the upper side. Whereas the dorsal side provides camouflage for the spiders during the day and its colour and its variability is adaptive in response to the environment, this is not the case for the underside that is not exposed to predators during the day. The Enamel Spider, *Plebs bradleyi*, is the largest of all *Plebs* and occurs in the south-eastern parts of the country.

The small species of the genus *Cyclosa* occur predominantly in the tropics and subtropics of the country. Females are characterised by the shape of the cephalothorax in which the head region is separated from the back area by deep grooves. Males, in contrast, have a flat carapace with a very narrow eye region. Whilst the genus is fairly well defined, species-level taxonomy is poorly resolved. The genus includes species with a globular abdomen, such as *C. vallata* and *C. mulmeinensis*; species with a somewhat elongated abdomen and this may have terminal humps, such as in *C. trilobata* and *C. insulana*; and very long species such as *C. bifida* and *C. bacilliformis*. *Cyclosa trilobata* is the most widespread species and also occurs in New Zealand. The orb-web of *Cyclosa* is often tilted towards the horizontal. Spiders can be found in it day and night and accordingly they incorporate 'false spiders' as decorations. These are food remains that mimic the inhabitant, hiding the spider and distracting potential predators.

The Wrap-around Spiders, genus *Dolophones*, are one of the most intriguing araneid groups in the Australian landscape. They are largely Australian endemics and occur throughout the country. Although 17 species are currently named for the country, their taxonomy is poorly resolved. The genus is clearly much more diverse, in particular in the more arid parts of the country. Species are often identified based on their abdomen shape, but it is unclear if protuberances and stick-like outgrowths and turrets are species-specific. In other stick-mimics, for example in the genera *Acroaspis* and *Poltys*, the abdominal shape varies greatly within species. *Dolophones* wrap themselves invisibly around tree branches during the day in perfect camouflage and like many other members of the Araneinae are best collected at night from their orb-web under torch light.

Convergent evolution of body shapes and colours appears to have occurred frequently in the Araneinae. A case in point are the genera *Larinia* and *Lariniophora*, elongated green Orb-weaving Spiders that can often be found in grasslands. *Larinia* occur worldwide and the Australian fauna has most likely originated by invasion from the north. They mostly occur in the coastal regions. Based on male pedipalp morphology they are only remotely related to *Lariniophora*, an endemic genus with affinities to the Australian indigenous *Eriophora*. *Lariniophora ragnhildae*, the only species in the genus, has a north-western and central arid distribution. *Araneus talipedatus* and related species also have a similar green and elongated shape but belong to a very different, undescribed genus altogether.

Spiders in the genus *Poltys* are masters of camouflage. The genus, together with *Micropoltys*, is characterised by a wide separation of the lateral eyes, which is an unusual eye configuration within the Araneidae. They build finely meshed orb-webs at night and sit motionless in vegetation during the day. The shape of the abdomen in these spiders, very variable within species, resembles part of a twig, gall or piece of wood helping to make the spiders almost invisible in their resting position, with legs drawn tightly around their carapace. Adult males are much smaller than females and abandon web-building when searching for a mate. Eight species of *Poltys* are currently known from Australia and these show a mainly northern and eastern coastal distribution. *Poltys laciniosus* is the most common species and has been reported from all mainland states.

One of the more bizarre Orb-weaving Spiders currently listed in the Araneinae is *Paraplectanoides crassipes*. These little orange spiders with a raised head and dorsally flattened and rigid abdomen can be found around the eastern and southern coast of Australia, including Tasmania, where they live in mesic forests and heathlands. Females make an oval silk nest close to the ground under fallen branches and in shrubs. The nest comprises a system of radial threads and a hub under which the spider rests. Males are much smaller than females and almost entirely black. Despite their small size, females are thought to be very long-lived and have reached an age of six years in captivity. Not surprising when looking at the morphology and behaviour of this species, the placement in the Araneinae is challenged by molecular analyses, some of which place these as sister group to the Golden Orb-weavers (Nephilidae).

There are a number of very small, globular species of *Cyclosa* in Australia, including *C. vallata* and *C. mulmeinensis*. The identity of this female from Brisbane is unclear as species identification within this group is currently impossible because the type material has yet to be reviewed. [V.W. Framenau, Phoenix Environmental Sciences]

The Wrap-around Spiders (genus *Dolophones*), here a female from suburban Perth in Western Australia, are largely Australian endemics with historic records from the Moluccas (Indonesia) and New Caledonia.. They have a broad and flat abdomen, often armed with turret-like outgrowths that fake a twig in the spiders' resting position. The taxonomy of the genus is poorly resolved and species names are not used here for any *Dolophones*. Abdominal shape, historically used for identification, is not a reliable character in araneids in general. [V.W. Framenau, Phoenix Environmental Sciences]

This *Dolophones* female from Western Australia takes camouflage to a whole new level. Wrap-around Spiders build a very loose capture spiral in their nocturnal web and the often odd-looking spiders behave in a somewhat cumbersome manner in it. During the day, they press tightly against a twig or stick with their concave body. Nevertheless, they are the common prey of spider wasps (Pompilidae) which walk along the branches drumming their front legs and stirring the spider into action. [F. Bokhari]

This male Wrap-around Spider from the genus *Dolophones* has lost its right pedipalp, possibly during mating. The pedipalp configuration in *Dolophones* is characteristic as the members of this genus are the only Australian orb-weavers with more than two spines on the pedipalp patella. .[V.W. Framenau, Phoenix Environmental Sciences]

Larinia montagui can be found throughout Australia in addition to three other representatives of the genus. These spiders are common in grassland, for which their elongated, greenish morphology is a perfect adaptation in terms of camouflage. [F. Bokhari]

The leaf-curling araneine *Araneus dimidiatus* from eastern Australia represents a currently undescribed Australian genus of five species. A second species is named, *Araneus mulierarius*. [M. Kuntner]

Unlike spiders in the genus *Phonognatha*, which place a leaf-retreat in the centre of the web, *Araneus dimidiatus*, as illustrated here, suspends the leaf from the bridging thread at the top of the web. A signal thread stretches from the leaf to the centre of the web alerting the spider to when there is prey in the web. [M. Kuntner]

Spiders in the genus *Poltys* have a characteristic resting position in which they draw their long legs high above the carapace. In combination with the highly variable abdomen that imitates twigs or gumnuts, this adaptation renders the spiders practically invisible during the day. *Poltys laciniosus*, here a female from Western Australia, is the most common representative of the genus in Australia. [F. Bokhari]

Females of the Scorpion-tailed Spiders, here possibly *Arachnura higginsii* from Western Australia, develop their long tail gradually after each moult. They can be seen in their low orb-web during the day and the tiny males, which have a compressed tail looking like an accordion, are often seen in high numbers around the web. The taxonomy of the three Australian *Arachnura* is unresolved, but *A. higginsii* is assumed to be the most common species. [F. Bokhari]

Araneus albotriangulus is a common eastern Australian species with a characteristic abdominal pattern. It is the most common species in a group that includes about five similar species which are found along the east coast of Australia. [V.W. Framenau, Phoenix Environmental Sciences]

The shape of some Australian araneids baffles even the most experienced arachnologist. This unknown species from Western Australia has a stick-like extension on the abdomen to provide camouflage. Whilst this spider resembles *Dolophones*, it clearly belongs to a different genus based on eye pattern and abdominal shape. [F. Bokhari]

Spiders in the genus *Acroaspis*, here *A. olorina* from Boya in Western Australia, often have a highly elevated abdomen similar to *Poltys* or some *Dolophones*. The genus is widespread in Australia with a number of named and unnamed species. However, the status of the genus has not been revised and most described species such as *A. lancearia*, *A. mamillanus* and *A. tuberculifera* are currently placed in *Araneus*. *Heurodes turritus*, described based on an immature specimen from Tasmania, is also a representative of *Acroaspis*. [V.W. Framenau, Phoenix Environmental Sciences]

Below: An unknown species of *Acroaspis* from Western Australia has caught a wasp somewhat similar to its own size. Abdominal shapes in *Acroaspis* are variable and include humped varieties as illustrated here. [F. Bokhari]

Paraplectanoides crassipes is one of the most cryptic and enigmatic of the Australian Orb-weaving Spiders. It builds its nest in low coastal vegetation and under logs in moist forests. It occurs from Queensland southwards and along the southern Australian coast into south-west Western Australia, as well as in Tasmania. The placement of this species in the Araneidae has been questioned by recent molecular work. [V.W. Framenau, Phoenix Environmental Sciences]

In contrast to the orange-brown female, the male of *Paraplectanoides crassipes* has a black carapace and hardened black abdomen, decorated with two orange lateral spots. [V.W. Framenau, Phoenix Environmental Sciences]

Eriophora pustulosa, here a female from Victoria, is a common Australian spider that also occurs in New Zealand and other Pacific islands. This species is wrongly placed in *Eriophora* and represents an unnamed genus that is most diverse in south-eastern Australia, in particular in Tasmania. These spiders are medium-sized and have five characteristic humps at the back of the abdomen. *Araneus senicaudatus* from Western and South Australia and *Araneus sydneyicus*, which is found throughout southern Australia, also belong to this genus. [V.W. Framenau, Phoenix Environmental Sciences]

Araneus albidus is a common coastal species in eastern Australia and occurs in Queensland between Brisbane in the south and Mareeba in the north, often in coastal mangroves. However, the spider depicted here is its undescribed, almost indistinguishable Western Australian counterpart, which occurs at pretty much the same latitude and also predominantly in mangroves. Both represent a new genus and unusually within the subfamily Araneinae these species show distinct sexual size dimorphism, with males much smaller than females. In eastern Australia, this species can easily be mistaken for *Araneus dimidiatus*. [F. Bokhari]

There are a large number of green Australian spiders, such as this female from Western Australia, and the abdominal pattern of these spiders is hugely variable. This female may represent *Araneus eburneiventris*, the only named species of this group from the state. There are a number of species known in this group, such as *Araneus psittacinus*, *A. circulisparsus*, *A. ginninderanus* and others. The taxonomy of this group, which represents an undescribed genus, is completely unresolved and species identification, in particular based on live spiders, is best avoided. [F. Bokhari]

Opposite page: *Araneus cyrtarachnoides* is a tropical species that occurs in the Northern Territory and along the Queensland coast as far south as Cooloola. It has also been found in Papua New Guinea. It belongs to another undescribed genus and the specific name refers to its similarity to species in the genus *Cyrtarachne*. These species show some colour variation and some colour morphs may be mistaken for colour morphs of the green spiders related to *Araneus psittacinus*. However, *A. cyrtarachnoides* is much less hairy and very shiny. [P. Zborowski]

The subfamily **Argiopinae** is recognised by the curvature of the hind eye row. Unlike most other araneids, the lateral posterior eyes are situated in front of the anterior median eyes. The carapace of species in the genus *Argiope* is often clothed with silvery hairs reflected in the scientific name of the genus (*argentum* being Latin for silver). Species of *Argiope* tend to be diurnal, often build their web in the open exposed to the sun and have a strong tendency to decorate their webs with a stabilimentum. Its shape is very variable and can be cross-shaped as in the St Andrew's Cross Spiders (*A. keyserlingi*), spiral-shaped or circular. The taxonomy of *Argiope* is very well known in Australia with a total of 16 species named. There is not much support to maintain the two Australian *Gea* species, *G. heptagon* and *G. theridioides*, in a separate genus and these may be formally transferred to *Argiope* soon. The east-coast Ladder-web Spiders, genus *Telaprocera*, also have the argiopine eye configuration and are currently included in this subfamily; however, their morphology, in particular that of the male and female genitalia, is very dissimilar and these spiders may belong to a different, currently unnamed subfamily.

The St Andrew's Cross Spider, *Argiope keyserlingi*, here a female from Brisbane, is one of the most common member of the genus *Argiope* along the eastern coast of Australia. The position of the legs of *Argiope* in the web is characteristic, with two pairs each held together forming a cross. This orientation is often camouflaged by the cross-shaped stabilimentum in the web. [V.W. Framenau, Phoenix Environmental Sciences]

The stabilimenta in the webs of *Argiope* are often cross-shaped and hide the outline of the spider. Webs are built in open, often sun-exposed spaces, for example under the eaves of houses, where they commonly fall prey to Noisy Friarbirds. [P. Zborowski]

Argiope ocyaloides is a comparatively small species from tropical Queensland and Northern Territory. The spider incorporates a spiralled stabilimentum into the web, which is often built against the burnt bark of trees. [P. Zborowski]

The Tear-drop Spider, *Argiope protensa*, is one of the most common and widespread members of the genus *Argiope* in Australia and it occurs throughout the country. This species has a characteristic highly elongated abdomen, unlike any other species in the genus which occurs in Australia. [F. Bokhari]

The genus *Telaprocera*, here *T. maudae* from New South Wales, currently fits the concept of the subfamily Argiopinae based on the procurved posterior row of eyes. However, overall morphology, in particular genitalia, and web-building behaviour, are significantly different to those found in *Argiope* and *Gea*. Therefore these spiders may need to be accommodated in their own subfamily. *Telaprocera* is restricted to eastern Australia and members of this genus build ladder-shaped webs against the trunk of a tree. [A. Harmer]

The Australian Orb-weaving Spider fauna contains a large number of undescribed genera and species. The spider illustrated here has a typical argiopine eye pattern with the posterior lateral eyes situated in front of the posterior median eyes. However, genitalia are very different to *Argiope* and, like *Telaprocera*, it may belong to a new subfamily altogether. The species illustrated has a characteristically heart-shaped abdomen. It builds its orb-web against the trunk of a tree. Two very similar species are currently known, one from Western Australia, illustrated here, and one from Victoria. [F. Bokhari]

Two genera of the Tent Orb-weaver subfamily **Cyrtophorinae** occur in Australia, *Cyrtophora* (14 species) and *Cyrtobill* (one species). The web of these spiders is a tightly woven horizontal mesh with a permanent non-sticky spiral. Some species are brightly coloured and tend to stay in the hub during the day. *Cyrtophora* is largely tropical or subtropical, but one species, *C. parnasia*, has managed to adapt to temperate climates and is found throughout the country, including in Tasmania. *Cyrtobill darwini* is an unusual cyrtophorine spider that builds its tent-web in low vegetation, for example in spinifex grass, in arid areas of northern and central Australia. They have been shown to thermoregulate their body temperature by orientating their body position in relation to the position of the sun.

Cytophora moluccensis is the most colourful member of the genus and one of the largest *Cyrtophora* in Australia. This female from Brisbane has captured a large cicada hanging under her finely meshed tent-web. *Cytophora moluccensis* is a widely distributed species which occurs from India to Japan and Australia, and a number of subspecies are known. Distinct colour morphs have also been found in tropical Australia suggesting that different species may be present. *Cyrtophora moluccensis* can often be seen in considerable aggregations in which one web is supported by the threads of others. [V.W. Framenau, Phoenix Environmental Sciences]

Cyrtophora parnasia, here a female from south-west Western Australia, build non-sticky, finely-meshed horizontal orb-webs that are drawn up in the centre to form a tent. The snare also includes a tangle-web above the horizontal orb, increasing the capture perimeter of the web. [F. Bokhari]

Cyrtophora moluccensis currently includes a number a clearly distinguishable colour morphs distributed through northern Australia and it is perceivable that more than a single species is present. The spider illustrated here differs considerably from the female illustrated to the left. A comprehensive taxonomic study that addresses the variability in the genital morphology of the tiny males is required to elucidate relationships within this group. [P. Zborowski]

The Double-tailed Tent Spider, *Cyrtophora exanthematica*, here a female from Brisbane, occurs in the South-East Asian tropics and in Australia in the tropical north and along the Queensland coast into New South Wales. It cannot be mistaken for any other *Cyrtophora* due to its distinct two protuberances at the end of the abdomen. [V.W. Framenau, Phoenix Environmental Sciences]

Cyrtobill darwini is a tiny member of the subfamily Cyrtophorinae and the only species in the genus *Cyrtobill*. Like other cyrtophorines, this species constructs a finely-meshed, slightly cone-shaped horizontal orb-web with tangle threads above and below. Here, this female has suspended its eggsacs above the orb. The species is common in spinifex grasslands in the semi-arid and arid northern half of Australia. [V.W. Framenau, Phoenix Environmental Sciences]

The remarkable, ornate members of the Spiny Orb-weavers, subfamily **Gasteracanthinae**, are widely distributed in tropical regions of the world. In Australia they include the genera *Gasteracantha* and *Austracantha*, the latter only represented by a single but extremely widespread species, the Christmas or Jewel Spider, *A. minax*. Gasteracanthinae have a number of paired spiky protuberances around the abdomen, often unbelievably elongated in the females. In the inconspicuous males, which are often found in large numbers around a female web, the spikes are generally much smaller. These spiders usually spin strong orb-webs with a closely spaced sticky spiral. Unlike many orb-weavers, Spiny Orb-weavers tend to occur close to each other with their small vertical orb-webs often sharing a common support. These spiders are active during the day and their body shape and colours may have evolved to help them avoid predation.

The Christmas or Jewel Spider, *Austracantha minax*, is the most common Spiny Orb-weaver in Australia and occurs throughout the country. It is the only representative of the genus *Austracantha*, which differs from *Gasteracantha* by the lack of a sclerotised ring around the spinnerets and the lack of genital tubercle on the ventral side of the abdomen. [V.W. Framenau, Phoenix Environmental Sciences]

Male gasteracanthines, here *Austracantha minax*, are smaller than the females and have less pronounced spines. They can often be seen around the webs of the female in considerable numbers. [F. Bokhari]

Austracantha minax displays a number of different colour variations and black, melanic spiders are not uncommon. [F. Bokhari]

Many *Gasteracantha*, such as *G. quadrispinosa* (upper left), have an abdomen which is much wider than it is long and are very colourful. This is one of five species currently recognised from tropical Australia. The distributions of most Australian *Gasteracantha* species continue into South-East Asia. The images to the left and upper right are of unidentified *Gasteracantha* and these illustrate the morphological diversity within the genus. [all images: P. Zborowski]

There is a strong tendency towards web reduction in the **Cyrtarachninae**. Sexual size dimorphism is pronounced and males are often tiny. Consequently, males are unknown for many described species and taxonomy is solely based on females. Cyrtarachnines are usually tropical with the genera *Cyrtarachne* and *Pasilobus* mainly recorded from Queensland. The Two-spined Spiders, genus *Poecilopachys*, include at least five species in eastern Australia and are found as far south as Victoria. These species mainly differ in genital morphology and their taxonomy is poorly known. Almost all published photographs identify these spiders as *P. australasia*; however, nobody has ever ascertained the identity of this particular species against the specimen that was used to originally describe it. Therefore, we only provide genus-level identification for the Two-spined Spiders here. It has been reported that these spiders can change their colour in life by '*producing a definite flush*' but this phenomenon has not been observed by any of the authors of this book. Unusual within the Cyrtarachninae, *Poecilopachys* build nocturnal orb-webs.

The cyrtarachnine Two-spined Spiders, genus *Poecilopachys*, belong to the most spectacularly coloured spiders in Australia. Some reports state that these spiders can actively modify their colour pattern to some extent. The genus *Poecilopachys*, here a female from Melbourne in Victoria, has never received any taxonomic attention in Australia, but it is clear that a number of very similar species occur in this country. Similar to *Dolophones*, species-level identifications are not provided here and should be discouraged; most published images of *Poecilopachys* are questionably referred to *P. australasia*. [V.W. Framenau, Phoenix Environmental Sciences]

Some Two-spined Spiders, such as this *Poecilopachys* female from Queensland, have strong spiny hair on the abdomen. Males of *Poecilopachys* are tiny and very rare in collections, making taxonomic revisions of this genus difficult. [P. Zborowski]

The **Mastophorinae** are often treated as part of the Cyrtarachninae. They include the enigmatic Bola Spiders, which are only represented by the genus *Ordgarius* in Australia, and the Orchard Spiders, genus *Celaenia*. In Bola Spiders the orb-web is reduced to a single strand of silk to which glue droplets are attached. Not only have these spiders mastered the technique of catching prey by throwing this silk strand at their target, but they also use aggressive chemical mimicry by copying the pheromones of female noctuid moths in order to attract the male moths as prey. *Ordgarius* is sexually size dimorphic and males are minute in comparison to females. More intriguingly, males hatch as mature animals from the eggsac, a feature unique amongst spiders. The time delay between male and female maturation probably avoids inbreeding, but why this occurs only in these spiders remains unclear. Three species of *Ordgarius* are described from Australia: *O. furcatus* (New South Walse); the Magnificent Spider, *O. magnificus* (New South Wales and Queensland); and *O. monstrosus* (Queensland). The genus also occurs widely in Asia, including India and South-East Asia. The Orchard Spiders, genus *Celaenia*, also use aggressive chemical mimicry. At night these spiders hang upside down in the vegetation with their long spiny forelegs open and ready to capture the lured moths. Seven species of *Celaenia* are described for Australia of which *C. excavata*, the Bird-dropping Spider, is the most common.

Bird-dropping Spiders, *Caelenia excavata*, here a female from Western Australia, are the most common representatives of the genus *Celaenia* in Australia. Females may measure up to 12 mm in body length, whereas the males are tiny (2–3 mm). Mimicking bird droppings, the spiders hide during daytime in vegetation in open woodland, although they are also curiously common in orchards. At night, *Celaenia* hang on a single strand, emitting chemicals that mimic the pheromones of female moths. [V.W. Framenau, Phoenix Environmental Sciences]

Celaenia excavata can best be found by looking for the species' conspicuous eggs. Each female lays up to a dozen eggsacs suspended under leaves in vegetation. The mother can be seen in the background to the left. [P. Zborowski]

The Magnificent Spider, *Ordgarius magnificus*, has abandoned building an orb-web, instead they hunt by using a gluey drop on the end of a line which she spins around catching night active insects. A number or mastophorine genera world-wide have adopted this strategy, together referred to as Bola Spiders. Similar to *Celaenia*, these spiders mimic female moth pheromones, in particular those of noctuid moths. Female *Ordgarius* are up to 15 mm long. Males, with a body length of about 2 mm, are comparatively tiny and, uniquely amongst spiders, mature in the eggsac and hatch with fully developed genitalia. [R. J. Raven]

The Magnificent Spider, *Ordgarius magnificus*, creates large amphora-shaped eggsacs which can be up to five times the size of the female. [P. Zborowski]

The leaf-curling orb-weavers of the subfamily **Phonognathinae**, the genera *Phonognatha* and *Deliochus*, have repeatedly been moved between families, in particular between the Araneidae, the Long-jawed Spiders (Tetragnathidae) and the Golden Orb-weavers (Nephilidae). Recent molecular data suggest that these spiders do not to belong to any of them, but instead form part of the formally unrecognised family Zygiellidae. As the type genus of this family, *Zygiella*, is currently placed in the Araneidae, these spiders are listed here. Spiders in the genus *Phonognatha* incorporate a leaf into the centre of the orb-web in which the spiders hide during the day. As in many orb-weavers, web-construction occurs mainly at night. Spiders are not too choosy in the retreat they use, and have been reported to incorporate snail shells. Cohabitation of females and males has frequently been observed in both *Phonognatha* and *Deliochus*. This appears to represent mate-guarding, as males react aggressively to other approaching males. Cohabiting males often have lost their pedipalps, a phenomenon that seems to increase the eunuch's fighting ability when mate-guarding against males with pedipalps.

The Leaf-curling Spiders in the genus *Phonognatha*, such as *P. graeffei*, hide in a curled leaf which they attach near to the hub of their orb web. They can often be seen with just the forelegs sticking out of the leaf, waiting for prey. [M. Kuntner]

In contrast to the araneine *Araneus dimidiatus*, the leaf in the web of *Phonognatha* is placed in the vicinity of the hub. [M. Kuntner]

Phonoganta pallida is the only leaf-curling spider currently described from Western Australia; however, the taxonomy of the genus is currently unresolved. [F. Bokhari]

A *Phonognatha pallida* male sitting in front of a curled leave. Males abandon web-building and this male was sitting in front of a female in the leaf to guard her against rival males. [F. Bokhari]

Opposite page: Females of *Deliochus zelivira* are considerably larger than the males, as illustrated by this pair from Brisbane, Queensland. These spiders build a messy retreat in curled leafs bound together by silk. Males guard females if they survive mating, during which they often lose their pedipalps, similar to the male here. Eunuchs appear to be more competitive in defending the female from other potential mates. [V.W. Framenau, Phoenix Environmental Sciences]

NEPHILIDAE
Golden Orb-weavers, Hermit Spiders, Coin Spiders

- Eight eyes in two rows of four each
- Legs long and slender with numerous spines, tarsi with three claws
- Elongated or lobed abdomen
- Large golden orb-webs (*Nephila*), asymmetrical orbs against trees (*Nephilengys*) or arboricolous ladder-webs (*Herennia*)
- Body length: 3–40 mm

Australia:
Taxonomy revised
Current: 6 species in 3 genera
Estimated: 6 species in 4 genera
World: 61 species in 4 genera

The most common group of the family Nephilidae in Australia are the Golden Orb-weavers (genus *Nephila*), which are famous for their enormous golden orb-webs. Few Australians who enjoy spending time in the bush have avoided being caught in one of these extensive webs. However, the Nephilidae also include two other genera in Australia, both represented by a single species from the tropical north: *Nephilengys* (Hermit Spiders) and *Herennia* (Coin Spiders). Amongst all orb web-building spiders, those of the family Nephilidae are probably the most studied in relation to both systematics and behaviour.

Whilst few people would mistake the Golden Orb-weavers for anything but *Nephila*, the characters that unite the whole family Nephilidae are more subtle and may not necessarily help to identify *Nephilengys* and *Herennia* in the field. These include a striated cheliceral boss and a number of sexually dimorphic somatic traits, such as females with white sternal pigment and relatively small male chelicerae. There are also some behavioural peculiarities, including the presence of the temporary (auxiliary), non-sticky spiral in the finished web, and the construction of the sticky spiral with the fourth leg.

Nephilids occur predominantly in tropical rainforests and mangroves throughout the world's tropics and, despite showing a largely Gondwanan distribution, it is more likely that their biogeographic pattern is based on dispersal events with a post-Gondwanan origin of the family in Australasia. The Nephilidae currently include five genera worldwide, with *Clitaetra* (African and Indian

Most Nephilidae are found in the tropics, but the Australian Golden Orb-weaver, *Nephila edulis*, is found in a great range of climatic zones, including the arid interior, tropical savannahs, subtropical, Mediterranean and temperate coastal habitats, and subalpine locations. Unlike all other Golden Orb-weavers which occur in Australia, *N. edulis* has rarely been found outside this country. Females hang upside down in their golden web day and night. [F. Bokhari]

tropics) and *Nephilingis* (largely Afrotropical) in addition to the above-mentioned Australian representatives. However, it has been postulated that *Nephila* as currently circumscribed does not share a common ancestry, which would add a further currently unnamed genus to the Australian fauna for all but the Giant Golden Orb-weaver, *N. pilipes*.

By current definition, three species of *Nephila* occur in mainland Australia and Tasmania. The Australian Golden Orb-weaver (*N. edulis*) is most common and found throughout much of the country and into Tasmania. The Giant Golden Orb-weaver *(N. pilipes)* and the Humped Golden Orb-weaver (*N. plumipes*) are largely restricted to the tropical north of the country, but also occur south along the east coast into New South Wales. A fourth species, the Asian Golden Orb-weaver, *N. antipodiana*, has been found on Christmas Island.

Nephila females are very large spiders with silvery-grey to dark violet bodies and dark brown to black, long and slender legs that sometimes have yellow bands.

The males are tiny in comparison and uniformly orange-brown. *Nephila edulis* and *N. plumipes* are very similar but differ due to a conspicuous tubercle on the sternum of *N. plumipes* which is absent in *N. edulis*. The large golden orbs of *Nephila* are suspended within three-dimensional barrier webs. In remote, almost treeless parts of inland Australia, the supporting strands for a *Nephila edulis* web can extend for over 10 metres to the nearest tree. Often, *Nephila* webs can be found in large aggregations with one web using others for support. The spiders incorporate vertical strands of prey remains into their web, and feed on these during periods of food shortage. These do not necessarily act solely as food caches, as *Nephila edulis* also includes plant material. The rotting material may attract insect prey to the web. Similarly, the golden-yellow silk may lure herbivorous and pollinating insect prey to the spider webs. *Nephila* webs are very strong and in addition to the staple insect diet, these spiders are also known to feed on small birds, bats and snakes.

Nephilengys only includes two species: *N. malabarensis* ranges from India to China, Japan and eastern Indonesia, whereas *N. papuana* occurs in Papua New Guinea and northern Australia. Similar to *Nephila*, females are much larger than males. *Nephilengys* build their asymmetric orb-web against a tree trunk and a large branch. The web has a retreat in which the spider hides during daytime, unlike *Nephila* which inhabits the web during the day. *Nephilengys* mating strategies have been studied in detail. Males detach and lose their palps during or after mating, which renders them sterile eunuchs. Parts of the pedipalp act as plug in the female epigyne, blocking any mating attempt by subsequent males. Whilst many males fall victim to the female they mate with, those eunuchs which do survive appear to be better fighters to fend off rival males when guarding their mate after copulation.

Herennia, the Coin Spider, is represented by a single species in Australia, which is found in the Northern Territory and far northern Queensland. The genus mainly consists of Australasian island endemics. *Herennia* build an arboricolous ladder-web, i.e. an elongate orb-web with parallel vertical sides that is constructed close to a tree trunk. Similar to *Nephilengys*, the tiny *Herennia* males plug the female epigyne by genital mutilation and surviving males mate-guard the female.

Despite their size, only fairly aggressive handling will cause nephilid spiders to bite humans. The bite causes local pain, redness, swelling and blisters that normally disappear within a day. Occasionally nausea and dizziness have been reported after a bite.

The Giant Golden Orb-weaver, *N. pilipes*, here a female from Christmas Island, is found from South-East Asia into China and occurs in the Australian tropics and along the eastern coast into northern New South Wales. The species is mainly found in rainforest habitats, but may also be encountered in moist and well-shaded domestic gardens and parks. *Nephila pilipes* is the largest and most colourful of the Australian *Nephila* [V.W. Framenau, Phoenix Environmental Sciences]

This female Giant Golden Orb-weaver, *N. pilipes*, demonstrates the colour variations that occur in this species in comparison to the specimen from Christmas Island illustrated at the top of the page. Viewed from underneath, the leg joints of *N. pilipes* females are bright yellow, independent of any other colour pattern. Unlike any other *Nephila*, which place their eggsac in the vegetation near the web, females of the Giant Golden Orb-weaver construct the eggsac in a shallow depression excavated on the forest floor, possibly in response to high levels of predation. [P. Zborowski]

The Asian Golden Orb-weaver, *N. antipodiana*, reaches the southern limits of its distribution in Indonesia and Papua New Guinea, and the only Australian records are from Christmas Island. Nephilids display extraordinary sexual size dimorphism with females sometimes a magnitude larger than males. Evolutionary comparison with other spiders suggests that it is female gigantism rather than male dwarfism that is responsible for this dimorphism in nephilids. The tiny male on the back of this *N. antipodiana* from Christmas Island may be waiting for a chance of copulation, or it is guarding the female from rival males. Small males can often be found in large numbers in and around the webs of females, but should not be confused with the kleptoparasitic members of the genus *Argyrodes* (family Theridiidae) which are also commonly found in the *Nephila* webs. [V.W. Framenau, Phoenix Environmental Sciences]

The tiny silver, shining Silver Dewdrop Spiders, *Argyrodes* (family Theridiidae), in the bottom right corner often hunt in the webs of *Nephila* as kleptoparasites. Some even feed at the very mouth of the *Nephila* female. The little parasitic thieves usually eat only the insects that are too small for Golden Orb-weavers. [P. Zborowski]

Hermit Spiders, genus *Nephilengys*, here *N. papuana* from Cape York Peninsula, make an asymmetrical orb-web with a tubular retreat. The tube ends against a tree or hollow in wood. A tiny male approaches the female from the left. The web of *Nephilengys* is silver and the spiders tend to hide away in their retreat during the day [R.J. Raven]

LINYPHIIDAE
Sheet-web Spiders, Money Spiders

- Eight eyes in two rows
- Chelicerae with teeth and often with lateral stridulary striae
- Abdomen oval, uniformly greyish or with generally inconspicuous pattern
- Legs long and slender
- Sheet-web often with tangle mesh above
- Body length: 1.5–6 mm

Australia:
Taxonomy poorly resolved
Current: 34 species in 21 genera
Estimated: 200 species in 30 genera
World: 4,461 species in 589 genera

The comparative paucity of Sheet-web Spiders (family Linyphiidae) in Australia is in stark contrast to the family's dominance in the Northern Hemisphere. For example, almost half of the spider species of Central Europe are Sheet-web Spiders, but only 34 species are currently described from Australia; amongst these are a fair proportion of introduced species.

Sheet-web Spiders are small spiders which are similar to the Comb-footed Spiders (family Theridiidae); however, linyphiids have much spinier legs and no comb on the fourth tarsus. Family-defining characters relate to the male pedipalps, which have an intersegmental paracymbium and lack the median apophysis and conductor – the latter two are otherwise present in the Araneidae and most allied families (Araneoidea).

The Australian indigenous linyphiid fauna mainly consists of members in the subfamily **Linyphiinae**, although this subfamily does not represent a natural group. *Laperousea* and *Laetesia* appear to be common, at least in the southern parts of the country. *Laetesia* also maintains a diverse native fauna in New Zealand. Many Australian **Erigoninae**, the Money Spiders, are apparently introduced; these for example include *Araeoncus humilis* from the Palaearctic, and *Diplocephalus cristatus* and *Microctenonyx subitaneus* from the Holarctic. Other Money Spiders, for example *Erigone eisenschmidti* and *E. prominens* appear to be of Australasian origin. The **Mynogleninae** are the dominant subfamily of Linyphiidae in New Zealand, but only a single species in this subfamily is currently known from

Australia: *Haplinis australis*, which is endemic to Tasmania.

One characteristic of the Australian linyphiid fauna is that many genera described from here include only a single species worldwide. These include *Australolinyphia remota* from Queensland, *Chthiononetes tenuis* from Western Australia and *Palaeohyphantes simplicipalpis* from New South Wales. This may be an artefact of the poor knowledge of these spiders and more species in these genera may eventually be described.

Members of the Linyphiidae build a small sheet-web which is characteristically drawn up into a peak in the middle. The central area serves as a resting area for the spider which hangs upside-down in the shallow dome. When prey gets entangled in the web, the spiders run along the underside to their victim, bite it through the sheet-web and pull it through the web where it is securely wrapped. The damaged sheet is later repaired.

The Australian linyphiid fauna includes some troglobitic cave species, for example *Chthiononetes tenuis* from Cape Range in Western Australia and *Laetesia leo* from the South Australian part of the Nullarbor Plain.

Extensive aggregations of little sheet-webs can be the main evidence of the presence of the family Linyphiidae. The webs can be very common in wet meadows. In the early mornings when the dew still covers the plants, hundreds of small sheet-webs shine in the morning light. [R.J. Raven]

The typical web of spiders in the subfamily Linyphiinae consists of a sheet that is drawn up in the centre. Above the sheet, a three-dimensional tangle web assists in catching the prey. The spider sits under the centre of the sheet and attacks the prey from underneath. [R.J. Raven]

Laperousea is an indigenous Australian genus of Sheet-web Spiders, although the most common species, *L. blattifera*, has apparently naturally dispersed to New Zealand. This unidentified female from Evans Head, New South Wales, was collected hanging upside-down in her sheet-web between the bark of a tree (see below). [R.J. Raven]

The sheet-web of the *Laperousea* female illustrated above, constructed in a hollow of a tree trunk. [R.J. Raven]

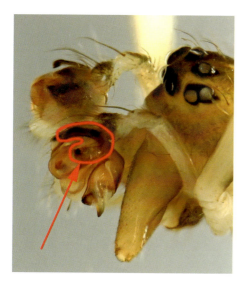

One of the most important characters that define the linyphiids is the separate paracymbium which is attached by a membrane. It is U- or J-shaped and opposes the cymbium of the male pedipalp. [B.C. Baehr]

Diplocephalus cristatus has a Holarctic distribution but has been introduced to Australia, New Zealand and the Falkland Islands. *Diplocephalus* translates as 'double-headed'. The males of many species of Money Spiders (subfamily Erigoninae) have extended head-structures, which produce cephalic secretions to which the females are attracted during mating. [B.C. Baehr]

Males of *Erigone*, including this specimen from Dalby, south-east Queensland, have rows of teeth on the outer side of their chelicerae and similarly, the edge of the carapace has pointed denticles. Three species of *Erigone* have been reported from Australia: the Holarctic *E. dentipalpis* has been introduced; *E. prominens* is apparently native to the Australasian region and occurs throughout Asia and in New Zealand; and *E. eisenschmidti* is only known from Queensland. Spiders in the subfamily Erigoninae, the Money Spiders, are small spiders that are able to balloon even as adults. [B.C. Baehr]

CYATHOLIPIDAE
No common name

- Eight eyes in two rows, lateral eyes contiguous and widely separated from middle eyes
- Carapace squat and heavily sclerotised, head region sometimes raised
- Sheet-webs of closely meshed fine silk in tree buttresses, against logs and in understory vegetation; some litter dwellers
- Body length: 2–5 mm

Australia:
Taxonomy poorly known
Current: 5 species in 5 genera
Estimated: 20 species in 10 genera
World: 58 species in 23 genera

The Cyatholipidae is a comparatively small family of spiders with Gondwanan affinities and is mainly known from southern temperate and tropical montane forests of Africa, including Madagascar, and humid forest habitats in Australia and New Zealand. However, the Australian and New Zealand faunas do not appear to be immediately related.

Cyatholipids could be confused with the Sheet-web Spiders (family Linyphiidae) or the tiny Ground Orb-web Spiders (family Anapidae). Family characteristics are subtle and include a greatly expanded cymbium in the male pedipalp, the lack of a claw on the female pedipalp, and the presence of a broad posterior tracheal spiracle. Therefore, these spiders are difficult to identify in the field. *Teemenaarus silvestris* and *Forstera daviesae* have a somewhat triangular abdomen when viewed from the side.

The documented diversity of cyatholipids in Australia is easily summarised. There are five different genera and each of these contains a single described species. Some of these spiders are only known from very limited material. *Matilda australia* is a leaf litter dweller from Queensland and New South Wales, but the genus includes at least another three undescribed species from Victoria. *Teemenaarus silvestris* is known from Queensland where it builds sheet-webs in tree trunks and buttresses in moist forests. *Tekellatus lamingtoniensis* was collected from low vegetation in Lamington National Park, southern Queensland, and similarly *Forstera daviesae* has only been found in Bulburin National Park in central eastern

Queensland. *Lordhowea nesiota* is endemic in leaf litter on Lord Howe Island. The limited number of species in each genus may reflect the poor taxonomic knowledge of the group and more species may eventually be described.

Cyatholipid sheet-webs are generally found in the understorey of humid forests, although *Matilda* and *Lordhowea* have been collected from litter. Webs are constructed in tree buttresses, against logs or embankments and in both woody and herbaceous vegetation in the shade. Cyatholipid webs are comprised of a fine mesh sheet, and often an under-sheet of a few lines, which is about one-half the length of the main sheet. *Teemenaarus silvestris* has been observed hanging under the sheet at night, but hiding in adjacent bark during the day. Eggsacs only include a few eggs and are attached to ventral threads of the web close to the substrate. The eggsac is very loosely woven and eggs can be seen through the silk.

This undescribed male cyatholipid spider from Western Australia, possibly in the genus *Matilda*, has a raised cephalic region of the carapace and a heavily sclerotised abdomen. The spider is small, only approximately 2 mm in body length. [V.W. Framenau, Phoenix Environmental Sciences]

TETRAGNATHIDAE
Long-jawed Spiders

- Eight eyes in two rows, both rows recurved
- Chelicerae short or long and well-developed with large teeth and long projecting spurs (only Tetragnathinae)
- Legs often long and slender, with three claws
- Vertical or horizontal widely or densely spaced orb-webs with open hub or webless
- Body length: 2–25 mm

Australia:
Partially revised
Current: 38 species in 8 genera
Estimated: 60 species in 10 genera
World: 957 species in 47 genera

The common name of Long-jawed Spiders for the family Tetragnathidae mainly refers to the genus *Tetragnatha* in the subfamily Tetragnathinae. The extremely elongated jaws of males and females in these spiders interlock during mating, possibly to avoid the male being sexually cannibalised by the female.

The Tetragnathidae are distributed all over the world with highest diversity in the tropics and subtropics. Many members of the family have a preference for riparian habitats and they occur near rivers, streams or other water bodies, where they spin their loosely woven orb-web vertically or horizontally over the surface of the water.

Four subfamilies of Long-jawed Spiders are known from Australia: the Tetragnathinae, Leucauginae, Metainae, and the informally termed *Nanometa* clade. However, we have included the Triangular Spiders, the Arkyinae, in the Tetragnathidae, as some recent evolutionary hypotheses suggest these to form a lineage basal to all other Long-jawed Spiders. This theory is favoured over a second hypothesis that places the Arkyinae together with the Pirate Spiders (family Mimetidae) as closest relatives to the Tetragnathidae.

In addition to the elongated fangs, in particular in males, one of the more notable morphological characters of the subfamily **Tetragnathinae** is a secondary simplification of the female reproductive organ to the haplogyne state. Female tetragnathines do not have an epigyne and the fertilisation duct is absent. This

The extremely elongated chelicerae are characteristic for many *Tetragnatha* species, including this one from north Queensland. The number, size and position of the denticles on the chelicerae can be used to identify species in the genus, in particular as females have haplogyne genitalia which do not allow species identification based on external morphology [P. Zborowski]

feature is paired with a close proximity of the embolus, and the conductor in the male pedipalp forming a twisted coil, a family characteristic of the Tetragnathidae. *Tetragnatha* is the only representative of the Tetragnathinae in Australia and includes about two dozen indigenous or Australasian species, in addition to at least two cosmopolitan representatives, *T. mandibulata* and *T. nitens*. Spiders in this genus disperse extremely well and are therefore found in almost every part the world.

The characteristic feature of the **Leucauginae** is two rows of long feathered trichobothria on the fourth leg femora; these can often be seen without magnification. Species in the genus *Leucauge* often display striking and conspicuous colours of silver, yellow, red and green. The web-orientation in leucaugines is often slanted and the spiders hang upside down in its hub. The subfamily has a pantropical distribution, although some species reach the temperate zones. The subfamily includes three genera in Australia: *Leucauge*, *Tylorida* and *Mesida*. Most common is probably *L. granulata*, whereas *L. decorata* is known mainly from the tropics. *Leucauge insularis* is only known from Lord Howe Island and Samoa.

The genus *Dolichognatha* is the only described representative of the subfamily **Metainae** in Australia. Within the Tetragnathidae, Metainae have well-sclerotised spermathecae and fertilization ducts in addition to other peculiarities of the female genitalia. *Dolichognatha* have large anterior median eyes on a slight tubercle and males have comparatively long chelicerae with enlarged cheliceral teeth. They construct densely woven horizontal orb-webs in vegetation at the base of trees or in canopies, otherwise little is known of the genus. Two species occur in Australia: *D. incanescens* and *D. raveni*, both of which are also found in New Guinea; and *D. incanescens* also occurs in Sri Lanka..

The **Nanometa** clade is an Australian group that includes the genera *Nanometa* and *Pinkfloydia*, both with a single described species from Western Australia, *N. gentilis*, and *P. harveii*. Females have denticles between the anterior and posterior rows of cheliceral teeth and males have stridulatory ridges on the covers of the booklung and small denticles on the mesal surface of the fourth coxae. Not much is known about the biology of both Australian species. Webs of juvenile *P. harveii* are horizontal with a closed hub and the temporary spiral is removed from the final web.

The subfamily **Arkyinae** was formerly placed in the Pirate Spiders (Mimetidae) and Orb-weaving Spiders (Araneidae) but is considered here to be part of the Tetragnathidae, although we accept that this systematic position is not settled. Arkyinae represent a conspicuous element of the Australasian region. They include two genera, the Triangular Spiders in the genus *Arkys* and members of the small genus *Demadiana*. These extraordinary spiders have a roughly rectangular carapace, sometimes with outgrowth near the eyes ('carapaceal horns') and a characteristic eye pattern with the posterior median eyes more spaced than the anterior median eyes. The frontal two pairs of legs of the Arkyinae are much larger than the rear two pairs and bear a row of strong spines that possibly assist in prey capture. *Arkys* includes 18 species in Australia, of which *A. walckenaeri* and *A. alticephala* are the most widespread and the only ones that are found in Western Australia in addition to the eastern states. *Demadiana* include very small, largely orange spiders and are found in the southern half of the country. *Arkys* and *Demadiana* have lost their ability to create an orb-web; instead, they hunt freely on vegetation and are frequently found on wattle (*Acacia*).

Long-jawed spiders in the genus *Tetragnatha*, such as this female from Western Australia, often rest hidden under a leaf or sitting camouflaged along stalks of the vegetation with one pair of legs directed to the back and two pairs to front. [F. Bokhari]

This still pale, freshly moulted *Tetragnatha* female slips carefully out of its old skin, securely suspended by a thread of silk. [F. Bokhari]

A *Tetragnatha* female from northern Queensland has laid an eggsac under leaves near the web. [P. Zborowski]

This dark coloured, slender *Tetragnatha* female placed a camouflaged eggsac on eucalypt bark. The eggsac is apparently afforded protection by the female. [P. Zborowski]

The relatively long legs and the body coloration of silver, black and yellow markings, make the identification this *Leucauge granulata* female from Western Australia fairly easy. The web is often more or less horizontal rather than vertical, and the spider rests upside down in the middle of the web. [F. Bokhari]

Triangular Spiders, here a female *Arkys lancearius* from Queensland in waiting position, are a typical sit-and-wait predator. They remain motionless until prey is close enough to be trapped by their two strong and spiny pairs of fore legs. *Arkys lancearius* is known to occur from New Guinea into New South Wales. [P. Zborowski]

Arkys walckenaeri, here a female from Western Australia, is one of the most common species within the genus. It has been reported from Tasmania and all the mainland states and territories except Northern Territory. [V.W. Framenau, Phoenix Environmental Sciences]

Opposite page: *Arkys*, here an unidentified species from Queensland, is a very diverse genus and does not only include triangular species. The species are very variable in body shapes and coloration, providing exceptional camouflage when hiding in vegetation. [P. Zborowski]

Spiders in the arkyine genus *Demadiana*, here a *Demadiana cerula* female from Western Australia, can readily be recognised by their unique coloration and dimpled carapace. *Demadiana* do not build webs but sit with the front legs stretched on vegetation at night, waiting for passing prey. [V.W. Framenau, Phoenix Environmental Sciences]

Demadiana males, here *Demadiana cerula* from Western Australia, look fairly similar to the female although they are a little bit smaller and the abdomen is flatter. Six species of *Demadiana* are known from Australia, but these spiders are rarely collected. Species identification requires the examination of female and male genitalia. [V.W. Framenau, Phoenix Environmental Sciences]

MIMETIDAE
Pirate Spiders

- Eight eyes in two rows, anterior median eyes usually largest
- First leg very long; tibia and metatarsus of first and second leg with a series of long, curved spines interspersed with shorter spines
- Chelicerae basally fused, promargin with peg teeth
- Aggressive vibratory mimicry and specialised predators on other spiders
- Body length: 4–8 mm

Australia:
Partially revised
Current: 29 species in 2 genera
Estimated: 50 species in 2 genera
World: 156 species in 13 genera

Pirate Spiders (family Mimetidae) have earned their colloquial name through their specialised predatory behaviour. They mainly prey on other spiders, in particular on Comb-footed Spiders (Theridiidae) and Orb-weaving Spiders (Araneidae). They have perfected the art of aggressive vibratory mimicry by pretending to unsuspicious spiders to be prey in their web. The approaching spider is then usually attacked by the Pirate Spider from the underside and immobilised by a quick bite. Pirate Spiders may also feed on insects which are already trapped in the host web, but they do not actively hunt them.

The specialised prey capture strategy is reflected in the morphology of the Pirate Spiders. They have conspicuous rows of raptorial spines on the front legs, which can be arranged to form a basket, trapping their victim after the attack.

Pirate Spiders have a worldwide distribution; however, they are most diverse in the southern hemisphere tropics. In Australia, two genera of Mimetidae are known, *Australomimetus* with 28 species and *Ero*, which includes a single species, *E. aphana*, which was apparently introduced from the Palaearctic. *Australomimetus* have a short row of small spines on the back margin of the first femur which are absent in *Ero*.

Australomimetus includes a number of widespread species in Australia. For example, the litter-dwelling *A. tasmaniensis* has so far been found in all mainland states, with the exception of South Australia, and also in Tasmania. Others have more localised distributions such as *A. stephanieae* which is known from only two localities in nature reserves in the Avon Wheatbelt of Western Australia. Species identification is difficult in the field, although colour patterns appear to be somewhat species specific. *Ero aphana* has confirmed isolated records from the Queensland coast and appears to be fairly common in south-western Western Australia.

Pirate spiders are mainly found in sclerophyllous vegetation and in rainforests. There are currently no records from the arid centre. Pirate Spider eggsacs are roughly spherical and are covered with a loose layer of white to brownish silk. They are attached by a short stalk on the underside of fallen logs or in tree trunks. Females of *Australomimetus* lay an unusually small number of eggs per sac; less than 25 eggs have been found in a variety of species from Western Australia.

Pirate Spiders, here an *Australomimetus* female from Queensland, often have a yellowish-brown speckled coloration and can be recognised by the distinct rows of spines on their long front legs; these rows consist of a series of a long spine, followed by three or four shorter ones, which form a cage around their prey. The body of this individual is about 4 mm long. [P. Zborowski]

The eggsacs of Pirate Spiders (family Mimetidae), here of an unknown *Australomimetus* from Toolangi in Victoria, are very characteristic and generally suspended on a thick strand of silk from the vegetation. The eggs are wrapped in a fluffy layer of silk which is surrounded by curly brown strands. The tufted nature of the silk may protect the eggs from mechanical damage and predators or parasites. [K. Walker].

HOLARCHAEIDAE
Minute Long-jawed Spiders

- Eight eyes in two rows; anterior median eyes smallest and closely spaced; posterior median eyes oval and well separated
- Raised front of carapace
- Elongate chelicerae arising from a distinct but ventrally unsclerotised foramen, without venom gland opening
- Abdomen spherical or globose
- Body length: 1–1.5 mm

Australia:
Partially revised
Current: 1 species in 1 genus
Estimated: 1 species in 1 genus
World: 2 species in 1 genus

With a total of two named species worldwide, the Minute Long-jawed Spiders (family Holarchaeidae) qualify as one of the smallest spider families known. At the same time, members of this cryptic spider family are tiny, generally less than 2 mm in body length. One species is known from Tasmania, *Holarchaea globosa*, in addition to a second species from New Zealand, *H. novaeseelandiae*.

The Holarchaeidae can be distinguished from all other spider families by elongate chelicerae arising from a foramen that is ventrally outlined only by an unsclerotised cuticle. Viewed from the front these chelicerae seem to be only loosely connected to the carapace by a comparatively large thin membrane. Like the Venomless Spiders (family Uloboridae) and the genus *Heptathela* in the Segmented Spiders (family Liphistiidae), holarchaeid spiders do not appear to have venom glands.

Very little is known of the biology of Holarchaeidae. All records of these spiders are from consistently humid or wet habitats. Most specimens of *H. globosa* have been found on ferns, such as the low-growing Hardwater Fern *Blechnum wattsii* in dark and wet *Nothofagus* forests or within moss and leaf litter in temperate rainforests. Several specimens have been collected from caves.

A paucity of silk spigots suggests that Holarchaeidae do not construct a prey capture web, and the absence of poison glands and other peculiar features of the chelicerae such as the lack of peg teeth, together with their minute size, appears to limit the prey they might capture to similar-sized arthropods such as springtails (Collembola), mites or possibly other small spiders.

The tiny *Holarchaea globosa* is only known from Tasmania, where it occurs in humid or wet conditions. The spiders do not have venom glands and the strategies they use to obtain their prey are unknown. Based on the reduced spinneret morphology it is unlikely that they construct a prey capture web. [M.G. Rix]

PARARCHAEIDAE
Tiny Thick-necked Spiders

- Eight eyes in two rows; anterior eye-row straight, posterior eye-row procurved
- Chelicerae elongated, promargin adjacent to fang usually with three groups of stout peg teeth, retrolateral surface of paturon with strong, smooth, moveable hairs
- Abdomen oval with sclerotised pits (sigillae)
- Leg tarsi with three claws, tarsi longer than metatarsi
- Free-living active hunters
- Body length: 1–3 mm

Australia:
Partially revised
current: 31 species in 5 genera
estimated: 50 species in 5 genera
World: 35 species in 7 genera

The Tiny Thick-necked Spiders (family Pararchaeidae) are very small, eight-eyed spiders with a bulky and raised cephalic region and elongated chelicerae. They are currently only known from Australia, New Caledonia and New Zealand. In Australia, families with similar spiders include the Assassin Spiders (Archaeidae), which have a more elongate neck-region, and the Holarchaeidae, which have an unsclerotised foramen to which the chelicerae attach. Another similar family, the Mecysmaucheniidae, has so far not been recorded from Australia.

Tiny Thick-necked Spiders are most diverse in Australia; however, one species is recorded from New Caledonia and three species are currently named from New Zealand. The genus *Anarchaea* includes four species from Tasmania, New South Wales and Queensland. Seven species of *Flavarchaea* have so far been named from all Australian states except the Northern and Australian Capital Territories; this genus also includes the New Caledonian representative of the family. *Nanarchaea* contains two species and is found from south-eastern Queensland through to Tasmania. *Ozarchaea* includes 15 Australian and one New Zealand species. *Westrarchaea* is endemic to south-west Western Australia and contains three species. More than half of the species are only known from one or two localities, suggesting that many more species await discovery.

Due to their small size, genus- and species-level identification of Tiny Thick-necked Spiders is difficult to impossible in the field. Characters that distinguish genera include the size and shape of an abdominal sclerotised plate (scute) in males, genitalic characters and to some extend coloration. Female Parachaeidae are rarely collected. They live in thick humid leaf litter, in moss or under bark, preferably in rainforests or other humid forests. In captivity, they have been successfully reared on a diet of springtails (Collembola). Females built a relatively small discoid eggsac surrounded by an extensive silken complex. This structure is at least five times larger than the female when she attaches it to the underside of a rock, log or bark.

This female Tiny Thick-necked Spider from Western Australia, possibly *Ozarchaea harveyi*, shows the raised head region and oval abdomen with dark sigillae, which are typical features for the family. Parachaeidae are tiny, only growing up to 3 mm long. [V.W. Framenau, Phoenix Environmental Sciences]

This preserved female of *Anarchaea raveni* from Lamington National Park, Queensland, has a paler head region than specimens in life. The chelicerae of parachaeid spiders appear to be specially adapted for catching fast-moving prey. When the prey touches the comb of specialised setae on the raised and opened chelicerae, they quickly snap together during a forward-moving attack. [B.C. Baehr]

Anarchaea raveni, here a female from Lamington National Park, is widespread in south-eastern Queensland. It occurs in thick leaf litter at the base of eucalypt and she-oak trees. The species occurs in suburban Brisbane bushland reserves, sometimes together with *Flavarchaea anzac*. [B.C. Baehr]

SYNOTAXIDAE
Chickenwire-web Spiders

- Eight eyes in two rows, anterior median eyes smallest
- Abdomen elongated with stridulatory organs
- Long legs, first leg longest, three tarsal claws
- Irregular sheet-web close to ground
- Body length: 1.5–5 mm

Australia:
Taxonomy poorly resolved
current: 9 species in 4 genera
estimated: 20 species in 5 genera
World: 82 species in 14 genera

The Chickenwire-web Spiders (family Synotaxidae) have long remained an elusive family and its members have repeatedly been included in a number of other families, such as the Sheet-web Spiders (Linyphiidae), Comb-footed Spiders (Theridiidae) or Daddy Long-legs Spiders (Pholcidae). This family has a typical southern temperate distribution characteristic for a Gondwanan heritage; it is currently known only from Australia, New Zealand, Chile and the Neotropics.

The rarely-collected spiders of the Synotaxidae have long, spineless legs, with the first pair generally the longest. Males often have a stridulatory organ system associated with the abdomen which acts against structures on the carapace, pedicel or the coxae of the fourth leg. The defining characters of the family, however, are within the male pedipalps, which have an incised retrolateral cymbial margin and an excavate paracymbium.

Two subfamilies have been established in the Synotaxidae: the **Physogleninae**, in Australia represented by *Tupua* and *Paratupua*, and the **Pahorinae**, currently only known from New Zealand. However, there are a number of unplaced genera within the family, including the Australian *Calcarsynotaxus* and *Microsynotaxus*.

Tupua and *Paratupua* both have a pair of anteriorly directed strong hairs along the midline of the ocular area but differ from each other in characters of male and female genitalia. *Tupua* is known only from four species in Tasmania. Three species have been collected in caves, and at least one, *T. troglodytes*, appears to be an obligate cave-dweller. *Paratupua* is only known from Victoria. Males in both genera are distinctly larger than females. *Calcarsynotaxus longipes* is known only from the Lamington Plateau in south-eastern Queensland and *C. benrobertsi* only from high elevations of the eastern Stirling Ranges in south-west Western Australia. *Microsynotaxus insolens* and *M. calliope* are so far known only from Kroombit Tops, north of Brisbane.

Members of the Synotaxidae are generally associated with temperate forests, where they construct their webs under logs or amongst grasses and moss. For example, *C. benrobertsi* was found under damp, shaded leaves of sedges. The webs differ between the subfamilies. The Physogleninae make an irregular web in contrast to the cone-shaped sheet-web of the New Zealand Pahorinae. Otherwise, little is known about the biology of the Australian Synotaxidae.

Calcarsynotaxus benrobertsi is the only Western Australian representative of the Synotaxidae and is only recorded from the top of Ellen Peak and the south-facing flank of Pyungoorup Peak in the eastern Stirling Ranges in the south-west of the state. [M.R. Rix]

MALKARIDAE
Shield Spiders

- Eight eyes in two recurved rows
- Carapace with numerous deep pits
- Tibiae and metatarsi of the first and second leg with prolateral pairs of long and short spines in a row; leg tarsi with three claws
- Abdomen broadly oval with dark orange sclerotised pits
- Free-living hunters
- Body length: 2–4 mm

Australia:
Taxonomically poorly known
current: 10 species in 3 genera
estimated: 70+ species in 3–4 genera
World: 11 species in 4 genera

The Shield Spiders (family Malkaridae) are an unmistakable family of small spiders with characteristic carapace pits. They have a southern temperate distribution with records from Australia, New Zealand and Chile.

In addition to the carapace pits, the Shield Spiders are characterised by a small, unsclerotised area situated just behind the epigastric furrow that is enclosed within an anterior scute, and that contains one or two internally protruding sclerites. A more subtle character is an enlarged conductor flange in the male pedipalp. Similar to the Pirate Spiders (family Mimetidae), the Shield Spiders have rows of long spines on the first and second legs which, in some species, are interspersed by shorter spines.

Two subfamilies occur in Australia. The **Malkarinae** include a single species from south-eastern Queensland, *Malkara loricata*. The second subfamily, the **Sternodinae**, differs from the Malkarinae by a greatly raised ocular area and the presence of a pair of sulci on the carapace margin between the pedipalps and first legs. They include *Carathea*, a genus with two species from Tasmania, and *Perissopmeros* with six species from south-eastern Australia and a single Western Australian species: *P. darwini*, currently only known from the southern face of Pyungoorup Peak in the Stirling Ranges. However, Shield Spiders have been collected along the entire east coast of Australia and the family is clearly much more diverse than current literature suggests.

Little is known about the biology of Shield Spiders. They are hunters in leaf litter of temperate and tropical rainforests and do not seem to build a prey capture web. In Western Australia, *P. darwini* was collected in a moist, shaded creekline.

This *Malkara loricata* male from Palmerston National Park, south-eastern Queensland, has the anterior scute covering the lower part of the abdomen, including the pedicel, which is typical for the Shield Spiders. The abdominal surface is also slightly sclerotised with numerous darker disks. [B.C. Baehr]

The genus *Perissopmeros*, here an unidentified female from eastern Australia, belongs to the subfamily Sternodinae and this subfamily is characterised by the greatly raised ocular area, i.e. the eyes sit on an elevated tubercle. *Perissopmeros* occurs in eastern and south-western Australia. [N. Scharff]

THERIDIOSOMATIDAE
Ray Orb-weaving Spiders

- Eight eyes in two rows, anterior row recurved and posterior row straight or procurved, frontal median eyes and lateral eyes sometimes on slight tubercles
- Sternum with pits at the front
- Abdomen ovoid, sometimes with variously placed tubercles
- Tiny often cone-shaped orb-webs in humid shaded forests or in or near caves
- Body length: 0.5–2.5 mm

Australia:
Taxonomy poorly resolved
Current: 2 species in 2 genera
Estimated: 30 species in 4 genera
World: 101 species in 18 genera

The tiny Ray Orb-weaving Spiders (family Theridiosomatidae) belong to a group of related, minute orb-weaving spiders that, in Australia, also includes the Dwarf Orb-weavers (Symphytognathidae), Minute Clasping-weavers (Mysmenidae) and Ground Orb-weaving Spiders (Anapidae); together, these are referred to as 'symphytognathoids'. Some systematic analyses place the Ray Orb-weaving Spiders as a sister group to all other symphytognathoids, and therefore some comments on this grouping are given here.

All symphytognathoids are minute, often less than 2 mm in body length, with a domed sternum in lateral view. A fovea is absent on the carapace and the colulus has usually three or less setae (more in other orb-weaving spiders). The sternum margin at the back is truncated, not pointed as in many other spiders. Most symphytognathoids build three-dimensional orb-webs and females attach their eggsac at two separate points.

The most prominent character of the Theridiosomatidae is the presence of pit organs at the front of the sternum near the labium. Their leg tibiae have unusually long sensory hairs (trichobothria), especially on the third and fourth leg; here, the one furthest away from the body is exceptionally long. Ray orb-weaving Spiders also have a peculiar morphology of the male pedipalp which often appears disproportionately large in these spiders.

On a global scale, Ray Orb-weaving Spiders are largely tropical, although some species, in particular in the genus *Theridiosoma*, are also found in more temperate regions. They generally live in wet or humid, shaded forests. A number of species appear to be cave-dwellers or live around the entrances of caves.

There are only two species of Ray Orb-weaving Spiders described from Australia: *Theridiosoma circuloargenteum* from New South Wales and *Baalzebub brauni* from Queensland; however, the undescribed fauna is clearly much more diverse. Specimens of this family have been collected along the east coast from tropical Queensland into Tasmania and in caves in south-west Western Australia.

The orb-web of the Theridiosomatidae has a tension line at right angle to its plane that pulls the web into a cone. The spiders modify the hub of the web so that single radial threads are grouped and then connected in the centre where the tension line attaches. This design is referred to in the colloquial name Ray Orb-weaving Spiders. When prey hits the web, the spider holding the tension line releases it to catch the unsuspecting prey. Tension lines are absent in some *Baalzebub* species, but the web morphology of the Australian representatives is not known. The prey of these little spiders appears to be primarily small flies such as midges or other similarly weak-flying insects, although little is known about the general ecology of Ray Orb-weaving Spiders.

Baalzebub, here a male from Queensland, is one of only two genera of Ray Orb-weaving Spiders currently documented from Australia. These spiders are very small, often less than 2 mm in body length, and therefore rarely observed in the field. [B.C. Baehr]

MYSMENIDAE
Minute Clasping-weavers

- Eight eyes in two rows, eyes of males elevated or on a forward-directed mount
- Legs stout, tarsi with three claws
- Femoral spot on first leg in females (and sometimes males)
- Male metatarsal clasping spine on metatarsus and/or tibia of the first leg
- Abdomen soft, generally higher than it is long
- Day or night active, build tiny modified orb-webs in litter of humid habitats
- Body length: 0.5–2 mm

Australia:
Taxonomy poorly resolved
Current: 2 species in 1 genus
Estimated: 150 species in 10 genera
World: 131 species in 23 genera

The Minute Clasping-weavers (family Mysmenidae) are tiny symphytognathoid spiders. Males have a clasping spine on the metatarsus and/or the tibia of the first leg and females have a characteristic dark dot on the proximal-ventral surface of the first femur. In addition, the eyes of males are often elevated on long turrets. The soft abdomen is higher than it is long and often has an elevation or extension protruding from the back.

The Australian fauna includes two described species, *Mysmena tasmaniae* from Tasmania and *Mysmena leichhardti* from tropical northern Queensland; however, many more species await naming. For example, the genus *Trogloneta* has been reported a number of times from Australia. Generally recognisable by details of the genitalia and taking the size of these spiders into account, identification requires the use of a stereomicroscope.

Mysmenids are not uncommon in Australia and occur along the eastern coastal and mountainous regions from northern Queensland into Tasmania, but they have also been found in south-west Western Australia in the wider vicinity of Perth.

Mysmenidae live in rainforests or humid temperate forests. Here, most members of the family build tiny, three-dimensional, spherical orb-webs formed by a large number of out-of-plane radii in leaf litter or tree trunk crevices. Males, in addition to females and juveniles, were collected from webs. The webs of

Australian *Trogloneta* species are unknown, although some undescribed species have been collected suspended from single threads.

Mysmena leichhardti from Tasmania creates minute spherical, modified orb-webs beneath moss, leaf litter or in low crevices of tree trunks. Prey caught in the web is bitten and eaten without wrapping it up. [L. Lopardo]

The genus *Trogloneta*, here a male of an undescribed species from Lamington National Park in south-eastern Queensland, has currently no described species in Australia. The web architecture of *Trogloneta* is unknown; some specimens have been collected suspended from single silk threads. [B.C. Baehr]

This *Trogloneta* male belongs to a different species than that depicted in the image to the left. It has a more slender eye mount and a longer abdominal 'tail', but can only be confidently distinguished by its different pedipalp morphology. [B.C. Baehr]

The male of *Mysmena tasmaniae* lacks the highly elevated eye region that is typical for many members of the Minute Clasping-weavers (family Mysmenidae). This species is currently known from Tasmania only. It has been observed to mate in spring or early summer. The male stands in front of the female, stretches his pedipalps beneath her, and inserts them alternately into her epigyne. Three days after mating the female constructs loose eggsacs containing eight to ten eggs and suspends them under her tiny, horizontal web. [L. Lopardo]

ANAPIDAE
Ground Orb-weaving Spiders, Micro Gondwanan Spiders

- Eight or six eyes, anterior median eyes can be reduced in some species, other eyes grouped in three pairs
- Carapace with ocular region elevated, strongly in males and less so in females
- Abdomen oval; male with large dorsal scute; females without dorsal scute but with small sclerotised ring around pedicel
- Legs short, tarsi with three claws, metatarsi shorter than tarsi
- Horizontal orb- or sheet-web with central retreat in leaf litter or moss
- Body size: 0.5–2.25 mm

Australia:
Partially revised
current: 18 species in 25 genera
estimated: 150 species in 30 genera
World: 220 species in 57 genera

Within the Australian symphytognathoids, the Ground Orb-weaving Spiders (family Anapidae) are most closely related to the Dwarf Orb-weaving Spiders (Symphytognathidae). These families share a peculiar, enlarged cylindrical gland spigot base on the posterior lateral spinnerets of females, which is unusual in orb-weaving spiders. The Micro Gondwanan Spiders are often referred to as a separate family, the Micropholcommatidae, but are here included in the Anapidae based on the most recent, comprehensive systematic study. However, the debate regarding the systematic placement and rank of the Micro Gondwanan Spiders has not reached a consensus.

The Ground Orb-weaving Spiders are identified by a number of morphological characters compared to their symphytognathoid relatives, for example the concave labium that is fused to the sternum, pore-bearing depressions on the carapace and the absence of paracymbium on the male pedipalp. There are general morphological features that most anapids share, including small size (spiders rarely exceed 1.5 mm), a raised frontal area of the carapace and a slim or reduced female pedipalp. Depressions on the cuticle give the carapace a punctuate or rough appearance, and abdominal scutes, in particular in males, are common.

Ground Orb-weaving Spiders have a largely Gondwanan distribution with highest diversity in the southern continents, including in South America, Africa, Australia, New Guinea, New Caledonia and New Zealand. However, the family has also been recorded from Europe, Asia and North America.

The Anapidae belong to the better-known symphytognathoids in Australia based on the number of described species, although many species are yet to be named. Similar to other symphytognathoids, Ground Orb-weaving Spiders can be found along the east coast of Australia from tropical Queensland into Tasmania and in the south-western corner of Western Australia. They have also been recorded from caves on Christmas Island.

Relationships between many genera within the Anapidae remain unresolved, with the exception of those of the Micro Gondwanan Spiders that includes three different subfamilies: the Micropholcommatinae, Taphiassinae and Gigiellinae. Of these, the subfamily **Micropholcommatinae** is most diverse in Australia and includes nine genera (*Austropholcomma*, *Eperiella*, *Epigastrina*, *Eterosyncha*, *Micropholcomma*, *Normplatnicka*, *Patelliella*, *Raveniella* and *Rayforstia*) with 32 described species. Whilst some of these genera, such as *Micropholcomma*, are fairly widespread, some show endemic patterns. For example, *Austropholcomma* and *Normplatnicka* are only known from the temperate Walpole area in south-west Western Australia.

The subfamily **Taphiassinae** includes two genera of heavily punctuate spiders which lack an abdominal scute, *Taphiassa* (four species) and *Olgania* (five species), the latter of which is endemic to Tasmania. Spiders in the subfamily **Gigiellinae** have a posteriorly pointed sternum. In Australia, the subfamily only includes the genus *Gigiella* with a single species, *G. milledgei* from Victoria and Tasmania.

Endemicity levels are high at the genus level within the reminder of the Anapidae. *Tasmanapis* includes a single species, *T. strahan*, from north-western Tasmania; similarly, *Acrobleps*, with *A. hygrophilus* as its single species, is only known from that state; *Victanapis* has a single species, *V. warburton*, from Victoria; *Queenslanapis* has a single species, *Q. lamington*, in south-eastern Queensland; *Hickmanapis* includes two species only known from Tasmania; *Nortanapis* has a single species in northern Queensland, *N. almond*. *Risdonius* (three species) occurs from New South Wales into Tasmania; *Maxanapis* includes nine species from Queensland and New South Wales; *Octanapis* includes three species from Queensland to Victoria; *Spinanapis* includes nine species restricted to mountains of northern Queensland. In contrast, *Chasmocephalon* is widespread and occurs from Queensland to Victoria and in Western Australia.

The enigmatic *Pseudanapis aloha* has been collected in tropical northern Queensland. The species was initially described from Hawai'i but its biogeographic origins are unknown.

In Tasmania, a number of species have been exclusively found in caves and show varying levels of troglobitic adaptations, notably the reduction or complete loss of eyes. These troglobites include *Micropholcomma junee*, *Epigastrina loongana*, *E. typhlops* and *E. hastings*. All *Olgania* species have been exclusively recorded from caves, with the exception of *O. excavata* that has also been collected from moss in temperate rainforest.

Anapids are most common in leaf litter and moss on the floor of rainforests. Here, they build sheet-webs or horizontal orb-webs that may have additional radii and sticky spirals above the plane of the snare. However, the Tasmanian *Tasmanapis* constructs a planar orb-web similar to those built by most members of the Symphytognathidae.

Micropholcomma build irregular, three-dimensional tangle-webs similar to some Comb-footed Spiders (Theridiidae). Most other genera within the Micropholcommatinae construct horizontal sheet-webs. They are believed to feed on springtails and other small insects.

Acroplebs hygrophilus from Tasmania constructs the typical three-dimensional horizontal orb-web of the Ground Orb-weaving Spiders (family Anapidae). These webs are often tiny in diameter to accommodate spiders that are barely 1 mm long. [L. Lopardo]

The morning dew gives the web of this tiny anapid, *Chasmocephalon iluka*, a beautiful shine. The horizontal orb-web is made of extremely fine silk and has a three-dimensional tent-like framework above the orb web. The spiders generally hang upside down under the hub of the web. This web had a diameter less than 3 cm, but many anapid orb-webs are much smaller. [R.J. Raven]

The sheet-web of *Tasmanapis strahan* from Tasmania lacks the three-dimensional structural and sticky threads above the orb. [L. Lopardo]

Female Ground Orb-weaving Spiders, like this *Maxanapis burra* from Lamington National Park, south-east Queensland, generally have a much lower eye region than males and a softer abdomen with a small sclerotised ring around to the pedicel, but no dorsal abdominal scute. [B.C. Baehr]

Ground Orb-weaving Spiders, here a *Maxanapis burra* male from Lamington National Park, Queensland, have an elevated eye region, are reddish or dark chestnut brown and have heavily sclerotised abdominal scutes in males. This species occurs in Queensland and New South Wales. [B.C. Baehr]

This *Chasmocephalon iluka* male from Lamington National Park in south-eastern Queensland displays the typical features of the Anapidae, including a raised cephalic area of the carapace and the sclerotised plates (scutes) of the abdomen. The species is widespread in eastern Australia. [B.C. Baehr]

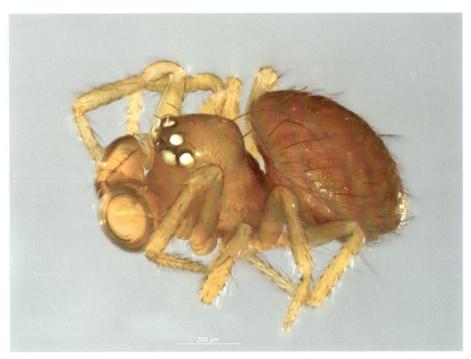

This *Micropholcomma* male from Lamington National Park in south-eastern Queensland, a relative of *Micropholcomma longissimum* from Victoria based on the long and tightly curled embolus of the pedipalp, shows the typical highly elevated cephalic area and very prominent dorsal and ventral scutes on the abdomen. This undescribed species is often found in moss or leaf litter in southern beech forests. [B.C. Baehr]

SYMPHYTOGNATHIDAE
Dwarf Orb-weaving Spiders

- Six or four eyes in triads or diads (eyes absent in troglobites)
- Labium fused to sternum and at least three times as wide as long
- Chelicerae fused at least at base
- Female pedipalps reduced or absent
- Planar orb-webs low in temperate or rainforest, some troglobites
- Body length: 0.35–1 mm

Australia:
Partially revised
currently: 8 species in 2 genera
estimated: 20 species in 4 genera
World: 68 species in 7 genera

Dwarf Orb-weaving Spiders (family Symphytognathidae) are tiny spiders with some unusual characters, in particular the reduction or lack of female pedipalps, the lack of booklungs (being so small these spiders appear to be able to breathe through their cuticle and tracheae) and fused chelicerae. The family was originally described from Australia based on spiders collected in Tasmania; however, Dwarf Orb-weaving Spiders are now known from the tropical, subtropical and southern temperate regions around the world.

Dwarf orb-weaving Spiders are extremely small spiders and a Pacific species in the genus *Patu* claims the world-record with a body length of 0.37 mm. Australian representatives are not much bigger; they are generally less than 1 mm long in both males and females. Unusually for spiders, the female pedipalps are reduced to a short, unsegmented lobe or absent altogether, a character otherwise only found in some Ground Orb-weavers (family Anapidae).

The Australian fauna consists of eight described species, four each in the genera *Anapistula* and *Symphytognatha*, although the local fauna is more diverse both at the genus and species level. *Anapistula* differs by a lower carapace and the retention of posterior spiracles. It is a largely tropical genus, but in Australia they have also been found in subterranean environments in the semi-arid zone. *Anapistula australia* is known from south-eastern Queensland; *A. troglobia* is only found in caves at Cape Range in Western Australia; and two species, *A. bifurcata* and *A. cuttacutta* occur in the Northern Territory, the latter also being a cave-dwelling troglobite.

Australian *Symphytognatha* have dark abdomens with dorsal and lateral pale stripes. They have been found in temperate forests around the country. *Symphytognatha blesti* has been recorded from New South Wales, *S. globosa* from Tasmania and *S. picta* is comparatively widespread in south-west Western Australia. *Symphytognatha fouldsi* is only known from one cave in Nambung National Park north of Perth in Western Australia. Undescribed species of *Symphytognatha* have been recorded from southern temperate forests of Victoria and other Dwarf Orb-weaving Spiders have been found in tropical Queensland.

Dwarf Orb-weaving Spiders are highly dependent on the very moist cool parts of the leaf litter in cooler, temperate forests, but also occur in tropical rainforests. Here, they generally build a horizontal orb-web, although *S. globosa* from Tasmania is reported to have a reduced web consisting of a few irregular, non-adhesive threads in a more or less horizontal plane. The spider is found in an inverted position under the hub. The species is most often found under loose stones in cool and shady situations, sometimes along the banks of creeks.

Dwarf Orb-weaving Spiders (family Symphytognathidae) are tiny spiders. Females have reduced or no pedipalps, as seen here in the undescribed specimen collected in subterranean traps in the central Pilbara region in northern Western Australia. Subterranean forms are not uncommon in the Symphytognathidae and these invariably have reduced eyes. The specimen illustrated here is completely eyeless. [A. Leung, Phoenix Environmental Sciences]

A Dwarf Orb-weaving Spider female from Queensland has suspended its eggsacs in the periphery of the horizontal orb-web. [L. Lopardo]

Typically, Dwarf Orb-weaving Spiders (family Symphytognathidae) construct a minute, horizontal orb-web as seen in the top of this image taken in Queensland. Some *Symphytognatha*, however, have been reported to build a snare of irregular threads as seen below the orb in this picture. Symphytognathids appear to tolerate each other's close proximity, even if individuals are not from the same species or possibly genus. [L. Lopardo]

This unidentified Dwarf Orb-weaving Spider male from tropical northern Queensland demonstrates the small size of these spiders. Unlike females, males of course have fully developed and functional pedipalps in this family, otherwise sexual reproduction would be impossible. [L. Lopardo]

NESTICIDAE
Scaffold-web Spiders

- Eight eyes in two rows, anterior median eyes small
- Carapace pear-shaped, labium thickened
- Abdomen more or less globular
- Legs comparatively long and slender, tarsus of fourth leg with comb of serrated bristles; female pedipalp claw elongated
- Cob- or scaffold-web of criss-cross threads and gummy droplets near attachment points
- Body length: 2–4 mm

Australia:
Taxonomy poorly resolved
Current: 1 species in 1 genus
Estimated: 10 species in 1 genus
World: 218 species in 9 genera

Scaffold-web Spiders (family Nesticidae) have traditionally been regarded as largely troglophile, because their preferred habitats are mainly caves, caverns and rock overhangs. However, this trait generally applies to the Holarctic fauna and towards the tropics these spiders are often found in leaf litter and near streams in rainforests.

Scaffold-web Spiders have long been suggested to be closely related to Comb-footed Spiders (family Theridiidae), as they also possess a row of serrate bristles on the tarsus of the fourth leg, construct a similar gum-footed web, and share peculiar morphological features of the spinnerets and the male pedipalp. However, molecular analyses have consistently rejected this association and the relationships of the Nesticidae to other araneoid spider families remain unresolved.

The Scaffold-web Spiders differ from the theridiids by having a thickened edge on the anterior rim of the labium. The comparatively long legs are covered with fairly long bristles, longer than in Comb-footed Spiders. Other differentiating features relate to the morphology of the pedipalps, in particular the presence of a typical nesticid paracymbium.

The Australian fauna consists of only a single described species, *Nesticella chillagoensis*, found at Royal Arch Cave near Chillagoe in northern Queensland, but undescribed, possibly litter-dwelling representatives of this genus have been reported elsewhere from northern Queensland. *Nesticella* is primarily an Asian-Oriental genus and represents a major lineage within the family that does not necessarily occupy caves.

With the exception of its apparent troglobitic lifestyle, reflected in reduced anterior median eyes, nothing is known of the biology of *Nesticella chillagoensis*.

Nesticellus chillagoensis, here the female specimen upon which the species description was based, is pale in coloration and has somewhat reduced eyes, consistent with its troglobitic lifestyle. It has so far only been recorded from a single cave in northern Queensland. [B.C. Baehr]

Nesticellus chillagoensis possesses a row of serrate bristles on the tarsus of the fourth leg. [B.C. Baehr]

THERIDIIDAE
Comb-footed spiders, Cob-web Spiders

- Eight eyes in two rows
- Legs often long and slender, generally without spines; tarsi with three claws
- Tarsi of fourth leg with comb of lightly curved serrated bristles
- Many webforms, including gum-footed cob- or sheet-webs or messy space-webs; some groups do not build their own web
- family members include kleptoparasites, araneophages, social spiders and those displaying maternal care
- Body length: 1–15 mm

Australia:
Taxonomy poorly resolved
Current: 93 species in 23 genera
Estimated: 500 species in 50 genera
World: 2,356 species in 121 genera

The Comb-footed Spiders (family Theridiidae) are an extremely diverse group of spiders with some remarkable representatives in Australia, including the notorious Redback Spider, the kleptoparasites in the genus *Argyrodes* and the social *Anelosimus*. Due to their enormous morphological and behavioural diversity, recognising a spider as a Comb-footed Spider is often difficult in the field. Their diagnostic feature is a line of enlarged saw-toothed bristles on the tarsus of the fourth leg ('comb'), which assists in pulling silk from the spinnerets to throw it over their prey. However, this comb is not present in all species and is often reduced or absent in males. Comb-footed Spiders generally lack spines on their legs, which helps to differentiate them from the similar Sheet-web Spiders (family Linyphiidae) or Scaffold-web Spiders (family Nesticidae).

The basic web of theridiid spiders appears to be a three-dimensional, messy cob-web in which the prey capture area is not limited to a single plane. This web has threads with sticky globules that attach to the substrate (gum-foot lines). However, the web has been modified in many lineages of the Comb-footed Spiders, in particular reductions are very common as detailed for the different subfamilies below.

The Comb-footed Spiders include the highly venomous Australian Redback Spider. The first bite of these spiders was recorded from Adelaide in medical journals in 1849, but the species was not described until German collectors took them at Rockhampton in Queensland and the species was described only more than 20 years after the initial record.

Australia includes a large indigenous Comb-footed Spider fauna and, as these spiders often disperse very well, there are many species in the Australian tropics of Asian or South-East Asian origin. The family also includes a considerable number of species that apparently have arrived on our shores mediated by human activity. These include the Brown Widow Spider (*Latrodectus geometricus*), Common or American House Spider (*Parasteatoda tepidariorum*), Red House Spider (*Nesticodes rufipes*) and the Cupboard Spiders (*Steatoda grossa* and *S. capensis*).

The Australian theridiid fauna is very diverse and many species and genera still await formal description. In addition, the tropical fauna includes many described species of Asian or South-East Asian origin that have not been listed for the country. The Australian Comb-footed Spiders belong to at least seven different subfamilies: Latrodectinae, Argyrodinae, Hadrotarsinae, Sphintharinae, Pholcommatinae, Theridiinae and Anelosiminae.

The Australian representatives of the **Latrodectinae** include the Australian Redback (*Latrodectus hasseltii*) and Brown Widow Spiders, the Cupboard Spiders (genus *Steatoda*) and members of the genus *Crustulina*. Spiders in this subfamily have a hairy carapace, three or more setae on a large colulus, and a peripheral retreat in the web. Latrodectines generally have a round to oval, shiny abdomen with few hairs. The Australian Redback Spider is the only indigenous representative of the cosmopolitan genus *Latrodectus* (the Black Widow Spiders) in Australia. The entire genus is of medical significance and the Australian Redback is no exception. Its venom includes the neurotoxic alpha-latrotoxin which attacks cell membranes resulting in excessive release of acetylcholine, norepinephrine and GABA, neurotransmitters of the nerve system. Pain is usually severe when bitten and systemic effects such as nausea, vomiting, abdominal or chest pain, headache and generalised sweating may occur. Fatal envenomations have occurred but antivenom has been available since the mid-1950s. The venom of the Redback Spider appears to be potent in a number of vertebrates, as these spiders are frequently reported to feed on reptiles, such as lizards and small snakes, or small mammals. However, the staple diet of these spiders are insects, in particular ants.

At least seven named species in the genus *Steatoda*, often referred to as

Australian Redback Spiders are unmistakable, with a brown to black abdomen, a red marking along its upper side and an hourglass-shaped orange to red spot on the underside. Whilst immature and male spiders are coloured in different shades of orange, white and black, all have the hourglass pattern that can be seen from underneath. [V.W. Framenau, Phoenix Environmental Sciences]

The colour patterns of male Australian Redback Spiders, here two photos of individuals taken in Perth, only remotely resemble those of adult females, although they still display the red hourglass pattern on the underside of the abdomen. Similarly, immature females have a variable pattern of white, black and red, unlike mature females. [V.W. Framenau, Phoenix Environmental Sciences]

The Cupboard Spider, *Steatoda grossa*, here a male (left) and female (right) from Perth, is a cosmopolitan species with synathropic tendencies. The white colour markings present in the male may not be very distinct and they are almost completely lacking in the female. [V.W. Framenau, Phoenix Environmental Sciences]

Females in the genus *Steatoda* are brown to black and sometimes have white spots and lines on the abdomen. The taxonomy of this genus, with the exception of two introduced species, is unresolved and a species-level identification of the illustrated female from Western Australia is not possible. [V.W. Framenau, Phoenix Environmental Sciences]

This male and female Comb-footed Spider from Western Australia are currently referred to *Crustulina*, based on the single described Australian species in the genus, *Crustulina bicruciata*, which was originally described from Western Australia. However, this generic placement appears incorrect, illustrating the poor taxonomic knowledge of this family in Australia. [V.W. Framenau, Phoenix Environmental Sciences]

Cupboard Spiders, occur in Australia. These include the cosmopolitan *S. grossa* and the originally African *S. capensis*. These spiders resemble the Australian Redback Spider in shape and behaviour, but they are generally uniformly dark brown to black and their abdomen is sometimes adorned with white spots and bands. In contrast to *Latrodectus*, the lateral eyes are touching each other or are separated by less than their diameter. The bite of *S. grossa* is generally less severe than that of the Australian Redback Spider. Symptoms include blistering and general unwellness that may last for several days.

A single species in the genus *Crustulina* is currently described from Australia, *C. bicruciata* from Western Australia. However, the placement of the species in this genus is historical and does not reflect its evolutionary relationships. True *Crustulina* have tubercles on the carapace as basis for fine hairs and females have a slerotised ring around the pedicel. The presence of this genus in Australia is currently unconfirmed.

Australian members of the subfamily **Argyrodinae** include the web-invading genus *Argyrodes* and the Whip Spiders, *Ariamnes*. The subfamily is identified by a number of characters, amongst others a projected clypeus and stalked, modified eggsacs. Argyrodines generally exploit other spiders either as kleptoparasites or by preying directly on them.

Argyrodes includes facultative kleptoparasites in other spiders' webs. Twelve species are listed for Australia, of which only six have received modern taxonomic treatments. The most widespread and probably best studied is *A. antipodianus*, the Dew-drop or Silver Tear-drop Spider, which is known from throughout Australia, New Zealand and New Caledonia. These spiders have been found in a variety of host webs, for example in those of large Orb-weaving Spiders with variable web architecture (such as *Eriophora* and *Cyrtophora*, family Araneidae) or in Golden Orb-weaver webs (*Nephila*, family Nephilidae). *Argyrodes* may show some plasticity in the prey they take and dependent on the prey size they may be considered commensals, i.e. their activity is not detrimental to the host, or kleptoparasites, which may drive the host to abandon the web. Some *Argyrodes* are reported to prey on the host itself. For example, *A. incursus* from New South Wales, including Lord Howe Island, is exclusively found in the web of the Comb-footed Spider *Parasteatoda mundula* where it preys on the host, its eggs and young and uses the host's leaf retreat to protect its own eggsacs. Kleptoparasites, such as

A. antipodianus, may construct their own sticky web in the barrier area of the host's web, although they also steal the silk of their host. This web can capture small prey but is also used to store stolen prey items and suspend the eggsacs.

There are three species of Whip Spiders, genus *Ariamnes*, described from Australia. They have a characteristically stick-like, sometimes vermiform abdomen and cannot be confused with any other spider in the country. Most species appear to be nocturnal. They construct simple non-sticky line-webs in low foliage, sometimes in the fringes of orb-webs, which they hold in their front tarsi. They predominantly catch flies and wandering male spiders that attempt to use the trap lines to travel.

Members of the subfamily **Hadrotarsinae** can by recognised by the presence of specialised, flat-tipped sensory setae on the tarsi of the first pair of legs. Some have characteristic kidney-shaped ('reniform') posterior median eyes and the pedipalps of some females have dorso-ventrally flattened pedipalp claws. Hadrotarsines are small spiders and, at large, webless hunters that specialise on ants as prey.

Five genera and 14 species are currently listed for the Hadrotarsinae in Australia, the genera being *Dipoena*, *Euryopis*, *Gmogala*, *Hadrotarsus* and *Yoroa*. However, the genus-level taxonomy is poorly resolved. Australian *Euryopis* may rightly belong to *Emertonella* and those species originally placed in *Trigonobothrys* and which are currently listed in *Dipoena* do not conform well to the circumscription of this genus. Some Australian *Dipoena* are *Phycosoma*, which itself is a senior synonym of *Trigonobothrys*.

Gmogala includes only a single species, *G. scarabaea*. This small species is widespread in Australia and has also been recorded from New Guinea. *Yoroa* had a modern taxonomic review and includes a single species from tropical Queensland, *Y. taylori*, in addition to a species from New Guinea. *Yoroa* lacks the typical reniform posterior median eyes of the Hadrotarsinae, as do spiders in the genera *Dipoena*, *Euryopis* and *Emertonella*.

The subfamily **Pholcommatinae** is mainly characterised by male pedipalp characters such as an upward-pointing hook on the ectal margin of the cymbium. Two genera are currently listed for Australia: *Enoplognatha*, with a single species, *E. bidens*, from Western Australia; and *Phoroncidia* with five species originally described from the eastern states. As is the case for many other Comb-footed Spiders, there are no modern taxonomic treatments for the Pholcommatinae in

The Dew-drop or Silver Tear-drop Spider, *Argyrodes antipodianus*, here a female from Western Australia, is one of 12 species listed in the genus from Australia, but the diversity is probably much higher. This species has been recorded from most Australian states and it also occurs in New Zealand and New Caledonia. As with many other *Argyrodes*, it lives on the edges of the host's web and steals small items of prey. Some Silver Tear-drop Spiders hang by a thread from high on the web, and swing to the centre of the web, feeding at the very mouth of the host and drinking her pre-liquefied food. [F. Bokhari]

The fragile appearance of *Ariamnes colubrinus*, here a female with a lantern-shaped eggsac from Queensland, belies its aggressive behaviour of hunting much bigger spiders. The species constructs a very simple line-web of one or two strands in low vegetation and often near orb-webs. Flies and wandering male spiders are among their most common prey items. [R.J. Raven]

It appears that *Argyrodes antipodianus* is an opportunist hunter that is not limited to feeding on prey items caught in the host's web. In this case it seems that the host, the Tent Spider *Cyrtophora moluccensis*, has died and *Argyrodes* has started to eat one of the softer leg joints. It is possible that *Argyrodes* caused the large spider's death. Some species in the genus, such as *A. incursus*, appear to regularly attack their host. [R.J. Raven]

The Australian Redback Spider, here a female with eggsac from Queensland, loves houses and associated dwellings with their dry and hidden spaces and the warmth that roof cavities provide in cooler winters. One factor that supports often high population numbers is the prolific production of offspring. Females can store sperm and may construct multiple eggsacs over a period of two years. Each of these eggsacs, which are suspended in the web, may contain up to 300 eggs. Given enough space, the female makes a sheet-web with a set of short vertical threads of sticky gum-foot lines leading to the ground. The threads are weaker than those of the main web and act as trip snares. They break easily at the ground end, when prey hits the web. The sticky drops hold the prey and the stretched silk lifts it off the ground. Using this method, Redback Spiders have been seen trapping, killing and immobilising animals as large as rats and snakes. [R.J. Raven]

The Australian Redback Spider, *Latrodectus hasseltii*, can be found throughout Australia and copes with almost all climatic conditions in this country. They construct their tangled and gum-footed webs preferably low in the vegetation in protected, dark or shaded spots under loose bark or under logs and rocks. Comb-footed Spiders are easily transported, as their small webs can be tucked away unnoticed in tight corners. Human-mediated transport took the Australian Redback Spider to Belgium, where they apparently did not establish populations, but they are now well entrenched in Japan and New Zealand and on the south Atlantic island of Tristan da Cunha. [P. Zborowski]

Australia and therefore distribution patterns are difficult to establish. Species-level identification is almost impossible. *Phoroncidia* is a common genus with representatives throughout the country. These are small spiders with a sclerotised abdomen that is comparatively large in relation to the carapace, often high and may have multiple characteristic tubercles. Other *Phoroncidia* have a low abdomen with distinct spines. *Phoroncidia* have a highly specialised, reduced gum-foot web that only consists of one or sometimes a few threads fastened to the substrate at either side. The spider rests in the middle, holding it together with the opposite first and generally fourth legs.

Spiders in the subfamily **Spintharinae** are mainly characterised by features of the male genitalia. In addition, the dorsal edge of the comb on the fourth leg is notched, the colulus is small and the abdomen has characteristic humps. The Australian fauna consists of three genera: *Janula*, *Moneta* and *Thwaitesia*; however, no modern taxonomic treatment for these exists. Most spintharines make simple line-webs. For example, *Thwaitesia* makes an H-shaped web with two gumfoot lines which the spider holds with its front legs.

Eye-patterns are important for distinguishing genera in the Sphintharinae. *Janula* includes only a single described species in Australia, *J. bicornis*, from tropical Queensland. Spiders in the genus are small, with a body length of less than 4 mm, and have characteristic conical protrusions which carry the anterior median eyes. *Moneta* species may be recognised by having the eyes in dorsal view in two parallel rows and very short tarsi; it includes three species from throughout the country. In *Thwaitesia* the posterior median eyes have a distance of about one eye's diameter between them, in contrast to other spintharines in which the posterior median eyes are separated by a distance of less than one eye or a distance of twice or more one eye's diameter. The Twin-peaked Thwaithesia, *T. argentiopunctata*, is a prominent member of the genus from coastal Queensland.

The subfamily **Theridiinae** includes those Comb-footed Spiders without any trace of a colulus; more specifically, not even colulus hairs are present. In Australia, the subfamily includes the genera *Achaearanea*, *Cryptachaea*, *Chrysso*, *Nesticodes*, *Parasteatoda* and *Theridion*. Most species in this clade have long and thin legs. Within the Theridiinae, a compact, globular central retreat with support and gumfoot lines radiating from it in a star-shape is a common web type.

Theridion includes 29 species in Australia, almost all of which were described before or during the early 1900s. The genus was a dumping ground for many Europe-based taxonomists then lacking an appropriate genus-framework for the Theridiidae in this country. Species within this genus have generally little in common and therefore are difficult to circumscribe here. Similarly, the placement of four Australian species in *Achaearanea* may represent an historic artefact.

In contrast, species in *Parasteatoda* and *Cryptachaea* have been treated taxonomically. *Parasteatoda* includes the cosmopolitan and synanthropic Common House Spider, *P. tepidariorum*. *Parasteatoda decorata* occurs from New Guinea into Queensland and *P. mundula* is currently known from Indian and Pacific Ocean islands and coastal New South Wales. *Cryptachaea gigantipes* is a south-east Australian species; in contrast, *C. veruculata* is common throughout the country.

Nesticodes rufipes, the Red House Spider, is an introduced and synanthropic species that has mainly been reported from the Queensland coast. As it is also found in New Zealand, a wider distribution in Australia is likely. A single described species of *Chrysso* has been found in Queensland: *C. nigra*, the Cat-eye Spider. It has a distinct shiny black coloration with bright yellow-green legs. The species has a south-east Asian distribution. It provides maternal care for the young, which can often be found in the web of a female spider.

The spiders in the subfamily **Anelosiminae**, as with those in the Theridiinae, have a reduced or absent colulus; however, colulus hairs are still present. Within this subfamily, the genus *Anelosimus* includes many examples of sociality which has apparently evolved multiple times. *Anelosimus pratchetti* from New South Wales, including Lord Howe Island, appears subsocial which means that web-sharing does not occur over prolonged periods of the spider's life. Molecular studies suggest close relationships to representatives of the genus in Madagascar, a phenomenon which is possibly explained by long-distance dispersal.

The subfamily Theridiinae includes long-legged Comb-footed Spiders, with many being very similar to the female of an unidentified species from Dryandra Woodland in Western Australia which is illustrated here. The eggsac is spherical and covered with a strong layer of silk. [V.W. Framenau, Phoenix Environmental Sciences]

The Twin-peaked Thwaitesia, *Thwaitesia argentiopunctata*, has been recorded at sites along the Queensland coast. It is one of currently two described species in the genus from Australia; the other is *T. nigronodosa*, which was also originally described from Queensland. [R.J. Raven]

This tiny hadrotarsine male from Western Australia closely resembles *Dipoena setosus* from Tasmania, which was originally placed in the genus *Trigonobothrys*. However, *Trigonobothrys* is a synonym of *Phycosoma* which has different genital morphology and higher elevated carapace in males (see image below). Consequently, the generic placement of these small spiders remains unresolved. [V.W. Framenau, Phoenix Environmental Sciences]

An elevated, cylindrical carapace in males is characteristic of the genus *Phycosoma*. This genus is currently not listed with any described species from Australia. This male, possibly *P. oecobioides*, lives in the rainforest leaf litter of Lamington National Park in southern Queensland. The females lack this strange modification of the carapace. [B.C. Baehr]

Right: Most Australian species listed in *Euryopis* may rightly belong to the genus *Emertonella*, which differs from *Euryopis* in the higher head region and some male pedipalp characters. Members of the Hadrotarsinae are specialist ant-hunters (myrmecophages) and this little spider makes a meal of a *Camponotus* ant. [F. Bokhari]

Opposite page: The theridiine *Theridion zebrinum* was originally described from China and occurs throughout the South-East Asian region and into tropical Queensland. This female with eggsac was encountered in Mossman Gorge. The species has a distinct colour pattern with yellow lines on the abdomen and a 'happy-face' marking with a smiling mouth when viewed from the back. The web of *T. zebrinum* is constructed on the underside of a broad leaf. It consists of strong, almost parallel lines across the leaf, which are connected by zig-zag lines in between. Irregular webbing is under this cover. [P. Zborowski]

The Cat-eye Spider, *Chrysso nigra*, is distributed primarily in South-East Asia but is also not uncommon in Queensland. These small but distinctly coloured spiders display maternal care. The female, pictured above, can be seen with a number of her offspring in her web which is constructed under a leaf. [P. Zborowski]

Phoroncidia, here an unidentified female from Alfred Cove, Perth, Western Australia, includes five described species in Australia, but the diversity is likely to be much higher. The female illustrated may be *P. sextuberculata* but, lacking any modern taxonomic treatment, species-level identifications based on abdomen shape or coloration should be treated cautiously. *Phoroncidia* uses a single or few strands of silk covered with sticky droplets, here seen at the bottom left of the image, to capture prey at night. During the day the spider sits very well camouflaged in the vegetation. [F. Bokhari]

NICODAMIDAE
Red-and-black Spiders

- Eyes in two straight rows
- Carapace orange or red, abdomen black or iridescent blue, sometimes with red
- Legs comparatively long and slender, segments variably coloured in red and black
- Sheet-web
- Body length: 3–12 mm

Australia:
Taxonomy revised
current: 23 species in 7 genera
estimated: 25 species in 7 genera
World: 29 species in 9 genera

Red-and-black Spiders (family Nicodamidae) are boldly coloured spiders that immediately attract attention in the field. And whilst nicodamid spiders are readily recognised and share clear, family-specific traits, their systematic position and relationships to other spider families has long been puzzling. Members of the family have been placed in the Dictynidae, Theridiidae, Agelenidae, Zodariidae and Amaurobioidea. Current molecular studies suggest affinities with the orb-weaving spiders in the widest sense (Orbiculariae), although these relationships are by no means settled. For example, nicodamids possess two major ampullate spigots on the anterior lateral spinnerets, but all other orbicularians have only one. One aspect that may contribute to the confusion is that Nicodamidae, as currently defined, may not represent a single family. There is some molecular evidence that the cribellate New Zealand representative *Megadictyna* is not immediately related to the ecribellate Australian representatives.

Red-and-black Spiders generally have a bright orange-red cephalothorax and black, brown, purplish or iridescent blue abdomen, that sometimes also has some red patterning. Their leg segments are coloured in varying combinations of red and black. The male pedipalp morphology is unusual within spiders as the tibia has a large, often divided apophysis on the upper (dorsal) side, not towards the back (retrolateral). The tarsus and metatarsus of the fourth leg are without sensory hairs (trichobothria) and the chelicerae only have a single tooth.

The centre of diversity for the Red-and-black Spiders is clearly within Australia where 23 of the 29 described species occur, mainly in temperate to subtropical forests; however, the family is also present in New Guinea (four species in the genus *Dimidamus*) and New Zealand. There are two subfamilies, the ecribellate Nicodaminae and the cribellate Megadictyninae; the latter is endemic to New Zealand.

Genus and species identification in the field is difficult although some characters may assist. For example, males of the single species of *Durodamus*, *D. yeni*, which occurs in the more arid central regions from Queensland into South Australia, have a dorsal abdominal scute. With 11 species *Ambicodamus* is the most diverse genus of the family and occurs along the eastern coast of Australia into Tasmania and South Australia and also in south-west Western Australia, in areas where annual rainfall exceeds 500 mm. *Dimidamus* has one species each around the Queensland/New South Wales border and in Victoria, in addition to the New Guinea representatives. *Litodamus* is endemic to Tasmania, where three species have been reported from closed forests at higher altitude. *Nicodamus* includes two species with broadly eastern and western Australian distributions although both occur in South Australia. *Novodamus* and *Oncodamus* include two species each from closed forests in eastern Australia.

Nicodamids are most common in the semi-arid to temperate forests and bushland of eastern, southern and western Australia. They build small, sturdy sheet-webs at ground-level on stones or logs, or in low vegetation. With few exceptions, adults of most species can be found from spring into summer or autumn.

Dimidamus dimidiatus, here a male from Queensland, is a comparatively small Red-and-black Spider (family Nicodamidae) of 4.5 to 6 mm body length. The abdomen is bicoloured with the back half red. This species lives in forests along the east coast of Australia as far north as Jimna State Forest, Queensland, and as far south as Myall Lakes, New South Wales. The species appears to be mainly winter/spring mature with adults recorded from March into December. [R.J. Raven]

Nicodamus mainae, here a mature male, is widespread in south-west Western Australia from Coral Bay in the north into the Nullarbor Plain, where it also occurs in South Australia. Adults are mainly found in spring and summer. The second species of *Nicodamus*, *N. peregrinus*, is common in eastern Australia and the distributions of both species may overlap in South Australia [V.W. Framenau, Phoenix Environmental Sciences]

Ambicodamus marae, here a female from Kambalda, is restricted to the very south-west corner of Western Australia. Adults can be found throughout the year. [F. Bokhari]

DEINOPIDAE
Net-casting Spiders, Ogre-faced Spiders, Retarius Spider, Hump-backed Spiders

- Eight eyes; greatly enlarged posterior median eyes in *Deinopis*, anterior lateral eyes on distinct, ventrally oriented tubercles
- Body elongated
- Legs elongated, third pair shortest
- Cribellate; cribellum entire and broad
- Rectangular web suspended between first three pairs of legs
- Night active
- Body length: 5–28 mm

Australia:
Partially revised
Current: 13 species in 2 genera
Estimated: 25 species in 2 genera
World: 60 species in 2 genera

The prey capture strategy of the Net-casting Spiders (family Deinopidae) is unique amongst spiders and, similar to the Bola Spiders in the family Araneidae, they have taken their (reduced) orb-web 'into their own hands'. Net-casting Spiders hold their rectangular cribellate capture-web between their legs, suspended in a framework of what is believed to be a reduced orb. When potential prey approaches, they greatly expand the capture web by stretching their legs, dropping sufficiently by releasing their fourth tarsi from the supporting thread and throw it over the unsuspecting aerial or pedestrian prey.

Deinopids are long-bodied and long-legged spiders. The embolus of the male pedipalp is thin, relatively flat, and coils multiple times around a single tegular apophysis, allowing an extreme rotation of the bulb during copulation. Species in the genus *Deinopis*, the Ogre-face Spiders, can be recognised by their greatly enlarged posterior median eyes. Species in the genus *Menneus*, the Hump-backed Spiders, have normal-sized posterior median eyes and the carapace usually has a distinct posterior guanine patch. Spiders in the genus *Deinopis* are generally larger than those of *Menneus*, but sizes overlap.

The huge posterior median eyes of *Deinopis* are considered the largest ocelli of any invertebrate, with those of *D. subrufa* of up to 1.4 mm in diameter. Their photoreceptive capabilities facilitate visual predation under dark conditions for these nocturnal spiders. Remarkably, the spiders destroy most of the photosensitive membrane in these eyes at dawn and resynthesize it at dusk.

The distribution of *Deinopis* is circumtropical whereas *Menneus* is limited to Australia, New Guinea, New Caledonia and Africa. The taxonomy of *Deinopis* is unresolved. All Australian species were described before 1900 and therefore distribution patterns of the six recognised species remain obscure. Five of the seven Australian *Menneus* occur along the east coast, with varying ranges from Queensland into New South Wales (including Lord Howe Island). Two species, *M. quasimodo* and *M. wa*, have been recorded from Western Australia.

Net-casting Spiders, in particular those in the genus *Menneus*, are comparatively rarely collected taking into account their spectacular prey capture behaviour, possibly because they are very cryptic when hiding in vegetation during the day. They do not appear to be selective in their choice of prey, although *Deinopis* has been recorded to mainly consume cockroaches, ants and other spiders. The eggsacs of these spiders are a hard, brown sphere, which is attached to leaves in vegetation or buried in leaf litter. The hatching spiderlings remain briefly near the eggsac.

Net-casting Spiders in the genus *Deinopis*, here an unidentified male from Western Australia, are colloquially referred to as Ogre-faced Spiders. Species of *Deinopis* differ from those of the other Australian genus, *Menneus*, by the extremely enlarged posterior median eyes that facilitate visual hunting by these nocturnal spiders. The embolus of the male pedipalp is coiled multiple times around a single tegular apophysis. [F. Bokhari]

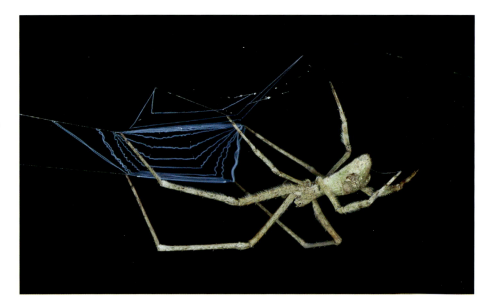

Spiders in the genus *Menneus*, here *M. aussie* photographed in Queensland, are known as Humpbacked Spiders as they often have protrusions on their dorsal abdomen. Whilst *Deinopis* regularly catch pedestrian prey, *Menneus* tends to be an aerial hunter, although these preferences are not mutually exclusive. [P. Zborowski]

The construction of the casting-net is an elaborate undertaking which commences with the construction of a temporary scaffold fixed to substrate. *Deinopis* has been reported to construct the scaffold against horizontal substrates, whereas *Menneus*, *M. aussie* is illustrated here, uses vertical structures. The casting-net is woven onto the scaffold but eventually cut from it. Spiders then keep it between their anterior legs, with their body suspended on a single thread to which they hold on with the fourth pair of legs. During attack, the legs let go of the suspension thread, giving the spider downward propulsion. [P. Zborowski]

Species of *Menneus*, here *Menneus aussie* from Queensland, have smaller eyes than *Deinopis*. They tend to be found in forest and riverine habitats. The cribellate silk, with which they construct their unique reduced orb-web, renders the snare a blue coloration. [P. Zborowski]

Along the east coast *Deinopis* are frequently found around houses, for example on screen doors, on the bark of trees and in low vegetation. The *Deinopis* female illustrated here was resting low on the bark of a eucalypt tree. [R.J. Raven]

ULOBORIDAE
Venomless Spiders, Feather-legged Spiders

- Eight eyes in two rows (*Miagrammopes* with four eyes in a single row, anterior eye row reduced)
- Venom glands absent
- Legs long without spines, tarsi with three claws; trichobothria on femora of second, third and fourth leg
- Cribellate; cribellum entire and calamistrum uniserrate
- Orb-web, triangle-web or single capture-thread
- Body length: 3–10 mm

Australia:
Taxonomy poorly resolved
Current: 11 species in 4 genera
Estimated: 50 species in 10 genera
World: 266 species in 18 genera

Most Venomless Spiders (family Uloboridae) build complete cribellate orb-webs, but there are many modifications to these, including the addition of cone-shaped structures and the incorporation of stabilimenta. Sometimes, the web is reduced to triangular segments or multiple- or single-capture threads. As their colloquial name suggests, Venomless Spiders do not have venom glands, a character they share with the unrelated Holarchaeidae, and therefore rely entirely on wrapping their prey for immobilisation.

Venomless Spiders have a worldwide distribution with the highest diversity in tropical and subtropical regions. The taxonomy of the family is poorly resolved in Australia with few modern descriptions. Interpreting the distribution patterns of the Australian species remains difficult in the absence of appropriate modern illustrations. Venomless Spider occur throughout Australia, but are rarely collected in the arid zone.

Most curious in relation to morphology and prey capture behaviour are the members of the genus *Miagrammopes*. Five species in this genus are currently described from Australia. Individuals of each of these species have only four eyes, as the anterior row of eyes is absent. They often have an elongated, almost stick-like body providing perfect camouflage in vegetation. The orb-web in *Miagrammopes* is usually reduced to a single, generally horizontal, strand with cribellate silk along most of its length or a non-sticky horizontal resting line with one or several

Miagrammopes, here an unidentified species from Western Australia, are the most curious of all Venomless Spiders (family Uloboridae) in Australia. They have only four eyes, widely spaced in a posterior eye row, as the anterior eyes are absent. The uloborid orb-web in *Miagrammopes* is often reduced to a single thread that is partly wrapped with cribellate silk. The spiders suspend themselves in the strand, literally becoming part of it. When prey touches the capture strand, *Miagrammopes* jerks on the thread putting the victim out of balance to quickly wrap it up. [F. Bokhari]

vertical capture-lines. The spiders usually hold the resting line and/or capture thread with their strong first and fourth pair of legs, becoming part of the snare itself. Prey capture involves rapid jerks of the capture line once prey touches it. The prey is enmeshed into the capture thread and subsequently wrapped in silk by the spider.

The genus *Philoponella* includes three described species in Australia. It is recognised by a nearly round carapace in males that has a broad and transverse thoracic groove. *Philoponella* are often found in web congregations, reflected in the name of one of the eastern Australian species, *P. congregabilis*. Cooperative prey capture on these web-congregations has been reported in species from overseas, but is not known from Australia.

Two species of *Uloborus* are described from Australia, *U. barbipes* and *U. canus*. *Uloborus barbipes* is characterised by brushes on the tibiae of the front legs. Spiders with this trait have been found throughout Australia, but it is unclear if they all represent the same species.

Purumitra grammicus is only known from offshore islands of the Great Barrier

Reef. They construct horizontal orb-webs with stabilimentum in understorey vegetation near the shoreline. A second species of the genus is known from The Philippines and Caroline Islands.

Zosis geniculata, the Grey House Spider, has a pantropical distribution and is largely synanthropic. In Australia it has been reported from Queensland and the Northern Territory. *Zosis geniculata* is common on ceilings where it produces pink, star-shaped eggsacs.

Most Venomless Spiders (family Uloboridae) construct regular orb-webs with cribellate capture threads. This orb-web is modified in many species, such as seen here in an unidentified species from near Pannawonica in the Pilbara region of Western Australia, by the incorporation of a stabilimentum of cribellate silk. [F. Bokhari]

This *Ulorborus* female from Karijini National Park in Western Australia may be *U. barbipes*, which was originally described from Queensland. The identification is based on the presence of brush-like setae on the tibiae of the first legs, to which the species name, 'barbed feet', refers to. However, the taxonomy of the Venomless Spiders in is poorly resolved and a species-level identification is not possible. [F. Bokhari]

HERSILIIDAE
Long-spinneret Bark Spiders, Two-tailed Spiders

- Eight eyes in two strongly recurved rows, posterior eyes on elevated mount
- Posterior lateral spinnerets extremely elongated, with spicules covering the whole length
- Metatarsi of first, second and fourth leg bi-articulate or flexible
- Active day and night without prey capture web
- Body length: 5–10 mm

Australia:
Taxonomy revised
Current: 55 species in 2 genera
Estimated: 60 species in 2 genera
World: 176 species in 15 genera

In Australia, the Long-spinneret Bark Spiders (family Hersiliidae) are arboricolous and predominantly found on eucalypt trees; however, worldwide this family also includes free-hunting rock-dwellers and ground-hunting web-builders. Based on the extremely elongated posterior lateral spinnerets, Long-spinneret Bark Spiders cannot be confused with any other spider family in Australia; however, finding these extremely cryptic species can be a challenge even for the most experienced naturalist.

The Hersiliidae have a predominantly southern tropical and sub-tropical distribution. Currently, there are two genera known from Australia. *Hersilia* occurs only in the northern parts of the Northern Territory and Western Australia, whereas *Tamopsis* is common and widely distributed throughout the country wherever host trees can be found; however, Long-spinneret Bark Spiders are not known from Tasmania. Genus-level identification is difficult in the field as the differentiating character refers to the articulation of the metatarsi and genital morphology. A good character to identify species groups within *Tamopsis* is the relative height of the eye area, which may be flat or strongly raised to a conspicuous eye mound. Species identification requires genital examination, in particular as coloration is extremely variable within species and changes in relation to the surface they inhabit.

Perfectly camouflaged by their mottled coloration, the spiders generally sit head down on tree trunks and branches, but can be at times seen on rocks or house walls. Draglines on the tree trunks may be the only evidence that gives away their presence. Long-spinneret Bark Spiders are very fast runners, especially when disturbed.

Similar to Wall Spiders (family Oecobiidae), Long-spinneret Bark Spiders encircle their prey whilst at the same time throwing silk at it with their extremely elongated spinnerets. This fixes the prey to the bark and once completely immobilised the spiders will bite through the restricting layer of silk.

Hersiliids attach their eggsacs to the substrate. They are of a variety of shapes, and may resemble a little volcano, small oval pockets, or be spherical and hang on a stalk from the vegetation.

This unidentified *Tamopsis* female from Western Australia is just about to finish its spherical eggsac. It will be attached, using the stalk seen at the top of the image, to bark or other parts of the vegetation. [F. Bokhari]

Above and opposite page below: Long-spinneret Bark Spiders are absolute masters of disguise and are able to actively adjust the shades of their coloration to the background. These two unidentified females from the Pilbara region in Western Australia inhabit more unusually patterned environments. [F. Bokhari]

Fickert's Long-spinneret Bark Spider (*Tamopsis fickerti*) is recorded from Queensland, New South Wales and Victoria. This female from Melbourne has woven a patterned sheet of silk on the bark surface on which it rests. [V.W. Framenau, Phoenix Environmental Sciences]

Not much of the prey, possibly a moth, can be recognised after this female Fickert's Long-spinneret Bark Spider (*Tamopsis fickerti*) has wrapped it up for consumption. Hersiliids capture their prey by speedily running around it, spinnerets facing the victim, and thereby covering it with silk from their enormously elongated posterior spinnerets. [V.W. Framenau, Phoenix Environmental Sciences]

The eye-pattern of Long-spinneret Bark Spiders is characteristic. Both eye rows are recurved and the posterior eyes are on an elevated mount as can be seen here in an unidentified *Tamopsis* male from Dryandra Woodland in Western Australia. [V.W. Framenau, Phoenix Environmental Sciences]

This beautiful, barely discernible female *Tamopsis facialis* minds four irregularly shaped eggsacs on eucalyptus bark. This species has been recorded from New South Wales, through South Australia and into Western Australia. [B.C. Baehr]

Opposite page: This unidentified *Tamopsis* female is practically invisible on the patchy bark of a eucalypt tree as its body is mottled with white, grey and earthy colours. [P. Zborowski]

OECOBIIDAE
Wall Spiders

- Eight eyes in two rows, anterior median and posterior lateral eyes fully developed, others degenerate
- Carapace oval- to kidney-shaped ('reniform'), generally wider than it is long
- Six spinnerets, posterior pair longest with end joint turned upwards
- Large anal tubercle above spinnerets fringed with two rows of hair
- Cribellate (*Oecobius*); cribellum partially divided, calamistrum degenerate, in two rows (absent in males)
- Sheet-web builders
- Synanthropic
- Body length: 1.5–4 mm

Australia:
Taxonomy revised
current: 5 species in 1 genus
estimated: 5 species in 1 genus
World: 110 species in 6 genera

The distinguishing feature of the Wall Spiders (family Oecobiidae) is a large two-jointed anal tubercle above the spinnerets which is fringed with two conspicuous rows of stout, curved bristles. However, it is not necessary to rely on this microscopic character to identify members of this family – oecobiids are very small spiders – as their overall appearance is very distinctive. The carapace is wider than it is long, with a protruding frontal tip and the eyes are situated towards the centre away from the frontal margin. The eyes are in a tight group but only the anterior median eyes and the posterior lateral eyes appear fully developed – all others are narrower and indistinct.

The Oecobiidae include cribellate and ecribellate spiders, but only the cribellate genus *Oecobius* is found in Australia. Five species have been recorded and all are synanthropic or at least partly synanthropic. Whether these species were introduced by humans is often difficult to judge, in particular for the pantropical species that may have dispersed into the country naturally. However, the most common species, *Oecobius navus*, is thought to have been introduced by humans. Identification by colour pattern is possible but should be confirmed by examination of the genitalia.

A male *Oecobius navus*, right, approaches a female that is still sitting under her silken retreat. Males make specialised mating webs although this is not evident in this image. [A. Lance]

The cosmopolitan and omnipresent *O. navus* occurs around buildings throughout Australia and is also found in New Zealand. *Oecobius putus* is possibly of African/Middle Eastern origin and also occurs east into India. There are records of this species from northern and south-west Western Australia. *Oecobius marathaus* was originally described from India, but is a now considered a pantropical species. It has been found in northern Australia and along the east coast as far south as the New South Wales border. *Oecobius concinnus*, a pantropical species, and *O. interpellator* have isolated records from the Northern Territory. When *O. interpellator* was initially described from Massachusetts, its presence in New Caledonia was already suggested.

Oecobius navus appears to tolerate a variety of climatic conditions and has been found into semi-arid environments. However, detailed field observations and laboratory experiments in suburban Perth suggest a preference for high humidity, low air temperature and shelter from sunlight and rainfall where populations persist. The spiders appear to be to some extent vulnerable to desiccation and thermal stress. Ants are one of the main prey items, but other insects and spiders are also taken.

Oecobius navus spins small star-shaped mesh- or sheet-webs on walls across cracks and in corners. It rests flat against the surface underneath it and rushes out when potential prey is detected. The spider overcomes its prey by combing silk with the bristles of the anal tubercle from their large posterior spinnerets whilst continuously encircling it. In Australia, the family shares this type of prey attack behaviour with the Long-spinneret Bark Spiders (family Hersiliidae); both are members of the superfamily Eresoidea.

Mating occurs in a special mating web constructed by the male. Multiple eggsacs are constructed by the female and attached to the substrate near the sheet, but each of these includes only about five to ten eggs.

This unidentified *Oecobius* female may represent *Oecobius putus* based on the lack of any dark patterning on the carapace and the comparatively large anterior median eyes. Species identification based on colour and eye pattern is possible in the Australian *Oecobius* species, but should be confirmed by examination of genitalia. [P. Zborowski]

Opposite page: A female *Oecobius navus* has overcome a colourful Pollen Beetle (family Melyridae). This photo illustrates the long posterior spinnerets of the Wall Spiders, from which silk is combed with the bristles of the anal tubercle. [A. Lance]

HAHNIIDAE
Comb-tailed Spiders, Dwarf Sheet Spiders

- Eight eyes in two rows
- 'Fishbone-pattern' on abdomen
- Six spinnerets in a single transverse row beneath abdomen, outermost longest
- Sheet-web builders with no retreat; some vagrant hunters
- Body length: 1–5 mm

Australia:
Taxonomy poorly resolved
current: 6 species in 3 genera
estimated: 120 species in 7 genera
World: 250 species in 27 genera

The Comb-tailed Spiders (family Hahniidae) are small and hence comparatively rarely collected in Australia. Their colloquial name originates in the comb-like arrangement of their spinnerets under the abdomen; these generally reach substantially beyond the tip of the abdomen. The outermost pair, the posterior lateral spinnerets, is longest due to a greatly elongated end-segment. Internally, the tracheal system is peculiar, as tracheoles extend through the pedicel into the cephalothorax.

Three genera include described species in Australia, but genus level identification requires an examination of genitalia under a stereomicroscope. *Alistra* is a largely Oriental-Australasian genus; *A. astrolomae* is known from Tasmania and *A. pusilla* occurs on Lord Howe Island. Seven species of *Alistra* are known from New Zealand. *Neoaviola* includes a single species worldwide, *N. insolens* from Victoria. *Scotospilus* includes three described species from Tasmania, but the genus has also been reported from New Zealand, India and Vietnam. This total account of six species, however, represents only a fraction of the diversity of Comb-tailed Spiders in Australia.

Comb-tailed Spiders are mainly known from tropical and temperate regions in Australia, and very few have been collected in the arid or semi-arid parts of the country. Most Hahniidae live near the ground in grass tussocks, low shrubs or moss, or under stones. They are often found in the vicinity of rivers and streams; however, they have also been collected from under the bark of trees. In the cold heaths of Tasmania's highlands these spiders are reproductively active from December to March. In Queensland, at higher altitudes, mature males can also be found throughout the extended summer, but at lower altitudes they are found all year round.

Little is known about the biology of Comb-tailed Spider species in Australia. Some are known to construct delicate sheet-webs, which are suspended in shallow depressions in the ground or between grass or moss. *Scotospilus bicolor* spins a small sheet-web under loose bark of eucalypts, in which the spider rests on the upper surface. The lenticular eggsac is usually attached to the substrate near the web.

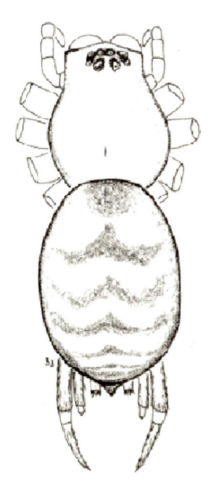

Above: The spinnerets of Comb-tailed Spiders, here details of an unidentified species from Stradbroke Island, Queensland, are arranged in a single row. The outermost spinnerets are the longest. [B.C. Baehr]

Left: Comb-tailed Spiders (family Hahniidae) are easily recognised by the arrangement of the spinnerets and the fishbone pattern on their dorsal abdomen, but they are difficult to distinguish in the field due to their small size. The genus- and species-level taxonomy is poorly resolved for the Australian species. [B.C. Baehr]

DICTYNIDAE
Mesh-web Spiders

- Six or eight eyes in two weakly curved rows, subequal in size
- Chelicerae S-shaped, strongly bowed in males
- Legs without spines, tarsi with three claws
- Cribellate; cribellum entire, calamistrum reduced
- Plant- (or rarely ground-) dwelling spiders with prey capture web forming ladder-shaped structures
- Body length: 2–5 mm

Australia:
Taxonomy poorly resolved
current: 3 species in 2 genera
estimated: 50 species in 4 genera
World: 575 species in 51 genera

Mesh-web Spiders (family Dictynidae) are small plant-dwelling spiders which construct ladder-like webs consisting of parallel threads criss-crossed with a hackled band of cribellate silk in grass or low shrubs. In New Zealand, species in the genus *Arangina* build their snares between alluvial gravel in riverbeds. Dictynidae are easily identified by the peculiar, bowed shape of the chelicerae in males, which are used to disable the female chelicerae during mating.

The Mesh-web Spiders together with the Comb-tailed Spiders (Hahniidae) and the Intertidal and House Spiders (Desidae) have been suggested to form a group of related spiders, the subfamily Dictynoidea, based on the presence of a strongly branched median pair of trachea.

Similar to the Sheet Orb-weaving Spiders (family Linyphiidae), the Mesh-web Spiders are most diverse in the Northern Hemisphere and the Australian fauna appears comparatively small. However, the taxonomy of the family is poorly resolved in Australia, where only three species are described, all based on historic studies from the end of the 19th century. Dictynidae can be found in all climatic zones throughout the country.

The endemic Australian genus *Callevophthalmus* includes *C. albus*, which has been reported from New South Wales, including Lord Howe Island, and Western Australia suggesting an Australia-wide distribution, and *C. maculatus* which so far has only been reported from New South Wales. *Sudesna anaulax* was described from Western Australia; the genus is otherwise known also from China, South-East Asia and India.

Males of Mesh-web Spiders, here an unidentified species from the Perth Hills in Western Australia, have strong, bowed chelicerae, which they use to embrace and disable the female chelicerae during mating. [F. Bokhari]

SPARASSIDAE
Huntsman Spiders, Giant Crab Spiders

- Eight eyes in two more or less straight rows
- Carapace broadly oval, flattened
- Legs long, directed sideward ('laterigrade'), tarsi with two claws and dense claw tufts, metatarsi and tarsi often with dense scopulae
- Light brown to brown, dark mottled, sometimes green
- Extremely fast runners
- Mostly habitat specialists living under bark or in narrow crevices in rock piles and rocky outcrops
- Night active hunters without prey capture web
- Body length: 6–40 mm

Australia:
Partially revised
Current: 150 species in 18 genera
Estimated: 200 species in 15 genera
World: 1,132 species in 84 genera

The Huntsman Spiders (family Sparassidae) belong to one of the most distinctive groups of the Australian spider fauna. Few Australians will not have had a sudden encounter with one of these large spiders, which may either have rushed out from behind a picture on the wall or from furniture, or may have dropped into the driver's or passenger's lap in a car. Huntsman Spiders are generally large spiders with a more or less flat body and a crab-like ('laterigrade') arrangement of the legs. This morphology is perfectly adapted to the natural habitat of many species, which is a life under the bark of trees or in small crevices under rocks. In addition to two tarsal claws, they have dense pads of hairs on the ends of their legs, which allow them to easily climb almost any vertical surface. They may even be seen scuttling on a ceiling.

Huntsman Spiders are found in the warm temperate to subtropical regions worldwide. Over 200 species are estimated to occur in Australia and they are found throughout the country from the tropics to high altitude regions of Tasmania.

Huntsman Spiders are night active hunters that do not build a prey capture web. They can easily be found at night with the use of a head torch as their eyes reflect light similar to those of Wolf Spiders (family Lycosidae). However, in contrast to

Huntsman Spiders (family Sparassidae) have their eight eyes arranged in two more or less straight rows. This arrangement is very different to that of the Wall Crab Spiders (family Selenopidae) with which they could be confused. Wall Crab Spiders have a single row of six eyes at the front with the fourth pair set back behind. [F. Bokhari]

Heteropoda venatoria, here photographed in the tropical forests of Christmas Island, is a pantropical species which occurs in tropical Australia and along the east coast into Brisbane. They differ from the most common native species by the white moustache just above the fangs. [V.W. Framenau, Phoenix Environmental Sciences]

Wolf Spiders, which are mainly ground hunters, the eye reflection of Huntsman Spiders will originate mainly from the vegetation. Upon closer examination, members of both families cannot be confused based on a very different eye-pattern. During the day Huntsman Spiders hide under the bark of trees but they also frequent tight spaces around houses, including behind picture frames, curtains and

This *Yiinthi lycodes* male from Cooktown in Queensland, looks and behaves like a Wolf Spider, which is reflected in the species' Latin name. It forages in the leaf litter of the rainforests of northern Australia and New Guinea. [R.J. Raven]

Based on the number of described species, *Heteropoda*, here an unidentified male from the Northern Territory, is the most diverse genus in Australia. *Heteropoda* occur mainly in the northern half of the country with a preference for subtropical and tropical rainforests. [P. Zborowski]

furniture, and in folded towels and clothes. Huntsman Spiders lay a variety of flat, disk-like eggsacs, which are usually attached under the bark of trees.

Despite their large size, Huntsman Spiders are not known to inflict a serious bite on humans. They often show very aggressive behaviour when disturbed and bites are relatively frequent, for example when people pick up logs under which they hide, or if they cause stress to a spider that was hiding in washing on the clothes line. Effects are local, including puncture marks and minor bleeding, with associated pain which only lasts for a short time. Systemic effects are very rare but may include nausea and headache.

The Australian fauna of Huntsman Spiders belongs to two different subfamilies, the Heteropodinae and the Deleninae, with the latter apparently most diverse in Australia. Differences between the subfamilies relate to details of the genitalia in addition to cheliceral dentition and size of the lateral eyes. Males in the Heteropodinae have an uncoiled embolus, whereas it is a multiple-stacked coil in the Deleninae; the female epigyne lacks a sclerotised rim in the Heteropodinae which is present in the Deleninae. The spiders in the subfamily Heteropodinae are mainly found in the northern half of the country and dominate the tropical sparassid fauna, whereas the Deleninae are found throughout.

The **Heteropodinae** include five genera in Australia: *Heteropoda*, *Yiinthi*, *Pandercetes*, *Keilira* and *Irileka*. Of these, *Heteropoda* is the most diverse with 41 species. The genus occurs mainly in the northern half of the country. It includes the pantropical *H. venatoria*. Males of these species have been reported to use substrate-borne vibration, mainly abdominal drumming, in the presence of a female. The signal conveys to the female that he is not prey and may help also her in deciding if he is a worthy father for her offspring. Similar behaviours have been studied in many other spiders such as Wolf Spiders (Lycosidae) and Jumping Spiders (Salticidae).

Members of *Yiinthi* are similar to *Heteropoda* and also occur in the tropics, where eight species have been reported from Western Australia through to Queensland. The carapace is centrally orange-brown and darker laterally and the abdomen also has a pale upper central area. One of the most distinctive Huntsman Spiders in the subfamily Heteropodinae is the Lichen Huntsman, *Pandercetes gracilis*. It can easily be distinguished from other Huntsman Spiders by its cryptic grey-green coloration and lateral fringes of hairs on the legs. The species occurs from Sulawesi south to New Guinea and along the Queensland coast.

Keilira includes the smallest Australian Huntsman Spiders, which have a body length of about 10 mm or less. Two species are currently described from Victoria and South Australia, but unnamed species have been recorded from south-western Western Australia and eastern Queensland. *Irileka iridescens*, the only representative of *Irileka*, is not much larger. This species has an iridescent red-brown coloration on the frontal parts of the carapace. Similar unnamed species appear to occur in Queensland.

The **Deleninae** is a diverse Australian subfamily of Huntsman Spiders which includes ten genera. However, based on molecular research this genus arrangement appears to inflate actual diversity at least in in relation to *Isopeda*, *Holconia* and *Isopedella*, which may only represent a single genus, and possibly in relation to *Neosparassus* and *Zachria*. It is therefore difficult to comment on genus-level characteristics. *Neosparassus* includes the Badge or Shield Huntsman Spiders, named for their conspicuous colour patterns on the underside of the abdomen. *Neosparassus diana* is the most common of these and occurs throughout southern Australia. In addition to the above two genus-complexes the Deleninae includes: *Pediana* with 10 species; the related *Beregama* with two species; and three species of the Giant Green Huntsman Spiders, *Typostola*. Whilst *Pediana* is found throughout the country, *Beregama* occurs in New Guinea and south along the Queensland Coast. *Typostola* are also more common in the northern half of Australia, but have been found into New South Wales and Victoria. The Giant Green Huntsman Spiders stand out by having green haemolymph which can be seen through the leg joints.

Most remarkably, the Deleninae include the social spiders of the genus *Delena*. *Delena cancerides* is the best studied of these. The colonies of these spiders consists of a single female and her numerous offspring. After the maternal female dies, the colony retreat is subsequently occupied by one of her adult daughters.

The listing of *Palystes pinnotheres*, the only representative of the subfamily **Palystinae** in Australia, is historical and therefore it is not clear whether the genus actually occurs in this country until a taxonomic re-assessment has occurred. *Palystes pinnotheres* was also reported from New Caledonia.

The male Lichen Huntsman, *Pandercetes gracilis*, is perfectly camouflaged on white bark lichen in north Queensland. A fringe of hairs along its outline eliminates shadows. It is the only representative of the genus in Australia, but other species are known from India and South-East Asia. [R. Farrow]

This green male of a Lichen Huntsman, *Pandercetes gracilis*, rests quietly on tree leaves in the day, covered in messy looking green tufts. On a more suitable background its irregular outline can make it virtually invisible to predators and prey. [R.J. Raven]

Huntsman Spiders are mostly solitary, but the Social Huntsman Spider, *Delena cancerides*, which prefers cooler dry climates, forms colonies beneath bark. The species is known from eucalypt forest in eastern and southern Australia. Many innocent campers and arachnologists have been showered by hundreds of young when they have pulled bark off a tree. Molecular data suggest that *Delena cancerides* does not represent a single species. It is also not the only social *Delena*; it shares its gregarious habits with *D. lapidicola* and *D. melanochelis*. [R.J. Raven]

The Shield or Badge Huntsman Spiders, genus *Neosparassus*, have a relatively higher head and the fangs look more impressive. The underside of the legs are often decorated with white spots. [P. Zborowski]

The Bark Huntsman Spiders, genus *Pediana*, here an unidentified female from central eastern Queensland, occurs throughout Australia. The most common species is *P. regina*, which has been found in Queensland, New South Wales and also northern Western Australia. As with many species of Huntsman Spiders, Bark Huntsman Spiders built their retreat under loose bark and hunt at night on the tree trunks. [R.J. Raven]

Isopeda leishmanni is one of the most frequently encountered Huntsman Spiders in the suburbs of Perth, where this image of a male was taken. The species' range extends into southern South Australia and Victoria. [V.W. Framenau, Phoenix Environmental Sciences]

This female Badge Huntsman Spider, *Neosparassus diana*, was photographed in Melbourne. It has a comparatively large abdomen suggesting that it is about to lay eggs. [V.W. Framenau, Phoenix Environmental Sciences]

The colloquial name Badge or Shield Huntsman Spiders for species in the genus *Neosparassus* (here an immature spider from Western Australia) refers to the colour pattern on the underside of the abdomen. Shield Huntsman Spiders build a small sphere of leaves in which they place the eggsac and stand and guard over it. [F. Bokhari]

Opposite page: The Grey Huntsman Spider, *Holconia immanis*, is one of the most common house spiders, hunting at night on walls and ceilings in eastern Australia. It is surefooted even on very smooth surfaces. Away from human dwellings, *Holconia* are at home beneath the loose bark of eucalypt trees, where they hide during the day. [J. Haider]

DESIDAE
Intertidal Spiders, House Spiders

- Eight eyes in two rows, occupying about half of head width
- Cribellum, if present, undivided
- Calamistrum proximal on metatarsus of fourth leg
- Spinnerets stout, broad, anterior pair contiguous
- Legs long or stout, with three tarsal claws and with or without scopula
- Night active hunters with retreats of varying size
- Body length: 5–22 mm

Australia:
Taxonomy recently partly revised
Current: 51 species in 12 genera
Estimated: 70 species in 15 genera
World: 182 species in 38 genera

There are considerable difficulties in delineating family limits within a large group of spiders currently referred to the superfamily Amaurobioidea, which includes the Australian Desidae as well as the families treated in the following four chapters, namely the Stiphidiidae, Amphinectidae, Agelenidae and Amaurobiidae. The fact that generally no single colloquial name exists for any of these families reflects the diversity of spiders within each of these families and the uncertainty if the respective included genera represent a group of evolutionary related species.

The Desidae, which include the House Spiders (genus *Badumna*) but also the Intertidal Spiders (genus *Desis*), are a good example. It is very difficult to characterise the Desidae morphologically and therefore typical representative genera are treated separately here. Often the inclusion of genera in the Desidae (or any of the other families mentioned above) must be taken more as an opinion of the scientist who worked on the group at the time than of any rigorous phylogenetic analysis.

In the absence of a systematic study, accepted subfamilies for the Desidae have not been proposed, although it is accepted that *Desis* itself is a highly derived genus within the current assortment of genera of the family. Some interrelationships of genera have been suggested, for example a 'badumnine' group that includes *Badumna*, *Phryganoporus* and *Forsterina*, based on a sinuous embolus of the male pedipalp, and a 'namandiine' group with spoon-shaped membranous median apophysis including the Australian *Namandia* and *Paramatachia*.

The Black House Spider, *Badumna insignis*, here a female from Queensland, is a dark robust spider with a dark brown front and a dark greyish back with lighter markings. *Badumna insignis* builds a funnel-shaped retreat attached to a sheet-web, which is densely layered with cribellate silk. They often do so around houses, where artificial nooks and crannies help them to fashion their retreats. [P. Zborowski]

Purely by nomenclatural rule, the Intertidal Spiders of the genus *Desis* must belong to the Desidae as the family name is based on this genus. These are ecribellate spiders that live in the intertidal zone of our seashores. Here, they build a silk-lined retreat in empty shells, cavities and holes in rocks or corals. The opening of the retreat is closed by the spider during high tide, and air trapped inside allows the spider to breath. There are published records of two species of *Desis* in Australia: *D. kenyone* from Tasmania and *D. hartmeyeri* from Western Australia. *Desis*, however, has been found around Australia and it is likely that more species in the genus occur. In the absence of a comprehensive taxonomic treatment it is

This unidentified *Badumna* female from northern Queensland hides during daytime under bark in her cribellate retreat. [R.J. Raven]

Phryganoporus candidus, here a female from Queensland, is common throughout the country. These spiders are about 5 mm long with a light grey pubescence.
[R.J. Raven]

difficult to judge the distribution of these spiders, although dispersal on floating objects may allow them to distribute themselves fairly widely.

The House Spiders of the genus *Badumna* are familiar to every Australian. Most common are the Black House Spider, *B. insignis*, and the Brown House Spider, *B. longinqua*. Both species differ in coloration, as their names suggest, with the Black House Spider darker overall. This is also the more widespread species, which appears to cope better with more arid conditions. Their cribellate, messy sheet-web, that often leads into a funnel-shaped retreat, can be found at or in almost any house in Australia. The web of the spider is, however, adaptable and spiders may build it simply in the corner between wall and ceiling without retreat. Bites of the Black and Brown House Spiders can be quite painful and can cause swelling and occasionally nausea, vomiting and sweating. A total of 14 species in the genus *Badumna* are described for Australia, but modern taxonomic treatments are lacking for most of them and their distribution patterns remain unknown.

The species of the genus *Phryganoporus* are apparently closely related to *Badumna* based on similarities in genital and overall morphology. They differ by the strong presence of white hairs and details in genital morphology. The genus includes four solitary species, but *P. candidus* is known for subsocial behaviour in which spiders of the same clutch remain together before they mature. Large aggregations of communal webs can often be observed, but social interactions are generally limited to immatures below the subadult stage. The species is found throughout Australia in almost all climatic zones but has not been reported from Tasmania. *Phryganoporus nigrinus* is found in open woodland and areas with shrubs in Western Australia, throughout the arid zone and into western Queensland and New South Wales. This solitary species lives in strong tubular retreats from which an irregular capture web originates. *Phryganoporus melanopygus* occurs in central Western Australia, *P. davidleei* mainly in southern South Australia and into Western Australia, and *P. vandiemeni* is known from Tasmania and Victoria's Wilsons Promontory.

Forsterina has morphological affinities with *Badumna* and *Phryganoporus* and includes seven described species in Australia; however, a recent taxonomic revision is not available.

The genera *Paramatachia*, with five species in Australia, and *Namandia*, which only includes a single named species, *N. periscelis*, represent the 'namandiine'

The intertidal spider, *Desis kenyone*, has been identified from Tasmania and the specimen in this image, photographed in Elwood, Victoria, possibly belongs to the same species. These spiders live in silk-lined hideouts in the intertidal zone, where they remain during high tide. They leave the retreat during low tide to forage on intertidal arthropods. Females with eggsac remain in the retreat until the spiderlings hatch. [G. Fitzpatrick]

spiders based on male pedipalp and spinneret confirmation. This informal group also includes a number of New Zealand genera. *Paramatachia*, the Cribellate Twig Spiders, are found in south-eastern Australia where individuals live in holes and crevices in the vegetation with webs that include ladder-like structures and incorporate cribellate zig-zag lines. Little is known about *Namandia periscelis* which is only recorded from Tasmania.

A number of other genera have been included in the Desidae, namely *Pitonga* with a single species, *P. woolwa*, from the tropical Northern Territory; *Colcarteria*, with three species from New South Wales; and *Taurongia* with two cribellate species from Victoria. *Epimecinus* includes a single species from Western Australia, *E. alkirna*, in addition to three species from New Caledonia. *Lastrygones* includes a single species, *L. setosus*, from Tasmania in addition to five

This unidentified, possibly new species of *Desis* lives amongst brain corals in the intertidal zone of northern Queensland. This female was captured south of Cairns; it was discovered at night at about 1.30 am at extreme low tide and during the full moon, and it was walking on the corals. [R.J. Raven]

New Zealand species. These ecribellate spiders have previously been included in the Oxypopidae, *Stiphidion* (then placed in the Psechridae), Perissoblemmidae, Toxopidae, and Zodariidae. They are agile hunters found in grassy habitats. *Lathyarcha* includes two species from eastern Australia and one from Western Australia. *Myro maculatus* from Tasmania is the only Australian species in the genus and is apparently related to *Ommatauxenus macrops*, also from Tasmania, as both genera were included in a subfamily Myroninae. *Paratheuma* is a Pacific genus. The only Australian representative, *P. australis*, can also be found in Fiji. These spiders live close to the high-tide mark among broken coral on the beach. The genus *Toxops* includes only a single species, *T. montanus* from Tasmania, as does *Cicirra*, with the single species *C. decemmaculata*. *Syrosis misella* has an unusual disjunct distribution as it has only been reported from New Caledonia and Western Australia.

The small species of *Paramatachia*, the Cribellate Twig Spiders, have a tiny retreat in insect holes left in twigs, from where the web originates. Parts of the web are shaped like a ladder with cribellate silk. [R.J. Raven]

Phryganoporus candidus builds conglomerates of messy cribellate webs that can be about 1 m wide in trees or shrubs. These spiders are subsocial and offspring of the same clutch stay together until they mature. [R.J. Raven]

Phryganoporus nigrinus constructs a tube-shaped retreat from which a messy, irregular web of cribellate silk is built into the vegetation. [V.W. Framenau, Phoenix Environmental Sciences]

Phryganoporus nigrinus is a solitary spider that occurs mainly in Western Australia and into the arid zone. [F. Bokhari]

STIPHIDIIDAE
Platform Spiders, Cone-web Spiders, Sombrero Spiders, Labyrinth Spiders

- Eight eyes in two rows
- Abdomen oval, grey with cinnamon and pale chevrons
- Legs slender, tarsi with three claws
- Cribellum divided if present, or absent
- Calamistrum consisting of single row of bristles, very short
- Sheet-web of varying shapes
- Body length: 4–20 mm

Australia:
Partially revised
Current: 93 species in 17 genera
Estimated: 130 species in 20 genera
World: 135 species in 22 genera

Members of the Stiphidiidae have received a number of colloquial names and these invariably refer to the impressive sheet-webs that some of these spiders construct, and which often have a genus-specific shape. The family has received considerable taxonomic attention and many genera and species are known from Australia; however, family uniting features are poorly defined, and taxonomic publications have often not referred to the family name but the superfamily Amaurobioidea. The family includes largely cribellate spiders and, if present, the cribellum is divided.

Species of the Stiphidiidae, in particular the smaller species, are often fairly 'nondescript' with a red-brown carapace and greyish abdomen which have an irregular lighter or darker pattern. Identification of genera and species in the field is often impossible as it relates to characters of the genitalia.

Stiphidiids have a southern distribution and are most common in temperate and subtropical rainforests of Australia, including in Tasmania. They also occur in New Guinea, New Zealand, New Caledonia, Mauritius and Madagascar.

Internal eye morphology, i.e. the distribution of the various types of reflective layers (tapetum) may help in delineating relationships between members of this family and their relatives. Three subfamilies have been established to accommodate stiphidiid genera, the Stiphidiinae, the Borralinae and the Kababininae; however, these have not been comprehensively tested with modern phylogenetic methods.

The subfamily **Stiphidiinae** is poorly circumscribed but here includes

This female of *Corasoides* from Kalamunda in Western Australia has made a meal of a *Camponotus* ant that apparently fell onto the web. *Corasoides* includes a single described species in Australia, but the genus is probably more diverse. [F. Bokhari]

The genus *Baiami*, here a *B. tegenaroides* female, is most diverse in Western Australia. The general carapace and abdomen pattern is characteristic for the genus that includes nine described species in Australia. [V.W. Framenau, Phoenix Environmental Sciences]

This male *Baiami volucripes* from Western Australia displays its large pedipalps; however, the pedipalp tibia is comparatively short in comparison to some other species in the genus. This species is a forest dweller but can commonly be found in or near the entrances to caves. [V.W. Framenau, Phoenix Environmental Sciences]

those genera traditionally included in the family, such as *Stiphidion*, *Baiami*, *Procambridgea* and *Tartarus*. Species in the genus *Baiami* are medium-sized to large, cribellate, web-building spiders of up to 13 mm in body length. The carapace is pale to dark greyish-brown and has a more or less distinct patch of darker pigment in front of the fovea. The abdomen is light to dark grey with a paler anterior mid-dorsal band. The nine species in the genus occur in south-western Western Australia into South Australia. The sheet-web of *Baiami* can be an impressive 1 m in diameter. The spider moves on the underside of the sheet. Species of the genus *Tartarus* had previously been included in *Baiami*. The genus now includes four cave-dwelling species from the Nullarbor Plain in Western Australia. They display typical adaptation for underground life such as lack of eyes and pigment and comparatively long legs.

Procambridgea includes small species of up to about 5 mm body length. The cribellum is divided but only present in females; males have a large colulus. They construct a sheet-web in hollows of fallen logs and the spiders rest on the underside. The 12 species of the genus have a coastal distribution in eastern Australia from central Queensland to Victoria. *Stiphidion* are cribellate spiders with a strongly

The Platform Spider, *Corasoides australis*, is found throughout eastern Australia. Its extensive sheet-web is strung out from embankments and tree buttresses. The large, very fast, striped spider runs on top of the web, and when disturbed retreats quickly to a small tube near the tree. [R.J. Raven]

recurved posterior eye row. The web is umbrella-shaped and reminiscent of a Sombrero hat. *Stiphidion* includes four species from the eastern coast, but is also found in Victoria, South Australia and Tasmania.

Corasoides has a southern Australian distribution but also occurs in rainforests in the tropics. Here, unlike many rainforest spiders, they may also occupy sandy heaths. These spiders cover their eggs in multiple layers of silk interspersed with substrate, such as soil, debris, dirt particles or sand. Unlike many other stiphidiids, *Corasoides* usually travels on the top of the web with enormous speed. The genus includes a single described species, *C. australis*, but is clearly more diverse. *Barahna* are small cribellate spiders. The eight species of the genus occur in wet sclerophyll vine scrub and open eucalypt forest from central eastern Queensland into Victoria.

Members of the **Borralinae** are gracile, cribellate spiders and all, with the exception of *Therlinya*, have a longitudinally striped pattern on the carapace. All members of the subfamily have a grate-shaped tapetum in all posterior eyes. The eight genera of the subfamily are widely distributed along the coastal and highland forest regions of eastern Australia from central Queensland into Victoria. *Therlinya* also occurs in Tasmania and the genus *Karriella* consists only of two species which are endemic to south-west Western Australia. Overall, genera in this subfamily show fairly localised distributions; the four species in *Borrala* are restricted to south-eastern Queensland and northern New South Wales; the two species of *Elleguna* occur in coastal areas of central Queensland; *Jamberoo*, with four species, ranges from central New South Wales into Victoria; and *Pillara*, with four species, is only found in central eastern New South Wales. Boralline spiders are forest-dwellers that construct simple, cribellate sheet-webs at logs, rocks and stable embankments. The sheet tapers into a short funnel-like entrance of stronger silk that leads into a sparsely silk-lined retreat hole. As with most stiphidiid, the spiders run upside-down under the sheet.

The subfamily **Kababininae** is poorly defined. It includes stiphidiids in which the carapace is highest in the fovea region. A cribellum may be present, except in the four species of the genus *Carbinea*. Coloration of the abdomen varies from pale to dark grey-black with an arrangement of light spots in vague chevron pattern. They occur in the wet tropics of northern to central eastern Queensland. In addition to *Carbinea*, the subfamily includes the cribellate *Kababina* with nine species; *Wabua* with 11 species; and *Malarina* with four species.

A Sombrero Spider male, genus *Stiphidion*, has a unique kind of web that consists of a small roughly circular sheet suspended above the substrate and joined to it via a wide cylindrical column of silk that has several arches near the ground. The spider rests and hunts within the space formed by the arches and column. Overall, the web is reminiscent of a sombrero hat, which is how the genus received its colloquial name. [both images: R.J. Raven]

AMPHINECTIDAE
Forest Hunters

- Eight eyes in two straight or slightly curved rows
- Legs strong, with three claws; sometimes with scopula
- Six spinnerets
- Cribellum divided, if present, or absent
- Calamistrum, if present, a single row of bristles
- Nocturnal hunters without prey capture web; hiding in silken retreat during the day
- Body length: 3–12 mm

Australia:
Taxonomy revised
Current: 33 species in 12 genera
Estimated: 40 species in 12 genera
World: 159 species in 32 genera

The Forest Hunters (family Amphinectidae) are ground-dwelling spiders found from tropical to temperate forests, although a number of species have been reported from caves. Forest Hunters are inconspicuous spiders that do not build a prey capture web. As with other families in the superfamily Amaurobioidea, the Amphinectidae are poorly circumscribed. The family includes large ecribellate but also cribellate spiders in Australia. They generally forage at night through leaf litter and hide during the daytime in burrow-like retreats. The cribellate representatives appear to construct a small sheet-web stretching from the retreat.

Forest Hunters are restricted to South America, south-eastern mainland Australia, Tasmania and New Zealand. The Australian amphinectids can be divided into two subfamilies, the Metaltellinae and the Tasmarubriinae, which are primarily identified through characters of the male genitalia.

Males in the **Metaltellinae** are easily recognised by the anticlockwise direction of the embolus of the left male pedipalp. The Australian metaltellines generally have a brown carapace, which is somewhat darker in the cephalic area. The abdomen is brown-black with lighter chevron pattern. The anterior median eyes are reduced.

The only cribellate genus of the family is *Quemusia*. These spiders are less than 5 mm long and occur along the Queensland and northern New South Wales coast.

Ecribellate genera include *Austmusia*, *Buyina*, *Cunnawarra*, *Jalkaburra*, *Keera*, *Magua* and *Peenaola*.

The subfamily **Tasmarubriinae** includes only ecribellate spiders. The male pedipalp has a short and thick embolus and the tegulum is divided. The subfamily is largely restricted to Tasmania, with a single species, *Tanganoides harveyi*, known from Victoria. *Tasmarubrius* include five Tasmanian species, *Tasmabrochus* and *Teeatta* three species each, and *Tanganoides* five Tasmanian representatives in addition to the above-mentioned Victorian species.

Forest Hunters (family Amphinectidae) are largely vagrant forest dwellers, but some live in caves, like this sub-adult male *Tanganoides clarkei*. This image was taken on the banks of Base Camp Tributary, deep in Exit Cave at Ida Bay, 1.8 km from the nearest entrance. [A. Clarke]

The European House Spider, *Tegenaria domestica* (family Agelenidae), has established populations in Australia with confirmed records from Tasmania and Victoria. It is a cosmopolitan, synanthropic species that is found in and around houses. They build sheet-webs with a large funnel that they add to constantly and which therefore can become fairly large. [R. Vetter]

AGELENIDAE
Funnel-web Weavers

- Eight eyes in two slightly procurved or straight rows
- Trichobothria on female pedipalp and male cymbium absent
- Abdomen with plumose hairs
- End segment of posterior spinnerets elongate
- Sheet-web with funnel retreat
- Body length: 8–12 mm

Australia:
Taxonomy of single indigenous species unclear
Current: 2 species in 2 genera
Estimated: 1 species in 1 genus
World: 1,156 species in 68 genera

The single confirmed member of the Funnel-web Weavers (family Agelenidae) in Australia is the cosmopolitan and synanthropic European House Spider, *Tegenaria domestica*. The family characterisation above refers to this species. The only published record is from Tasmania; however, the species was apparently also collected in Melbourne in the 1950s.

The European House Spider can easily be identified by the elongated endsegment of the posterior spinnerets, a character unique within Australian spiders. They are inconspicuous brownish spiders with a light chevron pattern on the abdomen. The European House Spider constructs sheet-webs which lead into a funnel where the spider resides and waits for prey to get entangled on the sheet. They are very fast movers once prey is detected. Males wandering in search of a mate may frequently get trapped in slippery bath tubs.

The second genus of the Agelenidae currently listed for Australia is *Oramia*, with *Oramia frequens* described from Lord Howe Island. However, these records are historical and the species was originally described in the genus *Amaurobius*. A taxonomic reassessment is required to confirm *Oramia* for Australia. The genus is currently known from New Zealand only where seven species are described. All are inhabitants of the spray zone of shingle beaches where they construct small webs between stones.

AMAUROBIIDAE
Hackled-mesh Weavers

- Eight eyes in two rows
- Indistinct brown coloration
- Median apophysis of male pedipalp sclerotised, variable plate-shaped
- Cribellate and ecribellate
- Tangle- or sheet-web with retreat or vagrant
- Body length: 1–10 mm

Australia:
Taxonomy poorly resolved, even at family level
Current: 41 species in 9 genera
Estimated: 100 species in 15 genera
World: 285 species in 52 genera

Invariably, the family Amaurobiidae in Australia serves as a 'dumping ground' for those amaurobioid spiders that cannot be placed in any of the other families belonging to this large group and treated previously, namely Desidae, Stiphidiidae, Amphinectidae and Agelenidae. It remains somewhat fruitless to characterise this family in the Australian context. Original descriptions of genera often refer to the superfamily Amaurobioidea, rather than explicitly naming a family.

The genera included in the family Amaurobiidae includes spiders with and without cribellum. They are overall brown, nondescript spiders, often with strong ventral spines on the first pair of legs. They are tangle- or sheet-web builders that may rest in a retreat, but the family also includes vagrant representatives. The New Zealand amaurobiids have been defined by male genital characters, including a sclerotised, variable plate-like median apophysis, and a simple tracheal system. Australian amaurobiids inhabit the ground, in particular the litter layer in forests, although some species have been collected from tree foliage.

The genera *Storenosoma* and *Oztira* contain free-living, ground-dwelling ecribellate spiders with strongly procurved eye rows. The posterior lateral eyes and sometimes the posterior median eyes are noticeably larger than those of the anterior row. The eye pattern and body coloration give them a superficial resemblance to Wolf Spiders (family Lycosidae). At present, they are only known from eastern and south-eastern Australia. Members of *Oztira* are small (< 2.5 mm) and can be differentiated from those of *Storenosoma* (3–6 mm) by smaller size

The genus *Midgee* includes very small amaurobiid spiders, such as *M. binnaburra* from south-eastern Queensland and north-eastern New South Wales. [B.C. Baehr]

and a distally somewhat swollen metatarsus of the first leg in males. Species-level identification within these genera requires examination of the genitalia.

Oztira is known from four species in disjunct patches from northern and south-eastern Queensland and Tasmania, whereas *Storenosoma* has a south-eastern distribution; its 13 species are found from south-eastern Queensland into Tasmania.

A number of tropical and subtropical amaurobiids appear closely related. The single species of *Bakala*, *B. episinoides*, is known from northern Queensland. Similarly, two species of *Manjala*, *M. pallida* and *M. spinosa*, occur in tropical Queensland, whereas the third species of the genus was found near Brisbane. *Midgee* includes very small, ecribellate spiders. Nine species occur from tropical eastern Queensland to central eastern New South Wales. A fourth genus, *Jamara*, with a single, tiny (ca. 1–1.2 mm long) cribellate species was described from moss on tree trunks or rocks at an altitude of about 1,500 m on Bellenden Ker and Bartle Frere in tropical Queensland. Both *Midgee* and *Jamara* have been referred to as Midgeeinae, although this subfamily name has not been formally established.

The genus *Daviesa* includes two tree-dwelling ecribellate species collected in rainforests from northern to south-eastern Queensland. They are about 10 mm in body length and are straw-coloured with little discernable colour pattern on the abdomen.

Wabarra is known from northern Queensland and one of the species, *W. caverna*, was found in limestone caves. *Dardurus* includes six species from eastern Australia with paired spines on the tibiae and metatarsi of the first and second legs. They build a short, U-shaped burrow with soil encrusting the web.

Species in the amaurobiid genus *Dardurus* from eastern Australia construct a U-shaped retreat door. [R.J. Raven]

CYCLOCTENIDAE
Scuttling Spiders

- Eight eyes in two strongly recurved rows; posterior eyes much larger than anterior eyes
- Legs long and more or less laterigrade (directed sideways); double row of spines on tibiae and metatarsi of the first leg; tarsi with three claws and no claw tufts
- Free-living nocturnal-hunting spiders without prey capture web
- Body length: 10–15 mm

Australia:
Taxonomy poorly resolved
Current: 7 species in 1 genus
Estimated: 30 species in 3 genera
World: 36 species in 5 genera

The common name Scuttling Spiders for members of the family Cycloctenidae refers to the rapid sideways scuttle of the spiders when disturbed. They are ground-dwelling spiders reminiscent of Wolf Spiders (family Lycosidae); however, their posterior eyes do not form a square as in the Australian representatives of Wolf Spiders, but are arranged in a trapezoid with the posterior lateral eyes furthest apart. Scuttling Spiders are medium-sized to large, somewhat flattened spiders that freely hunt in forest litter and on logs and bark, but have also been found in caves. They have an indistinct mottled brown coloration which provides good camouflage in their preferred habitats.

Scuttling Spiders are currently known from five genera in Australia, New Zealand and Indonesia (Java). In Australia, only the genus *Cycloctenus* has named species; however, the family has not been taxonomically treated and it is likely that it is more diverse at the genus level. These spiders are mainly found along the east coast of the country from tropical Queensland into Tasmania, but unnamed species of the family have also been found in south-west Western Australia.

Four species are described from Tasmania: *Cycloctenus montivagus*, *C. infrequens*, *C. flavus*, and *C. cryptophilus*. Two species were described from New South Wales: *C. abyssinus* from Jenolan Caves and *C. robustus* from Sydney. The locality of the seventh Australia representative, *C. flaviceps*, is unknown.

Females normally attach their lenticular eggsac beneath bark, camouflaging it with small debris. They remain until the young have hatched.

This unidentified male of *Cycloctenus* from Tasmania appears to favour fallen logs and bark to hunt. *Cycloctenus* is currently the only genus of Scuttling Spider (family Cycloctenidae) that has named species in Australia. The family is widely distributed in rainforests and temperate forests on the east coast of Australia, but has also been recorded from south-west Western Australia. [R.J. Raven]

An unidentified *Cycloctenus* from a cave at Cobberas, Alpine National Park in Victoria, is making a meal of a fungus gnat fly (family Mycetophilidae). [J. Finn]

ZODARIIDAE
Ant-eating Spiders

- Eight eyes in two procurved rows
- Chelicerae with strong lateral condyle
- Legs strong with spines; tarsi with three claws
- Median and posterior spinnerets reduced or absent, anterior spinnerets retractile (Lachesaninae) or on common base (Zodariinae)
- Day or night active hunters, without prey capture web
- Body length: 2–21 mm

Australia:
Partially revised
current: 252 species in 30 genera
estimated: 450 species in 35 genera
World: 1070 species in 78 genera

It is not surprising that the Ant-eating Spiders (family Zodariidae) belong to one of the most diverse and abundant spider families in Australia taking their close association with ants into account; these are probably one of the most dominant arthropod groups of this continent. They are largely ant and termite predators and live in close proximity to, or in their nests. They often mimic ant behaviour, for example by holding up their first pair of legs like the elbowed ant antennae, and some species have been shown to mimic ant pheromones to disguise themselves when invading ant nests to prey on the hosts.

Zodariidae are diagnosed by the absence of a serrula on the maxillae, the presence of lateral teeth on the tarsal claws, long anterior spinnerets, and their burrowing behaviour. They are often recognised by their attractive bright white, yellow, orange, or red spots, against a dark brown abdomen, and by their annulated legs.

The Ant-eating Spiders are found in all tropical and subtropical regions. Three subfamilies are known from Australia: the Cyriocteinae, Lachesaninae and Zodariinae.

The **Cyriocteinae** are characterised by a transverse row of six short, stout spines between the eye rows. *Cyrioctea raveni* from central eastern Queensland is the only described Australian species in the subfamily. Females are rarely collected as they are burrowing spiders that rarely emerge from their burrows.

The **Lachesaninae** are characterised by cylindrical, retractile anterior spinnerets.

They include a single Australian genus, *Australutica*, with four described species. The carapace and legs are yellow to orange, sometimes with darker areas around the eyes. Three species are known from South Australia, with the fourth collected from Moreton Island, Queensland. However, the Lachesaninae appear to be considerably more diverse both at the genus and species level.

Most Australian Ant-eating Spider species belong to the subfamily **Zodariinae** which have two strongly procurved eye rows and their anterior spinnerets on a common mound.

Two of the most diverse Australian genera are *Habronestes* and *Storena*. The genus *Habronestes* is identified by male pedipalp morphology. The cymbium has a large lateral fold and the tegulum is Y-shaped due to a mesal sclerotised outgrowth; in addition, the tegulum has a distal membranous appendage. The genus includes 50 named species; however, the taxonomy of central and Western Australian species has not been treated. *Habronestes* mainly inhabits semi-arid regions of Australia. Chemical mimicry has been studied in *Habronestes bradleyi*, a southern Australian species that mimics pheromones of the meat ant *Iridomyrmex purpureus*.

The elongated cymbium fold of *Habronestes* is shared with the genera *Neostorena*, *Asceua* and *Malinella*. *Neostorena* are found throughout Australia. They are burrowing spiders and some species apparently close their burrow with a lid, whilst others construct a palisade. The seven described species represent only a fraction of the true diversity of this genus. Both other genera are represented in Australia by a single tropical species each: *Asceua epugatrix* from Northern Territory and Queensland; and *Malinella zebra* from Queensland, which also occurs in New Guinea and the Solomon and Aru Islands. These genera also occur in South-East Asia and beyond.

The genus *Storena* is well defined by the presence of a pitted, central abdominal shield. The genus includes 41 described species from around Australia. The burrow of *Storena* species usually has a small palisade of twigs or litter around the entrance.

The genera *Notasteron* (two described species) appears to form a natural grouping with *Hetaerica* (two species) and *Storosa* (two species) based on the morphology of the sternum, labium and endites. These genera differ in particular by genitalic characters.

A large natural grouping within the Australian Zodariinae is the 'Asteron-complex', including several genera that share a peculiar male pedipalp morphology, namely a large, free-standing tegular apophysis that developed in the opposite direction to the embolus. This complex includes genera such as *Basasteron*, with the single species *B. leucosemum* from Lord Howe Island, *Cavasteron* (12 species from throughout Australia), *Euasteron* (17 species), *Holasteron* (16 species), *Leptasteron* (two species from Western Australia and New South Wales), *Masasteron* (21 species), *Minasteron* (three species), *Spinasteron* (19 species), *Tropasteron* (22 species) and others.

Zillimata is a peculiar genus that includes a single species, *Z. scintillans*, from southern Australia. These spiders have a deeply reticulated carapace that reflects light in a variety of green to purplish colours, possibly mimicking Green-headed Ants in the genus *Rhytidoponera*. In contrast, the only Australian species in *Cryptothele*, *C. doreyana*, belongs to a genus of spiders that cover themselves with soil and dirt for camouflage. These are rarely collected spiders and the records of *C. doreyana* from Queensland and New Guinea are based on historical sources.

Ant-eating Spiders in the Cyriocteinae and Lachesaninae are generally burrowing spiders whereas those in the Zodariinae tend to be day active or nocturnal, ground-dwelling hunters. Their venom is not known to be dangerous to humans.

Pentasteron, here an unidentified male from Western Australia feeding on a *Camponotus* ant, are dark slender Ant-eating Spiders with bright yellow or pale spots on their abdomen. They live on tree trunks and hunt termites or ants. [F. Bokhari]

All Zodariinae have their anterior spinnerets on a common base, which is one of the main characteristics of most Australian Ant-eating Spiders. [B.C. Baehr]

Ant-eating Spiders appear to be very efficient predators, as this *Habronestes hunti* female has killed a bull ant more than twice its own size. [I. Gunther]

Zillimata scintillans, here a female from Western Australia, occurs throughout southern semi-arid to arid Australia. The species epithet *scintillans* means 'sparkling' and refers to the violet and dark green reflections caused by the deeply reticulated carapace. These spiders appear to mimic Green-headed Ants, for example *Rhytidoponera metallica*, and the effect is enhanced by the position of the first pair of legs that imitate the elbowed antennae of the ants. [F. Bokhari]

This night active *Neostorena* male from Western Australia is a new species. It hides under eucalypt bark during the daytime. Only seven species in this genus are described for Australia but there are at least 50 more species awaiting description. [F. Bokhari]

Above and right: *Storena cyanea*, here a female from north Queensland, is a common species along the coast line of eastern and south-eastern Australia. The species has a bright red front including legs but a dark bluish head to which the species epithet '*cyanea*' refers. *Storena* species usually make a burrow surrounded by a small palisade of twigs or litter. These are often close to eucalypt trees, but also on open ground. [both images R.J. Raven]

Most of the day active hunters within the Ant-eating Spiders belong to the genus *Habronestes*, here illustrated by an unidentified female from Western Australia. To date, only the species from Queensland, New South Wales and Tasmania have been taxonomically treated, whereas the faunas of Western Australia, South Australia and the Northern Territory remain poorly known. [F. Bokhari]

This *Storena digitulus* male from north Queensland has a dark reddish head and legs. This species occurs throughout Queensland and can be found under bark at the base of eucalypt trees. The genus *Storena* includes some of the largest Ant-eating Spiders in Australia and these can be recognised by five bright yellow or red abdominal spots with a small leather-like, pitted scute in the centre. [P. Zborowski]

This *Habronestes* female from Western Australia displays the procurved eye row typical for Australian species in the subfamily Zodariinae. The big anterior median eyes occur only in the *Habronestes macedonensis*-group. All other *Habronestes* species have small anterior median eyes. [F. Bokhari]

The colourful *Habronestes hunti* is one of the most common species in eastern Australia. It is distributed from eastern New South Wales into south-eastern Queensland. [R.J. Raven]

Storena raveni, here a male and female prior to mating, is only known from western Queensland around Birdsville. [R.J. Raven]

This *Masasteron complector* male from Western Australia can easily be recognised by its huge pedipalps that look like deer antlers. These highly complicated features occur in all *Masasteron* species in a variety of shapes. *Masasteron complector* is a day active ant hunter with a wide distribution in central Western Australia. [V.W. Framenau, Phoenix Environmental Sciences]

LYCOSIDAE
Wolf Spiders

- Eight eyes in three rows; anterior row with four small eyes; second and third row form roughly a square on top of the carapace; posterior median eyes largest
- Legs with three tarsal claws
- Male pedipalp lacks retrolateral tibial apophysis
- Variable in coloration, often with light median band or folium pattern on abdomen
- Ground-living spiders; vagrant, in burrows or on sheet-webs in low vegetation or depressions in the soil
- Mobile brood care; females carry the eggsac fixed to the spinnerets and subsequently their young on the abdomen
- Body length: 1.5–35 mm

Australia:
Partially revised
Current: 167 species in 30 genera
Estimated: 400 species in 50 genera
World: 2400 species in 121 genera

Wolf Spiders (family Lycosidae) take parental care to the extreme. Not only do females carry their eggsacs attached to the spinnerets, but the emerging spiderlings immediately climb onto the mother's abdomen and stay there until they disperse after their second moult, about two weeks or more after hatching. The spiderlings may spread over her whole body if there is insufficient space on the abdomen. Nursery-web Spiders (family Pisauridae) and Daddy Long-legs Spiders (Pholcidae) also carry the eggsacs but, unlike Wolf Spiders, they only use their fangs. Females of the Scaffold Spiders (family Nesticidae) have also been reported to carry the eggsac on the spinnerets but the juveniles disperse immediately after hatching.

    This mobile parental care probably contributed to the ecological success of Wolf Spiders in naturally disturbed areas such as inundation zones of rivers and lakes. Females simply take their offspring to flee rising water levels during a flood. Wolf Spiders have the ability to detect polarised light and use this for orientation even if they cannot see the water directly. Young Wolf Spiders initially disperse by ballooning on gossamer threads. Massive sheets of gossamer combined with the

Hoggicosa forresti has partially black femora. It occurs in semi-arid to arid areas of southern Western Australia and into South Australia. [F. Bokhari]

The Desert or Bicoloured Wolf Spider, *Hoggicosa bicolor*, is probably the most readily recognised Wolf Spider in Australia. The female (left) has a cream-coloured carapace and the tips of its legs contrast with the deep black femora. In contrast, the male (right) is more uniformly drab brown, which is an unusual colour dimorphism in spiders since as a rule the males are generally more boldly marked. The genus includes ten species, all arid-zone specialists that can be found in all mainland states except New South Wales and Victoria. Males are characterised by a distinct patch of backwards-bent setae on the tip of the pedipalp cymbium. [V.W. Framenau, Phoenix Environmental Sciences]

The Carpet Wolf Spider, *Tapetosa darwini*, is the only representative of its genus. This species is an extreme habitat specialist and only occurs on granite outcrops in south-central Western Australia. It has an extremely flattened carapace and abdomen and is therefore exceptionally well adapted to hiding in the narrow cracks and crevices of exfoliating rock slabs on the outcrops. [V.W. Framenau, Phoenix Environmental Sciences]

The Shuttlecock Wolf Spider, *Mainosa longipes*, has a unique black coloration with light transverse lines on the abdomen. It builds turrets of acacia phyllodes around the entrance to its burrow which are reminiscent of a badminton shuttlecock. It is common from arid parts of Western Australia east into South Australia. [V.W. Framenau, Phoenix Environmental Sciences]

Wolf Spiders are not choosy when it comes to their diet, which mainly consists of insects and other spiders, including smaller individuals of their own species. They attack by simultaneously biting and wrapping the legs around their prey. This female *Venatrix arenaris* from Western Australia devours a moth larger than itself. Larger Wolf Spiders, such as *Venatrix lapidosa* in eastern Australia, and *Lycosa obscuroides*, have been reported to feed on amphibians, including Cane Toads. Sexual cannibalism, i.e. a female eating a male after mating, is not common, probably because males and females are of a similar size in Wolf Spiders. [F. Bokhari]

Tetralycosa alteripa, similar to other species in the genus, has adapted to cope with high salt levels in its environment and is restricted to the open playa of salt lakes in Western and South Australia. A female from Lake Lefroy, Western Australia, is shown here. Evidence of these spiders during the day includes a hive of mud with little pebbles in a semicircle around it, indicating burrow activity from the night. [V.W. Framenau, Phoenix Environmental Sciences]

spiders draglines can frequently be found in grasslands near inundation zones of rivers and lakes. Wolf Spiders appear to be one of the most abundant representatives observed on these sheets, in addition to Sheet-web Spiders (Linyphiidae). Wolf Spiders have been recorded as some of the earliest colonisers in the moon-like landscapes that are created after volcanic eruptions.

Wolf Spiders display a variety of hunting strategies. Some are sheet-web hunters, many are vagrant hunters that may hide in a temporary silk-lined retreat under a rock or log only briefly whilst carrying their eggsacs. Many of the larger Australian species live in burrows, which allows them to persevere even in the hottest environments by restricting their activity to the cooler nights. Species in the genera *Tetralycosa* and *Hogna* managed to adapt to a life in one of the most inhospitable places on earth, the playa of temporarily inundated salt lakes in Australia's arid zone.

Wolf Spiders occur throughout Australia, with habitat specialists known from sandy beaches (*Tetralycosa oraria* and *Costacosa torbjorni*) to the nival zone of the Australian Alps (*Tasmanicosa musgravei* and *Venatrix kosciuskoensis*).

The bites of Wolf Spiders, even the larger species, are not known to cause more than local effects in humans. However, dogs and cats bitten by Wolf Spiders have been reported to die within an hour.

Wolf Spiders belong to one of the most diverse spider families in Australia. Members of four subfamilies occur: the Zoicinae, Venoniinae, Artoriinae and Lycosinae. These subfamilies are mainly characterised by their genital morphology;

however, each subfamily can also be broadly characterised by morphological features and some life history characteristics.

The **Zoicinae** include the smallest of all Wolf Spiders in Australia with a body length of only 1–3 mm. *Zoica* is the only genus of this subfamily known from Australia and three species occur. These are all restricted to the tropics where they have been reported from Queensland, the Northern Territory and Western Australia. They are vagrant hunters and their minute eggsac generally contains less than a handful of eggs.

The **Venoniinae** are, by and large, also small spiders, being generally up to 5 mm in body length. The most common genus, *Venonia*, typically contains small black and somewhat elongated spiders with a white tip at the end of the abdomen. However only one species, *V. micarioides*, is widespread throughout the temperate zone of the country; all the other species are tropical. Members of the genus build small sheet-webs in low vegetation and depressions in the soil. *Anomalosa* includes two Australian species: *Anomalosa kochi* occurs along the Queensland coast, whereas *A. oz* has only been found south of the McPherson Range in New South Wales, Victoria and South Australia. They are similar to *Venonia* but have a narrow pale band along the centreline of their body. *Anomalosa* have also been anecdotally reported to build sheet-webs, although free-ranging populations have been observed. Two species of *Allotrochosina* occur in Australia: *A. karri* from Karri forests in south-west Western Australia and *A. walesiana* from New South Wales. The latter can grow up to 11 mm in body length, making it the largest venoniine spider in Australia. A third species occurs in New Zealand.

The **Artoriinae** are the second most diverse subfamily of Wolf Spiders in Australia. Members of this subfamily are generally small (3–10 mm) and have a light median band in the frontal half of the abdomen, although some species, for example in the genus *Tetralycosa*, are larger and the coloration is less distinct. Artoriinae are typically restricted to the tropical, coastal and temperate regions of Australia and do not occur in the arid zone. They include daytime active, vagrant spiders that generally occur in forests, woodlands or open, moderately moist habitats. As such, they can often be found in gardens and parklands. A number of genera have been described in the Artoriinae, including *Artoria*, *Artoriopsis*, *Dingosa*, *Kangarosa*, *Tetralycosa* and *Diahogna*. *Artoria* is, with 21 described species, the most diverse artoriine genus in Australia, but many more undescribed species

This *Hoggicosa castanea* female was photographed in suburban Adelaide. The species is common throughout the arid zone of Australia, where it usually resides in permanent burrows. *Hoggicosa* is a genus endemic to Australia and includes ten large species which are adapted to arid habitats. [V.W. Framenau, Phoenix Environmental Sciences]

Lycosa australicola has a very distinct black triangle on the frontal half of its abdomen and the broad pale median band on the carapace is enhanced by dark borders. This beautiful spider is common throughout the arid zone of Australia, although subtle differences in genital morphology suggest that more than one species is present. [V.W. Framenau, Phoenix Environmental Sciences]

Wolf Spiders, here Leuckart's Wolf Spider, *Tasmanicosa leuckartii*, can be identified by their unique eye pattern with the small anterior eyes in one almost straight line, the posterior median and lateral eyes form a square on the top of the carapace. [V.W. Framenau, Phoenix Environmental Sciences]

Venator immansueta is probably the most commonly encountered species of Wolf Spider in Western Australia, where it can be found throughout the south-west, and often in suburban parks and gardens. This spider can be recognised by the dark areas behind the head region. Its natural habitat includes open eucalypt woodlands, often on sandy soils, and it is therefore common on the Perth Coastal Plain. Like many Wolf Spiders in temperate latitudes, its lifecycle is highly synchronised with the seasons, and mature males and females can generally be found in autumn only. [V.W. Framenau, Phoenix Environmental Sciences]

The Grey Wolf Spider is common in south-eastern Australia, including Tasmania, where it can be found in dry, sun-exposed habitats with compacted soil, such as roadside verges or in parkland, or in dry eucalyptus woodlands. It covers the entrance of its burrow with a hinged, solid trapdoor, a habit that is otherwise uncommon in Wolf Spiders. Although it is comparatively common throughout its range, it has not been scientifically described. It has often been erroneously attributed the scientific name *Dingosa simsoni* which is a turret-building wolf spider from southern Australia. [V.W. Framenau, Phoenix Environmental Sciences]

are known from collections. They are generally found in woodlands and forests in the temperate zone. They freely roam in the litter zone. Habitat specialisation is not uncommon, for example *Artoria albopedipalpis* is restricted to riparian gravel banks in the Victorian Alps. The genus *Artoriopsis* can be recognised by a central, black diamond-shaped patch in the middle of the abdomen that is cut through by the pale median band. The genus includes seven described species with similar habitat preferences and similar coloration and species identification requires examination of male and female genitalia. *Artoriopsis expolita* is the most common species and it occurs in the southern half of Australia, including southern Queensland, in open, moderately moist environments. It is one of the most common species found on grass in urban gardens and parks.

The genus *Tetralycosa* is one of the most remarkable genera of the Artoriinae in Australia and it exclusively includes spiders that have evolved a high tolerance to salt. *Tetralycosa oraria* is only found along sandy beaches in the southern half of the country, including Tasmania. *Tetralycosa wundurra* is a south-western Western Australian species that is found in samphire vegetation near inland salt lakes and pans. *Tetralycosa alteripa* and *T. eyrei*, however, have taken their salt tolerance to a new level. They occur on the playa of salt lakes in Western and South Australia, where they hide in burrows during the extreme heat of the day and come out to forage at night. There are a number of undescribed salt lake specialists in the genus, some of these only known from single lakes.

The **Lycosinae** is the most diverse subfamily of Wolf Spiders in Australia and at the same time includes the largest species. Most species are burrowing and the burrows in some genera include unusual decorations such as turrets and pebbly walls. A few species are also known to construct a hinged trapdoor to seal the burrow. The Lycosinae are particularly dominant in semi-arid and arid environments where they hide in their burrow during the day but may leave it during the night to forage. Many may simply rest at the entrance of the burrow to wait for unsuspecting prey to pass by. Species in the genus *Tasmanicosa* have been reported to move from burrow to burrow and possibly occupy another spider's retreat ('burrow stealing'), indicating that burrows are not as permanent as those for spiders in other families, for example in the Trapdoor Spiders (Mygalomorphae).

The genus *Tasmanicosa* includes the most commonly encountered Wolf Spiders in Australia, the Garden Wolf Spider, *T. godeffroyi*, and Leuckart's Wolf

Venatrix amnicola is a habitat specialist from gravel banks along alpine rivers of the Great Dividing Range. Here, this species is more commonly found along the lowland stretches of the river, whereas the larger *Venatrix lapidosa*, at least in New South Wales and Victoria, occurs at higher altitudes. The mottled coloration of *V. amnicola* blends perfectly with the sandy and pebbly substrate, providing excellent camouflage. [V.W. Framenau, Phoenix Environmental Sciences]

Hogna crispipes is one of the most common Australian Wolf Spiders and it can also be found on Christmas Island in the Indian Ocean, New Zealand, and many Pacific Islands. Characteristic are the three dark spots in an otherwise lighter band along the carapace margin. This species typically inhabits well-watered, low vegetation habitats, such as those beside streams, creeks and springs, including in the arid zone throughout central Australia, and also sites near the coast. [V.W. Framenau, Phoenix Environmental Sciences]

Spider, *T. leuckartii*. Spiders in *Tasmanicosa* can be recognised by black and white radiating lines on the carapace, often referred to as a 'Union Jack pattern'. The genus includes about 20 species in Australia from largely temperate to semi-arid environments. Whilst these spiders are uniform in their upper coloration, the markings on the underside of the abdomen are often characteristic. For example, Leuckart's Wolf Spider has a pale central patch on an otherwise black venter unlike any other *Tasmanicosa*. Accurate species identification, however, may necessitate an examination of the genitalia, in particular in south-eastern Australia where a number of similar species co-exist.

The genus *Hoggicosa* includes some spectacularly marked spiders that are mainly found in Australia's arid and semi-arid environments. The genus is most diverse in central Western Australia. It includes one of the most distinguishable Australian lycosids, the Desert or Bicoloured Wolf Spider, *H. bicolor*. Females are uniformly cream-coloured with distinctly black leg femora and a black abdomen that has an cream median band of varying size. The coloration is sexually dimorphic as males are uniformly dull brown. The evolutionary significance of this reversed colour dimorphism (often males are the more colourful sex in spiders) is unknown. *Hoggicosa* currently includes ten Australian species.

Dingosa, with four Australian species, and *Mainosa*, only represented by the Shuttlecock Wolf Spider, *M. longipes*, construct characteristic walls or turrets around the entrance to the burrow on which *Dingosa* can sometimes be seen resting during the day. Representatives of *Dingosa*, similar to those of *Tasmanicosa*, have a Union Jack pattern on the carapace, but differ in having a serrated dark mark on the abdomen. *Mainosa longipes* is a black spider with very characteristic light transverse lines on the abdomen. Both have a similar distribution ranging from Western Australia into South Australia, although *Dingosa* has also been found in New South Wales, Victoria and Tasmania.

Hogna includes lycosine Wolf Spiders with very similar genital morphology, including a triangular tegular apophysis of the male pedipalp and an inverted T-shaped female epigyne. *Hogna crispipes* is one of its most common representatives and its extraordinary dispersal capabilities are demonstrated by its occurrence as far afield as Christmas Island in the Indian Ocean, New Zealand and, most likely, many Pacific islands. The species is very common in moderately moist, open habitat and occurs in many suburban parks and gardens. However, it also thrives along watercourses and other inland water bodies in the arid zone. In New Zealand it can commonly be encountered close to beaches. *Hogna* also includes some salt tolerant species. For example, *H. salifodina* occurs together with *Tetralycosa* species on inland salt lakes and *H. corallina* can be found on coral shingle beaches off the coast of Western Australia.

Molecular evidence indicates that most Australian genera of the Lycosinae have affinities with genera from South America, suggesting an evolutionary history dating back to Gondwana with diversification after the split of the southern supercontinent. In contrast, the genus *Venatrix* is related to northern hemisphere Wolf Spiders and its predecessors may have invaded Australia from the north. *Venatrix* includes 26 described Australian species. They are characterised by a compound claw on the tip of the male pedipalp. Many species have a characteristic pattern of white spots or lines on an otherwise black underside of the abdomen. *Venatrix lapidosa*, the Gravel Bank Huntress, is a habitat specialist on riparian gravel banks along the Great Dividing Range and similar riparian habitat preferences are evident for *V. arenaris* and *V. amnicola*. Most other *Venatrix* are found in the litter of sclerophyll forest.

A number of smaller genera have recently been established for Australian Lycosinae, including *Costacosa* that includes two species from coastal Western Australia, and *Knoelle* with a single northern Australian species, *K. clara*, that can be found from Western Australia to Queensland. However, many more genera and species in this subfamily await description.

The lifecycles of the Garden Wolf Spider, *Tasmanicosa godeffroyi*, and the Gravel Bank Huntress, *Venatrix lapidosa*, have been studied in detail in southeastern Australia and this research has revealed patterns highly synchronised with the seasons. These larger spiders may take more than a year to mature and females may live for another year or so. The lifecycle of *V. lapidosa* in Victoria, revealed by a long-term mark and resight study, is complex as two cohorts, autumn- and spring-maturing, live side-by-side in the same population.

Opposite page: *Venonia micarioides*, here an immature male in a prey capture sheet-web in a suburban Brisbane park, belongs to the few web-building Wolf Spiders. The species is widely distributed in temperate Australia where it builds the web in grass or depressions in the soil. It is the only representative of seven Australian *Venonia* species that is found outside the tropics. [V.W. Framenau, Phoenix Environmental Sciences]

The genus *Venatrix* is one of the few genera in the subfamily Lycosinae that has a distribution in the more temperate regions of eastern and western Australia. The genus occurs along the Great Dividing Range from Queensland to Victoria, in South Australia and Tasmania. Two species are known from south-western Western Australia. Many species, such as *Venatrix pictiventris* illustrated here, are forest-dwellers. A characteristic feature of *Venatrix* males is a distinct claw at the tip of their pedipalps. The ventral side of the abdomen is dark with two longitudinal light bands that may be reduced to white spots. [V.W. Framenau, Phoenix Environmental Sciences]

Artoriopsis expolita, here a male from Perth, is one of the most common members of the subfamily Artoriinae in Australia. A characteristic feature for this genus is a black diamond-shaped spot on the abdomen which is cut through by a pale band. This species occurs throughout the temperate parts of the country where it prefers open, moderately moist habitats and it is therefore common in suburban gardens and parks. It is one of seven *Artoriopsis* species from Australia. [V.W. Framenau, Phoenix Environmental Sciences]

Opposite page: The genus *Artoria* is the most speciose genus in the subfamily Artoriinae. *Artoria* morphology and coloration is fairly uniform. They are dark mottled brown in coloration sometimes with some longitudinal light pattern on the carapace and a light median band on the abdomen as seen here in *A. cingulipes* from south-west Western Australia. [V.W. Framenau, Phoenix Environmental Sciences]

Above: After hatching from the eggsac, the spiderlings climb onto the female Wolf Spider's abdomen where they stay for another two to four weeks. Such extreme parental care is unusual amongst spiders but is also known from scorpions. *Venatrix pullastra* is a small to medium-sized Wolf Spider from Western Australia, which is very common on lawns in suburban gardens and parklands in the south-west of the state. A very similar species, *Venatrix pseudospeciosa*, occupies the same ecological niche in eastern Australia. [V.W. Framenau, Phoenix Environmental Sciences]

Wolf Spiders are mostly earth-coloured spiders with patterns that help them blend into the background. This female Leuckart's Wolf Spider, *Tasmanicosa leuckartii*, shows the Union Jack pattern of white and black radial lines on its carapace, which is typical for this genus. It is one of the most common lycosids in open eucalypt woodland in southern Australia. The equally common Garden Wolf Spider, *T. godeffroyi*, is very similar in coloration. [V.W. Framenau, Phoenix Environmental Sciences]

PISAURIDAE
Fishing Spiders, Nursery-web Spiders

- Eight eyes in two or three rows; one pair of eyes sometimes on tubercle
- Legs long and strong
- Day or night time hunters with or without prey capture web
- Nursery-web for young
- Females carry eggsac with chelicerae and secured with thread to spinnerets
- Body length: 8–50 mm

Australia:
Taxonomy poorly resolved
Current: 17 species in 7 genera
Estimated: 50 species in 10 genera
World: 333 species in 48 genera

The Fishing Spiders, also referred to as Nursery-web Spiders (family Pisauridae), include semi-aquatic specialists that primarily hunt on the water's surface. These spiders can be seen at the shore with their front legs touching the surface of the water to detect the vibrations of potential prey. In this way they hunt aquatic insects or arthropods that have fallen into the water and have been observed to catch fish. They can walk on the water without breaking the surface tension but can also hunt underwater. Their dense hairs act like a plastron by trapping air and enabling the diver to breathe underwater. However, Pisauridae also includes web-building representatives that build sheet-webs to capture prey.

Female pisaurids carry their eggsac between the fangs until the spiderlings are about to hatch. At least the normally vagrant and often riparian members of the family build a three-dimensional web to which the female attaches the eggsac. The mother can often be seen near the web apparently guarding the young. The web helps the spiderlings to catch small flies to support the initial instars with food. This unusual behaviour of providing a specialised web for the rearing of the offspring led to these spiders being given the colloquial name Nursery-web Spider.

Fishing Spiders can be found worldwide. The named Australian fauna is small but many undescribed species are known from collections. They are mainly found in tropical and temperate climates, although these spiders have been recorded from near water in the arid zone. Two subfamilies are currently recognised for Australia, the Thalassiinae and the Pisaurinae, although no phylogenetic analysis has so far been conducted that appropriately delineates the Thalassiinae, which therefore represents a historic grouping of genera that may not be immediately related.

The **Thalassiinae** includes the typical Fishing Spiders, in Australia represented by seven named species in the worldwide genus *Dolomedes* and the Australian endemic genus *Megadolomedes*, which only includes a single species, *M. australianus*. *Dolomedes* are medium-sized to large spiders, typically with two light bands along the sides of their body. These spiders generally hunt at night and hide during the day under large rocks or boulders near the water's edge of the creeks and rivers they inhabit. *Megadolomedes* are impressive Fishing Spiders, and females may have a leg-span exceeding 150 mm. Males are much smaller than females, in contrast to those of *Dolomedes*, in which the males are almost equal in size to their female counterparts. *Megadolomedes* differs from *Dolomedes* also by flexible tarsi and details of the male pedipalp. The species occurs along the east Australian coast from tropical Queensland into Tasmania and inhabits areas with still to moderately fast running water. Before they reach maturity these spiders can often be seen high in vegetation overhanging water.

The subfamily **Pisaurinae** includes the sheet-web building Pisauridae in Australia, represented by four species of *Inola* and two species in the genus *Dendrolycosa*. *Inola* is apparently restricted to tropical Queensland, where they build sticky sheet-webs just outside of rainforests or in areas of rainforest with a broken canopy. A short funnel extends from the sheet-web to a retreat in a tree trunk or embankment. *Dendrolycosa* has also been recorded in the tropical parts of the Northern Territory and along the east coast into northern New South Wales. Members of the genus normally construct a sheet-web with a retreat in vegetation, but historical records suggest that *D. icadia*, the Tree Water Spider, has also been found under rocks. The distribution of this species is currently limited to Queensland.

The subfamily Pisaurinae also includes a typical Fishing Spider, *Perenethis venusta*, the only Australian representative of the genus. It is a widespread species which occurs from India to South-East Asia and northern Australia.

Hygropoda lineata, the only named Australian species in the genus *Hygropoda*, occurs in South-East Asia and into Queensland. Similar to *Perenethis*, they have a long, slender body, but with a very different coloration. *Hygropoda* constructs a sheet-web beside streams or other water bodies.

Fishing Spiders, such as this unidentified immature *Dolomedes* from Western Australia, can walk on the surface of the water, as the dense scopulae on their legs do not break the surface tension of the water. [F. Bokhari]

Dolomedes, here an unidentified immature male from the Murray River in south-west Western Australia, often live along fast-flowing rivers with rocky shores. Here, they hide under the larger boulders during the day and forage at the water's edge during the night. Collecting spiders on riparian gravel banks invariably results in finding *Dolomedes* under the larger rocks whereas the smaller rocks often harbour different species of Wolf Spiders (family Lycosidae). [V.W. Framenau, Phoenix Environmental Sciences]

The Giant Water Spider, *Megadolomedes australianus*, can dive under the surface. In this way it can hide in vegetation from predators, or is able to catch the aquatic insect larvae of dragonflies, damselflies or mayflies. The silver halo is a layer of air trapped in the dense layer of hairs that covers the spider's body, allowing it to breath whilst under water. [P. Zborowski]

This yellowish-olive coloured *Dolomedes facetus* lives at the edge of undisturbed freshwater ponds, lakes or slow flowing rivers in tropical northern Australia and along the Queensland coast. They are able to walk on water and even jump a distance twice their length when chasing insect prey such as water striders. [P. Zborowski]

Megadolomedes australianus, with the female leg span in excess of 150 mm, is one of the largest Australian pisaurids. The males are much smaller and reach a maximum leg span of about a third of that of the female. When females swim across the water, they put their first pair of legs together in front, and their back pair behind, and scull with the middle two pairs. [R.J. Raven]

This *Hygropoda lineata* female carries its eggsac between the chelicerae and, as typical for the Fishing Spiders, will have it safely secured with threads to the spinnerets. [P. Zborowski]

This big *Megadolomedes australianus* male is waiting at the edge of the water for prey. The long legs touch the water's surface to detect vibrations caused by potential prey such as aquatic insect larvae, water striders, or vertebrates, including prey items up to five times bigger than their own size. In the early days of Brisbane, horrified goldfish keepers would find their prized animals in the fangs of one of these giants at the water's edge. [P. Zborowski]

This slender green *Hygropoda lineata* female from Mossman, north Queensland, is sitting on an indistinct sheet-web on the top of a leaf. This species can be found from South-East Asia into Queensland. [P. Zborowski]

Females of the Pisauridae, the Fishing or Nursery-web Spiders, such as this unidentified *Hygrolycosa* female from north Queensland, carry the eggsac between the chelicerae. The tactic of mobile broodcare is particularly beneficial in dynamic environments such as near water, where there is a constant danger of flooding threatening the brood. [P. Zborowski]

Dendrolycosa icadia occurs along the east coast of Australia as far south as Fraser Island. Hundreds of webs can often be seen in the vegetation amongst the trees. Similar to spiders in the genus *Inola*, *Dendrolycosa* construct sheet-webs with funnel-like retreats. *Dendrolycosa icadia* webs are strong, up to 60–80 cm in diameter, and often built high in trees. The spider runs on the top of the web and when disturbed runs back to a small tubular leaf-coated retreat near a branch. [R.J. Raven]

CTENIDAE
Tropical Wolf Spiders

- Eight eyes in three rows, typically in a 2:4:2 pattern
- Carapace with deep long fovea
- Legs strong, with scopulae on metatarsi and tarsi; tarsi with two claws
- Strong paired spines on the underside of the tibiae and metatarsi of the first two pairs of legs
- Night active ground-living hunting spiders, without prey capture web
- Body length: 10–30 mm

Australia:
Partially revised
Current: 20 species in 5 genera
Estimated: 40 species in 6 genera
World: 490 species in 40 genera

Tropical Wolf Spiders (family Ctenidae) resemble and behave like Wolf Spiders (family Lycosidae), but differ in their eye pattern. Whereas Wolf Spiders have their eyes arranged in three rows with the posterior eye row forming a square on the carapace, Tropical Wolf Spiders have two recurved eye rows with the anterior lateral eyes sitting near the posterior median eyes. In addition, Tropical Wolf Spiders have only two tarsal claws (and claw tufts), whereas Wolf Spiders have three. Other ground-dwelling spiders in the superfamily Lycosoidea are similar, including the False Wolf Spiders (Miturgidae) and Spiny-leg Spiders (Zoridae), and it is these to which the Tropical Wolf Spiders are probably most closely related.

The Australian fauna of Tropical Wolf Spiders includes named species mainly from rainforests, heathland and open forests in tropical and subtropical Queensland, although the fauna is clearly much more diverse. The genus *Amauropelma* is probably a relatively recent invader from South-East Asia, and includes 16 species from tropical Queensland. These spiders are found in rainforest litter and one species, the eyeless *A. undara*, has only been found in caves.

Leptoctenus agalenoides is only known from eastern Queensland. Other species of the genus are known from the Americas and China. *Ctenus agroecoides* is only known from historical records from northern Queensland.

The eyeless *Janusia muiri* is only known from caves of the Nullarbor Plain in south-west Western Australia; however, additional blind *Janusia* have been found in other Western Australian caves. *Janusia muiri* appears to be a vagrant hunter that occurs from the deep into the twilight zone of caves where food supply is comparatively plentiful. Similarly, *Bengalla bertmaini* is eyeless. This species is currently only known from caves on Cape Range Peninsula in Western Australia.

This unidentified Tropical Wolf Spider, family Ctenidae, from Iron Range, north Queensland, most likely belongs to the genus *Anahita*, which does not have any described species listed from Australia. [R.J. Raven]

OXYOPIDAE
Lynx Spiders

- Eight eyes in four rows forming a hexagon
- Anterior spinnerets short, conical, close together
- Legs slender and spiny
- Mostly day active in vegetation without prey capture web
- Body length: 5–12 mm

Australia:
Partially revised
Current: 19 species in 4 genera
Estimated: 60 species in 6 genera
World: 447 species in 9 genera

The Lynx Spiders (family Oxyopidae) are a dominant family of spiders in vegetation and they typically exhibit a distinct hexagonal eye pattern and strongly spined legs. They approach their prey slowly, then jump suddenly. Lynx Spiders generally have a tropical and subtropical distribution and become quite rare in temperate regions. They are common in all vegetated terrestrial habitats throughout mainland Australia and Tasmania.

The Australian Lynx Spiders have been taxonomically revised in a thesis, but as most of the results of this thesis remain unpublished, taxonomic decisions of this work are not nomenclaturally valid.

The published record for Lynx Spiders currently lists four genera in Australia, including *Oxyopes* (14 species), *Peucetia* and *Hamataliwa* (two species each). The validity of the fourth genus, *Pseudohostus*, with the single Australian species *P. squamosus*, has been questioned as the type material consists of juveniles, most likely representing *Oxyopes*.

In contrast to *Oxyopes* and *Hamataliwa*, species in *Peucetia* lack teeth on the chelicerae margins and the posterior eye row is only slightly procurved. The genus is apparently restricted to the tropical and arid zone in the northern half of Australia, but these spiders are rarely collected

Hamataliwa are generally smaller (< 5.5 mm) than *Oxyopes* (> 5.5 mm) and otherwise differ in genital structures. *Hamataliwa cooki* occurs in tropical northern Queensland and Northern Territory and *H. monroei* along the Queensland coast south to Rockhampton.

The genus *Oxyopes* occurs throughout all climatic zones in Australia. Species identification generally relies on the examination of genitalia. Almost all members of the genus are widespread. Some, such as *O. macilentus*, *O. papuanus*, *O. elegans*, *O. gratus*, *O. punctatus* and *O. attenuatus* have a subtropical and/or tropical distribution in Queensland and the Northern Territory. *Oxyopes amoenus*, *O. variabilis* and *O. molarius* are found from eastern Queensland into the arid interior. *O. rubicundus* and *O. gracilipes* are distributed in southern Australia, with the latter also known from New Zealand. *Oxyopes dingo* is widespread throughout the arid centre.

The biology of Lynx Spiders is very uniform. They are common on most types of vegetation, especially on low shrubs and in the herbaceous layer such as on grasses and flowers or on crops. Many species occur in high densities in agricultural ecosystems and are thought to play an important role in integrated pest management.

Lynx Spiders do not build a prey capture web. Despite the lack of claw tufts or hairy scopulae on their feet, they are excellent climbers. They are largely active during the day and rest at night, when they can often be seen hanging from a silken thread which is attached under leaves or branches.

The eggsac is attached to grass, bark or leaves, the latter often folded to cover the eggs. The females stay with the eggsac until the spiderlings emerge. Females of *O. gracilipes* have been observed to open the eggsac to assist their offspring in hatching.

Lynx spiders (family Oxyopidae), here an unidentified *Oxyopes* from Western Australia, have eight eyes arranged in a characteristic hexagonal pattern and strong spines on their legs. [V. W. Framenau, Phoenix Environmental Sciences]

Female Lynx Spiders, here an unidentified *Oxyopes*, fix their eggsac to vegetation such as bark, grass phyllodes or leaves. The mother guards the eggsac until the young hatch. [F. Bokhari]

The iridescent blue pedipalps of this unidentified male *Oxyopes* from Queensland are most likely used in courtship behaviour. [P. Zborowski]

Right: A male *Oxyopes*, possibly *O. variabilis* or a related species, has caught a bee twice the size of its own body. Lynx Spiders are efficient predators in almost all types of vegetation but they are particularly abundant in the herbaceous layer of grass and flowers and in crops. [P. Zborowski]

Lynx Spiders, such as this unidentified *Oxyopes* female, trap their prey by placing their usually long, slender and spiny legs around it. The legs form a trap like a fishing basket, and the spider then strikes by pinching its fangs between the head and thorax. [P. Zborowski]

This male of *Oxyopes macilentus* or a related species has a very long, thin orange abdomen with pale stripes on each side. *Oxyopes macilentus* is found along the Queensland coast and into the Northern Territory and has also been recorded in New Guinea. [P. Zborowski]

MITURGIDAE
False Wolf Spiders, Prowling Spiders

- Eight equally-sized eyes in two rows
- Posterior lateral spinnerets with two segments, apical segment elongated or short; anterior lateral spinnerets conical, close together
- Legs long, two claws with or without claw tufts
- Night active hunters without prey capture web
- Sac-like retreat, often extensive, where the spiders hide during the day and females care for their eggsacs
- Body length: 6–30 mm

Australia:
Partially revised
Current: 28 species in 7 genera
Estimated: 160 species in 10 genera
World: 177 species in 28 genera

The limitations of the False Wolf or Prowling Spiders (family Miturgidae) are here based on systematic studies with Australian context, and therefore exclude the Long-legged Sac Spiders (genus *Cheiracanthium*), which are here treated as members of the Sac Spiders (Clubionidae). We acknowledge that this placement is not scientifically settled but it avoids, within this context, that the Miturgidae include spiders of very different ecologies and overall morphologies.

Within the superfamily Lycosoidea, the False Wolf Spiders are two-clawed spiders with grate-shaped tapetum in the secondary eyes, and a retrolateral tibial apophysis of the male pedipalp that has an unsclerotised portion. They differ from the Wolf Spiders (family Lycosidae) most evidently by the arrangement of the eyes, as the posterior eye row is slightly procurved to recurved and does not form a square.

Two subfamilies of False Wolf Spiders have been identified in Australia, the Miturginae and the Diaprograptinae. The Diaprograptinae have paired moveable claw tufts, whereas these are lacking in the Miturginae. These have their tarsal scopulae, patches of dense hair, extend below the tarsal claws. The family is very diverse but only a fraction of this diversity has been documented.

In Australia, *Miturga* is the only genus with named species in the **Miturginae**, however, the subfamily is clearly more diverse at the genus level. *Miturga* includes 15 species from throughout the country; however, a modern taxonomic treatment of *Miturga* is not available and therefore species identification not possible for most species.

The **Diaprograptinae** includes four genera in Australia. *Mituliodon* includes the most widespread of all False Wolf Spiders, *M. tarantulinus*, which occurs around Australia but rarely within the semi-arid or arid interior. As with many other False Wolf Spiders, it is a nocturnal ground-dweller in forest litter that is rarely seen up in the vegetation. *Diaprograpta* includes five species, which have so far been found in Queensland, Victoria and Western Australia, but the genus possibly occurs in all other mainland states. *Eupograpta* includes two species, one each from Western Australia (*E. kottae*) and western Queensland (*E. anhat*). The most common species of *Mitzoruga*, *M. insularis*, has been found throughout southern Western Australia, South Australia and Victoria, whereas *M. marmoreus* is a central Australian species. Disjunct records of *M. elapines* from north-east Queensland and near Adelaide suggest a wider distribution in between these localities. The smallest species of the Miturgidae is *N. fishburni* from south-eastern Queensland.

False Wolf Spiders are night active, fast-moving ground-hunting spiders. They are found in temperate and semi-arid to arid landscapes and less common in rainforests. Many species occur in the dry interior and several species have at times been found together.

Whilst the Miturgidae include fairly large spiders, the venom of species in this family does not appear to be very potent for humans. Effects after envenomation by *M. tarantulinus* include localised pain and in rare cases systemic effects such as dizziness, light-headedness or euphoria.

False Wolf Spiders construct a silken retreat in which they hide during the day. This female *Mituliodon tarantulinus* was found in a silken tube caring for her eggsac (which is visible in the background) in suburban Carlisle, Western Australia. [V.W. Framenau, Phoenix Environmental Sciences]

Mituliodon tarantulinus, here a female from Western Australia, is widespread in coastal Australia, including Tasmania. *Mituliodon* are large spiders with mottled brown coloration. The underside of the abdomen is dark-brown to black and has four white spots arranged in a central square. [F. Bokhari]

Below: False Wolf Spiders (family Miturgidae), in contrast to Wolf Spiders (family Lycosidae), have two rows of small eyes as seen here in an unidentified male from Dryandra Woodland in Western Australia. [V.W. Framenau, Phoenix Environmental Sciences]

This female miturgid from Newman in the Pilbara region of Western Australia belongs to an undescribed species and genus with high species diversity in Western Australia. [F. Bokhari]

This *Miturga lineata* male is a typical representative of the striped spiders in the genus *Miturga*. The species is common in the eastern states and has been found into Western Australia along the south coast. [R.J. Raven]

Nuliodon fisburni is, with a body length of about 10 mm, the smallest of the Miturgidae. It is found amongst fallen leaves in open forests along the Queensland coast. [R.J. Raven]

ZORIDAE
Spiny-leg Spiders, Wandering Ghosts

- Eight eyes in two strongly recurved rows
- Carapace flattened, sub-circular
- Legs fairly long, tibiae and metatarsi of first and second legs with pairs of strong ventral spines; tarsi with two claws and claw tufts, tarsi and distal part of metatarsi with scopulae
- Extremely fast day or night active hunters in sunny and open spaces without prey capture web
- Body length: 4–11 mm

> **Australia:**
> Partially revised
> current: 21 species in 8 genera
> estimated: 70 species in 10 genera
> **World:** 79 species in 14 genera

Spiny-leg Spiders (family Zoridae) are among the relatives of the Wolf Spider superfamily, Lycosoidea. They include generally day active, vagrant hunters that run with high speed and prefer sunny and open spaces. The taxonomy of the family is poorly resolved at the species level, but a key to seven Australian genera exists. Even the validity of the family is in question as it may be regarded part of the Miturgidae. The eye positionings of some representatives of the family resembles those of Wolf Spiders (Lycosidae), but Spiny-leg Spiders have only two tarsal claws, in contrast to the three in Wolf Spiders.

Spiny-leg Spiders are found worldwide with the type genus of the family, *Zora*, mainly limited to the Palaearctic region. Otherwise, the family is reported from the Americas, Africa and South-East Asia. Australia hosts most of the described genera and all species reported from New Zealand are apparently emigrants from Australia.

Seven genera are currently recognised from Australia. Species in *Hestimodema*, *Odomasta* and *Thasyraea* have all eyes of similar size, whereas in all other genera the posterior eyes are much larger than the anterior ones. *Hestimodema* includes two described species from Western Australia: *H. ambigua* and *H. latevittata*; *Odomasta*, a single species, *O. guttipes*, from Tasmania; and *Thasyraea*, two species originally described from Queensland (*T. ornata*) and New South Wales (*T. lepida*). The elongated spiders of *Thasyraea* have often been misidentified as *Tibellus tenellus* in the Running Crab Spiders (family Philodromidae).

Of the 'large-eyed' zorids, *Argoctenus* and *Tuxoctenus* have only two to four pairs of spines on the tibiae of the first and second legs, whereas *Simonus* and *Elassoctenus* have more than five pairs. *Argoctenus* is the most diverse genus with ten described species. These spiders often have a characteristic, elongated bell-shaped dark mark on the abdomen. *Tuxoctenus* (three described species) also has a characteristic coloration with longitudinal lines of white hair on carapace and abdomen. *Tuxoctenus linnaei* is known from southern Western Australia into South Australia, *T. mcdonaldae* throughout northern Australia and *T. gloverae* is limited in its distribution to south-eastern Queensland. Undescribed species of the genus are known from south-eastern Australia.

Elassoctenus and *Simonus* are genera from Western Australia, and each has a single described species from the state: *E. harpax* and *S. lineatus*. *Elassoctenus* is uniformly mottled brown-grey in colour whereas *Simonus* has longitudinal bands.

Odo australiensis is the only representative of the genus. Its record from central Australia is historic and the species is probably misplaced as the genus is otherwise mainly known from South America.

Little is known about the biology of Spiny-leg Spiders in Australia, although they are commonly found throughout the country.

This unidentified *Elassoctenus* female from south-west Western Australia was photographed in open sclerophyll eucalypt forest, a habitat in which this species is not uncommon. [V.W. Framenau, Phoenix Environmental Sciences]

Elassoctenus harpax is an extremely fast daytime hunter on open ground. The species occurs in south-west Western Australia. [V.W. Framenau, Phoenix Environmental Sciences]

The eyes of Spiny-leg Spiders (family Zoridae) are arranged in two strongly recurved rows. This *Elassoctenus harpax* female has larger posterior than anterior eyes, although this size difference is not characteristic for all genera of the family. [V.W. Framenau, Phoenix Environmental Sciences]

This unidentified Spiny-leg Spider from Western Australia, currently referred to the genus *Odo*, lacks the tufts that are typical for some of the genera in the family. However, the eye-pattern identifies this species as member of the Zoridae. [V.W. Framenau, Phoenix Environmental Sciences]

The genus *Argoctenus*, here a male of an unidentified species from Western Australia, is characterised by a dark, elongated and white-edged patch on the abdomen. [V.W. Framenau, Phoenix Environmental Sciences]

THOMISIDAE
Crab Spiders, Flower Spiders

- Eight eyes in two rows, lateral eyes on tubercles
- All spinnerets short, conical, close together
- Legs stout, orientated sideways ('laterigrade'); first two pair of legs often longest; two tarsal claws
- Semi-sedentary ambushers; mostly day active without prey capture web
- Sac-like retreat where the spiders hide during the night and lay their eggsac
- Body length: 2–23 mm

Australia:
Taxonomy poorly resolved
Current: 122 species in 23 genera
Estimated: 200 species in 25 genera
World: 2,153 species in 174 genera

The Crab or Flower Spiders (family Thomisidae) are master ambushers and their behavioural repertoire rivals that of members of any other spider family. Some Crab Spiders (for example *Diaea*, *Runcinia* and *Thomisus*) are able to adjust their colour to that of their host flower, providing unparalleled camouflage; the silk of others (*Phrynarachne*) mimics the smell of faeces or rotting fruit to attract flies; some Crab Spiders (*Poecilothomisus*) pretend to be dead to lure bigger spiders; and others (*Amyciaea*) imitate their preferred prey, ants, for ease of access to an almost unlimited food supply. They can overwhelm ants, butterflies and bees three times their own size. In addition, Crab Spiders belong to one of the few families with social aggregations. In Australia this behaviour is otherwise known only in Comb-footed Spiders (Theridiidae), Huntsman Spiders (Sparassidae) and Intertidal and House Spiders (Desidae).

Many Crab Spiders are readily recognised as such. Their first two pairs of legs are longer and stronger than the two rear pairs and all are directed to the side ('laterigrade'). But even in absence of this typical appearance, Crab Spiders can be recognised by the comparatively large lateral eyes that sit on elevated tubercles.

Whilst the Crab Spiders represent a well-supported evolutionary unit, modern phylogenetic studies based on molecular and morphological data suggest that traditional subfamily arrangements do not reflect the evolutionary history of the family. However, due to the lack of an alternative arrangement, and in order to facilitate an overview of the diverse Australian fauna of Crab Spiders, these traditional subfamilies are referred to here. Four subfamilies occur in Australia, the Bominae, Dietinae, Thomisinae and Stephanopinae.

The taxonomy of the Australian Thomisidae is poorly resolved both at the genus and species level. Many species have not been taxonomically treated and in particular the genus *Diaea* has been used by early European arachnologists as dumping ground to place species of unknown affinity.

The subfamily **Bominae** includes the two genera in Australia, *Bomis* and *Corynethrix*. These are small spiders with thick and short legs, but relatively long patellae. The carapace is covered by granulations or small tubercles. *Corynethrix* differs from *Bomis* by having a flatter carapace with a lower clypeus. *Bomis* has been reported from along the east coast, whereas *Corynethrix obscura* is only known from Queensland and New South Wales.

The subfamily **Dietinae** includes the Green Tree Ant-mimicking Spider, *Amyciaea albomaculata*, and a similarly green spider, *Oxytate isolata*, with an elongated abdomen. Whilst *Amyciaea* is commonly reported from tropical Australia wherever its preferred prey, the Green Tree Ant, *Oecophylla smaragdina*, occurs, *O. isolata* is only known from the Montebello Islands off the north-west Western Australian coast, from where it was originally described; however, unidentified species of the genus have also been found in Queensland.

The **Thomisinae** include the typical Crab Spiders, those of often crab-like appearance. Many of these are colourful and some are able to change colour. Eleven genera include described species of this subfamily in Australia. *Diaea* is the largest genus in Australia with 31 described species. The genus occurs throughout the country. However, only a few modern taxonomic descriptions exist for certain species, including those of the subsocial *D. ergandros* which occurs from Queensland south into Tasmania, *D. megagyna* from New England in New South Wales into Queensland, and *D. socialis* from Western Australia. In these social Crab Spiders, the females, similar to those in solitary species, deposit their eggsac in a curled leaf. However, the female then adds further leaves to the nest, and after the offspring hatch, they eventually participate in nest-building behaviour and continue to do so after the mother has died. The family group stays together until maturity, when males leave the nest to search for mates, although some mate with their nestmates.

Above and right: The Green Tree Ant-mimicking Spider, *Amyciaea albomaculata*, closely matches in colour and morphology the Green Tree Ant, *Oecophylla smaragdina*, on which it preys. The big black spots on the abdomen resemble the eyes of green ants. The spider hangs on a thread of silk from branches on which the tracks of the Green Tree Ant are located and attacks secured by its line. After the ant is immobilised the spider will take its victim to a leaf for consumption. However, even the best disguise does not always guarantee success and the spiders occasionally fall victim to the ants. [P. Zborowski]

This Western Australian Crab Spider, possibly from the genus *Stephanopis*, has conical horns above and between the eyes. Overall, the knobbly surface of these spiders contributes to their great camouflage. [F. Bokhari]

This female *Stephanopis*, possibly *S. cambridgei*, from Western Australia, has successfully attacked a cockroach. In contrast to other Crab Spiders, those in the subfamily Stephanopinae have teeth on the chelicerae margins which assist in chewing their prey. [F. Bokhari]

Opposite page and right: Crab Spiders in the genus *Phrynarachne* look like bird droppings. In addition, they apparently use a bed of white silk that smells like bird droppings. This attracts insects such as flies, which expect to feed on bird excrement, and which the spider then traps with its strong front legs. The spiders also create several decoy webs across adjoining leaves to confuse their own predators. The image on the right shows a fly lured to the spider's safe hunting position. [P. Zborowski]

Cymbacha is a largely Australian Crab Spider genus, although some species also occur in neighbouring countries to the north. Seven species are described from the country but no modern taxonomic treatment exists. Similarly, *Tharpyna* includes mainly Australian representatives. Nine species are described from this country, of which *T. campestrata* is possibly the most common species. It has two characteristic white spots on the abdomen. The genus is otherwise also known from Indonesia and India. The genus *Porropis* was described to accommodate four Australian species, but it is also found in New Guinea. *Porropis flavifrons* from eastern Australia is characterised by a yellow clypeus contrasting with the dark brown carapace.

Runcinia includes an elongated Crab Spider, *R. acuminata*, that has apparently reached Australia through the tropics, as it is also found in Japan and New Guinea. Likewise, *Thomisus* only includes a single species in this country, *T. spectabilis*, that is found from India through to Australia. *Poecilothomisus* only includes a single species of spectacular Crab Spider from Northern Australia, *P. speciosus*. The abdomen is yellow with a white centre in which black spots provide a spectacular contrast.

Zygometis includes a single species, *Z. lactea*, which occurs from Thailand into and throughout Australia. These spiders are of whitish coloration with characteristic brown longitudinal bands on the carapace. Probably some of the more unusual members of the Thomisinae are the members of the genus *Tmarus*. In contrast to most other spiders in the genus, the typical Flower Spiders, *Tmarus* ambushes prey along the branches and twigs of trees and shrubs. Camouflage in these spiders is therefore enhanced by an elongated abdomen and in resting position these spiders orientate their front legs along the twig upon which they sit.

Spiders in the subfamily **Stephanopinae** differ from those of all other Crab Spiders in the presence of strong teeth on the margins of the chelicerae, which help in chewing and therefore externally digesting their prey. These spiders are often very unlike the typical Crab or Flower Spider. They include many bark-dwellers and their external lumpy morphology and drab coloration provide perfect camouflage. The subfamily is well represented in Australia with at least four genera.

Stephanopis is a large genus with a distribution generally limited to the southern hemisphere. A total of 27 species is currently described from throughout Australia but the taxonomy of the genus is unresolved and accurate species identification impossible. These spiders are very variable in their body shapes and colours, and can often be seen attaching substrate such as soil and litter to their cuticle to enhance camouflage. *Stephanopis cambridgei* appears to be one of the more common species and occurs along the east coast and into south-west Western Australia, but without modern taxonomic treatment any species-level identification in the genus should be conducted cautiously.

Sidymella includes Crab Spiders with a triangular abdomen which is truncated or concave at the back. Species in this genus have been found in South America, New Zealand and Australia. Eight species are described from Australia, but species identification is hindered by the lack of a modern taxonomic treatment. Behavioural observations on the genus from New Zealand suggest that the truncated abdomen is beneficial in order to stabilise the spider's position in a behavioural sequence after falling accidentally on its back.

Only two species of *Synalus* are currently described from Australia, where the genus is endemic; *S. angustus*, originally described from New South Wales, and *S. terrosus* from Tasmania. However, the genus appears to be more diverse and can be found throughout the country. Species identification is impossible as a modern taxonomic treatment of the genus has not been published. *Synalus* includes elongated Crab Spiders generally found on the bark of trees and shrubs. They build their retreat under bark.

Tharralea is a tropical genus with mainly South-East Asian representatives, although three species are also described from Madagascar. Two species have been described from tropical Queensland, but without taxonomic review these are impossible to identify.

The Bird-dung Crab Spiders, genus *Phrynarachne*, have no described species listed for Australia, but are here illustrated from Queensland. Species-level identification is currently not possible, but the biology of species in the genus is nevertheless fascinating. These spiders have a knobbly, marmorated body surface mimicking bird droppings. In addition the spider produces odours which are attractive to flies, allowing it to hunt without moving from its cryptic position.

This female *Zygometis lactea* from Western Australia shows the typical colour patterns of the species, including two dark brown longitudinal bands on the carapace. The coloration of the abdomen is somewhat variable. This species occurs throughout Australia and is also found into Thailand in South-East Asia. [F. Bokhari]

This Crab Spider in the genus *Diaea*, possibly *Diaea prasina*, is in its typical ambush position with widely opened front legs. These mostly day active Crab Spiders are often found in flowers or on leaves or bark, matching the colour of their background. Some species in the subfamily Thomisinae, including some *Diaea*, can adapt their colour to that of the background. [P. Zborowski]

Left: A female Ornate Bark Spider of the genus *Tharpyna* hides partially concealed under eucalypt bark and rushes out to seize an unwary ant. [P. Zborowski]

Opposite page: *Zygometis lactea* shows what Crab or Flower Spiders are capable of when it comes to taking prey. These spiders are skilled ambushers and can overcome prey much bigger than themselves with a surprise attack using their two strong pairs of front legs. Here a female spider has ambushed a horsefly at least twice its own size. [P. Zborowski]

The White Crab Spider, *Thomisus spectabilis*, can often be seen in white flowers. Here it stands in complete contrast to the backgrounds, and thus contradicts its reputation as a well-camouflaged spider. It is not only the colour, but more so the scent of flowers that plays an important part in the decision regarding which flower to inhabit. This way these spiders apparently exploit the same signal that bees use to discriminate between high quality and low quality flowers [P. Zborowski]

The White Crab Spider, *Thomisus spectabilis*, is the only representative of its genus in Australia. This species has an extended distribution and can be found from India throughout South-East Asia and into Australia, where it is mainly found in the northern half of the country. [P. Zborowski]

This female low-headed and beautifully ornate unidentified *Cymbacha* has launched out from its retreat to take the enormous winged Green Tree Ant queen. [P. Zborowski]

Tmarus, here an unidentified female from Western Australia, are elongated Crab Spiders in the subfamily Thomisinae. These spiders can often be found along small branches and twigs in trees and shrubs where they ambush their prey. Its long two pairs of front legs are typically extended towards the front. [V.W. Framenau, Phoenix Environmental Sciences]

Subadult female *Stephanopis* with a small adult male on her back. In Crab Spiders, males are often much smaller than females and can frequently be observed sitting on the back of a subadult female waiting for her last moult. [P. Zborowski]

Tharpyna campestrata, here a female from Western Australia, is probably the most widespread species of *Tharpyna* in Australia. [V.W. Framenau, Phoenix Environmental Sciences]

Members of the genus *Stephanopis*, here an unidentified female from south-west Western Australia, are bark-dwellers. Species identification in the genus is almost impossible due to the lack of a modern taxonomic treatment. [V.W. Framenau, Phoenix Environmental Sciences]

Like many other tree-, shrub- and foliage-dwelling Crab Spiders, members of the genus *Tmarus*, like this unidentified female, spend the daytime in a retreat made of a rolled-up leaf, in between their nocturnal hunting expeditions. [P. Zborowski]

The genus *Cymbacha* includes ornate brownish Crab Spiders with circular patterns on the abdomen, as seen in this female from South Australia. The genus has not received a modern taxonomic assessment and identifications based on colour pattern should be taken cautiously. [A. Lance]

Species in the genus *Stephanopis*, here an unidentified female from Western Australia, are often encrusted with bark or soil to provide perfect camouflage against their environment. This species appears to be a soil- rather than a bark-dweller. [F. Bokhari]

Synalus, here an unidentified species from Western Australia, are elongated and cryptic Crab Spiders in the subfamily Stephanopinae. Although only two species are currently described, the genus is much more diverse. [V.W. Framenau, Phoenix Environmental Sciences]

Stephanopis, like many Crab Spiders, are masters of disguise. Here an unidentified species of the genus from Queensland sits beautifully camouflaged against the recently burned eucalypt bark. [P. Zborowski]

PSECHRIDAE
Pseudo-Orbweaving Spiders, Lace-sheet Weaving Spiders

- Eight eyes of similar size; anterior row of eyes recurved, posterior row of eyes recurved or straight
- Body generally slender, abdomen ovoid to elongated
- Legs very long, tarsi generally flexible
- Pseudo-orbwebs (*Fecenia*) or horizontal sheet-web (*Psechrus*)
- Body length: 7–32 mm

Australia:
Taxonomy revised
Current: 2 species in 2 genera
Estimated: 2 species in 2 genera
World: 50 species in 2 genera

The Pseudo-Orbweaving and Lace-sheet Weaving Spiders (family Psechridae) are a family of web-building spiders with a centre of distribution in South-East Asia. The members of one of the two genera in the family, *Fecenia* (Pseudo-Orbweaving Spiders), build vertical prey capture webs which are reminiscent of the orb-webs of the Orbiculariae. However, this web type has in all likelihood independently evolved as the Psechridae's closest relatives are possibly within the Wolf Spiders and allies (superfamily Lycosoidea). The second genus of the family, *Psechrus* (Lace-sheet Weaving Spiders), builds large, cribellate and horizontal sheet-webs.

Psechridae include cribellate spiders with three tarsal claws and distal claw tufts. They have a rectangular calamistrum with at least three rows of setae and secondary eyes with a grate-shaped tapetum. They include medium-sized to large long-legged spiders which are distributed from India eastwards into the islands of the western Pacific. Some systematic studies suggest that *Fecenia* and *Psechrus* may not necessarily be immediately related but instead may represent separate evolutionary lines within the Lycosoidea.

In Australia, Psechridae have only been found at the very northern tip of mainland Queensland and on islands further north. *Fecenia ochracea* has been collected at Cape York and on Torres Strait islands. *Psechrus argentatus* is a common species in New Guinea. It has not been recorded recently from Australia, but it is likely that this species occurs on islands of the Torres Strait similar to *Fecenia ochreata*.

In addition to the difference in the prey capture web, *Psechrus* differs from *Fecenia* in having a higher cephalic region of the carapace, smaller anterior median eyes and a white longitudinal line on the underside of the abdomen. The Lace-sheet Weaving Spiders generally live in shady habitats near the ground, such as between tree-roots or underneath dead wood and rocks in rainforest and other evergreen forests. The horizontal sheet-web may reach up to 1.2 m or more in length. The web has a tubular retreat into the substrate. Spiders move upside down underneath the web. Females carry their eggsacs between their chelicerae.

The Pseudo-orbweaving Spiders, *Fecenia*, have a comparatively flat carapace. Adults and later instars construct a vertical pseudo-orbweb with non-adhesive supporting threads radiating from a central retreat. The cribellate capture silk, in contrast to true orb-weavers, is not spun as complete, uninterrupted spiral, but is formed of bands of silk that go back and forth across the radiating lines. The web includes a rolled-up leaf at the centre as a retreat. The web is constructed in shrubs and trees, including in their canopies. Early instars do not build a pseudo-orb, but remain in a conical tube-retreat amongst irregular webbing.

Females in the genus *Psechrus*, here *P. senoculatus* from China, in lieu of images lacking of the only possible Australian representative *P. argentatus*, build large cribellate sheet-webs. They carry their eggsac between the chelicerae in a similar way to the Fishing or Nursery-web Spiders (family Pisauridae). [P. Jäger]

Opposite page: The pseudo-orb of spiders in the genus *Fecenia*, here that of *F. cylindrata* in Laos, differs from the orbweb in the Orbiculariae considerably in its architecture; in particular, the radial threads are less regular and the sticky spiral is actually not a continuous spiral but zig-zagging cribellate silk. However, the construction of the vertical pseudo-orb represents an intriguing example of convergent evolution to the orbicularian orb and demonstrates how efficient this prey capture model is. In addition, curled leaves as a retreat within the web are also used by orbicularians, for example in the Orb-weaving Spiders (family Araneidae). [P. Jäger]

ZOROPSIDAE
False Wolf Spiders, False Huntsman Spiders

- Eight eyes in two recurved rows, lateral eyes largest
- Male abdomen with frontal scute
- First and second pair of legs directed sideways ('laterigrade'), tibiae and metatarsi of first and second leg with 4–5 pairs of strong spines
- Cribellum present or absent, absent in all Australian representatives
- Body length: 8–15 mm

Australia:
Taxonomy revised
Current: 27 species in 6 genera
Estimated: 35 species in 2 genera
World: 51 species in 2 genera

The False Wolf or False Huntsman Spiders (family Zoropsidae) include ground-dwelling members of the Lycosoidea (Wolf Spiders and allies) with a vague resemblance to the Huntsman Spiders due to the sideways-oriented first and second pairs of legs. In Australia, the majority of described species are from montane rainforests in Queensland and northern New South Wales.

False Wolf Spiders are characterised by a basal fracture on the tibiae in males, a frontal abdominal scute in males, a truncated apical cymbium of the male pedipalp and relatively larger anterior lateral eyes in comparison to the anterior median eyes. All Australian representatives belong to a single subfamily, the Zoropsinae. These have two recurved eye rows, and generally sideways-oriented ('laterigrade') first and second legs, which are armed with pairs of strong spines on tibiae and metatarsi.

Six genera of False Wolf Spiders are currently described from Australia. These differ in details of the tarsal organ, namely the presence and shape of a tarsal rod, and details of male and female genitalia.

Birrana includes a single species, *B. bulburin* from Bulburin State Forest in south-eastern Queensland. *Huntia* is only known from a species in south-west Western Australia (*H. deepensis*) and a cave-dwelling representative from eastern Victoria (*H. murrindal*). *Kilyana* males do not have a tarsal rod. The genus includes ten species from rainforests within a range from central eastern Queensland to north-eastern New South Wales. *Krukt* is identified by the peculiar shape of the male pedipalp cymbium, which is narrowed at the base. The genus includes five species from the montane rainforest in north Queensland. Similarly, the eight species of *Megateg* are restricted to north-east Queensland.

Uliodon ferrugineus is currently listed for Australia based on the species' historical description; however, it appears that the genus *Uliodon* is restricted to New Zealand. Species identification and genus affinities of this species remain unresolved.

Little is known about the biology of the False Wolf Spiders. Their preferred habitat is montane and lowland rainforests where they are vagrant hunters.

The genus *Kilyana*, here *K. hendersoni*, includes ten species from rainforests in mid-eastern Queensland to north-eastern New South Wales. *Kilyana hendersoni* is found in rainforests around Brisbane and Mt. Glorious. [P. Belfield]

TENGELLIDAE
False Water Spiders, Host Spiders

- Eyes in two recurved rows, equal in size
- Long legs, three long tarsal claws
- Night active, ground-living hunters, without prey capture web
- Most are found in rainforest or at least in moist habitats
- Body length: 5–10 mm

Australia:
Partially revised
Current: 6 species in 1 genus
Estimated: 20 species in 3 genera
World: 57 species in 9 genera

The False Water Spiders (family Tengellidae) form part of the superfamily Lycosoidea and can therefore easily be confused with families such as the Wolf Spiders (Lycosidae), Fishing or Nursery-Web Spiders (Pisauridae) and Tropical Wolf Spiders (Ctenidae). However, they differ from Wolf Spiders by the presence of a retrolateral tibial apophysis on the male pedipalp, from the Fishing Spiders by the presence of a retrocoxal hymen and from the Tropical Wolf Spiders by the presence of a grate-shaped tapetum in the secondary eyes.

False Water Spiders have been recorded mainly from the New World, but include the monotypic *Calamistrula* from Madagascar and *Wiltona* from New Zealand. In Australia, a single genus, *Austrotengella* has been described including six species from south-east Queensland and north-east New South Wales.

Austrotengella are small to medium-sized spiders of about up to 10 mm in body length. They are generally drably coloured with a brown donut-shaped band in the head region and annulated legs. Species identification requires a stereomicroscope to examine female and male genitalia.

Austrotengella are litter hunters in moist habitats, in particular in subtropical rainforests. Females remain with the soil- and bark-encrusted eggsac, which is attached to the underside of a log or rock.

Austrotengella hackerae, here a female from Mt. Glorious near Brisbane, is the most widely distributed species of False Wolf Spider in Australia, but it is known only from south-eastern Queensland. Females weave their disc-like eggsacs to the underside of rocks and logs and encrust it with soil and debris. [R.J. Raven]

ANYPHAENIDAE
Ghost Spiders, Phantom Spiders, Sea-shore Spiders

- Eight eyes in two rows
- Tracheal spiracle situated at about one third of abdomen length
- Spinnerets conical, equal in size
- Legs stout, with two claws and claw tufts composed of lamelliform setae
- Body length: 6–15 mm

Australia:
Taxonomy poorly resolved
Current: 2 species in 1 genus
Estimated: 20 species in 2 genera
World: 521 species in 56 genera

The Ghost or Phantom Spiders (family Anyphaenidae) are free-hunting spiders that construct silken retreats on leaves, under bark or under rocks. The Australian and New Zealand faunas, however, only include the single genus *Amaurobioides*, the Sea-shore Spiders, which are specialist hunters in the littoral marine zone.

Spiders in the family Anyphaenidae can easily be separated from members of all other spider families due to the presence of a wide tracheal spiracle, a slit-like incision supplying the respiratory system, close to the spinnerets at about one third of the way down the length of the abdomen. The carapace is dark brown and the abdomen has a light chevron pattern.

Amaurobioides has an apparent Gondwanan distribution as the genus is found in South Australia, Tasmania, New Zealand, Chile and southern Africa. *Amaurobioides isolata* (South Australia) and *A. litoralis* (Tasmania) are the only representatives known from Australia, although the series of specimens on which *A. litoralis* was described, apparently includes two different species.

Sea-shore Spiders are nocturnal and can be seen wandering over rocks at night. They live in the marine spray zone where they construct tough silken retreats in rock fissures and crevices at or somewhat below the mean high-tide level. This retreat is about 3–5 cm long. The eggsac is lenticular and is attached to the inner surface of the retreat. Young spiders were found in retreats with their mother, but it is not known how long they remain there prior to dispersal.

The Tasmanian species, *Amaurobioides litoralis*, here a female, lives in the cracks of rocks in marine littoral zones. The coloration of spiders in *Amaurobioides* is uniform with a dark brown carapace and light chevron pattern on the abdomen. [B.C. Baehr]

Amaurobioides litoralis lives in the cracks of rocks in the marine spray zone, where it builds a watertight silk retreat in which enough air is trapped to survive the flooded periods at high tide. Here they also construct their eggsacs. [B.C. Baehr]

CLUBIONIDAE
Sac Spiders

- Eight small eyes in two rows
- Anterior lateral spinnerets conical and close together
- Legs long; two tarsal claws and claw tufts
- Night active hunters without prey capture web
- Sac-like retreat where the spiders hide during the day; females guard their eggsac
- Body length: 5–20 mm

Australia:
Taxonomy poorly resolved
Current: 35 species in 3 genera
Estimated: 150 species in 6 genera
World: 775 species in 17 genera

The common name Sac Spiders (family Clubionidae) refers to the sac-like retreat in which spiders of this family hide during the day. These mostly long-legged, fragile-looking spiders are generally pale or cinnamon coloured, sometimes with a weak abdominal pattern. The chelicerae are often darker coloured and protrude forwards from underneath the carapace.

Sac Spiders occur worldwide. In Australia the family includes two subfamilies, the Clubioninae and Eutichurinae. Clubioninae have a thoracic groove, which is absent in the Eutichurinae. In addition, the posterior eye row is usually wider than the anterior one in the Clubioninae, whereas it is not or only barely wider in the Eutichurinae.

The **Clubioninae** include the genera *Clubiona* and *Pteroneta* with described species in Australia. In contrast to *Clubiona*, *Pteroneta* have brushes of hairs on the tarsi of the second leg and the carapace has bluish spots caused by blue lobes of the mid-gut diverticula shining through the cuticle.

Clubiona is a very large genus with a worldwide distribution. In Australia 17 species have been named; however, species identification is almost impossible for any of these as a modern taxonomic revision of the genus in Australia has not been published. In Australia, *Clubiona* is generally associated with the bark of trees, in particular the loose, corticating bark of eucalypt trees. A study on *C. robusta* in South Australia showed that the spiders construct different types of retreats

As in many spiders, male Sac Spiders, here an unidentified *Cheiracanthium* from Western Australia, often have a more distinctive abdominal pattern than their female counterparts. [V. W. Framenau, Phoenix Environmental Sciences]

Long-legged or Slender Sac Spiders, here an unidentified *Cheiracanthium* male from South Australia feeding on a tipulid fly, often have very long and strong fangs which easily penetrate human skin. Bites from these spiders in Australia have been reported as being painful with localised redness and itchiness and may lead to systemic effects such as headache and nausea. [A. Lance]

This unidentified *Clubiona* female from Western Australia hides in a sac-shaped retreat under bark during the day, where it protects its disc-like eggsac. [V.W. Framenau, Phoenix Environmental Sciences]

Sac spiders, here an unidentified female from Western Australia, are nocturnal. The underside of all tarsi and metatarsi are covered by scopulae of dense hairs, enabling them to easily climb slippery surfaces. [V.W. Framenau, Phoenix Environmental Sciences]

Sac Spiders, here an unidentified *Clubiona* female, have comparatively small eyes, equal in size and arranged in two rows. Clubionidae are fairly uniform in their light brown coloration, often with a darker pattern on the abdomen. [F. Bokhari]

The genus *Calamoneta*, here an unidentified female from northern Queensland, does not have any described species in Australia. Spiders in the genus have long and slender legs and a greenish body. Slim conical spinnerets are typical for these clubionids. [P. Zborowski]

for broodcare and moulting. Broodcare requires stronger retreats, possibly to maintain favourable conditions for mother, eggs and juveniles to avoid the risk of desiccation. Females may lay two clutches per year in South Australia and juveniles remain in the nest for two moults and disperse as third instar.

The genus *Pteroneta* occurs only in northern Australia. A single species, *P. spinosa*, has been described from northern Queensland, and it is known to occur between Cairns and Cape York.

The systematic placement of the subfamily **Eutichurinae** either in the False Wolf Spiders (Miturgidae) or Sac Spiders is unsettled. The subfamily has also been considered a distinct taxon at the family level, the Eutichuridae. We follow studies within an Australasian context, which place this subfamily into the Clubionidae. In Australia, the subfamily is represented by the genus *Cheiracanthium*, the Slender or Long-legged Sac Spiders. Similar to *Clubiona*, there is a considerable fauna of described *Cheiracanthium* in Australia, but species identification of the 15 species is impossible as no modern taxonomic treatment exists.

In contrast to *Clubiona*, which appears to be mainly associated with trees, *Cheiracanthium* is more often found in the ground layer of forests and in herbaceous vegetation. Silken retreats may be constructed under rocks, in man-made structures or in the vegetation, generally in rolled leaves. However, habitat preferences of *Clubiona* and *Cheiracanthium* are not mutually exclusive and spiders appear to be somewhat versatile in their choice of habitat.

The eutichurine genus *Calamoneta* is only known from two described species from Indonesia, but the genus has also been reported from northern Queensland. The spinnerets of these spiders are long and conical and males in the genus have a very long and flexible first pair of legs.

The genus *Dorymetaecus* is unplaced within the Sac Spiders and includes a single species from Lord Howe Island, *D. spinnipes*. However, its placement in the Clubionidae is doubtful as the original description states that "*the genus appears to fall between groups Miturgeae and Zorae*", suggesting it to be associated with the Lycosoidea, i.e. Wolf Spiders and relatives.

Sac Spiders, in particular in the genus *Cheiracanthium*, have long and powerful fangs and can inflict a painful bite in humans. Local pain after a *Cheiracanthium* bite may last more than two hours and is accompanied by redness and swelling of the bite site. In some cases, systemic effects such as headache and nausea may be observed.

CORINNIDAE
Swift Spiders, Ant-mimics

- Eight eyes in two rows, posterior eye row generally procurved
- Anterior spinnerets short, conical, contiguous
- Legs slender, with two tarsal claws
- Male pedipalp bulb with corkscrew-shaped embolus (Castianeirinae)
- Day active without prey capture web, very fast runners
- Sac-like retreat in leaves and plant debris, where the spiders hide during the night and deposit their eggsac
- Body length: 3–12 mm

Australia:
Taxonomy revised
Current: 92 species in 16 genera
Estimated: 120 species in 16 genera
World: 1,150 species in 98 genera

The Swift Spiders (family Corinnidae) include extraordinarily fast ground-hunting spiders. As they are active during the day they are often seen between leaf litter, on tree trunks and between low vegetation, but also on open ground, for example around houses. Many are Batesian mimics of ants or other Hymenoptera, confusing potential predators with busy, ant-like bursts of speed.

As relatives of the Sac Spiders (family Clubionidae), Swift Spiders have a comparable eye pattern of similar-sized eyes in two rows. They have elongated bodies with long legs. The abdomen may be partly sclerotised, in particular around the pedicel.

Three subfamilies are recognised from Australia. The Castianeirinae, characterised by a short, corkscrew-shaped embolus of the male pedipalp, includes the majority of the indigenous Australian Swift Spider fauna. The Corinninae and Oedignathinae mainly include introduced cosmopolitan or tropical species and these are best identified based on species-specific characters.

The **Castianeirinae** include 13 genera in Australia, of which *Poecilipta* (26 species), *Battalus* (11 species), *Leichhardteus* (11 species) and *Nyssus* (10 species)

Opposite page: *Nyssus coloripes* is very common throughout Australia. The species differs from *N. funereus* by the different abdominal pattern and the orange front legs. These place *N. coloripes* in a mimicry chain involving other insects such as wasps and beetles (see page 368). [P. Zborowski]

Poecilipta smaragdinea from south-west Western Australia is a spectacular mimic of the Green-headed Ant, *Rhytidoponera metallica*. [V.W. Framenau, Phoenix Environmental Sciences]

The Yellow-horned Clerid Beetle, *Trogodendron fasciculatum*, is often found in burnt areas after a fire, and it is part of the mimicry chain with *Nyssus coloripes* and the Spider Wasp, *Fabriogenia*. [P. Zborowski]

This Spider Wasp (Pompilidae, Pepsinae), most probably a species of *Fabriogenia*, hunts spiders. With a nearly identical colour pattern to *Nyssus coloripes*, it is a rare example of a prey species, the spider, imitating one of its natural enemies, a wasp. However, the spider probably mimics the wasp to avoid predation (Batesian mimicry). [P. Zborowski]

are the most species rich. *Disupunna*, *Iridosupunna*, *Kolora*, *Nucastia*, *Ozcopa* and *Ticopa* each include between two and seven species from throughout the country. *Poecilipta* is the most species-rich genus of all Australian Swift Spiders. These are gracile spiders with slender legs.

Nyssus includes some of the most widespread and recognisable Australian Swift Spiders. They are black with white species-specific markings on the carapace and abdomen. Both *N. funereus* and *N. coloripes* are widespread throughout Australia, including Tasmania, and also occur in New Zealand.

Leichhardteus differs from all other Australian Castianeirinae by an enlarged pedipalp femur in males and the presence of four pairs of ventral spines on the tibiae of the first and second legs. The carapace is yellow-orange to dark brown, the legs yellow-orange to yellow-brown with or without dark markings and the abdomen is dark brown with or without pale spots or chevrons. These spiders are mainly found in eastern Australia with some rainforest species only known from very small ranges.

Copa, an otherwise African and Sri Lankan genus, only includes *Copa kabana*. *Medmassa* is represented only by *M. deelemanae* from the northern Torres Strait islands and *Leptopicia* includes only *L. bimaculata* from Queensland.

The **Corinninae** include only the introduced, cosmopolitan *Creugas gulosus*. These spiders have the tibiae of the first and second leg ventrally with 5–7 pairs of strong spines. The carapace is silvery-black, the abdomen somewhat lighter and the legs are brown. The species has so far been recorded from Queensland, New South Wales, the Northern Territory and Western Australia, but may occur elsewhere.

The **Oedignathinae** include *Oedignatha* and *Koppe*. *Oedignatha scrobiculata* occurs on Christmas Island, in the Northern Territory and Queensland, including some coral islands, as far south as Capricorn Cays. This species occurs from India into South-East Asia and has also been found in the Seychelles. It has a heavily sclerotised abdomen and paired spines on the tibiae of the first and second leg. *Koppe toddae* is only found in northern Queensland. Recent phylogenetic studies suggest that the subfamily Oedignathinae may rightly belong to the Spiny-legged Sac Spiders (family Liocranidae).

Swift Spiders inhabit a variety of habitats, including tropical and temperate rainforest, open eucalyptus forest, swamps, semi-arid areas, deserts and intertidal or littoral and riparian zones. The spiders construct a retreat in the substrate or rolled-up leaves where they also deposit their eggsac.

Leichhardteus garretti is found in rainforests throughout Queensland. This is a dark cinnamon-brown male with its characteristic white markings. [R.J. Raven]

Leichhardteus conopalpis has a distinct dark cephalic area of the carapace contrasting with an orange-brown base tone. The species is widely distributed in eastern Australia where it occurs in chenopod shrubland. Members of the genus *Leichhardteus* can be recognised by the enlarged pedipalp femur in males, which may have a conical protrusion in some species, as in *L. conopalpis*. [R.J. Raven]

Members of the genus *Poecilipta*, here an unidentified female from Queensland, are long-legged spiders, running around with their front legs held up to look like elbowed ant antennae. They dash around with ants, live with ants and may hunt ants. *Poecilipta* is an Australian endemic, and with 26 described species the most species-rich Swift Spider genus in Australia. [R.J. Raven]

Nyssus funereus, here a female from Queensland, is one of the most common Swift Spiders in Australia and it occurs throughout the country. It has also been collected in New Zealand. The species is completely black with white marks shaped by silvery scaly setae. A common and widely distributed spider, it is often found running on bark or between vegetation and is a mimic of a mutilid wasp. [P. Zborowski]

LIOCRANIDAE
Spiny-legged Sac Spiders

- Eight eyes in two rows, anterior row straight, posterior row procurved or recurved
- Carapace generally longer than it is wide
- Tibiae and metatarsi of first and second leg often with pairs of long spines; two tarsal claws
- Abdomen ovoid, generally without scute (in particular in females)
- Ground-dwelling hunting spiders
- Body length: 5–12 mm

Australia:
Taxonomy poorly resolved
Current: 1 species in 1 genus
Estimated: 20 species in 5 genera
World: 171 species in 27 genera

The Spiny-legged Sac Spiders (family Liocranidae) are a poorly diagnosed family of small to medium-sized ground hunters. They lack true claw tufts but have tenent hairs on their tarsi. Liocranidae do not have extensive abdominal sclerotisation (at least in females), as is typical in many Swift Spiders (family Corinnidae).

The Spiny-legged Sac Spiders are largely Holarctic and Afrotropical, with some species known from India and South-East Asia, and it remains unclear if the family occurs in Australia. The Australian fauna currently includes a single species only, *Liparochrysis resplendens*, which has not been recorded since its original description at the beginning of the 1900s. Nothing is known about the biology of this species. No modern description of the species is available and therefore it remains undiagnosible without re-examining the specimen on which the description was based on. It may not be a member of the Liocranidae.

The subfamily Oedignathinae with the genera *Oedignatha* and *Koppe*, which here have been included in the Swift Spiders (Corinnidae), may rightly belong to the Spiny-legged Sac Spiders.

SELENOPIDAE
Wall Crab Spiders

- Eight eyes in two rows, anterior row with six eyes, posterior row with two eyes
- Carapace and abdomen flattened
- Legs directed sideways ('laterigrade')
- Pale to medium brown, mottled dark brown to black
- Extremely fast runners
- Habitat specialists living in narrow crevices in rock piles and rocky outcrops or under bark in tropical to dry sclerophyll forests
- Night active hunters without prey capture web
- Body length: 3–12 mm

Australia:
Partially revised
Current: 37 species in 1 genus
Estimated: 70 species in 1 genus
World: 265 species in 10 genera

The legs of Wall Crab Spiders (family Selenopidae) are directed sideways, like those of crabs ('laterigrade'), and within the spiders they are similar to Huntsman Spiders (family Sparassidae) and some Crab Spiders (Thomisidae). This feature allows these spiders to move exceptionally fast in any direction. Like Huntsman Spiders they are flat and perfectly adapted to their main habitats of rocky outcrops, breakaways, scree slopes, and the underside of the bark of trees. With this similar morphology and ecology, these spiders may be confused with Huntsman Spiders, but selenopids have a very different eye pattern, which consists of a single recurved row of six eyes with the fourth pair situated behind. Huntsman Spiders have two rows of four eyes. The cryptic nature, perfect camouflage and high speed of Wall Crab Spiders are possibly responsible for the fact that they are rarely collected.

Selenopids are found in the tropical and subtropical regions worldwide, and occur throughout mainland Australia. In the semi-arid and arid landscapes they can often be found on rocky outcrops or along breakaways. Many of these rock dwellers have small ranges due to the isolation of their habitats. In contrast, the bark-dwelling species are often common in temperate and dry sclerophyll forests and these species are often widespread. Wall Crab Spiders have so far not been found in Tasmania.

The highest diversity of Wall Crab Spiders in Australia is reported from the Pilbara region of Western Australia where these spiders are targeted within surveys for environmental assessment studies for large-scale resources projects. However, there is no reason to believe that these spiders are not similarly diverse and abundant in other rangelands throughout the arid and semi-arid zones of Australia.

Leg spination is one of the primary characters that differentiates the selenopid genera; however, the Australian fauna consists only of a single genus, *Karaops*. Species identification generally requires the use of a stereomicroscope to examine details of the male and female genitalia.

Little is known about the biology of *Karaops*. Females construct a disc-shaped, smooth and papery eggsac, which is secured against the substrate under rocks and under bark. Females have been observed to guard their eggsacs but it is not known when they abandon their offspring.

Karaops is the only genus of Wall Crab Spiders in Australia. Spiders in *Karaops*, as seen in this unidentified female from Western Australia, generally have a mottled brown, grey or black pattern that provides camouflage in their particular habitat, which here is the bark of a eucalypt tree. [F. Bokhari]

This unidentified immature *Karaops* from Fitzgerald River National Park, Western Australia, was found in leaf litter and is possibly one of the bark-dwelling species. The colour pattern is less distinct than in the other species illustrated here. [V.W. Framenau, Phoenix Environmental Sciences]

The flat body of *Karaops jarrit* helps it to vanish quickly into cracks or under bark. This long-legged species is not uncommon in the Jarrah and Karri forests of south-west Western Australia where the spiders live under bark. [V.W. Framenau, Phoenix Environmental Sciences]

Opposite page bottom: Wall Crab Spiders are similar to Huntsman Spiders (family Sparassidae), both in general appearance and habitat preferences. However, they differ distinctly in the arrangement of the eyes. Wall Crab Spiders have six eyes in their first row and two eyes set back behind at the side. [F. Bokhari]

SALTICIDAE
Jumping Spiders

- Eight eyes in three or four rows, anterior median eyes large
- Anterior spinnerets short, conical, close together
- Legs stout, two tarsal claws and dense claw tufts
- Mostly day active ambushers without prey capture web
- Sac-like retreat where the spiders hide during the night and care for their eggsac
- Body length: 2–15 mm

Australia:
Partially revised
Current: 385 species in 85 genera
Estimated: 1,000 species in 95 genera
World: 5,615 species in 592 genera

The Jumping Spiders (family Salticidae) require almost no introduction. These are spiders which use visual cues for foraging and mating, facilitated by the excellent vision of their enlarged anterior median eyes. As this is also the sensory channel that humans use, much of the behavioural repertoire of the Jumping Spiders is open to us for interpretation, without the need for a complex laboratory set-up. However, vision is not the only way for these spiders to communicate. Their mating behaviour, for example, also includes complex behavioural sequences employing other communication channels, including tactile signals or vibratory cues such as drumming on the surface with pedipalps or abdomen. These are often also used in other spiders with poorer vision. The Jumping Spiders' superior sight, combined with strong legs, let them jump many times their body length while very accurately targeting their prey.

Jumping Spiders are readily recognised by their enlarged anterior median eyes. However, they display a great diversity of body shapes, colour patterns and behaviours. The evolutionary variation of these spiders, through adding acute vision to their senses, has been so successful that they are the most species-rich of all spider families. This also applies to Australia where they are the most diverse of all spider families in terms of the number of described species. It is impossible within the scope of this book to do more than scratch the surface of this remarkable diversity.

Jumping Spiders are generally sexually dimorphic, with males often

These elongated and flattened Jumping Spiders in the genus *Holoplathys* from Western Australia are closely related to similar species in the genera *Paraplatoides* and *Zebraplatys*. These spiders generally hunt on trees, with a retreat under bark, where the females build their disc-like eggsacs and care for their young. [F. Bokhari]

Jumping Spiders have greatly enlarged anterior median eyes with superior vision. Amongst some of the more unusual features of their eyes is the ability to see colours, including ultraviolet light, and to perceive depth. The latter is of great importance for prey capture, as the spiders have to judge how far to jump in an attack. Lacking strong muscles, their ability to jump often many times their own length is based on the build up of hydraulic pressure using hemolymph. [V.W. Framenau, Phoenix Environmental Sciences]

The agile Bronze Aussie Jumper, *Helpis minitabunda*, here a male from Brisbane, is mainly found in eastern Australia, although the species has also been recorded from Western Australia, New Guinea and New Zealand. This spider has an elongated body and, as in many other jumping spiders, the male has more distinct colour patterns than the female. [V.W. Framenau, Phoenix Environmental Sciences]

Ocrisiona jovialis is widely distributed in southern Australia. This image shows a female from Melbourne. There is much variation in the colour of individuals and future taxonomic revision of these spiders may show that more than one species is involved. [V. W. Framenau, Phoenix Environmental Sciences]

Opisthoncus, here a female from Western Australia, is a diverse genus in Australia with the taxonomy of the many undescribed species as yet unresolved. *Opisthoncus* often have a distinct 'pseudo-eye', a dark and elevated spot, between the last pair of eyes. [V.W. Framenau, Phoenix Environmental Sciences]

The highly enlarged chelicerae of this male **Opisthoncus,** or a related genus from northern Queensland, shows a big single tooth at the lower front of the chelicerae. [P. Zborowski]

spectacularly more colourful than their female counterparts, and these colour patterns may be exaggerated by exuberant hairy decorations in males. Males of the genus *Maratus* have abdominal flaps that they spread when courting a female, amplifying the signal displayed by the extremely colourful abdomen. Sexual selection plays an important part in maintaining this dimorphism, as females may be able to discriminate between different quality mates by their coloration. In addition, sexual selection has also been suggested as one of the driving forces for Jumping Spider diversity.

Jumping Spiders have largely abandoned the prey capture web, although some species such as the tropical *Portia fimbriata,* which occurs throughout the tropics of Australia, may construct a platform web as a base for their pursuit of other spiders. Prey specialisation is not uncommon in Jumping Spiders. For example, *Cosmophasis bitaeniata* lives inside the colonies of the Green Tree Ant, *Oecophylla smaragdina*, feeding on their larvae. The spider stimulates minor workers to release the larva they are carrying by drumming on their antennae and head. By handling and eating the ant larvae, *Cosmophasis* acquires the colony-specific hydrocarbon profile of the ants.

Traditionally, the Jumping Spiders have been broken up into three broad groups, depending on the number of teeth that they have on the back edge of the cheliceral groove. Some have many teeth (Pluridentati), some have one fused tooth (Fissidentati) and others have a single tooth (Unidentati). It is now clear that these do not represent coherent units in terms of evolution, but there is no doubt that such a classification helps to break this massive group of spiders into manageable units for easier identification.

Although it is impossible to provide a stable subfamily arrangement for Jumping Spiders, molecular systematic studies have revealed broad continental patterns for some groups. A group termed the **Astioida** appears to represent many Australasian genera, with few genera of this group known from outside of Australia, New Zealand and nearby islands. More widespread genera are the ant-mimicking *Myrmarachne* and the small spiders of the genus *Neon*. Typical representatives of the Australian fauna include the genera *Adoxotoma* (9 species), *Helpis* (7 species), *Jacksonoides* (7 species), *Sondra* (15 species), *Holoplatys* (36 species), *Opisthoncus* (30 species), *Simaetha* (10 species), *Simaethula* (7 species), *Mopsus* (one species, *M. mormon*), *Sandalodes* (5 species), and *Ligonopes* (4 species).

In addition, the **Euophryinae** are well represented in Australasia, although this subfamily also occurs in the Americas and elsewhere. Australian Euophryinae include *Cytaea* (10 species), *Hypoblemum* (2 species), *Jotus* (6 species), *Maratus* (34 species), *Prostheclina* (7 species), *Omoedus* (13 species), *Saitis* (8 species) and *Servaea* (6 species).

The **Spartaeinae** have traditionally been identified by a character of the male pedipalp, i.e. a furrow on the tegulum. They are considered one of the more basal lineages of the Jumping Spiders, having separated from the rest early in the evolutionary history. However, they include one of the most advanced spiders based on behavioural complexity, the Fringed Jumping Spider, *Portia fimbriata*. This species mainly occurs in the northern parts of Australia but is also found in South-East Asia. *Portia* is a spider-hunter and as such it is enormously resourceful. Its instinctive predation tactics have been shown to be extremely adaptable by trial and error, a behaviour likened to learning. *Portia* is not choosey when it comes to its prey and takes both vagrant hunters and invades the webs of web-building species.

The **Heliophaninae** include *Afraflacilla* (7 species), *Cosmophasis* (10 species) and *Menemerus* (4 species).

Many unplaced indigenous genera of Australian Jumping Spiders are recorded from the country and some subfamilies are only represented by introduced species. For example, *Asemonea stella* in the subfamily **Lyssomaninae** was imported from Africa. Adanson's House Jumper, *Hasarius adansoni*, representing the informal **Hasariae**, is a circumtropical spider often associated with houses.

Jumping Spiders cause about five per cent of spider bites in humans in Australia. In general these spiders inflict minor pain with only minor effects such as redness and minor swelling.

A female unidentified *Simaethula* is inconspicuously coloured. It is well camouflaged and, with the false eyes on its rear, confusing to its predators. The genus has not been taxonomically revised and species identification is difficult to impossible. [P. Zborowski]

The genus *Ligonipes*, here a female from northern Queensland found on bark, includes ant-mimics closely related to *Myrmarachne*. [P. Zborowski]

Jumping Spiders often display distinct sexual dimorphism. In the Monkey-faced Jumping Spider, *Mopsus mormon*, the female (left), although colourful, lacks the dark front legs and only the male (right) has the white bushes (beard) beside its eyes. Many male traits are a product of sexual selection, i.e. exaggerated male traits are an advantage either in a direct competition between males or in courting a female. [P. Zborowski]

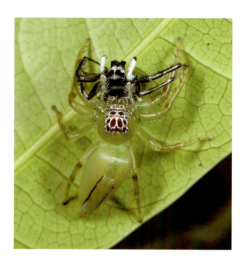 

This female Monkey-faced Jumping Spider, *Mopsus mormon* (left), has taken one of the colourful ant-mimicking Jumping Spiders, *Cosmophasis micans*. The male (right), however, has shown its cannibalistic behaviour and taken the young of its own species. *Mopsus mormon* is common on foliage in the tropics and as far south as Brisbane. [P. Zborowski]

This unidentified *Cosmophasis* female from north Queenland is minute, measuring only 3 mm in body length when adult. [P. Zborowski]

The males of *Copocrossa tenuilineata*, a conspicuous Jumping Spider from northern Queensland, have extremely elongated front legs. This is a sexually dimorphic trait that plays a role either in male-male competition, or in the mating display for a female. [P. Zborowski]

Opposite page: The bearded male of the Monkey-faced Jumping Spider, *Mopsus mormon*, shows the unique ability of Jumping Spiders to turn the cephalothorax at a different angle to the body and therefore facilitate orientation through using visual cues. [P. Zborowski]

The Fringed Jumping Spider, *Portia fimbriata*, is a prey specialist and mainly hunts other spiders. A multitude of behavioural studies on these fascinating spiders has shown an adaptability of behaviour unlike in any other spider. *Portia* may stalk prey, invade webs of other spiders effortlessly without getting caught, and at the same time may produce deceptive vibratory signals to the web owner. They may also construct their own prey capture web, very unlike other Jumping Spiders. There appear to be regional differences in the behavioural patterns of these spiders. In this image, a female has invaded the flimsy sheet-web of a Fishing or Nursery-web Spider (family Pisauridae) and made a meal of its inhabitant. [P. Zborowski]

Like many Jumping Spiders, the Fringed Jumping Spider, *Portia fimbriata*, is sexually dimorphic, i.e. males look different to females. Exaggerated signals may be important in male-male competition, although fights between males are usually short in this species. [P. Zborowski]

Opposite page: The Green Ant-mimicking Jumping Spider, *Cosmophasis bitaeniata*, is a nest associate of the Green Tree Ant, *Oecophylla smaragdina*. It steals ant larvae from minor workers and avoids attack from the ants by chemically mimicking their cuticular hydrocarbon 'smell'. [P. Zborowski]

The Metallic Green Jumping Spider, *Cosmophasis micans*, is found from northern to central eastern Queensland. The male (left) has overcome a winged ant, the female (right) displays a slightly different colour pattern on the abdomen [P. Zborowski]

Spiders in the genus *Omoedus*, here a female from Queensland with characteristic black and white stripes, are common on eucalypt bark, where they mainly hunt ants. Their eggsac contains about 20 eggs and is protected in a small cell within a roll of the bark, or in the gap between the bark and the tree. [P. Zborowski]

A male (left) and female (right) of *Maratus chrysomelas* illustrate the distinct sexual dimorphism in Jumping Spiders. Mature males need to catch a female's attention to be accepted as mates in their short life-span, whereas the female's main role is to remain inconspicuous to predators when caring for the brood. Males generally find females through pheromones on the female's drag- or safety-line. [Left: F. Bokhari; Right: V.W. Framenau, Phoenix Environmental Sciences]

The genus *Myrmarachne* includes many ant mimics; however, it appears that they do not mimic ants to exploit and prey on them, but that the spiders disguise themselves as dangerous or bad-tasting to avoid predators (Batesian mimicry). Here the mimic is at the top of the image with the ant below. [P. Zborowski]

Ant mimicry by Jumping Spiders in the genus *Myrmarachne* is not only limited to body form, but extends into the spiders' behaviour, as they hold their front pair of legs in the typical elbowed fashion of ant antennae. In the rainforests of north Queensland, this pair of model (right) plus mimic (left) are quite hard to tell apart. The taxonomy of the genus *Myrmarachne* is very difficult as the same species may mimic different ants throughout their life stages. [P. Zborowski]

Male Peacock Spiders (of the genus *Maratus*) come in a wide array of colours. These images show species recorded from Western Australia, with *M. mungaich* or a related species from near Perth (top), *M. sarahae* from the Stirling Ranges (centre) and an undescribed species from near Eucla (bottom). [V.W. Framenau, Phoenix Environmental Sciences]

Above and left: The males of the Peacock Spiders, genus *Maratus*, here *M. pavonis* from Western Australia, are arguably the most spectacularly coloured of all Australian Jumping Spiders. *Maratus* is endemic to Australia and currently includes 36 described species, but the genus is likely to be more diverse. Male Peacock Spiders have incredibly coloured abdomens, and also possess flaps on the side of the abdomen, which they display in courtship to make their abdomen bigger. Their visual display also includes waving their third pair of legs, which have their own ornamentations. [Left: V.W. Framenau, Phoenix Environmental Sciences; Right: F. Bokhari]

PHILODROMIDAE
Running Crab Spiders

- Eight eyes in two strongly recurved rows; anterior and posterior median eyes forming a square
- Carapace flattened, without fovea
- Abdomen ovoid or elongated
- First two pairs of legs, in particular the second pair, longer than the third and fourth pair; two tarsal claws and dense tufts
- Vagrant hunters on vegetation
- Body length: 8–25 mm

Australia:
Taxonomy poorly resolved
Current: 5 species in 3 genera
Estimated: 20 species in 5 genera
World: 542 species in 29 genera

The Running Crab Spiders (family Philodromidae) superficially resemble the Crab Spiders (family Thomisidae) and these were for a long time believed to represent their closest relatives. However, Running Crab Spiders are more closely related to the Sac Spiders (Clubionidae) and Ground Spiders (Gnaphosidae) and allies, whereas the Crab Spiders are more closely related to the Wolf Spiders and allies (superfamily Lycosoidea).

The Running Crab Spiders are a diverse spider family worldwide but only a few species have been described from Australia. These species have not had modern taxonomic treatments and therefore identification is difficult.

All five Australian representatives of Running Crab Spider belong to the subfamily **Philodrominae**. The genus *Gephyrota* includes the single species *G. limbata*, originally described from Queensland. *Philodromus* includes three species, *P. austerus* and *P. planus*, both originally described from Queensland and the latter also reported from New Guinea, and *P. luteovirescens*, described from Tasmania. It is unlikely that the true identity of *P. luteovirescens* can be established as the original specimen on which the spider was described has been lost.

Tibellus tenellus is the most common and most recognisable of all Australian Running Crab Spiders, and the only representative of the genus *Tibellus* in the country. These spiders have an elongated body with a greenish-brown coloration which is typical for spiders inhabiting grasslands. It is widespread and has been recorded from eastern Australia and south-west Western Australia. It has been historically recorded in the Eastern Palearctic from Russia and China, although a review of Eastern Palearctic *Tibellus* argues that *T. tenellus* is absent from the region. Only a comprehensive review of the genus *Tibellus*, including *T. tenellus*, which was originally described from Queensland, can solve the distribution limits of the species.

Little is known about the biology of Australian Running Crab Spiders. Members of the family are generally hunters on the ground and in vegetation. They are more active hunters than the sit-and-wait predators in the Crab Spiders (Thomisidae). *Tibellus* are mainly known from grassy habitats. Males of European species have been reported to tie females down with silk before mating, a behaviour otherwise also reported from Crab Spiders. Females fix the round, discoid eggsacs to the substrate.

Tibellus tenellus, here a female from Western Australia, is the most common Running Crab Spider in Australia. The species has an elongated body with characteristic greenish-brown colour and a pattern which includes a forked dark band on the carapace. The species is a typical inhabitant of grassland but was here photographed on the branch of a shrub. [V.W. Framenau, Phoenix Environmental Sciences]

Tibellus tenellus is often confused with members of the genus *Thasyraea* in the Spiny-leg Spiders (family Zoridae). However, it differs distinctly in the eye arrangement and colour pattern. [A. Lance]

Blind Ground Spiders (family Gnaphosidae) have been found in arid Western Australia. The female illustrated here was collected in an exploration boreholes in the western Pilbara region in Western Australia. This spider inhabits the subterranean fissures, possibly feeding on a diverse troglofauna that includes Short-tailed Whipscorpions (Schizomida), cockroaches and other smaller spiders. [V.W. Framenau, Phoenix Environmental Sciences]

GNAPHOSIDAE
Ground Spiders

- Eight eyes in two rows; posterior median eyes flattened, irregularly shaped and with silvery shine
- Cylindrical anterior lateral spinnerets separated by more than their diameter and with greatly enlarged and widened piriform gland spigots
- Legs slender or stout with two tarsal claws; sideways orientated ('laterigrade') in *Hemicloea*
- Night active hunters without prey capture web
- Sac-like retreat where the spiders rest during the day and females tend to the eggsac
- Body length: 3–25 mm

> **Australia:**
> Taxonomy poorly resolved
> Current: 49 species in 15 genera
> Estimated: 500 species in 24 genera
> **World:** 2,147 species in 121 genera

The Ground Spiders (family Gnaphosidae) are a species-rich, free hunting element of the Australian spider fauna, although they generally live a cryptic life in leaf litter, under bark or under rocks. The taxonomy of this family is poorly resolved and only a few species have received a modern taxonomic treatment.

The Ground Spiders are one of seven Australian families that belong to the superfamily Gnaphosoidea, the Ground Spiders and allies. These are treated in the last chapters of this book and therefore briefly characterised here. Gnaphosoidea have flattened posterior median eyes that have lost the dome-shaped focusing lense and are often irregularly shaped, for example oval rather than round, and reflect a silvery shine. These eyes appear able to detect polarised light. Within this superfamily, four families form the 'lower' gnaphosoids, which retain a complete ring of seta-bearing cuticle on the anterior lateral spinnerets, the Termite Hunters (Ammoxenidae), the Long-jawed Ground Spiders (Gallieniellidae), Scorpion Spiders (Trochanteriidae) and the Swift Ground Spiders (Cithaeronidae). In contrast, in the 'higher' gnaphosoids, the sclerotised ring on the anterior lateral spinnerets is reduced; these include the White-tailed Spiders (Lamponidae), Long-spinneret Ground Spiders (Prodidomidae) and Ground Spiders (Gnaphosidae).

Ground Spiders can be identified by the greatly enlarged and widened piriform gland spigots on the anterior lateral spinnerets. This microscopic character can hardly be used for the identification of these spiders in the field. However, these spiders generally have cylindrical anterior spinnerets that are separated by at least their diameter and ovoid silvery posterior median eyes. The outer edge of the maxillae, where the pedipalps emerge, are generally noticeably indented.

The family includes a number of very different spiders in Australia. At large, they are small to medium-sized inconspicuous ground-dwelling hunters, but the Australian fauna includes some remarkable exceptions, including *Eilica* with its bright red markings, the contrasty white-marked *Ceryerda,* and the large and flattened species in the genus *Hemicloea*.

A stable subfamily arrangement for the Ground Spiders that accommodates the Australian fauna does not exist and few Australian genera have received modern taxonomic diagnoses. Species identification is virtually impossible.

Anzacia is one of the Ground Spider genera with recent taxonomic studies, at least for one of its species groups, the *A. perexigua*-group, which includes five of the 13 Australian species in the genus. They are small spiders (3–7 mm long) that are characterised by the combined presence of slightly notched trochanters, a preening brush on the metatarsi of the third and fourth leg, and lanceolate iridescent hairs covering the dorsal surface of the carapace and abdomen, in addition to some specific genitalic characters. *Anzacia* is found throughout the country.

Some *Eilica* can be recognised by the presence of two or three translucent laminae on the cheliceral retromargin. The chelicerae extend considerably beyond the edge of the carapace. The spiders are fairly small, less than 10 mm, and have pale or red spots on the abdomen. Seven species of *Eilica* are described from Australia, although the diversity within the genus is probably higher. Most species appear widespread and occur in or into the semi-arid and arid regions of the country. *Eilica* can be observed near meat ant nests (*Iridomyrmex*) apparently feeding on these ferocious predators.

The genus *Hemicloea* includes flattened Ground Spiders that generally rest under the bark of eucalypt trees. These spiders are often confused with the flattened members of the Scorpion Spiders (Trochanteriidae) and one of the trochanteriid genus names, *Hemicloeina*, adds to this confusion. However, *Hemicloea* differs from the trochanteriids by the spinneret characters listed above. *Hemicloea* mainly includes Australian representatives and 12 species are known from this country. One common eastern Australian species, the Flattened Bark Spider, *H. rogenhoferi*, is also found in New Zealand. Species identification is almost impossible as no modern taxonomic treatment of the genus exists. The genus presumably includes many undescribed species.

Ground Spiders are generally active at night. They are vagrant hunters that have a silky retreat where they hide during the day and deposit their eggsac. Ground Spiders are commonly found under stones and under bark. Many species are adapted to dry conditions and this group is therefore well represented in the arid and semi-arid Australian interior. However, gnaphosids can also be found in rainforests, vine thickets and eucalypt forests.

This male *Ceryerda* from northern Western Australia has long legs in contrasting colours in addition to light patches on the carapace and abdomen. The genus *Ceryerda* currently includes only a single described species, *C. cursitans*; however, true species diversity is considerably higher. [F. Bokhari]

The genus *Ceryerda*, here an unidentified male from the Pilbara region in Western Australia, includes unusually contrasting spiders in the family Gnaphosidae. This male has dense brushes of white hairs on its front legs. Similar brushes are known from males in other spiders and are generally used to augment their mating displays. [F. Bokhari]

Members of the genus *Hemicloea*, here an unidentified female from south-west Western Australia, have sideways directed legs. They spend the day under the bark of trees, but at night they are extremely fast hunters on the surface of tree trunks. *Hemicloea* are often confused with the flattened Scorpion Spiders (Trochanteriidae), for example in the genus *Rebilus*. [V.W. Framenau, Phoenix Environmental Sciences]

Most members of the Gnaphosidae, such as this unidentified male from suburban Perth, are inconspicuous, drably coloured ground-dwellers. They may have silvery scaly hair that renders a silvery shine. The family is well adapted to arid conditions and a large undocumented fauna exists in Australia. [V.W. Framenau, Phoenix Environmental Sciences]

This unidentified *Eilica* male from Western Australia is one of the more conspicuous Ground Spiders, displaying an orange-red carapace and yellow spots on the abdomen. *Eilica* occur throughout the country but the diversity is probably much higher than suggested by the seven species so far described. [V.W. Framenau, Phoenix Environmental Sciences]

This female *Intruda signata* shows the general, inconspicuous appearance of Ground Spiders (Gnaphosidae). This species has a characteristic pattern of light chevrons on the abdomen. *Intruda signata* has a largely southern Australian distribution and has also been recorded from New Zealand. Little is known about the biology of the species, but in New Zealand it was recorded from long grass in a garden. [R.J. Raven]

PRODIDOMIDAE
Long-spinneret Ground Spiders

- Eight eyes in two rows, sub-equal in size
- Greatly elongated anterior lateral spinnerets, which originate far in advance of the other four spinnerets (except in *Prodidomus*)
- Long and slender legs with two tarsal claws
- Ground-living hunters without prey capture web
- Body length: 1.8–5 mm

Australia:
Taxonomy revised
Current: 142 species in 7 genera
Estimated: 170 species in 8 genera
World: 304 species in 31 genera

The Long-spinneret Ground Spiders (family Prodidomidae) are fast running ground-dwellers without webs. Most Australian species possess extremely long anterior lateral spinnerets that originate half or two-thirds of the way along the underside of the abdomen. Together with the Ground Spiders (Gnaphosidae) and White-tailed Spiders (Lamponidae) they belong to the 'higher' Gnaphosoidea.

Most Australian Long-spinneret Ground Spiders belong to the subfamily **Molycriinae**, which includes those species with elongated anterior lateral spinnerets: *Cryptoerithus* (19 species), *Molycria* (36 species), *Myandra* (4 species), *Nomindra* (16 species), *Wesmaldra* (14) and *Wydundra* (45 species). Morphological differences between these genera are related to the arrangement and shape of the eyes, the arrangement of the spinnerets, and also to size difference. The subfamily **Prodidominae** includes spiders without elongated spinnerets, and only includes a single genus, *Prodidomus,* which in Australia is represented by eight species. However, *Prodidomus* have greatly enlarged posterior lateral spinnerets, which is unique within the Long-spinneret Ground Spiders.

Molycriine Long-spinneret Ground Spiders are common throughout Australia, but most species are only known from very restricted distributions. Among the more widespread species around Australia are *Molycria quadricauda* (southern Australia into mid-central Queensland), *Myandra bicincta* (all of Australia except the tropical north) and *Nomindra flavipes* (south-western Australia into South Australia). The small day-active species of the genera *Myandra* and *Nomindra* have at least parts of their bodies covered with iridescent scales or plumose setae. They have been found amongst ants, mimicking their behaviour and appearance. The mimicry is not just for protection, as the spiders apparently eat their ant hosts.

Like the Molycriinae, *Prodidomus* may be found in soil embankments where they rest deep in the cracks. The genus is largely restricted to the northern half of Australia. *Prodidomus rufus* is a widespread species worldwide and possibly synanthropic.

Molcyria vokes is a common litter-dwelling spider in Western Australia. This female from Gwambygine Pool Reserve has lost its right front leg but makes up for it with its remaining seven long legs. [V.W. Framenau, Phoenix Environmental Sciences]

Molycria stanisici is dark grey with a pale spot at the end of the abdomen. It occurs only around Brisbane and is found in litter amongst ants. [R.J. Raven]

This *Molycria quadricauda* female displays the greatly elongated anterior lateral spinnerets, which originate far in advance of the other four spinnerets, a feature which is typical for most groups within the Prodidomidae. *Molycria quadricauda* is one of the most common Long-spinneret Ground Spiders, with a distribution covering Queensland, New South Wales, Victoria, South Australia and southern Western Australia. [B.C. Baehr]

LAMPONIDAE
White-tailed Spiders

- Eight eyes in two rows, posterior median eyes oval
- Pair of oval sclerites just behind the epigastric furrow on the underside of the abdomen
- Legs with two tarsal claws
- Sac-like retreat where the spiders hide during the day and rear their young
- Night active without prey capture web
- Body length: 3–13 mm

Australia:
Taxonomy revised
Current: 188 species in 22 genera
Estimated: 200 species in 24 genera
World: 192 species in 23 genera

The White-tailed Spiders (family Lamponidae) are generally dark-coloured ground-dwelling spiders, often with a conspicuous white spot at the back of their abdomen just above the spinnerets. The White-tailed Spiders are thought to be the sister group of the Ground Spiders (Gnaphosidae) and Long-spinneret Ground Spiders (Prodidomidae) combined. Together they are regarded as the 'higher' Gnaphosoidea based on the reduced sclerotised ring of the anterior lateral spinnerets.

Most White-tailed Spiders can be recognised by a pair of large, oval sclerites situated just behind the epigastric furrow on the underside of the abdomen, although these sclerites are inconspicuous in the small species of the subfamily Pseudolamponinae.

The White-tailed Spiders are restricted to Australia, New Guinea, New Caledonia and New Zealand, although the New Zealand fauna only includes the probably human-introduced, partially synanthropic *Lampona cylindrata* and *L. murina*. The only genus of the family that does not occur in Australia is *Centrocalia*, which is endemic to New Caledonia with three species.

The White-tailed Spiders include three subfamilies, the Lamponinae, the Centrothelinae, and the Pseudolamponinae. The Lamponinae have a peculiar, evenly rectangular endite and tubular pedicel sclerites and the Centrothelinae have posterior median spinnerets each with longitudinal row of three heavily enlarged cylindrical gland spigots. Females in this subfamily have an anterior abdominal scute. The Pseudolamponinae are characterised by the loss of leg spines.

This elongated, unidentified male White-tailed Spider, possibly *Lampona cylindrata*, pulls the left third leg through its chelicerae for cleaning. This individual was encountered in dry sclerophyll forest near the Stirling Ranges in south-west Western Australia. [V.W. Framenau, Phoenix Environmental Sciences]

The **Lamponinae** includes the most common White-tailed Spiders, including those partially synanthropic spiders in the genus *Lampona*. *Lampona cylindrata* is common throughout southern Australia and *L. murina* occurs only along the east coast, being most common in Queensland and becoming less common towards New South Wales and into Victoria. A third related species, *L. papua*, is endemic to New Guinea. Overall, *Lampona* includes 56 species in Australia. Other lamponinae genera include: *Lamponata* with a single species, *L. daviesae*, from throughout mainland Australia; *Lamponega*, with three species from Western and South Australia; *Lamponella*, with ten species from coastal eastern and western Australia; *Lamponicta*, with *L. cobon* from southern Australia; and *Lamponina*, with six species from mainly semi-arid and arid landscapes. *Lamponoides coottha* and *Lamponova way* are largely eastern Australian, whereas *Lamponusa gleneagle* is from Western Australia.

Lampona cylindrata, here a female photographed in Perth, is one of the most common White-tailed Spiders in Australia. Due to its synanthropic habits it is often encountered by people inside houses or sheds. This species is common in the southern half of Australia, whereas the closely related *L. murina* only occurs in eastern Australia. [V.W. Framenau, Phoenix Environmental Sciences]

Platylampona mezappa is an unusually flattened lamponine White-tailed Spider from Queensland and New South Wales. Within the Gnaphosoidea, this morphological adaptation to live under bark and in rock crevices has evolved at least three times as it is also found in *Hemicloea* in the Ground Spiders (Gnaphosidae) and most Scorpion Spiders (Trochanteriidae).

The **Centrothelinae** includes 87 species in ten genera of White-tailed Spiders in Australia. *Asadipus*, with ten species, occurs throughout the country, *Bigenditia* includes two species from western and eastern Australia respectively, *Centroina* (11 species), *Centrothele* (ten species), *Graycassis* (ten species) and *Queenvic* (three species) are mainly restricted to eastern Australia, although single species may be found elsewhere. *Centsymplia gloriosus* occurs in south-eastern Queensland. *Longepi* (eight species) and *Prinosternum* (three species) are found in south-eastern and south-western Australia. The largest genus of the subfamily, *Notsodipus*, includes 18 species from throughout the country.

Lampona includes 56 species in Australia, such as this unidentified female from the Weld Range in the mid-west of Western Australia. Colour patterns are variable in the genus, but a white spot at the end of the abdomen is generally present. [F. Bokhari]

The **Pseudolamponinae** are small spiders of about 2–4 mm in body length. Two genera are found in Australia, *Paralampona* with eight species and *Pseudolampona* with 20 species. These spiders are rarely collected and occur in the arid and semi-arid zones.

White-tailed Spiders generally live in forest landscapes or in shrubland. Some species are partially synanthropic and can be found in and around buildings, most notably *L. cylindrata* and *L. murina*. Most species are active at night. During the day they hide away in a silken retreat under bark or stones. White-tailed Spiders hunt other spiders and this includes other synanthropic species such as Jumping Spiders (Salticidae), Australian Redback Spiders (*Latrodectus*), Daddy Long-legs Spiders (Pholcidae) and Black and Brown House Spiders (*Badumna*). *Lampona* eggsacs are placed in a web retreat and are usually semicircular or oval and attached to the substrate.

Bites by White-tailed Spiders have been implicated in causing severe necrotic ulcerations in humans. However, a study of more than 100 confirmed bites by *Lampona* species, i.e. where the spider was caught and identified by an arachnologists, did not result in ulcerations, but mainly caused localised pain, that was in some cases severe, and minor skin lesions. Systemic effects such as nausea and headaches were reported in some cases. Analyses of the venom of these spiders did not isolate a necrotising component. However, *Lampona* bites are frequent due to their synanthropic habits. People are mainly bitten by spiders hiding indoors, for example in bedding or within clothes left on the floor.

This unidentified species of *Lamponina*, possibly *L. elongata*, was encountered near Mt Magnet in Western Australia. In this genus, the legs originate in circular openings fully surrounded by a sclerotised cuticle, as the sternum is fused with the lateral sclerites. White-tailed Spiders are very diverse in Australia and the family is estimated to include about 200 species across the country. [F. Bokhari]

Opposite page: The genus *Lampona*, here an unidentified female from Queensland, is probably the most common genus in the family Lamponidae in Australia. [P. Zborowski]

AMMOXENIDAE
Termite Hunters

- Eight eyes in two rows, almost equal in size
- Carapace covered in club setae (*Austrammo*)
- Abdomen covered in scale-like setae, iridescent (*Austrammo*); males with scute (*Barrowammo*)
- Reduced female pedipalp claw
- Litter dwellers without prey capture web
- Body length: 2–7 mm

Australia:
Taxonomy revised
Current: 5 species in 2 genera
Estimated: 10 species in 2 genera
World: 18 species in 4 genera

The Termite Hunters (family Ammoxenidae) are only known from southern Africa and Australia. They are somewhat inconspicuous spiders and rarely collected. As 'lower gnaphosoids' they retain a distal segment on the anterior lateral spinnerets. This group also includes the following families that are treated in the final chapters of this book: Swift Ground Spiders (Cithaeronidae), Long-jawed Ground Spiders (Gallieniellidae) and Scorpion Spiders (Trochanteriidae).

Termite Hunters differ from the other lower gnaphosoids in a greatly reduced female pedipalp claw and specialised setae around the tip of the palpal tarsus in both sexes. The Ammoxenidae lack the elongated fangs of Long-jawed Ground Spiders and Scorpion Spiders and the pseudosegmented tarsi of the Swift Ground Spiders. Ammoxenidae are very similar to Ground Spiders (family Gnaphosidae) in the field, however, Termite Hunters have large scale-like setae on the abdomen, which are not found in the Ground Spiders.

The Australian fauna consists of only five named species in two genera, *Austrammo* and *Barrowammo*. *Austrammo* differs from *Barrowammo* by the presence of a patch of dense setae on tip of the male and female pedipalp tarsis. *Austrammo harveyi* occurs in the southern half of Western Australia into South Australia, *A. monteithi* is known from mainland eastern Australia, *A. hirsti* has been found in South Australia and Tasmania and *A. rossi* in the northern half of Western Australia. *Barrowammo* is an endemic genus on Barrow Island off the north-west Western Australian coast and includes a single species, *B. waldockae*. Males of *B. waldockae* have a dorsal abdominal scute and a median apophysis on the male pedipalp, which are both absent in *Austrammo*.

Little is known about the biology of Termite Hunters. *Austrammo* are found in leaf litter but do not appear to be very habitat specific, a point which is illustrated by the wide distributions of some of its members. They have been collected in open forests, but also near salt lakes and in dune vegetation.

This *Austrammo harveyi* female was found in leaf litter just north of the Stirling Ranges in Western Australia. The beauty of these small and inconspicuous spiders is in the detail. Large scale-like setae give the abdomen a silvery shine and, similarly, the carapace and legs are partially covered with silvery hairs. [V.W. Framenau, Phoenix Environmental Sciences]

GALLIENIELLIDAE
Long-jawed Ground Spiders

- Eight eyes in two rows of four each
- Carapace longer than wide, fovea short, surface finely reticulate
- Legs long, two tarsal claws without claw tufts
- Long slender chelicere with long fangs parallel to the body
- Orange to dark brown, abdomen can be black with white lateral spots
- Extremely fast, night active hunters without prey capture web
- Body length: 3–9 mm

Australia:
Taxonomy revised
Current: 27 species in 5 genera
Estimated: 40 species in 6 genera
World: 55 species in 10 genera

Long-jawed Ground Spiders (family Gallieniellidae) are often misidentified as mygalomorph spiders based on the longitudinal orientation of their fangs. However, in contrast to mygalomorph spiders they only have a single pair of booklungs and as members of a different suborder, differ in many other aspects such as genital and spinneret morphology. The orientation of the fangs distinguishes the Long-jawed Ground Spiders from all other 'lower' gnaphosoids, i.e. Termite Hunters (Ammoxenidae), Scorpion Spiders (Trochanteriidae) and Swift Ground Spiders (Cithaeronidae).

Long-jawed Ground Spiders appear to have Gondwanan affinities as they are found in Africa, Madagascar, South America and Australia. Australia has the most diverse fauna with five described genera. *Meedo* includes spiders that do not have any leg spines. The 13 species of the genus can be found throughout the country. Other genera differ mainly in details of the genitalia. *Neeto* is largely a south-eastern Australian genus, although one of the seven species, *N. arid*, is only found in Western Australia. *Oreo* includes five species that are found throughout the country. *Peeto rodmani* is only known from Queensland and *Questo annuello* from Victoria.

The gallieniellids, until their long chelicerae are noticed, seem like many other spiders. Like the Ground Spiders, the Gallieniellidae have no strong tufts on the legs and cannot climb smooth surfaces.

Gallieniellids are ground-dwelling spiders that are usually found in leaf litter. They are often found in company of ants, upon which they most probably prey.

This female of *Meedo broadwater* from Lake Broadwater in southern Queensland illustrates the main characteristic of the genus, the spineless legs. The species is common in south-eastern Queensland. The genus *Meedo*, with 13 species, is the largest Australian genus in the Gallieniellidae. [R.J. Raven]

The longitudinally directed fangs of the Gallieniellidae, here a male of *Oreo muncoonie*, are reminiscent of those of the mygalomorph spiders and the distinguishing character of the Long-jawed Ground Spiders (family Gallieniellidae) within the Araneomorphae. Species in *Oreo* have extremely long chelicerae without any teeth. [B.C. Baehr]

TROCHANTERIIDAE
Scorpion Spiders

- Eight eyes in two rows, posterior row wider than anterior row, occupying most of carapace width
- Extremely flat body
- Chelicerae large with constriction at base
- Legs directed sidewards
- Anterior lateral spinnerets conical with distal article
- Nocturnal active hunters without prey capture web
- Body length: 2–25 mm

Australia:
Recently revised
Current: 115 species in 15 genera
Estimated: 150 species in 15 genera
World: 152 species in 19 genera

The Scorpion Spiders (family Trochanteriidae) are free-living hunters that can fold their legs over their body like a scorpion. They differ from the other 'lower' Gnaphosoidea, the Termite Hunters (Ammoxenidae), Long-jawed Ground Spiders (Gallieniellidae) and Swift Ground Spiders (Cithaeronidae), in having a greatly flattened carapace and eyes occupying most of the carapace width.

Scorpion Spiders conquered the harsh habitats in Australia's Outback by adapting their body shape to inhabit the extremely narrow spaces between bark layers of eucalypt trunks and tight crevices under the exfoliating slabs of rocky outcrops. Trochanteriids are known throughout Australia and are represented by three subfamilies, the Trochanteriinae, the Trachycosminae and the Morebilinae.

The **Trochanteriinae** includes spiders with a strongly ridged posterior margin of the carapace. The subfamily includes 25 species in the genus *Desognaphosa*, five species in the genus *Tinytrema*, the introduced *Platyoides walteri* and two blind species, *Olin platnicki* from caves on Christmas Island and Indonesia, and *Desognanops humphreysi* from subterranean habitats in central Western Australia. The carapace of species in *Desognaphosa* is less flattened than that of *Tinytrema*, and the spiders are generally larger with a body length of ca. 4–10 mm. Species of *Desognaphosa* have only been found in eastern Queensland and north-eastern New South Wales. Species of *Tinytrema* are very small spiders of less than 4 mm body length. The most common species is *T. sandy* that can be found throughout the southern half of Australia. Other species have more localised distributions or are only known from few specimens.

Spiders in the subfamily **Trachycosminae** have only slightly sideways directed legs and less enlarged chelicerae that point more downwards than forwards. Three genera are listed in the subfamily from Australia. The four species of *Trachycosmus* lack leg spines. *Trochycosmus sculptilis* is the most widerspread species and can be found in eastern and south-eastern Australia and also occurs in south-western Western Australia. *Trachytrema* includes two species, *T. castaneum* from Western Australia and *T. garnet* that is found from northern Queensland to north-eastern New South Wales. *Trachyspina* is, with eight species, the largest genus in the subfamily. These spiders have a pale grey abdomen, almost the whole body is covered with short and clubbed setae and the leg spines are short. The genus is mainly known from Western Australia into South Australia and the Northern Territory.

The members of the **Morebilinae** are characterised by the presence of a retrolateral apophysis in the male pedipalp. Many members of this subfamily have been misidentified as *Hemicloea* in the Ground Spiders (family Gnaphosidae), but the morphology of the spinnerets identifies them as 'lower' gnaphosoid Scorpion Spiders. Eight genera are known in the subfamily, *Boolathana* (two species), *Fissarena* (nine species), *Hemicloeina* (eight species), *Longrita* (nine species), *Morebilus* (13 species), *Platorish* (five species), *Pyrnus* (five species) and *Rebilus* (17 species). *Morebilus* includes the largest Scorpion Spiders which can reach up to 25 mm in body length. Most species are from eastern Australia, although *M. diversus* is widespread in the northern half of the country. *Longrita* can be recognised by the elongated tibial apophysis in males that nearly reaches the tip of the cymbium. *Boolathana* is a Western Australian genus with two species, *B. mainae* and *B. spiralis*, and *Rebilus* is only found in Queensland and New South Wales.

The dorsoventrally flattened Scorpion Spiders are night active hunters on tree trunks or rocky outcrops. In the daytime they hide under bark or rock crevices in a small web retreats, where females also care for their disk-shaped eggsacs.

This *Rebilus glorious* male from Mount Glorious near Brisbane is resting on *Melaleuca*, which supplies perfect daytime hiding spots beneath the bark. This species is only found in south-eastern Queensland. [R.J. Raven]

The genus *Tinytrema*, here the male of *T. yarra* from suburban Perth, currently includes five Australian species. Spiders in this genus are very small (less than 4 mm long) and extremely flat. Anecdotal evidence suggests that they mimic the behaviour of ants. [V.W. Framenau, Phoenix Environmental Sciences]

CITHAERONIDAE
Swift Ground Spiders

- Eight relatively large eyes in two slightly procured rows
- Cephalothorax rounded in dorsal view
- Abdomen ovoid, males with dorsal scute
- Legs long, pseudosegmented tarsi with two claws
- Nocturnal hunter without prey capture web; silken retreat during the day
- Body length: 4–7 mm

Australia: Single introduced species
World: 7 species in 2 genera

The Swift Ground Spiders (family Cithaeronidae) are represented in Australia only by a single introduced species, *Cithaeron predonius*. The only records of the species in this country are from the Northern Territory. They are generally pale yellowish spiders, although variable in coloration, with long, pseudosegmented tarsi. This character separates them from the other 'lower' gnaphosoid families, the Termite Hunters (Ammoxenidae), Long-jawed Ground Spiders (Gallieniellidae) and Scorpion Spiders (Trochanteriidae).

Cithaeron predonius is known from north-eastern and western Africa, south-eastern Europe (Greece), the Middle East, India, Malaysia, Singapore, North America (Florida) and South America (Brazil). In particular the American and Australian records suggest human mediated dispersal.

Swift Ground Spiders are fast-moving, nocturnal hunters that rest during the day in silken retreats under rocks. They reportedly have a preference for hot, rocky or stony places; however, here they seem to seek damp microhabitats. They have been reported from gravelly or rocky riverbeds and in Africa they have also been reported from bushveld and humid savanna to riverine forest. In Florida, the first spiders were detected and collected from inside buildings.

Cithaeron predonius, here a male photographed in Florida, have extremely long legs with pseudosegmented tarsi which allow them to run with enormous speed. This at least partially synanthropic, almost cosmopolitan species has so far only been recorded from the Northern Territory in Australia. [J. Koerner, John Koerner Photography, Old Town, Florida]

Page 416: The genus *Argoctenus* is diverse in Australia; it is part of the Spiny-leg Spiders or Wandering Ghosts (family Zoridae). The tufts of hair on the abdomen are not uncommon in the genus. This individual is an unidentified female from suburban Melbourne. [V.W. Framenau, Phoenix Environmental Sciences]

PART 4
FURTHER READING

Spiders are arachnids

Harvey, M. S. 2002. The neglected cousins: what do we know about the smaller arachnid orders? *Journal of Arachnology* 30: 357–372.

Beccaloni, J. 2009. *Arachnids*. CSIRO Publishing, Melbourne, Vic.

INTRODUCTION

Main, B. Y. 1964. *Spiders of Australia. A guide to their identification with brief notes on the natural history of common forms*. Jacaranda Press, Sydney.

Main, B. Y. 1976. *Spiders*. Collins, Sydney.

Mascord, R. E. 1970. *Australian Spiders in Colour*. Reed, Sydney.

Mascord, R. E. 1980. *Spiders of Australia. A Field Guide*. Reed, Sydney.

Main, B. Y. 1981. Australian spiders: diversity, distribution and ecology. *In:* Keast, A. (ed.), *Ecological biogeography of Australia*. W. Junk, The Hague, Netherlands, pp. 809–852.

Davies, V. T. 1986. *Australian spiders. Collection, preservation and identification*. Queensland Museum Booklet No. 14, Queensland Museum, Brisbane.

Harvey, M. S. (ed.). 1995. *Australasian spiders and their relatives: papers honouring Barbara York Main*. Records of the Western Australian Museum, Supplement 52. Western Australian Museum, Perth.

Forster, R. & Forster L. 1999 (reprinted in hardback in 2005). *Spiders of New Zealand and their world-wide kin*. University of Otago Press in association with Otago Museum, Dunedin, New Zealand.

Raven, R. J., Baehr, B. C. & Harvey, M. S. 2002. *Spiders of Australia: interactive identification to subfamily*. ABRS Identification Series. CSIRO Publishing, Collingwood.

Agnarsson, I., Coddington, J.A., & Kuntner, M., 2013. Systematics: progress in the study of spider diversity and evolution. In: Penney, D. (ed.), *Spider research in the 21st century: trends and perspectives*. Siri Scientific Press, Manchester, pp. 58–111.

Framenau, V.W. 2014 (updated regularly). Checklist of Australian Spiders. http://www.australasian-arachnology.org/download/checklist_australian_spiders.pdf

MYGALOMORPHAE

Raven, R. J. 1985. The spider infraorder Mygalomorphae (Araneae): cladistics and systematics. *Bulletin of the American Museum of Natural History* 182: 1–180.

Goloboff, P. A. 1993. A reanalysis of mygalomorph spider families (Araneae). *American Museum Novitates* 3056: 1–32.

Raven, R. J. 2000. Taxonomica Araneae I: Barychelidae, Theraphosidae, Nemesiidae and Dipluridae (Araneae). *Memoirs of the Queensland Museum* 45: 569–575.

Hedin, M. & Bond, J. E. 2006. Molecular phylogenetics of the spider infraorder Mygalomorphae using nuclear rRNA genes (18S and 28S): conflict and agreement with current systems of classification. *Molecular Phylogenetics and Evolution* 41: 454–471.

Bond, J. E., Hendrixson, B. E., Hamilton, C. A. & Hedin, M. 2012. A reconsideration of the classification of the spider infraorder Mygalomorphae (Arachnida: Araneae) based on three nuclear genes and morphology. *PLOS One* 7: e38753.

Hexathelidae

Raven, R. J. 1978. Systematics of the spider subfamily Hexathelinae (Dipluridae: Mygalomorphae: Arachnida). *Australian Journal of Zoology, Supplement* 65: 1–75.

Raven, R. J. 1980. The evolution and biogeography of the mygalomorph spider family Hexathelidae (Araneae, Chelicerata). *Journal of Arachnology* 8: 251–266.

Gray, M. R. 1988. Aspects of the systematics of the Australian funnel web spiders (Araneae: Hexathelidae: Atracinae) based upon morphological and electrophoretic data. *Australian Entomological Society Miscellaneous Publications* 5: 113–125.

Raven, R. J. 2000. A new species of funnel-web spider (*Hadronyche*: Hexathelidae: Mygalomorphae) from north Queensland. *Memoirs of the Queensland Museum* 46: 225–230.

Isbister, G. K., Gray, M. R., Balit, C. R., Raven, R. J., Stokes, B. J., Porges, K., Tankel, A. S., Turner, E., White, J. & Fisher, M. McD. 2005. Funnel-web spider bite: as systemic review of recorded clinical cases. *Medical Journal of Australia* 128: 407–411.

Gray, M. R. 2010. A revision of the Australian Funnel-web Spiders (Hexathelidae: Atracinae). *Records of the Australian Museum* 62: 285–392.

Beavis, A. S., Sunnucks,

P. & Rowell, D. M. 2011. Microhabitat preferences drive phylogeographic disparities in two Australian funnel web spiders. *Biological Journal of the Linnean Society* 104: 805–819.

Dipluridae

Main, B. Y. 1969. A blind mygalomorph spider from a Nullarbor Plain cave. *Journal of the Royal Society of Western Australia* 52: 9–11.

Raven, R. J. 1984. Systematics of the Australian curtain-web spiders (Ischnothelinae: Dipluridae: Chelicerata). *Australian Journal of Zoology, Supplementary Series* 93: 1–102.

Raven, R. J. 1985. A new and interesting species of *Cethegus* (Ischnothelinae: Dipluridae) from South Australia. *Records of the South Australian Museum* 19: 15–17.

Raven, R. J. 1993. The biodiversity of Australian mygalomorph spiders. I. Two new species of *Namirea* (Araneae: Dipluridae). *Memoirs of the Queensland Museum* 34: 81–88.

Main, B. Y. 1993. Biogeographic significance of the Nullarbor cave mygalomorph spider *Troglodiplura* and its taxonomic affinities. *Journal of the Royal Society of Western Australia* 76: 77–85.

Main, B. Y. & Gray, M. R. 1985. Further studies on the systematics of Australian Diplurinae (Chelicerata: Mygalomorphae: Dipluridae): description of the male of *Troglodiplura lowryi*, with notes on its affinities. *Psyche* 92: 151–162.

Raven, R. J. 1979. Systematics of the mygalomorph spider genus *Masteria* (Masteriinae: Dipluridae: Arachnida).
Australian Journal of Zoology 27: 623–636.

Actinopodidae

Womersley, H. 1943. A revision of the spiders of the genus *Missulena* Walckenaer 1805. *Records of the South Australian Museum* 7: 249–269.

Faulder, R. J. 1995. Two new species of the Australian spider genus *Missulena* Walckenaer (Araneae: Actinopodidae). *Records of the Western Australian Museum, Supplement* 52: 73–78.

Main, B. Y. 1996. Biosystematics of Australian mygalomorph spiders: description of a new species of *Missulena* from southwestern Australia (Araneae: Mygalomorphae: Actinopodidae). *Records of the Western Australian Museum* 17: 355–359.

Harms, D. & Framenau, V. W. 2013. New species of Mouse Spiders (Araneae: Mygalomorphae: Actinopodidae: *Missulena*) from the Pilbara region, Western Australia. *Zootaxa* 3637: 521–540.

Miglio, L. T., Harms, D., Framenau, V.W. & Harvey, M.S. 2014. Four new species of the mouse spider genus *Missulena* (Araneae: Mygalomorphae: Actinopodidae) from Western Australia. *ZooKeys*.

Ctenizidae

Main, B. Y. 1957. Occurrence of the trap-door spider *Conothele malayana* (Doleschall) in Australia (Mygalomorphae: Ctenizidae). *Western Australian Naturalist* 5: 209–216.

Main, B. Y. 1985. Further studies on the systematics of ctenizid trapdoor spiders: a review of the Australian genera (Araneae: Mygalomorphae: Ctenizidae). *Australian Journal of Zoology, Supplementary Series* 108: 1–84.

Migidae

Raven, R. J. 1984. Systematics and biogeography of the mygalomorph spider family Migidae (Araneae) in Australia. *Australian Journal of Zoology* 32: 379–390.

Raven, R. J. & Churchill, T. B. 1989. A new species of *Migas* (Araneae, Migidae), with notes on *Heteromigas* in Tasmania. *Bulletin of the British arachnological Society* 8: 5–8.

Main, B. Y. 1991. Occurrence of the trapdoor spider genus *Moggridgea* in Australia with descriptions of two new species (Araneae: Mygalomorphae: Migidae). *Journal of Natural History,* 25: 383–397.

Cooper, S. J., Harvey, M.S., Saint, K. M. & Main, B. Y. 2011. Deep phylogeographic structuring of populations of the trapdoor spider *Moggridgea tingle* (Migidae) from southwestern Australia: evidence for long-term refugia within refugia. *Molecular Ecology* 20: 3219–3236.

Idiopidae

Main, B. Y. 1952. Notes on the genus *Idiosoma*, a supposedly rare Western Australian trap-door spider. *Western Australian Naturalist* 3: 130–137.

Main, B. Y. 1957. Biology of aganippine trapdoor

spiders (Mygalomorphae: Ctenizidae). *Australian Journal of Zoology* 5: 402–473.

Main, B. Y. 1969. The trap-door spider genus *Cataxia* Rainbow (Mygalomorphae: Ctenizidae)–taxonomy and natural history. *Journal of the Australian Entomological Society* 8: 192–209.

Main, B. Y. 1978. Biology of the arid-adapted Australian trapdoor spider *Anidiops villosus* (Rainbow). *Bulletin of the British arachnological Society* 4: 161–175.

Main, B. Y. 1983. Systematics of the trapdoor spider genus *Homogona* Rainbow (Mygalomorphae: Ctenizidae: Homogoninae). *Journal of the Australian Entomological Society* 22: 81–92.

Main, B. Y. 1985. Further studies on the systematics of ctenizid trapdoor spiders: a review of the Australian genera (Araneae: Mygalomorphae: Ctenizidae). *Australian Journal of Zoology, Supplementary Series* 108: 1–84.

Main, B. Y. 1985. Further studies on the systematics of Australian ctenizid trapdoor spiders: description of a new species of *Homogona* Rainbow from Victoria (Mygalomorphae: Ctenizidae). *Victorian Naturalist* 102: 16–19.

Wishart, G. 1992. New species of the trapdoor spider genus *Misgolas* Karsch (Mygalomorphae: Idiopidae) with a review of the tube-building species. *Records of the Australian Museum* 44: 263–278.

Main, B. Y. 1995. Biosystematics of Australian mygalomorph spiders: two new species of *Arbanitis* from Victoria (Mygalomorphae: Idiopidae). *Victorian Naturalist* 112: 202–207.

Main, B. Y. 2000. Biosystematics of two new species of unusually coloured Australian mygalomorph spiders, *Arbanitis* (Araneae: Idiopidae), from south-western Australia. *Journal of the Royal Society of Western Australia* 83: 93–97.

Wishart, G. 2006. Trapdoor spiders of the genus *Misgolas* (Mygalomorphae: Idiopidae) in the Sydney region, Australia, with notes on synonymies attributed to *M. rapax*. *Records of the Australian Museum* 58: 1–18.

Raven, R. J. & Wishart, G. 2006. The trapdoor spider *Arbanitis* L. Koch (Idiopidae: Mygalomorphae) in Australia. *Memoirs of the Queensland Museum* 51: 531–557.

Wishart, G. & Rowell, D. M. 2008. Trapdoor spiders of the genus *Misgolas* (Mygalomorphae: Idiopidae) from eastern New South Wales, with notes on genetic variation. *Records of the Australian Museum* 60: 45–86.

Wishart, G. 2011. Trapdoor spiders of the genus *Misgolas* (Mygalomorphae: Idiopidae) in the Illawarra and South Coast Regions of New South Wales, Australia. *Records of the Australian Museum* 63: 33–51.

Nemesiidae

Raven, R. J. 1981. A review of the Australian genera of the mygalomorph spider subfamily Diplurinae (Dipluridae: Chelicerata). *Australian Journal of Zoology* 29: 321–363.

Raven, R. J. 1982. On the mygalomorph spider genus *Xamiatus* Raven (Diplurinae: Dipluridae) with the description of a new species. *Memoirs of the Queensland Museum* 20: 473–478.

Raven, R. J. 1982. Systematics of the Australian mygalomorph spider genus *Ixamatus* Simon (Diplurinae: Dipluridae: Chelicerata). *Australian Journal of Zoology* 30: 1035–1067.

Main, B. Y. 1983. Further studies on the systematics of Australian Diplurinae (Chelicerata: Mygalomorphae: Dipluridae): two new genera from south Western Australia. *Journal of Natural History* 17: 923–949.

Raven, R. J. 1984. A revision of the *Aname maculata* species group (Dipluridae, Araneae) with notes on biogeography. *Journal of Arachnology* 12: 177–193.

Main, B. Y. 1985. Further studies on Australian Diplurinae: a review of the genera of the Teylini (Araneae: Mygalomorphae: Dipluridae). *Australian Journal of Zoology* 33: 743–759.

Raven, R. J. 1985. A revision of the *Aname pallida* species-group in northern Australia. *Australian Journal of Zoology* 33: 377–409.

Raven, R. J. 1985. Two new species of *Ixamatus* Simon from eastern Australia (Nemesiidae, Mygalomorphae, Araneae). *Journal of Arachnology* 13: 285–290.

Main, B. Y. 1986. Further studies on the systematics of Australian Diplurinae (Araneae: Mygalomorphae: Dipluridae): a new genus from south-western Australia. *Records of the Western Australian Museum* 12: 395–402.

Main, B. Y. 2004. Biosystematics of Australian mygalomorph spiders: descriptions of three new species of *Teyl* from Victoria (Araneae: Nemesiidae). *Memoirs of the Museum*

Victoria 61: 47–55.
Main, B. Y. & Framenau, V. W. 2009. A new genus of mygalomorph spider from the Great Victoria Desert and neighbouring arid country in south-eastern Western Australia (Araneae: Nemesiidae). *Records of the Western Australian Museum* 25: 277–285.
Harvey, F. S. B., Framenau, V. W., Wojcieszek, J. M., Rix, M. G. & Harvey, M. S. 2012. Molecular and morphological characterisation of new species in the trapdoor spider genus *Aname* (Araneae: Mygalomorphae: Nemesiidae) from the Pilbara bioregion of Western Australia. *Zootaxa* 3383: 15–38.
Main, B. Y. 2012. Description and biogeographic implications of a new species of the *Chenistonia maculata* group from south-western Western Australia and rediagnosis of *Chenistonia* (Araneae: Mygalomorphae: Nemesiidae). *Records of the Western Australian Museum* 27: 176–181.

Barychelidae

Raven, R. J. 1988. A revision of the mygalomorph spider genus *Idioctis* (Araneae, Barychelidae). *American Museum Novitates* 2929: 1–14.
Raven, R. J. 1990. A revision of the Australian spider genus *Trittame* Koch (Mygalomorphae: Barychelidae) and a new related genus. *Invertebrate Taxonomy* 4: 21–54.
Churchill, T. B. & Raven, R. J. 1992. Systematics of the intertidal trapdoor spider genus *Idioctis* (Mygalomorphae: Barychelidae) in the western Pacific with a new genus from the northeast. *Memoirs of the Queensland Museum* 32: 9–30.
Raven, R. J. 1994. Mygalomorph spiders of the Barychelidae in Australia and the western Pacific. *Memoirs of the Queensland Museum* 35: 291–706.

Theraphosidae

McKeown, K. C. 1939. Bird-catching spiders. *Emu* 39: 111–124.
Kotzman, M. 1990. Annual activity patterns of the Australian tarantula *Selenocosmia stirlingi* (Araneae, Theraphosidae) in an arid area. *Journal of Arachnology* 18: 123–130.
Raven, R. J. 2005. A new tarantula species from northern Australia (Araneae, Theraphosidae). *Zootaxa* 1004: 15-28.

ARANEOMORPHAE

Forster, R. R., Platnick, N. I. & Gray, M. R. 1987. A review of the spider superfamilies Hypochiloidea and Austrochiloidea. *Bulletin of the American Museum of Natural History* 185: 1–116.

Austrochilidae

Doran, N.E., Richardson, A.M.M. and Swain, R. (1999). The Biology of *Hickmania troglodytes*, the Tasmanian Cave Spider. Pp. 330-332. In *The Other 99%. The Conservation and Biodiversity of Invertebrates*. W. Ponder and D. Lunney (eds). Transactions of the Royal Society of New South Wales.
Clarke, A.K. (2006) *Cavernicole Diversity and Ecology in Tasmania*, (unpublished MSc thesis), School of Zoology, University of Tasmania, 394pp.
Doran, N.E., Kiernan, K., Swain, R. and Richardson, A.M.M. (1999). *Hickmania troglodytes*, the Tasmanian cave spider, and its potential role in cave management. *Journal of Insect Conservation* 3: 257-262
Forster, R. R., Platnick, N. I. & Gray, M. R. 1987. A review of the spider superfamilies Hypochiloidea and Austrochiloidea (Araneae, Araneomorphae). *Bulletin of the American Museum of Natural History*. 185: 1–116.
Higgins, E. & Petterd, W. 1884. Description of a new cave-inhabiting spider, together with notes on mammalian remains from a recently discovered cave in the Chudleigh district. *Papers and Proceedings of the Royal Society of Tasmania*, 1883 [1884]: 191–192.

Gradungulidae

Forster, R. R. & Gray, M. R. 1979. *Progradungula*, a new cribellate genus of the spider family Gradungulidae (Araneae). *Australian Journal of Zoology* 27: 1051–1071.
Forster, R. R., Platnick, N. I. & Gray, M. R. 1987. A review of the spider superfamilies Hypochiloidea and Austrochiloidea. *Bulletin of the American Museum of Natural History* 185: 1–116.
Michalik, P., Piacentini, L., Lipke, E. & Ramírez, M. J. 2013. The enigmatic Otway odd-clawed spider (*Progradungula otwayensis* Milledge, 1997, Gradungulidae, Araneae): natural history, first description of the female and micro-computed tomography of the male palpal organ.

ZooKeys 335: 101–112. Milledge, G. A. 1997. A new species of *Progradungula* Forster and Gray (Araneae: Gradungulidae) from Victoria. *Memoirs of the Museum of Victoria* 56: 65–68.

Haplogynae

Platnick, N. I., Coddington, J. A., Forster, R. R. and Griswold, C. E. 1991. Spinneret morphology and the phylogeny of haplogyne spiders. *American Museum Novitates* 3016: 1–73.
Ramírez, M. J. 2000: Respiratory system morphology and the phylogeny of haplogyne spiders (Araneae, Araneomorphae). *Journal of Arachnology* 28: 149–157.

Filistatidae

Savory, T. H. 1943. On Arachnida from Christmas Island. *Annals and Magazine of Natural History* 10: 355–360.
Gray, M. R. 1994. A review of the filistatid spiders (Araneae: Filistatidae) of Australia. *Records of the Australian Museum.* 46: 39-61.
Gray, M. R. 1995. Morphology and relationships within the spider family Filistatidae (Araneae, Araneomorphae). *Records of the Western Australian Museum, Supplement* 52: 79–89.

Sicariidae

Gertsch, W. J. & Ennik, F. 1983. The spider genus *Loxosceles* in North America, Central America, and the West Indies (Araneae, Loxoscelidae). *Bulletin of the American Museum of Natural History* 175: 264–360.
Harvey, M. S. 1996. The first record of the fiddle-back spider *Loxosceles rufescens* (Araneae: Sicariidae) from Western Australia. *Records of the Western Australian Museum* 18: 223–224.
Vetter, R.S. 2008. Spider of the genus *Loxosceles* (Araneae, Sicariidae): a review of biological, medical and psychological aspects regarding envenomations. *Journal of Arachnology* 36, 150–163.
Binford, G. J., Callahan, M. S., Bodner, M. R., Rynerson, M. R., Núñez, P. B., Ellison, C. E. & Duncan, R. P. 2008. Phylogenetic relationships of *Loxosceles* and *Sicarius* spiders are consistent with Western Gondwanan vicariance. *Molecular Phylogenetics and Evolution* 49: 538–553.

Scytodidae

Gilbert, C. & Rayor, L. S. 1985. Predatory behavior of spitting spiders (Araneae: Scytodidae) and the evolution of prey wrapping. *Journal of Arachnology* 13: 231–241.
Suter, R. B. & Stratton, G. E. 2009. Spitting performance parameters and their biomechanical implications in the spitting spider, *Scytodes thoracica*. *Journal of Insect Science* 9: 1–15.

Periegopidae

Forster, R. R. 1995. The Australasian spider family Periegopidae Simon, 1893 (Araneae: Sicarioidea). *Records of the Western Australian Museum, Supplement* 52: 91–105.
Labarque F. M. & Ramírez M. J. 2012. The placement of the spider genus *Periegops* and the phylogeny of Scytodoidea (Araneae: Araneomorphae). *Zootaxa* 3312: 1–44.
Vink, C. J., Dupérré, N. & Malumbres-Olarte, J. 2013. Periegopidae (Arachnida: Araneae). *Fauna of New Zealand* 70: 1–41.

Pholcidae

Huber, B. A. 2001. The pholcids of Australia (Araneae; Pholcidae): taxonomy, biogeography, and relationships. *Bulletin of the American Museum of natural History* 260: 1–144.
Bruvo-Mađarić, B., Huber, B. A., Steinacher, A. & Pass, G. 2005. Phylogeny of pholcid spiders (Araneae: Pholcidae): combined analysis using morphology and molecules. *Molecular Phylogenetics and Evolution* 37: 661–673.
Huber, B. A. 2011. Phylogeny and classification of Pholcidae (Araneae): an update. *Journal of Arachnology* 39: 211–222.

Ochyroceratidae

Edwards. R. L., Edwards, E. H. & Edwards, A. D. 2003. Observations of *Theotima minutissimus* (Araneae, Ochyroceratidae), a parthenogenetic spider. *Journal of Arachnology* 31: 274–277.

Tetrablemmidae

Butler, L. S. G. 1932. Studies in Australian spiders. No. 2. *Proceedings of the Royal Society of Victoria* 44: 103–117.
Lehtinen, P. T. 1981. Spiders of the Oriental-Australian region. III. Tetrablemmidae, with a world revision. *Acta zoologica fennica* 162: 1–151.
Burger, M. 2008. Two new

species of armoured spiders from Malaysia and Australia (Arachnida: Araneae: Tetrablemmidae). *Bulletin of the British arachnological Society* 14: 253–261.

Burger, M., Harvey, M. S. & Stevens, N. 2010. A new species of blind subterranean *Tetrablemma* (Araneae: Tetrablemmidae) from Australia. *Journal of Arachnology* 38: 146–149.

Segestriidae

Main, B. Y. 1954. Spiders and Opiliones. Part 6 of *The Archipelago of the Recherche*. *Australian Geographical Society Reports* 1: 37–53.

Dysderidae

Vetter, R. S. & Isbister, G. K. 2006. Verified bites by the woodlouse spider, *Dysdera crocata*. *Toxicon* 47: 826–829.

Oonopidae

Hickman, V. V. 1979. Some Tasmanian spiders of the families Oonopidae, Anapidae and Mysmenidae. *Papers and Proceedings of the Royal Society of Tasmania* 113: 53–79.

Harvey, M. S. 1987. *Grymeus*, a new genus of pouched oonopid spider from Australia (Chelicerata: Araneae). *Memoirs of the Museum of Victoria* 48: 123–130.

Harvey, M. S. & Edward, K. L. 2007. Three new species of cavernicolous goblin spiders (Araneae, Oonopidae) from Australia. *Records of the Western Australian Museum* 24: 9–7.

Ott, R. & Harvey, M. S. 2008. A new species of *Pelicinus* from Barrow Island, Western Australia (Araneae: Oonopidae). *Arthropoda Selecta* 17: 81–85.

Ott, R. & Harvey, M. S. 2008. A new species of *Xestaspis* (Araneae: Oonopidae) from the Pilbara region of Western Australia. *Records of the Western Australian Museum* 24: 337–342.

Edward, K. L. & Harvey, M. S. 2009. A new species of *Ischnothyreus* (Araneae: Oonopidae) from monsoon rainforest of northern Australia. *Records of the Western Australian Museum* 25: 287–294.

Baehr, B. & Harvey, M. S. 2010. Two new species of the endemic Australian Goblin Spider genus *Cavisternum* (Araneae: Oonopidae) from Queensland. *Australian Entomologist* 37: 171–177.

Baehr, B., Harvey, M. S. & Smith, H. M. 2010. The goblin spiders of the new endemic Australian genus *Cavisternum* (Araneae: Oonopidae). *American Museum Novitates* 3684: 1–40.

Platnick, N. I., Dupérré, N., Ott, R. & Kranz-Baltensperger, Y. 2011. The goblin spider genus *Brignolia* (Araneae, Oonopidae). *Bulletin of the American Museum of Natural History* 349: 1–131.

Baehr, B. C., Harvey, M. S. & Thoma, M. 2012. The new Australasian goblin spider genus *Prethopalpus* (Araneae, Oonopidae). *Bulletin of the American Museum of Natural History* 369: 1–113.

Baehr, B. C., Raven, R. J. & Whyte, R. 2013. Biodiversity discovery program Bush Blitz yields a new species of goblin spider, *Cavisternum attenboroughi* (Araneae: Oonopidae), from the Northern Territory. *Zootaxa* 3616: 396–400.

Baehr, B. C., Harvey M. S., Smith H. M. & Ott, R. 2013. The goblin spider genus *Opopaea* in Australia and the Pacific islands (Araneae: Oonopidae). *Memoirs of the Queensland Museum*, 58: 101–332.

Harvey, M. S. & Baehr, B. C. 2013. Two new species of the goblin spider genus *Cavisternum* from tropical Australia (Araneae: Oonopidae). *Memoirs of the Queensland Museum, Nature* 58: 353–360.

Edward, K. L. & Harvey, M. S. 2014. Australian goblin spiders of the genus *Ischnothyreus* (Araneae, Oonopidae). *Bulletin of the American Museum of Natural History* 389: 1-144.

Orsolobidae

Forster, R. R. & Platnick, N. I. 1985. A review of the austral spider family Orsolobidae (Arachnida, Araneae), with notes on the superfamily Dysderoidea. *Bulletin of the American Museum of natural History* 181: 1–230.

Baehr, B. C. &. Smith, H. M. 2008. Three new species of the Australian orsolobid genus *Hickmanolobus* (Araneae: Orsolobidae). *Records of the Western Australian Museum* 24: 325–336.

Baehr, B. C., Raven, R. J. & Hebron, W. 2011. Orsolobidae of the IBISCA-Queensland project at Lamington National Park. *Memoirs of the Queensland Museum, Nature* 55: 439–449.

Entelegynae

Griswold, C. D., Coddington, J. A., Platnick, N. I. & Forster, R. R. 1999.

Towards a phylogeny of entelegyne spiders (Araneae, Araneomorphae, Entelegynae). *Journal of Arachnology* 27: 53–63.

Griswold, C. E., Ramírez, M. J., Coddington, J. & Platnick, N. I. 2005. Atlas of phylogenetic data for entelegyne spiders (Araneae: Araneomorphae: Entelegynae) with comments on their phylogeny. *Proceedings of the California Academy of Sciences* 56 (Supplement II): 1–324.

Dimitrov, D., Lopardo, L., Giribet, G., Arnedo, M. A., Alvarez-Padilla, F. & Hormiga, G. 2012. Tangle in a sparse spider web: single origin of orb weavers and their spinning work unravelled by denser taxonomic sampling. *Proceedings of the Royal Society* B 279: 1341–1350.

Archaeidae

Forster, R. R. & Platnick, N. I. 1984. A review of the archaeid spiders and their relatives, with notes on the limits of the superfamily Palpimanoidea (Arachnida, Araneae). *Bulletin of the American Museum of natural History* 178: 1–106.

Platnick, N. I. 1991. On Western Australian *Austrarchaea* (Araneae, Archaeidae). *Bulletin of the Brirish Arachnological Society* 8: 259–261.

Rix, M. G. & Harvey, M. S.. 2011. Australian assassins, Part I: A review of the assassin spiders (Araneae, Archaeidae) of mid-eastern Australia. *ZooKeys* 123: 1–100.

Rix, M. G. & Harvey, M. S. 2012. Phylogeny and historical biogeography of ancient assassin spiders (Araneae: Archaeidae) in the Australian mesic zone: evidence for Miocene speciation within Tertiary refugia. *Molecular Phylogenetics and Evolution* 62: 375–396.

Rix, M. G. & Harvey, M. S. 2012. Australian assassins, part II: a review of the new assassin spider genus *Zephyrarchaea* (Araneae, Archaeidae) from southern Australia. *ZooKeys* 191: 1–62.

Rix, M. G. & Harvey, M. S. 2012. Australian assassins, part III: a review of the assassin spiders (Araneae, Archaeidae) of tropical north-eastern Queensland. *ZooKeys* 218: 1–55.

Stenochilidae

Platnick, N. I. & Shadab, M. U. 1974. A revision of the spider family Stenochilidae (Arachnida, Araneae). *American Museum Novitates* 2556: 1–106.

Lchtinen, P. T. 1982. Spiders of the Oriental-Australian region. IV. Stenochilidae. *Annales Zoologici Fennici* 19: 115–128.

Araneidae

Dahl, F. 1914. Die Gasteracanthen des Berliner Zoologischen Museums und deren geographische Verbreitung. *Mitteilungen des Zoologischen Museums Berlin* 7: 235–301.

Longman, H.A. 1922. The magnificent spider: *Dicrostichus magnificus* Rainbow: notes on cocoon spinning and methods of catching prey. *Proceedings of the Royal Society of Queensland* 33: 91–98.

Musgrave, A. 1973. The Two-spined Spider. *Australian Museum Leaflet* 9.

Hickman, V. V. 1976. On *Paraplectanoides crassipes* Keyserling (Araneae: Araneidae). *Bulletin of the British arachnological Society* 3: 166–174.

Davies, V. T. 1980. Two large Australian orb-weaving spiders, *Eriophora transmarina* (Keyserling 1865) and *Eriophora biapicata* (L. Koch 1871). *Memoirs of the Queensland Museum* 20: 125–133.

Levi, H. W. 1983. The orb-weaver genera *Argiope*, *Gea*, and *Neogea* from the Western Pacific Region (Araneae: Araneidae, Argiopinae). *Bulletin of the Museum of Comparative Zoology* 150: 247–338.

Davies, V. T. 1988. An illustrated guide to the genera of orb-weaving spiders in Australia. *Memoirs of the Queensland Museum* 25: 273–332.

Coddington, J. A. 1989. Spinneret silk spigot morphology: evidence for the monophyly of orbweaving spiders, Cyrtophorinae (Araneidae), and the group Theridiidae plus Nesticidae. *Journal of Arachnology* 17: 71–95.

Elgar, M. A. 1991. Sexual cannibalism, size dimorphism, and courtship behaviour in orb-weaving spiders (Araneidae). *Evolution* 45: 444–448.

Humphreys, W. F. 1991. Thermal behaviour of a small spider (Araneae: Araneidae: Araneinae) on horizontal webs in semi-arid Western Australia. *Behavioral Ecology and Sociobiology* 28: 47–54.

Hormiga, G., Eberhard, W. G. & Coddington, J. A. 1995. Web-construction behaviour in Australian *Phonognatha* and the phylogeny of nephiline and tetragnathid spiders (Araneae: Tetragnathidae). *Australian Journal of Zoology* 43: 313–364.

Elgar, M. A. & Bathgate, R. 1996. Female receptivity and male mate-guarding in the jewel spider *Gasteracantha minax* Thorell (Araneidae). *Journal of Insect Behaviour* 9: 729–738.

Scharff, N. & Coddington, J. A. 1997. A phylogenetic analysis of the orb-weaving spider family Araneidae (Arachnida, Araneae). *Zoological Journal of the Linnean Society* 120: 355–434.

Fahey, B. F. & Elgar, M. A. 1997. Sexual cohabituation as mate-guarding in the leaf-curling spider *Phonognatha graeffei* Keyserling (Araneoidea, Araneae). *Behavioural Ecology and Sociobiology* 40: 127–133.

Herberstein, M. E., Abernethy, K. E., Backhouse, K., Bradford, H., Crespigny, F. E. d., Luckock, P. R. & Elgar, M. A. 1998. The effect of feeding history on prey capture behaviour in the orb-web spider *Argiope keyserlingi* Karsch (Araneae: Araneidae). *Ethology* 104: 565–571.

Herberstein, M. E., Craig, C. L. & Elgar, M. A. 2000. Foraging strategies and feeding regimes: web and decoration investment in *Argiope keyserlingii* (Araneae: Araneidae). *Evolutionary Ecology Research* 2: 69–80.

Hormiga, G., Scharff, N. & Coddington, J. A. 2000. The phylogenetic basis of sexual size dimorphism in orb-weaving spiders (Araneae, Orbiculariae). *Systematic Biology* 49: 435–462.

Herberstein, M. E. & Fleisch, A. F. 2003. Effect of abiotic factors on the foraging strategy of the orb-web spider *Argiope keyserlingi* (Araneae: Araneidae). *Austral Ecology* 28: 622–828.

Smith, H. M. 2005. A preliminary study of the relationships of taxa included in the tribe Poltyini (Araneae, Araneidae). *Journal of Arachnology* 33: 468–481.

Smith, H. M. 2006. A revision of the genus *Poltys* in Australasia (Araneae: Araneidae). *Records of the Australian Museum* 58: 43–96.

Framenau, V. W. 2008. The male of the orb-weaving spider *Cyrtophora unicolor* (Araneae, Araneidae). *Journal of Arachnology* 36: 131–135.

Framenau, V. W. & Scharff, N. 2008. The orb-weaving spider genus *Larinia* in Australia (Araneae: Araneidae). *Arthropod Systematics and Phylogeny* 66: 227-250.

Harmer, A. M. T. & Framenau, V. W. 2008. *Telaprocera* (Araneae: Araneidae), a new genus of Australian orb-web spiders with highly elongated webs. *Zootaxa* 1956: 59–80.

Smith, H. M. 2008. Synonymy of *Homalopoltys* (Araneae: Araneidae) with the genus *Dolichognatha* (Araneae: Tetragnathidae) and descriptions of two new species. *Zootaxa* 1775: 1–24.

Framenau, V. W. & Scharff, N. 2009. *Cyrtobill darwini*, a new species in a new orb-weaving spider genus from Australia (Araneae, Araneidae, Cyrtophorinae). *Records of the Western Australian Museum* 25: 315–328.

Framenau, V. W., Scharff, N. & Levi, H. W. 2009. Not from "Down Under": new synonymies and combinations for orb-weaving spiders (Araneae: Araneidae) erroneously reported from Australia. *Zootaxa* 2073: 22–30.

Framenau, V. W., Dupérré, N., Blackledge, T. A. & Vink, C. J. 2010. Systematics of the new Australasian Orb-weaving Spider genus *Backobourkia* (Araneae: Araneidae: Araneinae). *Arthropod Systematics and Phylogeny* 68: 79–111.

Smith, H. M. & Levi, H. W. 2010. Review of the genus *Micropoltys* (Chelicerata: Araneae: Araneidae). *Arthropod Systematics and Phylogeny* 68: 291–307.

Elgar, M. A. & Walter, A. 2011. Signals for damage control: web decorations in *Argiope keyserlingi* (Araneae: Araneidae). *Behavioral Ecology and Sociobiology* 65: 1909–1915.

Framenau, V. W. 2011. Description of a new orb-weaving spider species representing the first record of *Novaranea* in Australia (Araneae: Araneidae: Araneinae). *Zootaxa* 2793: 47–55.

Framenau, V. W. 2011. *Lariniophora*, a new monotypic orb-weaving spider genus from Australia (Araneae: Araneidae: Araneinae). *Records of the Western Australian Museum* 26: 191–2011.

Joseph, M. M. & Framenau, V. W. 2012. Systematic review of a new orb-weaving spider genus (Araneae: Araneidae), with special reference to the Australasian-Pacific and South-East Asian fauna. *Zoological Journal of the Linnean Society* 166: 279–341.

Nephilidae

Schneider, J.M., Herberstein, M.E., De Crespigny, F.C., Ramamurthy, S. & Elgar, M.A. 2000. Sperm competition and small size advantage for males of the golden orbweb spider *Nephila edulis*. *Journal of Evolutionary Biology* 13: 939–946.

Schneider, J. M., Thomas, M. L. & Elgar, M. A. 2001. Ectotomised conductors in the golden orb-web spider, *Nephila plumipes* (Araneoidea): a male adaptation to sexual conflict. *Behavioural Ecology and Sociobiology* 49: 410–415.

Elgar, M. A., Bruce, M. J., de Crespigny, F. E. C., Cutler, A. R., Cutler, C. L., Gaskett, A. C., Herberstein, M. E., Ramamurthy, S. & Schneider, J. M. 2003. Male mate choice and patterns of paternity in the polyandrous, sexually cannibalistic orb-web spider *Nephila plumipes*. *Australian Journal of Zoology* 51: 357–365.

Kuntner, M. 2005. A revision of *Herennia* (Araneae: Nephilidae: Nephilinae), the Australasian 'coin spiders'. *Invertebrate Systematics* 19: 391–436.

Kuntner, M. 2007. A monograph of *Nephilengys*, the pantropical 'hermit spiders' (Araneae, Nephildae, Nephilinae). *Systematic Entomology* 32: 95–135.

Harvey, M. S., Austin, A. D. & Adams, M. 2007. The systematics and biology of the spider genus *Nephila* (Araneae: Nephilidae) in the Australasian region. *Invertebrate Systematics* 21: 407–451.

Kuntner, M., Coddington, J.A., Hormiga, G., 2008. Phylogeny of extant nephilid orbweaving spiders (Araneae, Nephilidae): testing morphological and ethological homologies. *Cladistics* 24: 147–217.

Schneider, J.M., Herberstein, M.E., Bruce, M.J., Kasumovic, M.M., Thomas, M.L. & Elgar, M.A. 2008. Male copulation frequency, sperm competition and genital damage in the golden orb-web spider (*Nephila plumipes*). *Australian Journal of Zoology* 56: 233–238.

Kuntner, M., Arnedo, M. A., Trontelj, P., Lokovšek, T. & Agnarsson, I. 2013. A molecular phylogeny of nephilid spiders: evolutionary history of a model lineage. *Molecular Phylogenetics and Evolution* 69: 961–979.

Linyphiidae

Helsdingen, P. J. v. 1972. An account of money spiders from down under (Araneida, Linyphiidae). *Zoologische Mededelingen* 47: 369–390.

Wunderlich, J. 1976. Spinnen aus Australien. 2. Linyphiidae (Arachnida: Araneida). *Senckenbergiana biologica* 57: 125–142.

Millidge, A. F. 1988. Spiders of New Zealand. Part VI. Family Linyphiidae. *Otago Museum Bulletin* 6: 35–67.

Millidge, A. F. 1993. Three new species of the spider family Linyphiidae from Australia (Araneae). *Records of the Western Australian Museum* 16: 211–219.

Hormiga, G. 1994. Cladistics and the comparative morphology of linyphiid spiders and their relatives (Araneae, Araneoidea, Linyphiidae). *Zoological Journal of the Linnean Society* 111: 1–71.

Blest, A. D. & Vink, C. J. 2003. New Zealand spiders: Linyphiidae, Mynogleninae, Linyphiinae. *Records of the Canterbury Museum, Supplement* 17: 1–30.

Brennan, K. E. C. 2004. A further record of the spider *Microctenonyx subitaneus* (Araneae: Linyphiidae: Erigoninae) in Australia. *Records of the Western Australian Museum* 22: 163–164.

Arnedo, M.A., Hormiga, G., Scharff, N., 2009. Higher-level phylogenetics of linyphiid spiders (Araneae, Linyphiidae) based on morphological and molecular evidence. *Cladistics* 25, 231–262.

Frick, H. & Scharff, N. 2013. Phantoms of Gondwana?—phylogeny of the spider subfamily Mynogleninae (Araneae: Linyphiidae). *Cladistics* 30: 67–106.

Scharff, N. & Hormiga, G. 2013. On the Australian linyphiid spider *Alaxchelicera ordinaria* Butler, 1932 (Araneae). *Zootaxa* 3750: 193–196.

Cyatholipidae

Wunderlich, J. 1978. Zur Kenntnis der Cyatholipinae Simon 1894 (Arachnida: Araneida: ?Tetragnathidae). *Zoologische Beiträge* (N.F.) 24: 33–41.

Davies, V. T. 1978. A new family of spiders (Araneae: Teemenaariidae). *Symposium of the Zoological Society London* 42: 293–302.

Forster, R. R. 1988. The spiders of New Zealand: Part VI. Family Cyatholipidae. *Otago Museum Bulletin* 6: 7–34.

Griswold, C. D. 2001. A monograph of the living world genera and Afrotropical species of cyatholipid spiders (Araneae, Orbiculariae, Araneoidea, Cyatholipidae). *Memoirs of the California Academy of Sciences* 26: 1–251.

Tetragnathidae

Okuma, C. 1987. A revision of the Australasian species of the genus *Tetragnatha* (Araneae, Tetragnathidae). *ESAKIA* 25: 37–96.

Hormiga, G., Eberhard, W. G. & Coddington, J. A. 1995. Web-construction behaviour in Australian *Phonognatha* and the phylogeny of nephiline and tetragnathid spiders (Araneae: Tetragnathidae). *Australian Journal of Zoology* 43: 313–364.

Smith, H. M. 2008. Synonymy of *Homalopoltys* (Araneae: Araneidae) with the genus *Dolichognatha* (Araneae: Tetragnathidae) and descriptions of two new species. *Zootaxa* 1775: 1–24.

Dimitrov, D. & Hormiga, G. 2011. An extraordinary new genus of spiders from Western Australia with an expanded hypothesis on the phylogeny of Tetragnathidae (Araneae). *Zoological Journal of the Linnean Society* 161: 735–768.

Alvarez-Padilla, F., Dimitrov, D., Giribet, G., Hormiga, G., 2009. Phylogenetic relationships of the spider family Tetragnathidae (Araneae, Araneoidea) based on morphological and DNA sequence data. *Cladistics* 25, 109–146.

Álvarez-Padilla, F. & Hormiga, G. 2011. Morphological and phylogenetic atlas of the orb-weaving spider family Tetragnathidae (Araneae: Araneoidea). *Zoological Journal of the Linnean Society* 162: 713–879.

Mimetidae

Heimer, S. 1986. Notes on the spider family Mimetidae with description of a new genus from Australia (Arachnida, Araneae). *Entomologische Abhandlungen des Museums für Naturkunde Dresden* 49: 113–137.

Heimer, S. 1989. Some new mimetid spiders from North Queensland, Australia (Arachnida, Araneae, Mimetidae). *Memoirs of the Queensland Museum* 27: 433–435.

Harms, D. & Harvey, M. S. 2009. A review of the pirate spiders of Tasmania (Arachnida, Mimetidae, Australomimetus) with description of a new species. *Journal of Arachnology* 37: 188–205.

Harms, D. & Harvey, M. S. 2009. Australian pirates: systematics and phylogeny of the Australasian pirate spiders (Araneae: Mimetidae), with a description of the Western Australian fauna. *Invertebrate Systematics* 23: 231–280.

Harms, D. & Dunlop, J. A. 2009. A revision of the fossil pirate spiders (Arachnida: Araneae: Mimetidae). *Palaeontology* 52: 779–802.

Townley, M. A. & Tillinghast, E. K. 2009. Developmental changes in spider spinning fields: a comparison between *Mimetus* and *Araneus* (Araneae: Mimetidae, Araneidae). *Biological Journal of the Linnean Society* 98: 343–383.

Jackson R. R. & Whitehouse, M. E. A. 1986. The biology of New Zealand and Queensland pirate spiders (Araneae, Mimetidae): aggressive mimicry, araneophagy and prey specialization. *Journal of Zoology* 210: 279–303.

Holarchaeidae

Forster, R. R. 1955. Spiders of the family Archaeidae from Australia and New Zealand. *Transactions of the Royal Society of New Zealand* 83: 391–403.

Hickman, V. V. 1981. New Tasmanian spiders of the families Archaeidae, Cycloctenidae, Amaurobiidae and Micropholcommatidae. *Papers and Proceedings of the Royal Society of Tasmania* 115: 47–68.

Forster, R. R. & Platnick, N. I. 1984. A review of the archaeid spiders and their relatives, with notes on the limits of the superfamily Palpimanoidea (Arachnida, Araneae). *Bulletin of the American Museum of Natural History* 178: 1–106.

Rix, M. G. 2005. A review of the Tasmanian species of Pararcheidae and Holarchaeidae (Arachnida, Araneae). *Journal of Arachnology* 33: 135–152.

Pararchaeidae

Forster, R. R. & Platnick, N. I. 1984. A review of the archaeid spiders and their relatives, with notes on the limits of the superfamily Palpimanoidea (Arachnida, Araneae). *Bulletin of the American Museum of natural History* **178**: 1–106.

Hickman, V. V. 1969. New species of Toxopidae and Archaeidae (Araneae). *Papers and Proceedings of the Royal Society of Tasmania* **103**: 1–11.

Rix, M. G. 2005. A review of the Tasmanian species of Pararcheidae and Holarchaeidae (Arachnida, Araneae). *Journal of Arachnology* 33: 135–152.

Rix, M. G. 2006. Systematics of the Australasian spider family Pararchaeidae (Arachnida: Araneae). *Invertebrate Systematics* 20: 203-254.

Synotaxidae

Wunderlich J. 1995. Description of the new genus *Calcarsynotaxus* from Australia (Arachnida: Araneae: Synotaxidae). *Beiträge zur Araneologie* 4: 539–542

Forster, R.R., Platnick, N. I. & Coddington, J. 1990. A proposal and review of the spider family Synotaxidae (Araneae, Araneoidea), with notes on theridiid interrelationships. *Bulletin of the American Museum of natural History* 193: 1–116.

Agnarsson, I. 2003. The phylogenetic placement and circumscription of the genus *Synotaxus* (Araneae: Synotaxidae), a new species from Guyana, and notes on theridioid phylogeny. *Invertebrate Systematics* 17: 719–734.

Wunderlich, J. 2008. Descriptions of fossil spider (Araneae) taxa mainly in Baltic amber, as well as on certain related extant taxa. *Beiträge zur Araneologie* 5: 44–139.

Rix, M.G., Roberts, J.D., Harvey M.S. 2009. The spider families Synotaxidae and Malkaridae (Arachnida: Araneae: Araneoidea) in Western Australia. *Records of the Western Australian Museum* 25: 295–304.

Malkaridae

Davies, V. T. 1980. *Malkara loricata*, a new spider (Araneidae: Malkarinae) from Australia. *Verhandlungen des 8. Internationalen Arachnologen-Kongreß, Wien*, 377–382.

Moran, R. J. 1986. The Sternodidae (Araneae: Araneomorpha), a new family of spiders from eastern Australia. *Bulletin of the British arachnological Society* 7: 87–96.

Rix, M. G., Roberts, J. D. & Harvey, M. S. 2009. The spider families Synotaxidae and Malkaridae (Arachnida: Araneae: Araneoidea) in Western Australia. *Records of the Western Australian Museum* 25: 295–304.

Platnick, N. I. & Forster, R. R. 1987. On the first American spiders of the subfamily Sternodinae (Araneae, Malkaridae). *American Museum Novitates* 2894: 1–12.

Theridiosomatidae

Wunderlich, J. 1976. Spinnen aus Australien. 1. Uloboridae, Theridiosomatidae and Symphytognathidae (Arachnida: Araneida). *Senckenbergiana biologica* 57: 113–124.

Coddington, J. A. 1986. The genera of the spider family Theridiosomatidae. *Smithsonians Contributions to Zoology* 422: 1–96.

Mysmenidae

Hickman, V. V. 1979. Some Tasmanian spiders of the families Oonopidae, Anapidae and Mysmenidae. *Papers and Proceedings of the Royal Society of Tasmania* 113: 53–79.

Lopardo, L., Giribet, G. & Hormiga, G. 2011, Morphology to the rescue: molecular data and the signal of morphological characters in combined phylogenetic analyses-a case study from mysmenid spiders (Araneae, Mysmenidae), with comments on the evolution of web architecture. *Cladistics* 27: 278–330.

Lopardo, L. & Michalik, P. 2013. First description of a mysmenid spider species from mainland Australia and new data for *Mysmena tasmaniae* Hickman, 1979 (Araneae, Mysmenidae). *Memoirs of the Queensland Museum, Nature* 58: 381–396.

Anapidae

Hickman, V. V. 1979. Some Tasmanian spiders of the families Oonopidae, Anapidae and Mysmenidae. *Papers and Proceedings of the Royal Society of Tasmania* 113: 53–79.

Hickman, V. V. 1981. New Tasmanian spiders of the families Archaeidae, Cycloctenidae, Amaurobiidae and Micropholcommatidae. *Papers and Proceedings of the Royal Society of Tasmania* 115: 47–68.

Platnick, N. I. & Forster, R. R. 1989. A revision of the temperate South American and Australasian spiders of the family Anapidae (Araneae, Araneoidea). *Bulletin of the American Museum of Natural History* 190: 1–139.

Rix, M. G. 2008. Molecular phylogenetics of the spider family Micropholcommatidae (Arachnida: Araneae) using nuclear rRNA genes (18S and 28S). *Molecular Phylogenetics and Evolution* 46: 1031–1048.

Lopardo, L. & Hormiga, G. 2008. Phylogenetic placement of the Tasmanian spider *Acrobleps hygrophilus* (Araneae, Anapidae) with comments on the evolution of the capture web in Araneoidea. *Cladistics* 24: 1–33.

Rix, M. G. 2008. A new species of *Micropholcomma* (Araneae: Araneoidea: Micropholcommatidae) from Western Australia. *Records*

of the Western Australian Museum 24: 343–248.
Rix, M. G. & Harvey, M. S. 2010. The spider family Micropholcommatidae (Arachnida, Araneae, Araneoidea): a relimitation and revision at the generic level. *ZooKeys* 36: 1–321.
Rix, M. G., Harvey, M. S. & Roberts, J. D. 2010. A revision of the textricellin spider genus *Raveniella* (Araneae : Araneoidea : Micropholcommatidae): exploring patterns of phylogeny and biogeography in an Australian biodiversity hotspot. *Invertebrate Systematics* 24: 209–237.
Lopardo, L., Giribet, G. & Hormiga, G. 2011. Morphology to the rescue: molecular data and the signal of morphological characters in combined phylogenetic analyses – a case study from mysmenid spiders (Araneae, Mysmenidae), with comments on the evolution of web architecture. *Cladistics* 27: 278–330.

Symphytognathidae

Hickman, V. V. 1931. A new family of spiders. *Proceedings of the Royal Society B* 1931: 1321–1328.
Forster, R. R. & Platnick, N. I. 1977. A review of the spider family Symphytognathidae (Arachnida, Araneae). *American Museum Novitates* 2619: 1–29.
Harvey, M. S. 1992. A new species of *Symphytognatha* Hickman (Araneae: Symphytognathidae) from Western Australia. *Records of the Western Australian Museum* 15: 685–689.
Harvey, M. S. 1998. A review of the Australasian species of *Anapistula* Gertsch (Araneae: Symphytognathidae). *Records of the Western Australian Museum* 19: 111–120.
Harvey, M. S. 2001. Notes on the spider genus *Symphytognatha* (Araneae: Symphytognathidae) in Western Australia. *Records of the Western Australian Museum* 20: 345–347.

Nesticidae

Lehtinen, P. T. & Saaristo, M. I. 1980. Spiders of the Oriental-Australian region. II. Nesticidae. *Annales Zoologici Fennici* 17: 47–66.
Wunderlich, J. 1995. First endemic Australian Oecobiidae and Nesticidae (Arachnida: Araneae). *Memoirs of the Queensland Museum* 38: 691–692.
Vink, C. J. & Dupérré, N. 2011. *Nesticus eremita* (Araneae: Nesticidae): redescription of a potentially invasive European spider found in New Zealand. *Journal of Arachnology* 39: 511–514.

Theridiidae

Hickman, V. V. 1943. On some new Hadrotarsidae (Araneae) with notes on their internal anatomy. *Papers and Proceedings of the Royal Society of Tasmania* 1942: 147–160.
Hickman, V. V. 1951. New Phoroncidiinae and the affinities of the New Zealand spider *Atkinsonia nana* Cambridge. *Papers and Proceedings of the Royal Society of Tasmania* 1950: 3–24.
Wunderlich, J. 1976. Spinnen aus Australien. 1. Uloboridae, Theridiosomatidae and Symphytognathidae (Arachnida: Araneida). *Senckenbergiana biologica* 57: 113–124.
Wunderlich, J. 1978. Zu Taxonomie und Synonymie der Taxa Hadrotarsidae, *Lucarachne* Bryant 1940 und *Flegia* C. L. Koch & Berendt 1854 (Arachnida: Araneida: Theridiidae). *Zoologische Beiträge* (N.F.) 24: 25–31.
Downes M. F. 1984. Egg sac 'theft' among *Latrodectus hasselti* females (Araneae, Theridiidae). *Journal of Arachnology* 12: 244.
Downes M. F. 1987. Postembryonic development of *Latrodectus hasselti* Thorell (Araneae, Theridiidae). *Journal of Arachnology* 14: 293–301
Whitehouse, M. E. A. 1988. Factors influencing specificity and choice of host in *Argyrodes antipodianus* (Theridiidae, Araneae). *Journal of Arachnology* 16: 349–355.
Gray, M. R. & Anderson, G. J. 1989. A new Australian species of *Argyrodes* Simon (Araneoidea: Theridiidae) which preys on its host. *Proceedings of the Linnean Society of New South Wales* 111: 25–30.
Elgar, M. A. 1993. Interspecific associations involving spiders: kleptoparasitism, mimicry and mutualism. *Memoirs of the Queensland Museum* 33: 411–430.
Forster L. M. 1995. The behavioural ecology of *Latrodectus hasselti* (Thorell), the Australian redback spider (Araneae: Theridiidae): a review. *Records of the Western Australian Museum, Supplement* 52:13–24
Grostal, P. & Walter, D.E. 1997. Kleptoparasites or commensals? Effects of *Argyrodes antipodianus* (Araneae: Theridiidae) on *Nephila plumipes* (Araneae: Tetragnathidae). *Oecologia* 111: 570–574.

Grostal, P. 1999. Five species of kleptobiotic *Argyrodes* Simon (Theridiidae: Araneae) from eastern Australia: descriptions and ecology with special reference to southeastern Queensland. *Memoirs of the Queensland Museum* 43: 621–638.

Harvey, M. S. & Waldock, J. M. 2000. Review of the spider genus *Yoroa* Baert (Araneae: Theridiidae: Hadrotarsinae). *Australian Journal of Entomology* 39: 58–61.

Isbister G. K. & Gray, M. R. 2003. Latrodectism: a prospective cohort study of bites by formally identified redback spiders. *Medical Journal of Australia* 179:88–91.

Fitzgerald, B. M. & Sirvid, P. J. 2003. The genus *Trigonobothrys* in New Zealand and a redescription of *Achaearanea blattea* (Theridiidae: Araneae). *Tuhinga* 14: 25–33

Arnedo, M. A., Coddington, J. A., Agnarsson, I. & Gillespie, R. G. 2004. From a comb to a tree: phylogenetic relationships of the comb-footed spiders (Araneae, Theridiidae) inferred from nuclear and mitochondrial genes. *Molecular Phylogenetics and Evolution* 31: 225–245.

Fitzgerald, B. M. & Sirvid, P. J. 2004 Notes on the genus *Phycosoma* Cambridge, 1879, senior synonym of *Trigonobothrys* Simon, 1889 (Theridiidae: Araneae). *Tuhinga* 15: 7–12.

Wunderlich, J. 2008. On extant and fossil (Eocene) European comb-footed spiders (Araneae: Theridiidae), with notes on their subfamilies, and with descriptions of new taxa. *Beiträge zur Araneologie* 5: 140–469.

Vink, C. J., Derraik, J. G. B., Phillips, C. B. & Sirvid, P. J. 2011. The invasive Australian redback spider, *Latrodectus hasseltii* Thorell 1870, (Araneae: Theridiidae): current and potential distributions, and likely impacts. *Biological Invasions* 13, 1003–1019.

Agnarsson, I. 2012. Systematics of new subsocial and solitary Australasian *Anelosimus* species (Araneae: Theridiidae). *Invertebrate Systematics* **26:** 1–16.

Agnarsson I. 2012. A new phylogeny of *Anelosimus* and the placement and behavior of *Anelosimus vierae* n. sp. from Uruguay (Araneae: Theridiidae). *Journal of Arachnology* 40: 78–84.

Smith, H. M., Vink, C. J., Fitzgerald, B. M. & Sirvid, P. J. 2012. Redescription and generic placement of the spider *Cryptachaea gigantipes* (Keyserling, 1890) (Araneae: Theridiidae) and notes on related synanthropic species in Australasia. *Zootaxa* 3507: 38–56.

Nicodamidae

Harvey, M. S. 1995. The systematics of the spider family Nicodamidae (Araneae: Amaurobioidea). *Invertebrate Taxonomy* 9: 279–386.

Brennan, K. E. C. 1999. Discovery of the spider *Ambicodamus marae* (Araneae: Nicodamidae) in the northern jarrah forest of Western Australia. *Records of the Western Australian Museum* 19: 323–325.

Deinopidae

Roberts, N. L. 1954. The Australian Netting Spider, *Deinopis subrufus*. *Proceedings of the Royal Zoological Society (NSW)* 54: 24–33.

Clyne, D. 1967. Notes on construction of the net and spermweb of a cribellate spider *Dinopis subrufus*. *Australian Zoologist* 14: 189–198.

Blest, A. D. & Land, M. F. 1977. The physiological optics of *Dinopis subrufus* L. Koch: a fish lens in a spider. *Proceedings of the Royal Society B (London)* 196: 197–222.

Blest, A. D. 1978. The rapid synthesis and destruction of photoreceptor membrane by a dinopid spider: a daily cycle. *Proceedings of the Royal Society B (London)* 200: 463–483.

Austin, A. D. & Blest, A. D. 1979. The biology of two Australian species of dinopid spider. *Journal of Zoology, London* 189: 145–156.

Raven, R. J. 1982. More on Dinopidae. *Australasian Arachnology* 9: 5.

Coddington, J. A., Kuntner, M. & Opell, B. D. 2012. Systematics of the spider family Deinopidae with a revision of the genus *Menneus*. *Smithsonian Contributions to Zoology* 636: 1–61.

Morrison, R. no date. Meet the toolmaking genius of the animal world. http://regmorrison.edublogs.org/files/2011/01/netcaster_1-155r96i.pdf (accessed 22 November 2013).

Uloboridae

Lubin, Y. D., Eberhard, W. G. & Montgomery, G. G. 1978. Webs of *Miagrammopes* (Araneae: Uloboridae) in the Neotropics. *Psyche* 85: 1–23.

Opell, B. D. 1984. Phylogenetic review of the genus *Miagrammopes* (sensu lato) (Araneae, Uloboridae). *Journal or Arachnology* 12: 229–240.

Opell, B. D. & Eberhard, W. G. 1984. Resting postures of orb-weaving spiders (Araneae, Uloboridae). *Journal of Arachnology* 11: 369–376.

Opell, B. D., T. W. Schoener, S. L. Keen & Davies, V. T. 1995. The new species *Purumitra australiensis* (Araneae, Uloboridae) with notes on its natural history. *Journal of Arachnology* 23: 127–129.

Wunderlich, J. 1976. Spinnen aus Australien. 1. Uloboridae, Theridiosomatidae und Symphytognathidae (Arachnida: Araneida). *Senckenbergiana biologica* 57: 113–124.

Hersiliidae

Baehr, B. & Baehr, M. 1987. The Australian Hersiliidae (Arachnida: Araneae): taxonomy, phylogeny, zoogeography. *Invertebrate Taxonomy* 1: 351–437.

Baehr, B. & Baehr, M. 1988. On Australian Hersiliidae from the South Australian Museum (Arachnida: Araneae). Supplement to the revision of the Australian Hersiliidae. *Records of the South Australian Museum* 22: 13–20.

Baehr, B. & Baehr, M. 1989. Three new species of genus *Tamopsis* Baehr and Baehr from Western Australia (Arachnida, Araneae, Hersiliidae). Second supplement to the revision of the Australian Hersiliidae. *Records of the Western Australian Museum* 14: 309–320.

Baehr, B. & Baehr, M. 1992. New species and new records of genus *Tamopsis* Baehr and Baehr (Arachnida, Araneae, Hersiliidae). Third supplement to the revision of the Australian Hersiliidae. *Records of the Western Australian Museum* 16: 61–77.

Baehr, B. & Baehr, M. 1993. Further new species and new records of Hersiliidae from Australia, with an updated key to all Australian species (Arachnida, Araneae, Hersiliidae). Fourth supplement to the revision of the Australian Hersiliidae. *Records of the Western Australian Museum* 16: 347–391.

Baehr, B. & Baehr, M. 1995. New species and new records of Hersiliidae from Australia (Arachnida, Araneae, Hersiliidae). Fifth supplement to the revision of the Australian Hersiliidae. *Records of the Western Australian Museum, Supplement* 52: 107–118.

Baehr, B. 1998. The genus *Hersilia*: phylogeny and distribution in Australia and New Guinea (Arachnida, Araneae, Hersiliidae). In: Selden, P. A. (ed.) *Proceedings of the 17th Europpean Colloquium of Arachnology, Edinburgh 1997*, pp. 61–65.

Baehr, B. & Baehr, M. 1998. New species and new records of Hersiliidae from Australia (Arachnida: Araneae: Hersiliidae). Sixth supplement to the revision of the Australian Hersiliidae. *Records of the Western Australian Museum* 19: 13–38.

Oecobiidae

Butler, S. G. 1929. Studies in Victorian Spiders, No. 1. *Proceedings of the Royal Society of Victoria* 42: 41–52.

Shear, W. A. 1970. The spider family Oecobiidae in North America, Mexico and the West Indies. *Bulletin of the Museum of Comparative Zoology at Harvard College* 140: 129–164

Wunderlich, J. 1995. First endemic Australian Oecobiidae and Nesticidae (Arachnida: Araneae). *Memoirs of the Queensland Museum* 38: 691–692.

Santos A. & Gonzaga M. O. 2003. On the spider genus *Oecobius* Lucas, 1846 in South America (Araneae, Oecobiidae). *Journal of Natural History* 37, 239–252.

Voss, S. C., Main, B. Y. & Dadour, I. R. 2007. Habitat preferences of the urban wall spider *Oecobius navus* (Araneae, Oecobiidae). *Australian Journal of Entomology* 46: 261–268.

Hahniidae

Rainbow, W. J. 1920. Arachnida from Lord Howe and Norfolk Islands. *Records of the South Australian Museum* 1: 229-272.

Butler, S. G. 1929. Studies in Victorian Spiders, No. 1. *Proceedings of the Royal Society of Victoria* 42: 41–52.

Hickman, V. V. 1948. Tasmanian Araneae of the family Hahniidae with notes on their respiratory systems. *Papers and Proceedings of the Royal Society of Tasmania* 1947: 21–35.

Forster, R. R. 1970. The spiders of New Zealand. Part. III. Desidae, Dictynidae, Hahniidae, Aumaurobioididae, Nicodamidae. *Otago Museum Bulletin* 3: 1–184.

Dictynidae

Lehtinen, P. T. 1967. Classification of the cribellate spiders and some allied families, with notes on the evolution of the suborder Araneomorpha. *Annales Zooogici Fennici* 4: 199–468.

Forster, R. R. 1970. The spiders of New Zealand. Part. III. Desidae, Dictynidae, Hahniidae, Aumaurobioididae, Nicodamidae. *Otago Museum Bulletin* 3: 1–184.

Sparassidae

Rovner, J. S. 1980. Vibration in *Heteropoda venatoria* (Sparassidae): a third method of sound production in spiders. *Journal of Arachnology* 8: 193–200.

Rowell, D. M., 1988. The chromosomal constitution of *Delena cancerides* Walck. (Araneae: Sparassidae) and its role in the maintenance of social behaviour. *Australian Entomological Society Miscellaneous Publication* 5: 107–111.

Hirst, D. B. 1989. A revision of the genus *Pediana* Simon (Heteropodidae: Araneae) in Australia. *Records of the South Australian Museum* 23: 113–126.

Hirst, D. B. 1989. A new genus of huntsman spider (Heteropodidae: Araneae) from south eastern Australia. *Transactions of the Royal Society of South Australia* 113: 7–13.

Hirst, D. 1990. A review of the genus *Isopeda* L. Koch (Heteropodidae: Araneae) in Australasia with descriptions of two new genera. *Records of the South Australian Museum* 24: 11–26.

Rowell, D. M., 1990. Fixed fusion heterozygosity in *Delena cancerides* Walck. (Araneae: Sparassidae): an alternative to speciation by monobrachial fusion. *Genetica* 80: 139–157.

Hirst, D. B. 1991. Revision of Australian species of the genus *Holconia* Thorell (Heteropodidae: Araneae). *Records of the South Australian Museum* 24: 91–109.

Hirst, D. B. 1991. Revision of the Australian genera *Eodelena* Hogg and *Zachria* L. Koch (Heteropodidae: Araneae). *Records of the South Australian Museum* 24: 91–109.

Davies, V. T. 1994. The huntsman spiders *Heteropoda* Latreille and *Yiinthi* gen. nov. (Araneae: Heteropodidae) in Australia. *Memoirs of the Queensland Museum* 35: 75–122.

Hirst, D. B. 1992. Revision of the genus *Isopeda* Koch (Heteropodidae: Araneae) in Australia. *Invertebrate Taxonomy* 6: 337–387.

Hirst, D. B. 1993. Revision of the genus *Isopedella* (Araneae: Heteropodidae). *Invertebrate Taxonomy* 7: 33–87.

Hirst, D. B. 1995. Further studies on the Australian Heteropodidae (Araneae): a new species of *Pediana* Simon, and description of the male *Zachria flavicoma* L. Koch. *Records of the Western Australian Museum, Supplement* 52: 145–149.

Rowell, D. M. & Aviles, L., 1995. Sociality in a bark-dwelling huntsman spider from Australia, *Delena cancerides* Walckenaer (Araneae: Sparassidae). *Insectes Sociaux* 42: 287–302.

Hirst, D. B. 1996. New species of *Pediana* (Heteropodidae, Araneae) Simon from central and northern Australia. *Records of the South Australian Museum* 29: 153–164.

Hirst, D. B. 1998. *Irileka*, a new heteropodine genus (Araneae: Heteropodidae) from Western Australia. *Records of the Western Australian Museum* 19: 141–144.

Hirst, D. B. 1999. Revision of *Typostola* Simon (Araneae: Heteropodidae) in Australasia. *Memoirs of the Queensland Museum* 43: 639–648.

Isbister, G. K & Hirst, D. 2003. A prospective study of definite bites by spiders of the family Sparassidae (huntsmen spiders) with identification to species level. *Toxicon* 42: 163–171.

Yip, E. C., Rowell, D. M. & Rayor, L. S. 2012. Behavioural and molecular evidence for selective immigration and group regulation in the social huntsman spider, *Delena cancerides* (Araneae: Sparassidae). *Biological Journal of the Linnean Society* 106: 749–762.

Agnarsson I, & Rayor L. 2013. A molecular phylogeny of the Australian huntsman spiders (Sparassidae, Deleninae): implications for taxonomy and social behaviour. *Molecular Phylogenetics and Evolution* 69: 895–905.

Desidae

Davies, V. T. 1984. *Pitonga* gen. nov., a spider (Amaurobiidae: Desinae) from Northern Australia. *Memoirs of the Queensland Museum* 21: 261–269.

Gray, M. R. 1992. New desid spiders (Araneae: Desidae) from New Caledonia and Eastern Australia. *Records of the Australian Museum* 44: 253–262.

Downes, M. F. 1993. The life history of *Badumna candida* (Araneae: Amaurobioidea). *Australian Journal of Zoology* 41: 441–466.

Downes, M. F. 1994. Tolerance, interattraction and co-operation in the behaviour of the social spider *Phryganoporus candidus* (Araneae: Desidae). *Bulletin of the British arachnological Society* 9: 309–317.

Downes, M. F. 1994. Courtship and mating in the

social spider *Phryganoporus candidus* (Araneae: Desidae). *Bulletin of the British arachnological Society* 9: 277–280.

Downes, M. F. 1994. The nest of the social spider *Phryganoporus candidus* (Araneidae: Desidae): structure, annual growth cycle and host plant relationship. *Australian Journal of Zoology* 42: 237–259.

Gray, M. R. 2002. The taxonomy and distribution of the spider genus *Phryganoporus* Simon (Araneae: Amaurobioidea: Desidae). *Records of the Australian Museum* 54: 275–292.

Gray, M. & Smith, H. M. 2008. A new subfamily of spiders with grate-shaped tapeta from Australia and Papua New Guinea (Araneae: Stiphidiidae: Borralinae). *Records of the Australian Museum* 60: 13–44.

Stiphidiidae

Gray, M. R. 1973. Cavernicolous spiders from the Nullarbor Plain and south-west Australia. *Journal of the Australian Entomological Society* 12: 207–221.

Gray, M. R. 1981. A revision of the spider genus *Baiami* Lehtinen (Araneae, Amaurobioidea). *Records of the Australian Museum* 33: 779–802.

Davies, V. T. 1988. Three new species of the spider genus *Stiphidion* (Araneae: Amaurobioidea: Stiphidiidae) from Australia. *Memoirs of the Queensland Museum* 25: 265-271.

Gray, M. R. 1992. The troglobitic spider genus *Tartarus* Gray with a cladistic analysis of *Tartarus* and *Baiami* Lehtinen (Araneae: Stiphidiidae). *Proceedings of the Linnean Society of New South Wales* 113: 165–173.

Davies, V. T. 1995. A tiny litter spider (Araneae: Amaurobioidea) from Australian rainforests. *Records of the Western Australian Museum, Supplement* 52: 119–129.

Davies, V. T. 1995. A new spider genus (Araneae: Amaurobioidea: Amphinectidae) from the wet tropics of Australia. *Memoirs of the Queensland Museum* 38: 463–469.

Davies, V. T. 1999. *Carbinea*, a new spider genus from north Queensland, Australia (Araneae, Amaurobioidea, Kababininae). *Journal of Arachnology* 27: 25–36.

Davies, V. T. & Lambkin, C. L. 2000. *Malarina*, a new spider genus (Araneae: Amaurobioidea: Kababinae) from the wet tropics of Queensland, Australia. *Memoirs of the Queensland Museum* 45: 273–283.

Davies, V. T. & Lambkin, C. L. 2000. *Wabua*, a new spider genus (Araneae: Amaurobioidea: Kababinae) from north Queensland, Australia. *Memoirs of the Queensland Museum* 46: 129–147.

Davies, V. T. & Lambkin, C. L. 2001. A revision of *Procambridgea* Forster & Wilton, (Araneae: Amaurobioidea: Stiphidiidae). *Memoirs of the Queensland Museum* 46: 443–459.

Gray, M. R. & Smith, H. M. 2002. *Therlinya*, a new genus of spiders from eastern Australia (Araneae: Amaurobioidea). *Records of the Australian Museum* 54: 293–312.

Davies, V. T. 2003. *Barahna*, a new spider genus from eastern Australia (Araneae: Amauroboidea). *Memoirs of the Queensland Museum* 49: 237–250.

Gray, M. & Smith, H. M. 2004. The "striped" group of stiphidiid spiders: two new genera from northeastern New South Wales, Australia (Araneae: Stiphidiidae: Amaurobioidea). *Records of the Australian Museum* 56: 123–138.

Gray, M. & Smith, H. M. 2008. A new subfamily of spiders with grate-shaped tapeta from Australia and Papua New Guinea (Araneae: Stiphidiidae: Borralinae). *Records of the Australian Museum* 60: 13–44.

Amphinectidae

Gray, M. R. 1983. A new genus of spiders of the subfamily Metaltellinae (Araneae, Amaurobioidea) from southeastern Australia. *Proceedings of the Linnean Society of New South Wales* 106: 275–285.

Davies, V. T. 2005. *Teeatta*, a new spider genus from Tasmania, Australia (Amaurobioidea: Amphinectidae: Tasmarubriinae). *Memoirs of the Queensland Museum* 50: 195-199.

Davies, V. T. 2003. *Tangana*, a new spider genus from Australia (Amaurobioidea: Amphinectidae: Tasmarubriinae). *Memoirs of the Queensland Museum* 49: 251–259.

Davies, V. T. 2002. *Tasmabrochus*, a new spider genus from Tasmania, Australia (Araneae, Amphinectidae, Tasmarubriinae). *Journal of Arachnology* 30: 219–226.

Davies, V. T. 1998. A

revision of the Australian metaltellines (Araneae: Amaurobioidea: Amphinectidae: Metaltellinae). *Invertebrate Taxonomy* 12: 211–243.

Agelenidae

Rainbow, W. J. 1920. Arachnida from Lord Howe and Norfolk Islands. *Records of the South Australian Museum* 1: 229–272.
Hickman, V. V. 1967. *Some common Spiders of Tasmania*. Tasmanian Museum and Art Gallery, Hobart.

Amaurobiidae

Davies, V. T. 1976. *Dardurus*, a new genus of amaurobiid spider from eastern Australia, with descriptions of six new species. *Memoirs of the Queensland Museum* 17: 399–411.
Davies, V. T. 1990. Two new spider genera (Araneae: Amaurobiidae) from rainforests of Australia. *Proceedings of XI International Congress of Arachnology. Turku, Finland*: 95–102.
Davies, V. T. 1993. A new spider genus (Araneae: Amaurobioidea) from rainforests of Queensland, Australia. *Memoirs of the Queensland Museum* 33: 483–489.
Davies, V. T. 1995. A tiny litter spider (Araneae: Amaurobioidea) from Australian rainforests. *Records of the Western Australian Museum, Supplement* 52: 119–129.
Davies, V. T. 1995. A tiny cribellate spider, *Jamara* gen. nov. (Araneae: Amaurobioidea: Midgeeinae) from northern Queensland. *Memoirs of the Queensland Museum* 38: 93–96.
Davies, V. T. 1996. A new genus (Araneae: Amaurobioidea) from Australia with a rainforest species and a relict species from limestone caves. *Revue Suisse de Zoologie* vol. hors. ser.: 125–133.
Milledge, G. A. 2011. A revision of *Storenosoma* Hogg and description of a new genus, *Oztira* (Araneae: Amaurobiidae). *Records of the Australian Museum* 63: 1–32.

Cycloctenidae

Hickman, V. V. 1981. New Tasmanian spiders of the families Archaeidae, Cycloctenidae, Amaurobiidae and Micropholcommatidae. *Papers and Proceedings of the Royal Society of Tasmania* 115: 47–68.

Zodariidae

Pickard-Cambridge, O. 1869. Descriptions and sketches of some new species of Araneidea, with characters of a new genus. *Annals and Magazine of Natural History, Series 4* 3: 52–74.
Platnick, N. I. & Griffin, E. 1988. On the first African and Australian spiders of the genus *Cyrioctea* (Araneae: Zodariidae). *Journal of the New York Entomological Society* 96: 359–362.
Jocqué, R. 1991. A generic revision of the spider family Zodariidae (Araneae). *Bulletin of the American Museum of Natural History* 201: 1–160.
Jocqué, R. & Baehr, B. 1992. A revision of the Australian spider genus *Storena* (Araneae: Zodariidae). *Invertebrate Taxonomy* 6: 953–1004.
Jocqué, R. 1995. Note on Australian Zodariidae (Aranae), I. New taxa and key to the genera. *Records of the Australian Museum* 47: 117–140.
Jocqué, R. 1995. Notes on Australian Zodariidae, II. Redescriptions and new records. *Records of the Australian Museum* 47: 141–160.
Jocqué, R. & Baehr, B. 1995. A supplement to the revision of the Australian spider genus *Storena* (Araneae: Zodariidae). *Records of the Western Australian Museum, Supplement* 52: 135–144.
Allan, R.A., Elgar, M.A. and Capon, R.J. 1996. Exploitation of an ant chemical alarm signal by the zodariid spider *Habronestes bradleyi* Walckenaer. *Proceedings of the Royal Society of London, Series B* 263: 69–73.
Baehr, B. & Jocqué, R. 2000. Revisions of genera in the *Asteron*-complex (Araneae: Zodariidae). The new genera *Cavasteron* and *Minasteron*. *Records of the Western Australian Museum* 20: 1–30.
Raven, R. J. & Baehr, B. C. 2000. Revised status of the genus *Hetaerica* Rainbow (Aranеae: Zodariidae). *Memoirs of the Queensland Museum* 45: 577–583.
Baehr, B. & Jocqué, R. 2001. Revisions of genera in the *Asteron*-complex (Araneae: Zodariidae): new genera *Pentasteron, Phenasteron, Leptasteron* and *Subasteron*. *Memoirs of the Queensland Museum* 46: 359–385.
Jocqué, R. & Baehr, B. 2001. Revisions of genera in the *Asteron*-complex (Araneae: Zodariidae). *Asteron* Jocqué and the new genus *Pseudasteron*. *Records of the Australian Museum* 53: 21–36.
Baehr, B. 2003. Three new endemic genera of the

Asteron-complex (Araneae: Zodariidae) from Australia: *Basasteron*, *Euasteron* and *Spinasteron*. *Memoirs of the Queensland Museum* 49: 1–27.

Baehr, B. 2003. *Tropasteron* gen. nov. of the *Asteron*-complex (Araneae: Zodariidae) from tropical Queensland. *Memoirs of the Queensland Museum* 49: 29–64.

Baehr, B. 2003. Revision of the Australian spider genus *Habronestes* (Araneae: Zodariidae). Species of New South Wales and the Australian Capital Territory. *Records of the Australian Museum* 55: 343–376.

Baehr, B. & Churchill, T. B. 2003. Revision of the endemic Australian genus *Spinasteron* (Araneae: Zodariidae): taxonomy, phylogeny and biogeography. *Invertebrate Systematics* 17: 641–665.

Baehr, B. 2004. Revision of the new Australian genus *Holasteron* (Araneae: Zodariidae): taxonomy, phylogeny and biogeography. *Memoirs of the Queensland Museum* 49: 495–519.

Baehr, B. 2004. The systematics of a new Australian genus of ant spiders *Masasteron* (Araneae: Zodariidae). *Invertebrate Systematics* 18: 661–691.

Baehr, B. 2005. The generic relationships of the new endemic Australian ant spider genus *Notasteron* (Araneae, Zodariidae). *Journal of Arachnology* 33: 445–455.

Jocqué, R. & Churchill, T. B. 2005. On the new genus *Tropizodium* (Araneae: Zodariidae), representing the femoral organ clade in Australia and the Pacific. *Zootaxa* 944: 1–10.

Baehr, B. C. 2008. Revision of the Australian ant spider genus *Habronestes* L. Koch 1872 (Araneae: Zodariidae): III. The *Habronestes macedonensis*-group in Queensland and New South Wales. *Memoirs of the Queensland Museum* 52: 65–87.

Baehr, B. C. & Raven, R. J. 2009. Revision of the Australian spider genus *Habronestes* L. Koch, 1872 (Araneae: Zodariidae). Species of Tasmania. *Contributions to Natural History* 12: 127–151.

Baehr, B. C. & Whyte, R. 2012. Biodiversity discovery program Bush Blitz supplies missing ant spider females (Araneae: Zodariidae) from Victoria. *Australian Entomologist* 39: 97–104.

Lycosidae

Hogg, H. R. 1905. On some South Australian Spiders of the Family Lycosidae. *Proceedings of the Zoological Society London* 1905: 569-590.

McKay, R. J. 1973. The wolf spiders of Australia (Araneae: Lycosidae): 1. The *bicolor* group. *Memoirs of the Queensland Museum* 16: 375–398.

McKay, R. J. 1974. The wolf spiders of Australia (Araneae: Lycosidae): 2. The *arenaris* group. *Memoirs of the Queensland Museum* 17: 1–19.

Humphreys, W. F. 1974. Behavioural thermoregulation in a wolf spider. *Nature* 251: 502–503.

McKay, R. J. 1974. The wolf spiders of Australia (Araneae: Lycosidae): 3. A coral shingle inhabiting species from Western Australia. *Memoirs of the Queensland Museum* 17: 21–26.

McKay, R. J. 1974. The wolf spiders of Australia (Araneae: Lycosidae): 4. Three new species from Mount Kosciusko, N.S.W. *Memoirs of the Queensland Museum* 17: 27–36.

McKay, R. J. 1975. The wolf spiders of Australia (Araneae: Lycosidae): 5. Two new species of the *bicolor* group. *Memoirs of the Queensland Museum* 17: 313–318.

McKay, R. J. 1975. The wolf spiders of Australia (Araneae: Lycosidae): 6. The *leuckartii* group. *Memoirs of the Queensland Museum* 17: 319–328.

Humphreys, W. F. 1976. The population dynamics of an Australian wolf spider, *Geolycosa godeffroyi* (L. Koch 1865) (Araneae: Lycosidae). *Journal of Animal Ecology* 45: 59–80.

McKay, R. J. 1976. The wolf spiders of Australia (Araneae: Lycosidae): 7. Two new species from Victoria. *Memoirs of the Queensland Museum* 17: 413–416.

McKay, R. J. 1976. The wolf spiders of Australia (Araneae: Lycosidae): 8. Two new species inhabiting salt lakes of Western Australia. *Memoirs of the Queensland Museum* 17: 417–423.

McKay, R. J. 1979. The wolf spiders of Australia (Araneae: Lycosidae): 9. *Pardosa serrata* (L. Koch 1877). *Memoirs of the Queensland Museum* 19: 225–229.

McKay, R. J. 1979. The wolf spiders of Australia (Araneae: Lycosidae): 10. A new species of the genus *Flanona* Simon. *Memoirs of the Queensland Museum* 19: 231–235.

McKay, R. J. 1979. The wolf spiders of Australia (Araneae: Lycosidae): 11. A new species from Lord Howe Island. *Memoirs of the Queensland Museum* 19: 237–240.

McKay, R. J. 1979. The wolf spiders of Australia (Araneae: Lycosidae): 12. Descriptions of some Western

Australian species. *Memoirs of the Queensland Museum* 19: 241–275.

McKay, R. J. 1979. The wolf spiders of Australia (Araneae: Lycosidae): 13. The genus *Trochosa*. *Memoirs of the Queensland Museum* 19: 277–298.

McKay, R. J. 1985. The wolf spiders of Australia (Araneae: Lycosidae): 14. A new species of the genus *Pardosa*. *Memoirs of the Queensland Museum* 22: 101–104.

Hudson, P. & Adams, M. 1996. Allozyme characterisation of the salt lake spiders (*Lycosa*: Lycosidae: Araneae) of southern Australia: systematic and population genetic implications. *Australian Journal of Zoology* 44: 535–567.

Hudson, P. 2000. First record of the salt lake wolf spider, *Lycosa salifodina* McKay, from Northern Territory, Australia. *Australasian Arachnology* 58: 5–6.

Framenau, V. W. & Vink, C. J. 2001. Revision of the wolf spider genus *Venatrix* Roewer (Araneae: Lycosidae). *Invertebrate Taxonomy* 15: 927–970.

Vink, C. J. 2001. A revision of the genus *Allotrochosina* Roewer (Lycosidae: Araneae). *Invertebrate Taxonomy* 15: 461-466.

Framenau, V. W. 2002. Review of the wolf spider genus *Artoria* Thorell (Araneae: Lycosidae). *Invertebrate Systematics* 16: 209–235.

Framenau, V. W. 2004 [imprint date 2003]. Two alpine wolf spiders of Australia: *Artoria alta* sp. nov., and the male of *Lycosa musgravei* McKay, 1974 (Araneae, Lycosidae). *Proceedings of the Royal Society of Victoria* 115: 27–34.

Isbister, G. K. & Framenau, V. W. 2004. Australian wolf spider bites (Lycosidae): clinical effects and influence of species on bite circumstances. *Journal of Toxicology, Clinical Toxicology* 42: 153–161.

Framenau, V. W. 2005. Gender specific differences in activity and home range reflect morphological dimorphism in wolf spiders (Araneae, Lycosidae). *Journal of Arachnology* 33: 334–346.

Framenau, V. W. 2005. The wolf spider genus *Artoria* Thorell in Australia: new synonymies and generic transfers (Araneae, Lycosidae). *Records of the Western Australian Museum* 22: 265–292.

Framenau, V. W. & Elgar, M. A. 2005. Cohort dependent life-history traits in a wolf spider (Araneae: Lycosidae) with bimodal life cycle. *Journal of Zoology* 265: 179–188.

Framenau, V. W. 2006. *Knoelle*, a new monotypic wolf spider genus from Australia (Araneae: Lycosidae). *Zootaxa* 1281: 55–67.

Framenau, V. W. 2006. *Mainosa*, a new genus for the Australian 'shuttlecock wolf spider' (Araneae, Lycosidae). *Journal of Arachnology* 34: 206–213.

Framenau, V. W. 2006. Revision of the Australian wolf spider genus *Anomalosa* Roewer, 1960 (Araneae: Lycosidae). *Zootaxa* 1304: 1–20.

Framenau, V. W. 2006. Revision of the wolf spider genus *Diahogna* Roewer, 1960 (Araneae, Lycosidae). *Journal of Natural History* 40: 273–292.

Framenau, V. W. 2006. The wolf spider genus *Venatrix* Roewer: new species, synonymies and generic transfers (Araneae, Lycosidae). *Records of the Western Australian Museum* 23: 145–166.

Framenau, V. W., Gotch, T. B. & Austin, A. D. 2006. The wolf spiders of artesian springs in arid South Australia, with a revalidation of *Tetralycosa* (Araneae, Lycosidae). *Journal of Arachnology* 34: 1–36.

Framenau, V. W. & Yoo, J.-S. 2006. Systematics of the new Australian wolf spider genus *Tuberculosa* (Araneae, Lycosidae). *Invertebrate Systematics* 20: 185–202.

Yoo, J.-S. & Framenau, V. W. 2006. Systematics and biogeography of the sheet-web building wolf spider genus *Venonia* (Araneae: Lycosidae). *Invertebrate Systematics* 20: 675–712.

Murphy, N.P., Framenau, V. W., Donnellan, S., Harvey, M. S., Park, Y.C. & Austin, A. 2006 Phylogenetic reconstruction of the wolf spiders (Araneae: Lycosidae) using scquences from the 12S rRNA, 28S rRNA and NADH1 genes: implications for classification, biogeography and the evolution of web building behavior. *Molecular Phylogenetics and Evolution* 38: 503-602.

Framenau, V. W. 2007. Revision of the new Australian genus *Artoriopsis* in a new subfamily of wolf spiders, Artoriinae (Araneae: Lycosidae). *Zootaxa* 1391: 1–34.

Framenau, V. W. & Baehr, B. C. 2007. Revision of the Australian wolf spider genus *Dingosa* Roewer, 1955 (Araneae, Lycosidae, Lycosinae). *Journal of Natural History* 41: 1603–1629.

Framenau, V. W. & Hebets, E. A. 2007. A review of leg ornamentation in male wolf spiders, with the description of a new species from Australia, *Artoria schizocoides* (Araneae, Lycosidae). *Journal of Arachnology* 35: 89–101.

Framenau, V. W. 2008. A new species in the wolf spider genus *Allotrochosina* from New South Wales, Australia (Araneae, Lycosidae). *Journal of Arachnology* 35: 463–469.

Framenau, V. W. 2008. A new wolf spider species of the genus *Artoria* from Western Australia (Araneae: Lycosidae). *Records of the Western Australian Museum* 24: 363–368.

Framenau, V. W., Main, B. Y., Waldock, J. M. & Harvey, M. S. 2009. *Tapetosa*, a new monotypic wolf spider genus from Western Australia (Araneae: Lycosidae: Lycosinae). *Records of the Western Australian Museum* 25: 309–314.

Framenau, V. W. 2010. Revision of the new Australian wolf spider genus *Kangarosa* (Araneae: Lycosidae: Artoriinae). *Arthropod Systematics and Phylogeny* 68: 113-142.

Langlands, P. & Framenau, V. W. 2010. Systematic revision of *Hoggicosa* Roewer, 1960, the Australian '*bicolor*' group of wolf spiders (Araneae: Lycosidae). *Zoological Journal of the Linnean Society* 158: 83–123.

Framenau, V. W. & Leung, A. E. 2013. *Costacosa*, a new genus of wolf spider (Araneae, Lycosidae) from coastal north-west Western Australia. *Records of the Western Australian Museum Supplement* 83: 173–184.

Pisauridae

Davies, V. T. & Raven, R. J. 1980. *Megadolomedes* nov. gen. (Araneae: Pisauridae) spiders, with a description of the male of the type-species *Dolomedes australianus* Koch 1865. *Memoirs of the Queensland Museum* 20: 135–141.

Davies, V.T. 1982. *Inola* nov. gen., a web-building pisaurid (Araneae: Pisauridae) from northern Australia with descriptions of three species. *Memoirs of the Queensland Museum* 20: 479–487.

Sierwald, P. 1990. Morphology and homologous features in the male palpal organ in Pisauridae and other spider families, with notes on the taxonomy of Pisauridae (Arachnida: Araneae). *Nemouria* 35: 1–59.

Sierwald, P. 1997. Phylogenetic analysis of pisaurine nursery web spiders, with revisions of *Tetragonophthalma* and *Perenethis* (Araneae, Lycosoidea, Pisauridae). *Journal of Arachnology* 25: 361–407.

Cerveira, A. & Jackson, R. R. 2002. Prey, predatory behaviour, and anti-predator defences of *Hygropoda dolomedes* and *Dendrolycosa* sp. (Araneae: Pisauridae), web-building pisaurid spiders from Australia and Sri Lanka. *New Zealand Journal of Zoology* 29: 119–133.

Tio, M. & Humphrey, M. 2010. Description of a new species of *Inola* Davies (Araneae: Pisauridae), the male of *I. subtilis* Davies and notes on their chromosomes. *Proceedings of the Linnean Society of New South Wales* 131: 37–42.

Jäger, P. 2011. Revision of the spider genera *Nilus* O. Pickard-Cambridge 1876, *Sphedanus* Thorell 1877 and *Dendrolycosa* Doleschall 1859 (Araneae: Pisauridae). *Zootaxa* 3046: 1–38.

Ctenidae

Gray, M. R. 1973. Cavernicolous spiders from the Nullarbor Plain and south-west Australia. *Journal of the Australian Entomological Society* 12: 207–221.

Gray, M. R. & Thompson, J. A. 2001. New lycosoid spiders from cave and surface habitats in southern Australia and Cape Range Peninsula (Araneae: Lycosoidea). *Records of the Western Australian Museum, Supplement* 64: 159–201.

Raven, R. J., Stumkat, K. & Gray, M. R. 2001. Revisions of Australian ground hunting spiders: I. *Amauropelma* gen. nov. (Araneomorphae: Ctenidae). *Records of the Western Australian Museum, Supplement* 64: 187–227.

Davila, D. S. 2003. Higher-level relationships of the spider family Ctenidae. *Bulletin of the American Museum of Natural History* 274: 1–86.

Oxyopidae

Cutler, B., Jennings, D. T. & Moody, M. J. 1977. Biology and habitats of the lynx spider *Oxyopes scalaris* Hentz (Araneae: Oxyopidae). *Entomological News* 88: 87–97.

Grimshaw, J. F. 1989. The genus *Hamataliwa* Keyserling (Araneae: Oxyopidae) in Australia with descriptions of two new species. *Journal of the Australian Entomological Society* 28: 181–186.

Grimshaw, J. F. 1991. Revision of the Oxyopidae (Araneae: Arachnida) of Australia. M.Sc. thesis, Department of Entomology, University of Queensland.

Vink, C. J. & Sirvid, P. J. 2000. New synonymy between

Oxyopes gracilipes (White) and *Oxyopes mundulus* L. Koch (Oxyopidae: Araneae). *Memoirs of the Queensland Museum* 45: 637–640.

Townsend, V. R., Felgenhauer, B. E. & Grimshaw, J. F. 2001 Comparative morphology of the Australian lynx spiders of the genus *Oxyopes* (Araneae: Oxyopidae). *Australian Journal of Zoology* 49: 561–576.

Miturgidae

Raven, R. J. & K. Stumkat. 2003. Problem solving in the spider families Miturgidae, Ctenidae and Psechridae (Araneae) in Australia and New Zealand. *Journal of Arachnology* 31: 105–121.

Raven, R. J. 2009. Revisions of Australian ground-hunting spiders: IV. The spider subfamily Diaprograptinae subfam. nov. (Araneomorphae: Miturgidae). *Zootaxa* 2035: 1–40.

Zoridae

Raven, R. J. 2008. Revisions of Australian ground-hunting spiders: III. *Tuxoctenus* gen. nov. (Araneomorphae: Zoridae). *Records of the Western Australian Museum* 24: 351–361.

Thomisidae

Simon, E. 1895. Descriptions d'arachnides nouveaux de la famille des Thomisidae. *Annales de la Société Entomologique de Belgique* 39: 432–443.

Rainbow, W. J. 1900. Two new thomisids. *Records of the Australian Museum* 3: 169–175.

Main, B. Y. 1988. The biology of a social thomisid spider. *In:* Austin, A. D. & Heather, N. W. (eds) *Australian Arachnology*. Australian Entomological Society, Brisbane, pp. 55–73.

Rowell, D. M. & Main, B. Y. 1992. Sex ratio in the social spider *Diaea socialis* (Araneae: Thomisidae). *Journal of Arachnology* 20: 200–206.

Evans, T. A. & Main, B. Y. 1993. Attraction between social crab spiders: evidence of pheromonal communication in *Diaea socialis* (Thomisidae). *Behavioural Ecology* 4: 99–105.

Evans, T. A. 1995. Two new social crab spiders (Thomisidae: *Diaea*) from eastern Australia, their natural history and geographic range. *Records of the Western Australian Museum, Supplement* 52: 151–158.

Evans, T. A. 2000. Male work and sex ratio in social crab spiders. *Insectes Sociaux* 47: 285–288.

Shield, J. M. & Strudwick, J. 2000. *Diasterea*, a new genus of flower spider (Thomisidae; Thomisinae) from eastern Australia and a description of the male *Diasterea lactea*. *Proceedings of the Royal Society of Australia* 111: 271–281.

Heiling, A. M., Cheng, K. & Herberstein, M. A. 2004. Exploitation of floral signals by crab spiders (*Thomisus spectabilis*, Thomisidae). *Behavioral Ecology* 15: 321–326.

Szymkowiak, P. 2007. Redescription of Australian crab spider *Diaea pulleinei* Rainbow, 1915 (Araneae: Thomisidae). *Zootaxa* 1425: 11–20.

Szymkowiak, P. 2007. Crab spiders (Araneae, Thomisidae) of Australia and New Guinea. Taxonomy of some species of *Diaea* as described by Kulczynski (1911). *Genus* Supplement 14: 53–58.

Szymkowiak, P. 2008. *Diaea kangarooblaszaki* sp. nov. from Kangaroo Island, South Australia (Araneae: Thomisidae). *Annales Zoologici, Warszawa* 58: 457–472.

Benjamin, S.P. 2011. Phylogenetics and comparative morphology of crab spiders (Araneae: Dionycha, Thomisidae). *Zootaxa* 3080: 1–108.

Szymkowiak, P. & Dymek, A. 2011. The redescription of *Corynethrix obscura* L. Koch, 1876 (Araneae: Thomisidae)—a crab spider of a monotypic genus from Australia. *Records of the Australian Museum* 63: 99–102.

Benjamin, S. P. 2011. Phylogenetics and comparative morphology of crab spiders (Araneae: Dionycha, Thomisidae). *Zootaxa* 3080: 1–108.

Psechridae

Bayer, S. 2011. Revision of the pseudo-orbweavers of the genus *Fecenia* Simon, 1887 (Araneae, Psechridae), with emphasis on their preepigyne. *Zookeys* 153:1–56.

Bayer, S. 2012. The lace-sheet-weavers—a long story (Araneae: Psechridae: *Psechrus*). *Zootaxa* 3379: 1–170.

Bayer, S. & Schönhofer, A. L. 2012. Phylogenetic relationships of the spider family Psechridae inferred from molecular data, with comments on the Lycosoidea (Arachnida: Araneae). *Invertebrate Systematics* 27: 53–80.

Agnarsson, I., Gregorič, M., Blackledge, T. A. & Kuntner, M. 2013. Phylogenetic placement of Pschridae and the convergent origin of orb-like spider webs. *Journal of Zoological Systematics and Evolutionary Research* 51: 100–106.

Zoropsidae

Gray, M. R. & Thompson, J. A. 2001. New lycosoid spiders from cave and surface habitats in southern Australia and Cape Range Peninsula (Araneae: Lycosoidea). *Records of the Western Australian Museum, Supplement* 64: 159–201.

Raven, R. J. & Stumkat, K. S. 2005. Revisions of Australian ground hunting spiders: II. Zoropsidae (Lycosoidea: Aranea). *Memoirs of the Queensland Museum* 50: 347–423.

Tengellidae

Raven, R. J. 2012. Revisions of Australian ground-hunting spiders. V. A new lycosoid genus from eastern Australia (Araneae: Tengellidae). *Zootaxa* 3305: 28–52.

Anyphaenidae

Hickman, V. V. 1949. Tasmanian littoral spiders with notes on their respiratory systems, habits and taxonomy. *Papers and Proceedings of the Royal Society of Tasmania* 1948: 31–43.

Forster, R. R. (1970). The spiders of New Zealand. Part III. *Otago Museum Bulletin* 3: 1–184.

Hirst, D. B. 1993. A new species of *Amaurobioides* Pickard-Cambridge (Anyphaenidae: Araneae) from South Australia. *Memoirs of the Queensland Museum* 33: 529–532.

Clubionidae

Austin, A. D. 1984. Life history of *Clubiona robusta* L. Koch and related species (Araneae, Clubionidae) in South Australia. *Journal of Arachnology* 12: 87–104.

Austin, A. D. 1993. Nest associates of *Clubiona robusta* L. Koch (Araneae: Clubionidae) in Australia. *Memoirs of the Queensland Museum* 33: 441–446.

Deeleman-Reinhold, C. L. 2001. Forest spiders of South East Asia. With a revision of the sac and ground spiders (*Araneae: Clubionidae, Corinnidae, Liocranidae, Gnaphosidae, Prodidomidae and Trochanterriidae* [sic]). Brill, Leiden.

Raven, R. J. & Stumkat, K. S. 2002. *Pteroneta* Deeleman-Reinhold and a remarkable sympatric *Clubiona* (Clubionidae: Araneomorphae: Arachnida) in northern Australia. *Memoirs of the Queensland Museum* 48: 199–206.

Vetter, R. S., Isbister, G. K., Bush, S. P. & Boutin, L. J. 2006. Verified bites by yellow sac spiders (genus *Cheiracanthium*) in the United States and Australia: where is the necrosis? *American Journal of Tropical Medicine and Hygiene* 74: 1043–1048.

Corinnidae

Baehr, B. & Raven, R. J. 2013: The new Australian Ground-Hunting Spider genus *Leichhardteus* (Araneae: Corinnidae). *Memoirs of the Queensland Museum, Nature* 58: 339–358.

Raven, R. J. 2014. Revision of the Australian Corinnidae. *Zootaxa*. In press.

Ramírez, M. J. 2014. The morphology and phylogeny of dionychan spiders (Araneae: Araneomorphae). *Bulletin of the American Museum of Natural History*. In press.

Liocranidae

Simon, E. 1909. Araneae, 2me partie. *In:* Michaelsen, W. & Hartmeyer, R. (eds) *Die Fauna Südwest-Australiens. Ergebnisse der Hamburger südwest-australischen Forschungsreise 1905.* Gustav Fischer, Jena, pp. 155–212.

Ramírez, M. J. 2014. The morphology and phylogeny of dionychan spiders (Araneae: Araneomorphae). *Bulletin of the American Museum of Natural History*. In press.

Selenopidae

Crews, S. C. & Harvey, M. S. 2011. The spider family Selenopidae (Arachnida, Araneae) in Australasia. *ZooKeys* 99: 1–103.

Crews, S. C. 2013. Thirteen new species of the spider genus *Karaops* (Araneae: Selenopidae) from Western Australia. *Zootaxa* 3647: 443–469.

Salticidae

Wanless, F. R. 1981. A revision of the spider genus *Cocalus* (Araneae: Salticidae). *Bulletin of the British Museum of Natural History* 41: 253–261.

Griswold, C. D. 1984. *Coccorchestes* Thorell newly

described from Australia (Araneae: Salticidae). *Bulletin of the British arachnological Society* 6: 147-148.

Żabka, M. 1987. Salticidae (Araneae) of Oriental, Australian and Pacific regions, I. Genera *Clynotis* and *Tara*. *Annales Zoologici* 40: 437–450.

Żabka, M. 1987. Salticidae (Araneae) of Oriental, Australian and Pacific Regions, II. Genera *Lycidas* and *Maratus*. *Annales Zoologici* 40: 451–482.

Wanless, F. R. 1988. A revision of the spider group Astieae (Araneae: Salticidae) in the Australian region. *New Zealand Journal of Zoology* 15: 81–172.

Żabka, M. 1988. Salticidae (Araneae) of Oriental, Australian and Pacific regions, III. *Annales Zoologici* 41: 421–479.

Davies, V. T. & Żabka, M. 1989. Illustrated key to the genera of jumping spiders (Araneae: Salticidae) in Australia. *Memoirs of the Queensland Museum* 27: 189–266.

Żabka, M. 1990. Salticidae (Arachnida: Araneae) of Oriental, Australian and Pacific regions, IV. Genus *Ocrisiona* Simon, 1901. *Records of the Australian Museum* 42: 27–43.

Żabka, M. 1991. Salticidae (Arachnida: Araneae) of Oriental, Australian and Pacific regions, V. Genus *Holoplatys* Simon, 1885. *Records of the Australian Museum* 43: 171–240.

Żabka, M. 1991. Salticidae (Arachnidae: Araneae) of Oriental, Australian and Pacific regions, VII. *Mopsolodes*, *Abracadabrella* and *Pseudosynagelides* - new genera from Australia. *Memoirs of the Queensland Museum* 30: 621–644.

Żabka, M. 1991. Studium taksonomiczno-zoogegraficzne nad Salticidae (Arachnida: Araneae) Australii. *Rozprawa Naukowa* 32: 1–110.

Żabka, M. 1992. Salticidae (Arachnida: Araneae) of Oriental, Australian and Pacific regions, VII. *Paraplatoides* and *Grayenulla* - new genera from Australia and New Caledonia. *Records of the Australian Museum* 44: 165–183.

Żabka, M. 1992. Salticidae (Arachnida: Araneae) of Oriental, Australian and Pacific regions, VIII. A new genus from Australia. *Records of the Western Australian Museum* 15: 673–684.

Żabka, M. 1993. Salticidae (Arachnida: Araneae) fo the Oriental, Australian and Pacific regions. IX. Genera *Afraflacilla* Berland & Millot 1941 and *Evarcha* Simon 1902. *Invertebrate Taxonomy* 7: 279–295.

Żabka, M. 1994. Salticidae (Arachnida: Araneae) of Oriental, Australian and Pacific regions, X. Genus *Simaetha* Thorell. *Records of the Western Australian Museum* 16: 499–534.

Żabka, M. 1995. Salticidae (Arachnida: Araneae) of Oriental, Australian and Pacific regions, XI. A new genus of Astieae from Western Australia. *Records of the Western Australian Museum, Supplement* 52: 159–164.

Waldock, J. M. 1995. A new species of *Maratus* from southwestern Australia (Araneae, Salticidae). *Records of the Western Australian Museum, Supplement* 52: 165–195.

Gardzinska, J. 1996. New species and records of Astieae (Araneae: Salticidae) from Australia and Papua New Guinea. *Memoirs of the Queensland Museum* 39: 297–305.

Rix, M. G. 1999. A new genus and species of ant-mimicking jumping spider (Araneae: Salticidae) form Southeast Queensland, with notes on its biology. *Memoirs of the Queensland Museum* 43: 827–832.

Szüts, T. 2000. An Afrotropical species, *Asemonea stella* (Araneae: Salticidae), found in Australia. *Folia Entomologica Hungarica* 61: 61–63.

Żabka, M. 2000. Salticidae (Arachnida: Araneae) of the Oriental, Australian and Pacific regions, XIII: the genus *Sandalodes* Keyserling. *Invertebrate Taxonomy* 14: 695–704.

Żabka, M. 2001. Salticidae (Arachnida: Araneae) from the Oriental, Australian and Pacific regions, XIV. The genus *Adoxotoma* Simon. *Records of the Western Australian Museum* 20: 323–332.

Masta, S. E. & Maddison, W. P. 2002. Sexual selection driving diversification in jumping spiders. *Proceedings of the National Academy of Sciences* 99: 4442–4447.

Żabka, M. 2002. Salticidae (Arachnida: Araneae) from the Oriental, Australian and Pacific regions, XV. New species of Astiae from Australia. *Records of the Australian Museum* 54: 257–268.

Waldock, J. 2002. Redescription of *Lycidas chrysomelas* (Simon) (Araneae: Salticidae). *Records of the Western Australian Museum* 21: 227–234.

Żabka, M. & Gray, M. R. 2002. Salticidae (Arachnida: Araneae) from Oriental, Australian and Pacific Regions, XVI. New species of *Grayenulla* and *Afraflacilla*. *Records of the Australian Museum* 54: 269–274.

Żabka, M. 2003. Salticidae (Arachnida: Araneae) from Oriental, Australian and Pacific regions, XVII. *Paraphilaeus*, a new genus from Australia. *Annales Zoologici, Warszawa* 53: 723–727.

Żabka, M. & Gray, M. R. 2004. Salticidae (Arachnida: Araneae) from the Oriental, Australian and Pacific regions, XVIII. *Huntiglennia* -- a new genus from Australia. *Annales Zoologici, Warszawa* 54: 587–590.

Richardson, B. J. & Żabka, M. 2007. A revision of the Australian jumping spider genus *Prostheclina* Keyserling, 1892 (Araneae: Salticidae). *Records of the Australian Museum* 59: 79–96.

Żabka, M. 2006. Salticidae (Arachnida: Araneae) from Oriental, Australian and Pacific regions. XIX. Genus *Pellenes* Simon, 1876 in Australia. *Annales Zoologici* 56: 567–573.

Waldock, J. M. 2008. A new species of *Maratus* (Araneae: Salticidae) from southwestern Australia. *Records of the Western Australian Museum* 24: 369–373.

Maddison, W. P. Bodner, M. R. & Needham, K. M. 2008. Salticid spider phylogeny revisited, with the discovery of a large Australasian clade. *Zootaxa* 1893: 49–64.

Waldock, J. M. 2009. A new species of jumping spider of the genus *Paraplatoides* (Araneae: Salticidae) from Western Australia. *Records of the Western Australian Museum* 25: 305–308.

Ceccarelli, F. S. 2010. New species of ant-mimicking jumping spiders of the genus *Myrmarachne* MacLeay, 1839 (Araneae: Salticidae) from north Queensland, Australia. *Australian Journal of Entomology* 49: 245–255.

Gardzinska, J. & Żabka, M. 2010. A new genus and five new species of Astieae (Araneae: Salticidae) from Australia, with remarks on distribution. *Zootaxa* 2526: 37–53.

Otto, J. C. & Hill, D. E. 2011. *Maratus vespertilio* (Simon 1901) (Araneae: Salticidae) from southern Australia. *Peckhamia* 92.1: 1–6.

Żabka, M. 2012. *Phlegra* Simon, 1876, *Phintella* Strand 1906 and *Yamangalea* Maddison, 2009 (Arachnida: Araneae: Salticidae)— new species and new generic records for Australia. *Zootaxa* 3176: 61–68.

Otto, J. C. & Hill, D. E. 2012. An illustrated review of the known peacock spiders of the genus *Maratus* from Australia, with description of a new species (Araneae: Salticidae: Euophryinae). *Peckhamia* 96.1: 1–27.

Otto, J. C. & Hill, D. E. 2012. Notes on *Maratus* Karsch 1878 and related jumping spiders from Australia, with five new species (Araneae: Salticidae: Euophryinae). *Peckhamia* 103.1: 1–81.

Richardson, B. J. & Gunter, N. L. 2012. Revision of Australian jumping spider genus *Servaea* Simon 1887 (Aranaea [sic]: Salticidae) including use of DNA sequence data and predicted distributions. *Zootaxa* 3350: 1–33.

Żabka, M. & Waldock, J. 2012. Salticidae (Arachnida: Araneae) from Oriental, Australian and Pacific regions. Genus *Cosmophasis* Simon, 1901. *Annales Zoologici, Warszawa* 62: 115–198.

Gardzińska, J. & Żabka, M. 2013. Redescription of the genus *Opisthoncus* L. Koch, 1880 (Araneae: Salticidae). *Zootaxa* 3717: 401–447.

Richardson, B. J. 2013. New unidentate jumping spider genera (Araneae: Salticidae) from Australia. *Zootaxa* 3716: 460–474.

Ruiz, G. R. S. & Brescovit, A. D. 2013. Revision of *Breda* and proposal of a new genus (Araneae: Salticidae). *Zootaxa* 3664: 401–433.

Waldock, J. 2013. A review of the peacock spiders of the *Maratus mungaich* species-group (Araneae: Salticidae), with descriptions of four new species. *Records of the Western Australian Museum* 28: 66–81.

Otto, J.C. & Hill, D.E. 2014 Spiders of the *mungaich* group from Western Australia (Araneae: Salticidae: Eurphryinae: *Maratus*), with one new species from Cape Arid. *Peckhamia* 112.1: 1–35.

Otto, J.C. & Hill, D.E. 2014. Description of a new peacock spider from Cape Le Grand, Western Australia, with observations on display by males and females and comparative notes on the related *Maratus volans* (Araneae: Salticidae: Euophryinae: *Maratus*). *Peckhamia* 114.1: 1–38.

Philodromidae

Koch, L. 1875. *Die Arachniden Australiens nach der Natur beschrieben und abgebildet. 1. Theil. 5. Lieferung*. Bauer und Raspe, Nürnberg, pp. 577–740.

Koch, L. 1876. *Die Arachniden Australiens nach der Natur beschrieben und abgebildet. 1. Theil. 6. Lieferung*. Bauer und Raspe, Nürnberg, pp. 741–888.

Efimik, V. E. 1999. A review of the spider genus

Tibellus Simon, 1875 of the East Palaearctic (Aranei: Philodromidae). *Arthropoda Selecta* 8: 103–124.

Gnaphosidae

Platnick, N. I. 1975. A revision of the spider genus *Eilica* (Araneae, Gnaphosidae). *American Museum Novitates* 2578: 1–19.

Platnick, N. I. 1978. On Australian *Eilica* (Araneae, Gnaphosidae). *Bulletin of the British Arachnological Society* 4: 226–227.

Forster, R. R. 1979. The spiders of New Zealand. Part V. Cycloctenidae, Gnaphosidae, Clubionidae. *Otago Museum Bulletin* 5: 1–95.

Platnick, N. I. 1988. A new spider of the Gondwanan genus *Eilica* from Victoria, Australia (Araneae: Gnaphosidae). *Memoirs of the Museum of Victoria* 49: 83–84.

Ovtsharenko, V. I. & Platnick, N. I. 1995. On the Australasian ground spider genera *Anzacia* and *Adelphodrassus* (Araneae, Gnaphosidae). *American Museum Novitates* 3154: 1–16.

Platnick, N. I. 1990. Spinneret morphology and the phylogeny of ground spiders (Araneae, Gnaphosoidea). *American Museum Novitates* 2978: 1–42.

Zakharov, B. P. & Ovtcharenko, V. I. 2011. Morphological organization of the male palpal organ in Australian ground spiders of the genera *Anzacia*, *Intruda*, *Zelanda*, and *Encoptarthria* (Araneae: Gnaphosidae). *Journal of Arachnology* 39: 327–336.

Prodidomidae

Platnick, N. I. & Baehr, B. C. 2006. A revision of the Australasian ground spiders of the family Prodidomidae (Araneae, Gnaphosoidea). *Bulletin of the American Museum of Natural History* 298: 1–287.

Platnick, N.I. & Baehr, B.C. 2013. New species and records of the molycriine ground spider genus *Wydundra* (Araneae: Prodidomidae) from northern Australia. *Memoirs of the Queensland Museum, Nature* 53: 93–103.

Lamponidae

Platnick, N. I. 2000. A relimitation and revision of the Australasian ground spider family Lamponidae (Araneae: Gnaphosoidea). *Bulletin of the American Museum of Natural History* 245: 1–330.

Platnick, N.I. 2004. On a third group of flattened ground spiders from Australia (Araneae, Lamponidae). *American Museum Novitates* 3462: 1–7.

Banks, J. Sirvid, P. & Vink, C. J. 2004. White-tailed spider bites-arachnophobic fallout? *New Zealand Medical Journal* 117: 1–7.

Isbister, G.K. and Gray, M.R. 2003. White-tail spider bite: a prospective study of 130 definite bites by *Lampona* species. *Medical Journal of Australia* 179: 199–202.

Ammoxenidae

Platnick, N. I. 2002. A revision of the Australasian ground spiders of the families Ammoxenidae, Cithaeronidae, Gallieniellidae, and Trochanteriidae (Araneae: Gnaphosoidea). *Bulletin of the American Museum of Natural History* 271: 1–243.

Gallieniellidae

Main, B. Y. 1987. A new genus of clubionoid spider from Western Australia (Arachnida: Araneomorphae). *Australian Entomological Magazine* 13: 77–81.

Platnick, N. I. 2002. A revision of the Australasian ground spiders of the families Ammoxenidae, Cithaeronidae, Gallieniellidae, and Trochanteriidae (Araneae: Gnaphosoidea). *Bulletin of the American Museum of Natural History* 271: 1–243.

Trochanteriidae

Platnick, N. I. 2002. A revision of the Australasian ground spiders of the families Ammoxenidae, Cithaeronidae, Gallieniellidae, and Trochanteriidae (Araneae: Gnaphosoidea). *Bulletin of the American Museum of Natural History* 271: 1–243.

Platnick, N. I. 2008. A new subterranean ground spider genus from Western Australia (Araneae: Trochanteriidae). *Invertebrate Systematics* 22: 295–299.

Cithaeronidae

Platnick, N. I. 2002. A revision of the Australasian ground spiders of the families Ammoxenidae, Cithaeronidae, Gallieniellidae, and Trochanteriidae (Araneae: Gnaphosoidea). *Bulletin of the American Museum of Natural History* 271: 1–243.

GLOSSARY

(→ refers to other entry in glossary)

abdomen: rear part of the body, connected to cephalothorax by the →pedicel; with heart, primary reproductive and respiratory organs, and silk glands and spinnerets; also called opisthosoma

aciniform gland: silk gland; in orb-weaving spiders producing prey-wrapping silk

aggregate gland: silk gland; in orb-weaving spiders producing the sticky droplets of the web

anterior: near the front end or head

annulated: with ring-like subdivisions, in spiders often referring to colour patterns around leg segments; rings of darker or lighter colour

apical: near the tip of an appendix, for example a leg; = →distal

apophysis: sclerotised (hardened) outgrowth of variable shape; plural: apophyses

Arachnida: →class of terrestrial arthropods characterised by eight legs; including the spiders, scorpions, mites, harvestmen, and others (anglicised: arachnids)

arachnology/arachnologist: the study of the →Arachnida/somebody studying the Arachnida

Araneae: the spiders; order of terrestrial arthropods within the Arachnida characterised by →pedipalps serving as secondary sexual organs in males, ability to spin silk from spinnerets on the →abdomen, and venom glands in the →chelicerae; sometimes also referred to as Araneida

araneology/araneologist: the study of spiders/somebody studying spiders

araneophage: feeding on spiders

Arthropoda: phylum of invertebrates characterised by jointed legs; including centipedes, millipedes, insects, crustaceans, spiders, scorpions, and others

ballooning: air-borne dispersal by some juvenile and small adult spiders facilitated by silk threads (→gossamer) released to catch air movement

basal: near the base of an appendix, for example a leg; = →proximal

Batesian mimicry: morphological and behavioural adaptations that imitate unpalatable species

booklung: paired respiratory organs of spiders made up of closely packed sheets of cuticle that contain →hemolymph on the underside of the abdomen; number of booklungs differs between spiders from none to two pairs

bulb: secondary sexual organ of male spiders situated in the →cymbium of the →pedipalp; with more or less S-shaped tubular duct (→sperm duct) that ends in a sharp hollow needle of varying length and shape, the →embolus, to transfer the semen

calamistrum: comb of setae on the →metatarsi of the fourth leg in →cribellate spiders

carapace: upper chitinous plate of the cephalothorax

cardiac mark: distinctly coloured elongated mark on the →anterior, upper surface of the abdomen overlying the heart

cephalothorax: frontal part of the body connected to abdomen by the →pedicel; including a frontal cephalic ('head') region with eyes and bearing →chelicerae and →pedipalps, and a rear thoracic region bearing the legs; includes the upper →carapace and the →sternum on the underside; also called →prosoma

chelicera: jaw; consisting of a large basal part, the →paturon, and the terminal →fang: plural: chelicerae

Chelicerata: subphylum of invertebrates characterised by a single pair of appendages, the →chelicerae in front of the mouth

chitin: tough, protective material primarily made up of nitrogen-containing polysaccharides, forming the main element of the spider exoskeleton

class: a taxonomic rank; a subdivision of a →phylum or subphylum, including a group of related →orders; the →Arachnida are the class to which the spiders belong

claw tufts: pair of adhesive hair clusters below the paired claws at the tip of the →tarsi

colulus: tiny unpaired lobe in front of the spinnerets; evolutionary equivalent (homologue) to the →anterior median spinnerets or the →cribellum

conductor: membranous structure in the male →pedipalp supporting the →embolus during insemination.

condyle: protrusion outside the base of the →chelicerae present in some spiders; sometimes called cheliceral boss

coxa: →basal most segment of the leg or

pedipalp connecting the leg to the body; followed by →trochanter; plural: coxae

cribellum: spinning plate evolutionary equivalent (homologue) to the →anterior median spinnerets; located in front of the spinnerets; only present in cribellate spiders, which also have a →calamistrum

cylindrical gland: silk gland; in orb-weaving spiders producing eggsac fibres

cymbium: the broadened, concave →tarsus of the male pedipalp containing the →bulb, the secondary sexual organs of the male.

dentate: with tooth-like, sclerotised projections

denticle: small sclerotised teeth-like outgrowth

distal: near the tip of an appendix, for example a leg; = →apical

dorsal: on the upper surface

ecdysis: moulting; periodic casting of the skin

embolus: terminal part of the →bulb accommodating the ejaculatory duct and inserted into the female genitalia during sperm transfer

endite: lobe of the →pedipalp →coxa forming a mouthpart of a spider; = →maxilla

Entelegynae: modern spiders in which female genitalia have a hardened, external genital plate, the →epigyne, and a separate fertilisation duct; anglicised: entelegynes

epigastric fold: fold or groove separating the frontal part of the abdomen underside (with →epigyne and →booklungs) from the rear part

epigyne: more or less →sclerotised external genital plate of variable shape associated with the reproductive openings of adult females of modern spiders

exoskeleton: hard, external cover of all arthropods

fang: needle-like part of each →chelicera; opening near its tip injects the venom

femur: third most basal part of the spider leg, between the →trochanter and the →patella; plural: femora

flagelliform gland: silk gland; in orb-weaving spiders producing the core fibre of the capture spiral

fovea: central depression of the →carapace which marks the internal attachment of gastric muscles

genitalia: reproductive organs

gossamer: specialised threads of silk; enables spiders air-borne dispersal (→ballooning)

gumfoot web: three-dimensional web that is connected to the surface with gluey tangle-threads (gumfoot threads) that pull walking prey off the ground

Haplogynae: modern spiders in which female genitalia lack a hardened, external genital plate, the →epigyne, and lack separate fertilisation ducts; anglicised: haplogynes

hemolymph: blood-like fluid in the circulatory system of the →Arthropoda

kleptoparasite: spiders stealing prey from other spiders

labium: lower lip of the mouth between the →endites, attached to the front of the →sternum

lamella: small and thin plate-like structure; plural: lamellae

lamina: two-dimensional layer

lateral: towards/along the side of the body or an appendix

major ampullate gland: silk gland; in orb-weaving spiders producing structural web-silk and dragline silk

maxilla: lobe of the →pedipalp →coxa forming a mouthpart of a spider; = →endite; plural: maxillae

median: towards/in the middle of the body or an appendix; = →mesal

median apophysis: sclerotised part of the male →pedipalp →bulb arising from the middle section, often interlocking with the other parts of the pedipalp or the female epigyne during copulation

mesal: towards/in the middle of the body or an appendix; = →median

metatarsus: sixth basal-most segment of the leg between →tibia and →tarsus; plural: metatarsi

minor ampullate gland: silk gland; in orb-weaving spiders producing the temporary capture spiral

order: a taxonomic rank; subdivision of a →class, including a group of related families; spiders are the order →Araneae

paracymbium: chitinous structure of the male pedipalp attached to the base of the cymbium

patella: fourth →basal most segment of the leg or pedipalp between the →femur and the →tibia

pedicel: narrow connection between →cephalothorax and →abdomen

pedipalp: second appendage of the →Chelicerata; in male spiders carrying the secondary sexual organs

pheromone: chemical substance which

influences the behaviour of another animal in the same species; often used to trigger a response in the opposite sex

phylogenetics: the study of evolutionary relationships between and within groups; adjective: phylogenetic

phylum: a taxonomic rank; a subdivision within a kingdom (for example the animals), including a group of related →orders; Arthropoda are the phylum to which the spiders belong

plumose: with thin feathery →setae

posterior: near/towards the rear end

procurved: an arc with ends curving ahead of its centre; in spiders used to describe the shape of an eye row

prolateral: at the side of an appendage, for example a leg, that faces the front of the animal

pyriform gland: silk gland; in orb-weaving spiders producing cementing silk to fix fibres

rastellum: patch of short spines forming a rake-like structure on the chelicerae

recurved: an arc with end curving behind its centre; in spiders used to describe the shape of an eye row

reniform: kidney-shaped

retrocoxal hymen: thin skin-like area on the back of the →coxa of the first leg

retrolateral: at the side of an appendage, for example a leg, that faces the rear of the animal

retrolateral tibial apophysis (RTA): apophysis on the →tibia of the male →pedipalp uniting an evolutionary unit of spiders, the RTA-clade

rugose: roughly wrinkled

scape: elongate projection from the midline of the female →epigyne

sclerite: hardened (→sclerotised) element of the male pedipalp bulb

sclerotised: chitinous, hardened structure

scopula: brush of hairs on the underside of the tarsus and metatarsus; plural: scopulae

scute: chitinous plates generally on the upper side of the →abdomen present in some spiders; also scutum, plural: scuta

serrula: serration on the margins of the →endites

seta: hair-like structure covering the exoskeleton of arthropods; colloquially 'hair'

sexual dimorphism: morphological differences between sexes of the same species

sigilla: impressed darker, sclerotised spots present on the upper surface of the abdomen or on the sternum marking points of internal muscle attachments; plural: sigillae

sperm transfer web: small web on which male spiders deposit their semen to take it into the →embolus of →pedipalp →bulb

spermatheca: internal receptacles of female spider genitalia that store sperm; plural: spermathecae

spiderling: immature spider, usually the form just emerged from the eggsac

spigot: small socket on the →spinnerets that produce silk

spine: a thick bristle

spinnerets: paired abdominal appendages of spiders through which silk strands are spun

stabilimentum: highly visible silk structure in the webs of some orb-web spider

sternum: chitinous plate covering the underside of the →cephalothorax

synonym: each of two or more scientific names of the same rank used to name the same taxon; the senior synonym is the name first established

synonymy: state of being a synonym

tapetum: reflective structure below the retina of spider eyes; plural: tapeta

tarsus: distal most segment of a leg articulated to the metatarsus; plural tarsi

taxon: taxonomic unit (eg. family, genus, species); plural: taxa

taxonomy: science classifying organisms; ideally, classifications are based on evolutionary units established through systematic or →phylogenetic research

tegulum: middle section of the male →pedipalp →bulb

tenent hairs: hairs with enlarged tip, sometimes secreting an adhesive fluid, growing in tufts on the feet of many spiders and insects

tibia: fifth →basal most segment of the spider leg or pedipalp between the →patella and →metatarsus; plural: tibiae

tracheal Spiracle: opening of the tracheae, respiratory tubes, on the underside of the →abdomen

trichobothrium: long and thin hair which are able to detect air movements and which rise from a socket on the leg; plural: trichobothria

trochanter: second basal most segment of the leg or pedipalp between the →coxa and →femur

ventral: on the underside

ACKNOWLEDGEMENTS

Australia's eminent arachnologist Robert Raven deserves a special mention for supporting this project. He shared much of his knowledge on spiders to improve the contents of many chapters of this book. He also facilitated access to many images of rarely illustrated species.

As nobody is an expert on all spider families, advice on and review of chapters were also sought from a number of local and international colleagues, including Ingi Agnarsson, Steffen Bayer, Danilo Harms, Mark Harvey, Gustavo Hormiga, Peter Jaeger, Matjaz Kuntner, Lara Lopardo, Martin Ramirez, Nikolaj Scharff, Michael Rix and Helen Smith. All are thanked for giving up some of their valuable time to support this publication.

In addition to the authors, many friends and colleagues provided images or access to them for this work, including Farhan Bokhari (72), Robert Raven (54 images), Juergen Haider (9), Lara Lopardo (7), Mike Gray, Allan Lance (both 6), Peter Langlands (5), Alan Clarke, Matjaz Kuntner (both 4), Peter Jäger, Heather McClennan, Michael Rix, (all 2), P. Belfield, Simon Blane, R. Farrow, Julian Finn, Gio Fitzpatrick, Ingrid Guenther, Aaron Harmer, John Koerner, Anna Leung, Kate Lowe, Jurgen Otto (title page), Bruce McQuillan, Nikolaj Scharff, Helen Smith, Rick Vetter and Ken Walker (all 1). Graham Milledge and Helen Smith facilitated obtaining images from the Australian Museum. Further assistance in obtaining photographs by providing details of photographers was provided by G.B. Edwards and Ken Walker. Volker Framenau also thanks those people who provided spider specimens for life images over the years, in particular David Knowles (Spineless Wonders, Perth) and Roy Teale and colleagues (Biota Environmental Sciences, Perth). Colleagues and friends from Western Australian Museum also provided a never-ending stream of material for photography, in particular Mark Harvey, Julianne Waldock and Michael Rix.

This work would not have been possible without the unwavering support of Volker Framenau's partner and soul mate Melissa Thomas. Their children Yannick, Bianca and Katya have seen less than normal of their father in the final stages of this book and an apology for that is in order. Volker also extends his gratitude to colleagues and friends at Phoenix Environmental Sciences, in particular to Karen Crews and Jarrad Clark, who gave him the freedom to pursue the compilation of this book at normal working hours. Volker also owes a great deal of gratitude to his scientific mentors. Mark Elgar taught him that 'the behaviour of a population is determined by that of its individuals' and Mark Harvey encouraged him to 'think phylogenetically'. Volker also learned much from the Australian Grande Dame of Arachnology, Barbara York Main.

Barbara Baehr thanks Ingrid Kern for supporting her as a good friend and helping her when it was needed most, and her sister Jutta Roesemann who supported here during this project whilst she was staying in Germany. Barbara also acknowledges contributions by Robert Wright, because he challenged her approach to the project from the beginning and forced her to think about a variety of aspects not previously considered. Barbara thanks the Australian Biological Resources Study's BushBlitz team, Jo Harding, Kate Gillespie and Mim Jambrecina, who stressed the importance of this work.

Paul Zborowski in particular acknowledges feedback on spiders by Marek Žabka and Christina Deeleman-Reinhold.

THE AUTHORS

Volker Framenau
Dr Volker W. Framenau is interested an all things spider. He is a professional zoologist who has published internationally on the taxonomy and systematics, ecology and behaviour of spiders and other invertebrates. His main passions are Wolf Spiders, Orb-weaving Spiders and Trapdoor Spiders. Volker worked at and holds adjunct positions at the University of Western Australia and the Western Australian Museum. Since 2011, he has been Director of Phoenix Environmental Sciences, a Perth-based environmental consultancy firm.

Barbara Baehr
Dr Barbara Baehr is an internationally recognised research scientist and spider taxonomist. Barbara has made major contributions to documenting invertebrate biodiversity by describing some 600 new spider species – most of them from Australia. Barbara was born and educated in Germany. Since 2000 she has been working in the Natural Environments Program of the Queensland Museum.

Paul Zborowski
Paul Zborowski is an entomologist and photographer, researching and illustrating invertebrates around the world. A passion for presenting the macro details of nature to a wide audience has resulted in 12 illustrated nature books, using the resources of his image bank www.close-up-photolibrary.com. He is a field based scientist, spending long periods in the bush in Australia and abroad, and a sometimes teacher, both of science and photography.

INDEX OF COMMON SPIDER FAMILY NAMES

Advanced Modern Spiders 137
Ant-eating Spiders 297
Ant-mimics 366
Armoured Spiders 123
Assassin Spiders 139
Australian Tarantulas 91
Barking Spiders 91
Bird-eating Spiders 91
Brush-footed Trapdoor Spiders 87
Chickenwire-web Spiders 208
Cob-web Spiders 229
Coin Spiders 180
Comb-footed Spiders 229
Comb-tailed Spiders 262
Cone-web Spiders 284
Cork-lid Trapdoor Spiders 68
Crab Spiders 339
Crevice Weavers 107
Curtain-web Spiders 59
Daddy Long-legs Spiders 119
Dwarf Orb-weaving Spiders 223
Dwarf Sheet Spiders 262
False Huntsman Spiders 356
False Water Spiders 358
False Wolf Spiders 331, 356
Feather-legged Spiders 250
Fiddle-back Spiders 110
Fishing Spiders 319
Flower Spiders 339
Forest Hunters 289
Funnel-web Spiders 54
Funnel-web Weavers 291
Ghost Spiders 360
Giant Crab Spiders 266
Goblin Spiders 129
Golden Orb-weavers 180
Ground Orb-weaving Spiders 217
Ground Spiders 393, 408
Hackled-mesh Weavers 292
Hermit Spiders 180
Host Spiders 358
House Spiders 276
Hump-backed Spiders 246
Huntsman Spiders 266
Intertidal Spiders 276
Jumping Spiders 376
Junction-web Weavers 99
Labyrinth Spiders 284
Lace-sheet Weaving Spider 353
Long-clawed Spiders 102
Long-jawed Spiders 192
Long-jawed Ground Spiders 408
Long-spinneret Bark Spiders 253
Long-spinneret Ground Spiders 398
Lynx Spiders 327
Mesh-web Spiders 264
Micro Gondwanan Spiders 217
Minute Clasping-weavers 214
Minute Long-jawed Spiders 202
Money Spiders 186
Mouse Spiders 63
Net-casting Spiders 246
Nursery-web Spiders 319
Ogre-faced Spiders 246
Orb-weaving Spiders 144
Pelican Spiders 139
Phantom Spiders 360
Pirate Spiders 200
Platform Spiders 284
Prowling Spiders 331
Pseudo-Orbweaving Spiders 353
Ray Orb-weaving Spiders 212
Recluse Spiders 110
Red-and-black Spiders 243
Relictual Spiders 115
Retarius Spider 246
Running Crab Spiders 390
Sac Spiders 362
Scaffold-web Spiders 227
Scorpion Spiders 411
Scuttling Spiders 295
Sea-shore spiders 360
Sheet-web Spiders 186
Shield Spiders 210
Six-eyed Ground Spiders 134
Sombrero Spiders 284
Spiny-leg Spiders 335
Spiny-legged Sac Spiders 371
Spitting Spiders 112
Swift Ground Spiders 414
Swift Spiders 366
Termite Hunters 406
Tiny Thick-necked Spiders 204
Trapdoor Spiders 51
Tree Trapdoor Spiders 72
Tropical Wolf Spiders 325
True Trapdoor Spiders 75
Tube-web Spiders 125
Two-tailed Spiders 253
Venomless Spiders 250
Wall Crab Spiders 372
Wall Spiders 258
Wandering Ghosts 335
Whistling Spiders 91
White-tailed Spiders 400
Wishbone Trapdoor Spiders 82
Wolf Spiders 304
Woodlouse Hunters 127

INDEX OF SCIENTIFIC SPIDER FAMILY NAMES

Actinopodidae 63
Agelenidae 291
Amaurobiidae 292
Ammoxenidae 406
Amphinectidae 289
Anapidae 217
Anyphaenidae 360
Araneidae 144
Archaeidae 139
Austrochilidae 99
Barychelidae 87
Cithaeronidae 414
Clubionidae 362
Corinnidae 366
Ctenidae 325
Ctenizidae 68
Cyatholipidae 190
Cycloctenidae 295
Deinopidae 246
Desidae 276
Dictynidae 264
Dipluridae 59
Dysderidae 127
Filistatidae 107
Gallieniellidae 408
Gnaphosidae 393
Gradungulidae 102
Hahniidae 262
Hersiliidae 253
Hexathelidae 54
Holarchaeidae 202
Idiopidae 75
Lamponidae 400
Linyphiidae 186
Liocranidae 371
Lycosidae 304
Malkaridae 210
Migidae 72
Mimetidae 200
Miturgidae 331
Mysmenidae 214
Nemesiidae 82
Nephilidae 180
Nesticidae 227
Nicodamidae 243
Ochyroceratidae 117
Oecobiidae 258
Oonopidae 129
Orsolobidae 134
Oxyopidae 327
Pararchaeidae 204
Periegopidae 115
Philodromidae 390
Pholcidae 119
Pisauridae 319
Prodidomidae 398
Psechridae 353
Salticidae 3760
Scytodidae 112
Segestriidae 125
Selenopidae 372
Sicariidae 110
Sparassidae 266
Stenochilidae 142
Stiphidiidae 284
Symphytognathidae 223
Synotaxidae 208
Tengellidae 358
Tetrablemmidae 123
Tetragnathidae 192
Theraphosidae 91
Theridiidae 229
Theridiosomatidae 212
Thomisidae 339
Trochanteriidae 411
Uloboridae 250
Zodariidae 297
Zoridae 335
Zoropsidae 356

448